# Beer Lover's New England

*Second Edition*

Norman Miller

Globe Pequot

Guilford, Connecticut

All the information in this guidebook is subject to change. We recommend that you call ahead to obtain current information before traveling.

Globe Pequot

An imprint of Rowman & Littlefield

Distributed by NATIONAL BOOK NETWORK



British Library Cataloguing in Publication Information Available

ISSN 2168-1341
ISBN 978-1-4930-0752-3 (paperback)
ISBN 978-1-4930-1968-7 (e-book)

∞™ The paper used in this publication meets the minimum requirements of American National Standard for Information Sciences—Permanence of Paper for Printed Library Materials, ANSI/NISO Z39.48-1992.

# Contents


## *Introduction* xii

## *How to Use This Guide* xiv

Glossary of Terms xiv
New England Beer News & Reviews xvii

## *Massachusetts* 1

**Breweries**

Backlash Beer Company 3
Bad Martha Beer Company 4
Banner Beer Company 5
Berkley Beer Company 6
Berkshire Brewing Company 7
Big Elm Brewing 9
Blatant Brewery 10
Blue Hills Brewery 11
Bog Iron Brewery 13
Boston Beer Company 14
Brewmaster Jack 15
Cape Ann Brewing Company 16
Cape Cod Beer 18
Cisco Brewers 20
Clown Shoes Beer 21
Cody Brewing Company 23
Element Brewing Company 25
Glass Bottom Brewery 27
Goodfellows Brewing Company 28
Harpoon Brewery 30
High & Mighty Beer Company 31
Idle Hands Craft Ales LLC 33
Jack's Abby Brewing 34
Kretschmann Brewing Company 36
Lefty's Brewing Company 37
Mayflower Brewing Company 39
Mercury Brewing Company 40
Mystic Brewery 42
Nashoba Valley Winery 44
Newburyport Brewing Company 45
Night Shift Brewery 47
Notch Brewing 49
Paper City Brewing Company 50
Percival Beer Company 52
Pioneer Brewing Company 52
Pretty Things Beer & Ale Project 54
Rapscallion 56
Riverwalk Brewing Company 57
Scantic River Brewery 59
Slumbrew: Somerville Brewing Company 60
Spencer Brewery 62
Tree House Brewing Company 62
Trillium Brewing Company 63
Wachusett Brewing Company 64
Wandering Star Brewing Company 66
Westfield River Brewing Company 67
Wormtown Brewing Company 68

**Brewpubs**

Amherst Brewing Company 71
Barrington Brewery & Restaurant 72
Beer Works 73
Cambridge Brewing Company 73
The Gardner Ale House 75
High Horse Brewing 76
John Harvard's Brew House 76
Northampton Brewery 77

Offshore Ale Company 78
Opa Opa Steakhouse & Brewery 80
The People's Pint 80
The Tap Brewpub 81
Watch City Brewing Company 83

**Beer Bars**

The Ale House 84
Armsby Abbey 85
British Beer Company 86
Bukowski's Tavern 87
Cambridge Common Restaurant 89
Deep Ellum 90
The Dive Bar 91
Green Street Grille 92
Horseshoe Pub & Restaurant 93
Jacob Wirth Restaurant 94
Lord Hobo 95
The Moan and Dove 96
Moe's Tavern 96
The Publick House & Monk's Cell 98
Sierra Grille 99
Sunset Grill & Tap 100
Yard House 101

*Maine* 103

**Breweries**

Allagash Brewing Company 105
Andrew's Brewing Company 106
Atlantic Brewing Company 108
Banded Horn Brewery Company 109
Bar Harbor Brewing Company 110
Baxter Brewing Company 111
Belfast Bay Brewing Company 113
Bissell Brothers 114
Black Bear Microbrewery 115
Boothbaby Craft Brewery 117
Bunker Brewing Company 117
D.L. Geary Brewing Company 118
Foundation Brewing Company 120
Friar's Brewhouse 120
Funky Bow Brewery and Beer Company 121
Gneiss Brewing Company 122
Gritty McDuff's Brewery 123
Maine Beer Company 125
Oak Pond Brewing Company 127
Oxbow Brewing Company 128
Peak Organic Brewing Company 130
Penobscot Bay Brewery 131
Rising Tide Brewing Company 133
Sebago Brewing Company 134
Sheepscot Valley Brewing Company 136
Shipyard Brewing Company 137
SoMe Brewing Company 139
Strong Brewing Company 140

**Brewpubs**

The Bag & Kettle Brewpub 141
Boon Island Ale House 142
Bray's Brewpub & Eatery 143
Federal Jack's Restaurant & Brew Pub 144
Geaghan's Restaurant & Pub 145
Kennebec River Pub & Brewery 146
Liberal Cup Public House and Brewery 148
Maine Coast Brewing Company 149
Marshall Wharf Brewing Company/ Three Tides Restaurant 150
The Run of the Mill 151
Sea Dog Brewing Company 152
Sunday River Brewing Company 153

### Beer Bars

The Badger Cafe & Pub 155
Ebenezer's Pub 155
The Great Lost Bear 157
Jimmy the Greek's 158
Novare Res Bier Café 159
Post Road Tavern 160
Three Dollar Dewey's 161

## Vermont 163

### Breweries

Drop-in Brewery 165
Fiddleheads Brewing Company 165
Foley Brothers Brewing 166
Four Quarters Brewing 167
14th Star Brewery 168
Hill Farmstead Brewery 169
Kingdom Brewing 171
Lawson's Finest Liquids 172
Long Trail Brewing Company 173
Lost Nation Brewing 175
Magic Hat Brewing Company 176
Northshire Brewery 178
Otter Creek Brewing/Wolaver's 179
Rock Art Brewery 181
Stone Corral Brewery 182
Switchback Brewing Company 183
Trout River Brewing Company 184

### Brewpubs

Bobcat Cafe & Brewery 187
Brewster River Pub & Brewery 188
Crop Bistro & Brewery 188
Jasper Murdock's Alehouse 190
Madison Brewing Company 191
McNeill's Brewery 192
Three Needs Brewery & Taproom 193
Trapp Family Lodge Brewery 193
Vermont Pub & Brewery 194
Whetstone Station Restaurant & Brewery 195
Zero Gravity Craft Brewery @ American Flatbread 196

### Beer Bars

Blackback Pub & Flyshop 197
Das Bierhaus 198
The Farmhouse Tap & Grill 199
Parker Pie Company 200
Three Penny Taproom 201

## New Hampshire 203

### Breweries

Agner & Wolf Brewing Corporation 204
Candia Road Brewing Company 205
Canterbury Aleworks 207
Great Rhythm Brewing Company 208
Henniker Brewing Company 208
Kelsen Brewing Company 209
Out.Haus Ales 210
Prodigal Brewery at Misty Mountain Farm 212
Redhook Ale Brewery 213
603 Brewery 214
Smuttynose Brewing Company 215
Squam Brewing Company 217
Stoneface Brewing Company 218
Throwback Brewery 219
Tuckerman Brewing Company 221
White Birch Brewing 222
Woodstock Inn Brewery 224

**Brewpubs**

Earth Eagle Brewings 226
Elm City Brewing Company 227
Flying Goose Brew Pub & Grill 228
Martha's Exchange 229
Milly's Tavern 230
Moat Mountain Smoke House & Brewing Company 231
Portsmouth Brewery 233
Schilling Beer Company 234
Seven Barrel Brewery 235

**Beer Bars**

The Barley House 236
Blue Mermaid Island Grill 237
Portsmouth Gas Light Co. 237
Strange Brew Tavern 238

## Connecticut 241

**Breweries**

Back East Brewing Company 242
Beaver Beer Company 243
Beer'd Brewing Company 244
Broad Brook Brewing Company 245
Black Hog Brewing Co. 246
Charter Oak Brewing Company 247
Cottrell Brewing Company 248
Firefly Hollow Brewing 250
Half Full Brewery 250
The Hartford Better Beer Company 251
New England Brewing Company 253
Olde Burnside Brewing Company 254
Relic Brewing Company 257
Shebeen Brewing Company 258
Stony Creek Brewery 259
Stubborn Beauty Brewing Company 260
Thimble Island Brewing Company 261
Thomas Hooker Brewing Company 262
Top Shelf Brewing Company 263
Two Roads Brewing Company 264

**Brewpubs**

Bru Room at BAR 266
The Cambridge House 266
City Steam Brewery Café 267
SBC Restaurant & Brewery 268
Willimantic Brewing Company 269

**Beer Bars**

The Cask Republic 270
Eli Cannon's Tap Room 271
MiKro Craft Beer Bar 272
Prime 16 273

## Rhode Island 275

**Breweries**

Bucket Brewery 277
Coastal Extreme Brewing Company 278
Foolproof Brewing Company 280
Grey Sail Brewing of Rhode Island 281
Narragansett Beer 282
Proclamation Ale Company 284
Ravenous Brewing Company 284
Revival Brewing Company 285

**Brewpubs**

Coddington Brewing Company 287
Mohegan Cafe & Brewery 288
Trinity Brewhouse 288
Union Station Brewery 290

**Beer Bars**
Doherty's East Avenue Irish Pub 291
English Cellar Alehouse 291
Julians 292
Pour Judgment Bar & Grill 293

## Beer Festivals 295

## BYOB: Brew Your Own Beer 303
Brew-on-Premises 303
Beer Recipe 306

## In the Kitchen 308
Pairing Beer with Food 308
Food Recipes 309

## Pub Crawls 318
Boston, MA 318
Cambridge, MA 320
Burlington, VT 322
New Haven, CT 324
Northampton, MA 326
Portland, ME 328
Portsmouth, NH 330
Providence, RI 332

## Appendix: Beer Lover's Pick List 336

## Index 340

# About the Author

**Norman Miller** grew up in the beer wasteland of Leominster, Massachusetts, where he still resides with his dog, Foxy, and his beer fridge, Beatrice. He writes the popular "Beer Nut" column that appears weekly in the *MetroWest Daily News* and the daily "Beer Nut" blog on wickedlocal.com. He developed his love of craft beer at the now-defunct Stone Coast Brewery in Laconia, New Hampshire, and thinks New England has developed into one of the great brewing regions in the US.

# Acknowledgments

Writing this book was a long process, and I have to thank a lot of people who made it possible. First, I want to thank my mother, Donna Miller, who convinced me, despite her not liking that I drink beer, to write this book. She passed away soon after the first edition of this book was released.

I also need to thank my good friend, Charlie Breitrose. If it weren't for having him as a drinking buddy in the early exploration of the craft beer, I probably would never have developed a love for beer.

I also would like to thank my editors at the *MetroWest Daily News* in Framingham, first for giving me my weekly "Beer Nut" column and, despite the tough times in the industry, allowing me to continue it all these years.

Much appreciation has to go out to all of the brewers and brewery employees and owners who helped me with this book, none more so than Will Meyers of the Cambridge Brewing Company. Every time I needed any information, he responded quickly with what I needed. He helped me with many different aspects of the book, and I can't thank him enough.

A lot of thanks has to go out to all of the New England breweries that have brewed and continued to make some phenomenal beers. If it weren't for them creating great beer, there would not be a need for a book like this. They have truly made New England a hotbed of brewing that is getting better and better every day.

Also important are the craft beer fans in New England. Better beer lovers demand more than what mass-produced beers offer. They aren't willing to settle for less than the best, and that forces the New England breweries to continue to strive toward greatness.

And finally, many thanks have to go out to my liver. If it weren't for my liver, it would not have been possible to drink more than 1,000 different beers brewed in New England, and that would be sad because I would be missing out on some truly phenomenal beers.

# Introduction

New England beer saved me from the mediocrity of flavorless, overpriced mixed drinks at bars. I hated beer while in college and wouldn't drink it. It wasn't snobbiness, it was flavor. Mass-produced beer didn't taste good to me, and why would I drink it? So I stuck to Captain Morgan's and Coke.

That was until I discovered the Stone Coast Brewery in Laconia, New Hampshire. I was working at a newspaper in the Granite State, and the Stone Coast, a brewpub, was the closest bar we could go to after deadline on Fridays. I remember looking at the beer list and seeing a beer called the Drunken Monkey Barleywine. I had no idea what a barleywine was, but I ordered it (how couldn't I, based on that name?) and tasted something I had never had before—a beer with flavor.

That started me on a journey of the exploration of the beer world. Sure, like all aspiring beer geeks, I fell in love with the California hop bombs, and the big, flavorful imperial stouts, but I always came back to New England breweries. Now, if you look in my beer fridge, most of it is New England beer. New England has truly turned into one of the great brewing regions in the country. You have the old standbys, such as Boston Beer Company (brewers of Samuel Adams Boston Lager) and Harpoon Brewery, both producing good solid beers, as well as branching out into more adventurous brews. And then you have exciting beer producers—Allagash Brewing Company in Maine that brews world class Belgian ales, Pretty Things Beer & Ale Project in Massachusetts that has some of the most exciting beers brewed anywhere in the US on the shelves, and the Narragansett Brewery of Rhode Island, which is trying to bring a classic New England brand back while introducing some of the best, easy-drinking seasonals on the market.

Don't forget about the brewpubs. Establishments throughout New England, such as the Cambridge Brewing Company and the Perfect Pear Cafe, combine quality beers brewed on the premises with delicious dishes, making them a one-stop destination for hungry craft beer lovers. Beer bars abound throughout the Northeast where you can get the latest and greatest local and imported beers on tap or in bottles.

Want to taste the best beer New England has to offer in one session? We're home to some of the best beer festivals in the country, from Beer Advocate's Extreme Beer Fest to the New England Real Ale Exhibition.

Ever thought about taking your love of craft beer to the next level and brewing your own? If you want to get your feet wet, stop by one of the handful of brew-on-premises establishments operating in New England to brew and bottle your own beer under the guidance of an expert. Go one step further and become a homebrewer, creating your own concoctions or trying one of the beer recipes available in this guide.

But the world of quality New England beer goes much further than brewing it and drinking it. Pair a dish with a good craft beer to take flavors to the next level, or better yet, cook with it! Try out some of the recipes on offer in the Food Recipes section to get a taste of classic New England food infused with its beer in your own kitchen.

This book is an exploration and celebration of New England beer from all angles. Maybe you'll find a brew you've never heard about, learn more about New England's proud brewing tradition, or be inspired to take a road trip to sample the best beer available in different regions, whether it's Massachusetts, Maine, Vermont, New Hampshire, Connecticut, or Rhode Island.

To us beer-loving New England natives and visitors alike: Cheers!

# How to Use This Guide

The brewery, brewpub, and beer bar listings in *Beer Lover's New England* are organized alphabetically within each state: Massachusetts, Maine, Vermont, New Hampshire, Connecticut, and Rhode Island. Every brewery profile contains a **Beer Lover's Pick,** a spotlight on the most outstanding beer being produced by its respective brewery, complete with tasting notes. You can find a complete list of Beer Lover's Picks organized by alphabetical order at the back of this guide in the Appendix.

In addition to the brewery, brewpub, and beer bar profiles that make up the bulk of this guide, you'll also find sections on:

**Beer Festivals:** A 12-pack of annual beer events is listed by month, with themes ranging from extreme craft beer to your typical outdoor summer fest.

**BYOB: Brew Your Own Beer:** This section celebrates the homebrewer, whether you're slightly interested in brewing your own beer or you're an avid hobbyist who's turned parts of your home into your own personal craft brewery. We've provided listings for brew-on-premises establishments for beginners and clone beer recipes for the advanced homebrewer.

**In the Kitchen:** It goes without saying that if you fancy yourself a bit of a beer lover, you might appreciate good food, too. And what goes better with a delicious meal than a glass (or two) of quality beer? Learn all about pairing types of food with styles of craft beer—complete with specific New England beer examples—and try your hand cooking with beer with the food recipes submitted by local chefs and beer enthusiasts.

**Pub Crawls:** In this itinerary-based section, we break down some of New England's greatest beer-centric cities into walkable tours where you can sample some of the best brew on offer throughout the region.

## Glossary of Terms

**ABV:** Alcohol by volume—the percentage of alcohol in a beer. A typical domestic beer is a little less than 5 percent ABV.

**Ale:** Beer brewed with top fermenting yeast. Quicker to brew than lagers, and most every craft beer is a style of ale. Popular styles of ales include pale ales, amber ales, stouts, and porters.

**Altbier:** A German style of ale, typically brown in color, smooth, and fruity.

**Barleywine:** Not a wine at all but a high-ABV ale that originated in England and is typically sweet. American versions often have large amounts of hops.

**Barrel of beer:** Production of beer is measured in barrels. A barrel equals 31 gallons.

**Beer:** An alcoholic beverage brewed with malt, water, hops, and yeast.

**Beer bar:** A bar that focuses on carrying craft or fine imported beers.

**Bitter:** An English bitter is an English style of ale, more hoppy than an English mild, but less hoppy than an IPA.

**Bock:** A German-style lager, typically stronger than the typical lager.

**Bomber:** Most beers are packaged in 12-ounce bottles. Bombers are 22-ounce bottles.

**Brewpub:** Typically a restaurant, but sometimes a bar, that brews its own beers on premises.

**Cask:** Also known as real ales, cask ales are naturally carbonated and are usually served with a hand pump rather than forced out with carbon dioxide or nitrogen.

**Clone beer:** A clone beer is a homebrew recipe based on a commericial beer.

**Contract brewery:** A company that does not have its own brewery and pays someone else to brew and bottle its beer.

**Craft beer:** High-quality, flavorful beer made by small breweries.

**Double:** Two meanings. Most often meant as a higher-alcohol version of a beer, most typically used in reference to a double, or imperial, IPA. Can also be used as an American translation of a Belgian dubbel, a style of Belgian ale.

**Gastropub:** A beer-centric bar or pub that exhibits the same amount of care selecting its foods as it does its beers.

**Growler:** A half-gallon jug of beer. Many brewpubs sell growlers of their beers to go.

**Gypsy brewer:** A company that does not own its own brewery, but rents space at an existing brewery to brew it themselves.

**Hops:** Hops are flowers used in beers to produce aroma, bitterness, and flavor. Nearly every beer in the world has hops.

**IBU:** International bittering units, which are used to measure how bitter a beer is.

**Imperial:** A higher alcohol version of a regular-strength beer.

**IPA:** India pale ale. A popular style of ale created in England that has taken a decidedly American twist over the years. Often bitter, thanks to more hops used than in other styles of beer.

**Kolsch:** A light, refreshing German-style ale.

**Lager:** Beer brewed with bottom fermenting yeast. Takes longer and is harder to brew than ales. Popular styles of lagers include black lagers, doppelbocks, pilsners, and Vienna lagers.

**Malt:** Typically barley malt, but sometimes wheat malt. Malt provides the fermentable sugar in beers. The more fermentable sugar, the higher the ABV in a beer. Without malt, a beer would be too bitter from the hops.

**Microbrewery:** A brewery that brews less than 15,000 barrels of beer a year.

**Nano-brewery:** A brewery that brews four barrels of beer per batch or less.

**Nitro draft:** Most beers that are served on draft use kegs pressurized with carbon dioxide. Occasionally, particularly with stouts, nitrogen is used, which helps create a more creamy body.

**Pilsner:** A style of German or Czeckolovian lager, usually light in color. Most mass-produced beers are based on this style.

**Porter:** A dark ale, similar to the stout but with less roasted characters.

**Pounders:** 16-ounce cans.

**Quad:** A strong Belgian-style ale, typically sweet and high in alcohol.

**Regional brewery:** A brewery that brews up to 6,000,000 barrels of beer a year.

**Russian imperial stout:** A stout is a dark, heavy beer. A Russian imperial stout is a higher-alcohol, thicker-bodied version of regular stouts.

**Saison:** Also known as a Belgian or French farmhouse ale. It can be fruity, and it can also be peppery. Usually refreshing.

**Seasonal:** A beer that is only brewed at a certain time of year to coincide with the seasons.

**Session beer:** A low-alcohol beer, one that you can have several of in one long "session" of drinking.

**Stout:** A dark beer brewed with roasted malts.

**Strong ale:** A style of ale that is typically both hoppy and malty and can be aged for years.

**Tap takeover:** An event where a bar or pub hosts a brewery and has several of its beers on tap.

**Triple (Tripel):** A Belgian-style ale, typically lighter in color than a dubbel but higher in alcohol.

**Wheat beer:** Beers, such as hefeweizens and witbiers, are brewed using wheat malt along with barley malt.

**Yeast:** The living organism in beer that causes the sugars to ferment and become alcohol.

## New England Beer News & Reviews

With the New England beer scene growing by leaps and bounds, the online beer community is keeping pace. There are numerous great beer blogs and websites worth checking out to get the latest news, information, reviews, and thoughts on beer. These eight are some of the best beer blogs out there, but search around and you may find your own favorite.

**Andy Crouch's BeerScribe.com, www.beerscribe.com:** Andy Crouch is one of the most knowledgeable people about beer in New England, and his articles are well written, informative, and entertaining. Crouch is a talented writer and has written two books, including *Great American Craft Beer*.

**Beer Advocate, www.beeradvocate.com:** There is simply not a better resource online anywhere for information about beer. Run by brothers Jason and Todd Alstrom, the site is a clearinghouse of beer news. Press releases about new beers are posted daily and every beer event—festivals, beer dinners, tastings—is listed. The Beer Fly is an essential tool when planning a beercation. There are also ample forums on numerous subjects where people get into debates, discuss new trends in beer, and share their latest beer hauls.

**The Beer Babe, www.thebeerbabe.com:** Meet Carla Companion, known in the beer world as the Beer Babe. This Maine-based blog is well organized and a fun read, with sections split up into different categories—reviews and beer adventures being two of them—so that it's easy to navigate.

**Beer Nut, http://blogs.wickedlocal.com/beernut:** Okay, self-promotion—this is my beer blog. It is updated daily with beer reviews, press releases, and information about upcoming events. Also features a weekly guest blog from Jack's Abby Brewing in Framingham and a weekly guest homebrewing blog.

**Connecticut Beer, www.connbeer.com:** If you want information about Connecticut beer, breweries, brewpubs, and bars, this is the place to go. Michael Walsh knows his stuff, and his passion for the local beer scene shows on his blog.

**Here for the Beer, www.hereforthebeer.com:** Here for the Beer is the brainchild of husband and wife Tim and Amy Brady of Vermont. The website is heavy on professional-quality videos of different bars and events the pair attends, as well as some of the most unique, and almost risqué, reviews on the web.

**Lost in the Beer Aisle, www.lostinthebeeraisle.com:** Blogger Josh Dion talks about beer from an everyman's perspective, posting honest reviews of what he thinks about craft beer. Numerous photos from different events and bars are always posted.

**Seacoast Beverage Lab, http://seacoastbeveragelab.com:** Brian Aldrich has one of the better-looking beer blogs in New England, and the content is pretty darn good, too. Heavy on reviews, it also has a calendar of events, a section on pub crawls, and beer news.

# Massachusetts

This isn't the Massachusetts beer lovers from the 1990s and early 2000s remember. From a region that was once known for its traditional English-style pale ales, mild IPAs, and blueberry beers, Massachusetts has become an area exploding with experimentation.

Breweries—from those established in the mid-1980s like Harpoon to those just starting in the last few years such as Wormtown Brewing Company—are taking some serious chances with the beers they produce. And now pretty much every region in the state has a great beer bar to go out to and grab your local favorite or imported beer, all served in the proper glassware. Brewpubs aren't letting this experimentation pass them by, be it the barrel-aging process going on at Cambridge Brewing Company or brewing hopless beers or beers with bacon at the Watch City Brewing Company in Waltham.

Massachusetts has truly become one of the brewing hubs in the US.

Massachusetts
N
VERMONT
NEW HAMPSHIRE
MASSACHUSETTS
NEW YORK
CONNECTICUT
RHODE ISLAND
ATLANTIC OCEAN
Massachusetts Bay
Cape Cod Bay
Buzzards Bay
Vineyard Sound
Nantucket Sound
Muskeget Channel
Rhode Island Sound
Block Island Sound
Martha's Vineyard
Nantucket Island
Connecticut River
Quabbin Reservoir
Mount Greylock
Manchester
Lowell
Plum Island
Ipswich
Gloucester
Beverly
Salem
Lexington
Bolton
Clinton
Concord
Cambridge
Boston
Wellesley
Quincy
Worcester
Sutton
Williamstown
Shelburne Falls
Deerfield
Pittsfield
Richmond
Lenox
Stockbridge
New Marlborough
Springfield
Brimfield
Provincetown
Truro
Wellfleet
Plymouth
Eastham
Brewster
Orleans
Sandwich
Yarmouth Port
South Yarmouth
Chatham
Hyannis Port
Dennis Port
Falmouth
Woods Hole
Providence
Fall River
Westport
North Dartmouth
New Bedford
Newport
Hartford
Waterbury
New Haven
Bridgeport
New London
0
20
40 miles

## BACKLASH BEER COMPANY

Contract brewed at Paper City Brewing Company in Holyoke, MA; (617) 615-9345; BacklashBeer.com

**Founded:** 2011 **Founder:** Maggie Foley, Helder Pimentel **Brewer:** Helder Pimentel **Flagship Beer:** Groundswell **Year-round Beers:** Convergence, Declaration **Seasonals/Special Releases:** Salute, Uprising! series, Apocalypse series **Tours:** None

Backlash Beer was one of the most anticipated breweries to open in Massachusetts when they released its first beer, **Groundswell,** in 2011. Founders Helder Pimentel and Maggie Foley used social media such as Twitter (@BackLashBeer) to get the word out about their beers months ahead of time, building up a fan base rarely seen for a brewery no one has ever tried before.

Backlash's beers did not disappoint. Groundswell was delightful Belgian blonde ale, spot on for the style. At 6.4 percent alcohol by volume (ABV), it's not too strong, but it has enough oomph to it for those who like bigger beer. The other year-round beers are **Convergence** and **Declaration.** Convergence is a 7 percent ABV Belgian-style saison. It's spicy and peppery and it finishes on the dry side. It pairs fantastically with roast chicken (author note: I know this from experience, it was great). Declaration is a 7.2 percent Belgian-style IPA. Belgian-style IPAs typically blend the hop characteristics of American hops with the spicy Belgian yeast. Declaration blends those flavors better than many of the style.

Backlash has also done two popular series of beers, the **Uprising! series** and the **Apocalypse series.** The Uprising! series based its beers on Backlash's Salute double IPA. Each beer features the same malt bill as Salute, but each of the beers—**Catalyst, Outbreak,** and

Massachusetts

**Riot**—featured several different hops, making each beer completely different. The Apocalypse series features four beers, **War,** which is a Rye farmhouse ale; **Famine,** which is a single hop tripel; **Conquest,** which is another Belgian IPA; and **Death,** an imperial stout.

Backlash contract brews its beers at Paper City Brewing Company in Holyoke, Massachusetts. All of Backlash's beers are available in 22-ounce bombers and on draft.

**Declaration**
**Style:** Belgian IPA
**ABV:** 7.2
**Availability:** Year-round
Not being a fan of the style, me picking this beer as the Beer Lover's Pick is showing how well-done this beer is. It blends the American and Belgian together perfectly, making this one of the best Belgian IPAs you'll find.

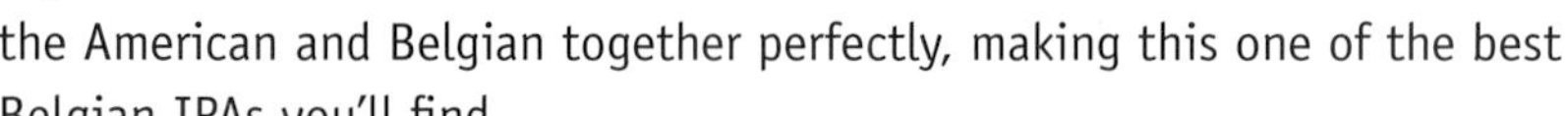

## BAD MARTHA BEER

Contract brewed at Mercury Brewing Company, Ipswich, MA; (617) 922-9242; BadMarthaBeer.com **Founded:** 2013 **Founder:** Jonathan Blum, Peter Rosbeck **Brewer:** Jared Ruben (develops recipes) **Flagship Beer:** Martha's Vineyard Ale **Year-round Beers:** Island IPA **Seasonals/Special Releases:** Vineyard Summer Ale **Tours:** None

They may have "bad" in its name, but Bad Martha Beer is doing a lot of good. Founded by Martha's Vineyard seasonal residents Jonathan Blum and Peter Rosbeck, Bad Martha Beer seeks to help those in need, donating the first 10 percent of all proceeds from the sales of its beers to food banks in whichever community the beers are sold.

Bad Martha Beer, although based in Martha's Vineyard, is actually brewed at Mercury Brewing Company in Ipswich. All of the beer recipes are created and developed by Jared Ruben, a former brewer at the popular Goose Island Brewing Company in Chicago, Illinois.

The brewery's flagship beer is the **Martha's Vineyard Ale,** a 5.3 percent alcohol by volume (ABV) Amber Ale. It has flavors of caramel and biscuits, with just a hint of hops in the finish. The **Island IPA** is a 5.5 percent ABV India pale ale. This beer has flavors of pear, grapefruit, and other tropical fruits. It has a slight bitterness, but it's balanced out by the bready malts. The brewery's one seasonal, **Vineyard Summer Ale,** is a hybrid style. It's brewed with pilsner malt and is similar to a pilsner, but brewed with ale yeast.

## BANNER BEER COMPANY

Based in Grafton, MA, brewed at Opa Opa in Williamsburg, MA; (617) 642-8079; BannerBeerCompany.com

**Founded:** 2013 **Founder:** Todd Charbonneau **Brewer:** Todd Charbonneau **Flagship Beer:** American Ale **Year-round Beers:** American Rye **Seasonals/Special Releases:** All-Nighter, American Summer **Tours:** None

Todd Charbonneau is not against high alcohol beers. As the former longtime head brewer at the Harpoon Brewery, he created some of the highest alcohol beers the Boston brewery's have ever produced.

But, Charbonneau is also the father of three and likes to exercise in the morning, and it is hard to deal with those responsibilities if your head is foggy after a night of drinking high-alcohol beer.

And that's where the idea of Banner Beer Company came from—low-alcohol beers with a lot of flavors. Banner Beer specializes in what is called "session beer." Session beers are meant to be drank over a long drinking session with friends, with the alcohol by volume (ABV) being low enough to not impair the drinker.

Banner's first beer was the **American Ale,** which is its flagship beer. It is a 3.5 percent ABV hoppy ale. It is amazingly easy to drink, and has a great hop presence

**American Rye**
**Style:** Rye Beer
**ABV:** 4 percent
**Availability:** Year-round
Many rye beers are high-alcohol IPAs, which sometimes mask the fantastic rye flavor. Banner's American Rye showcases the spicy peppery goodness. It's a dry beer that pairs well with grilled fish.

that does not overwhelm the rest of the beer. Banner's other year-round beer is the **American Rye,** a 4 percent ABV rye ale. The rye is spicy and dry. It has just a slight hop bite in the finish.

Banner also brews two seasonals, the **American Summer** and the **All-Nighter.** The American Summer is a 3.7 percent blonde ale. It is easy to drink, smooth, and flavorful. The All-Nighter is Banner's winter beer, and it's an English-style bitter. It is also Banner's strongest beer at 5 percent ABV. The beer is spot on for the style, flavorful with earthy and piney hops and enough malt backbone to make this a pleasant beer to drink. Banner's beers are available in both 22-ounce bottles and 12-ounce cans. It is also available on draft. Charbonneau brews the beers at Opa Opa's Williamsburg production facility.

## BERKLEY BEER COMPANY

17 Cotley St., Berkley, MA; (508) 326-9954; BerkleyBeer.com
**Founded**: 2012 **Founder:** Glenn Barboza **Brewer:** Glenn Barboza **Flagship Beer:** Berkley IPA **Year-round Beers:** Berkley Golden Ale **Seasonals/Special Releases:** Coffee Porter, Harvest Ale **Tours:** None

Located in the tiny farming community of Berkley, the Berkley Beer Company is almost a perfect mirror of its home community. It's small (a three-barrel nano brewery) and located on the farm. And, like many farmers, founder/brewer Glenn Barboza uses ingenuity to save money, using a wood burning system with reclaimed scrap and cord wood, to heat all of the brewery's water for brewing.

Founded in 2012, Berkley brews two year-round beers, the **Berkley IPA** and the **Golden Ale.** The Berkley IPA, which is 7 percent alcohol by volume (ABV), starts with a touch of malt sweetness, which is followed by a blast of citrus flavors, finishing on a pleasantly bitter note. It is nicely balanced and easy to drink for a beer as strong as it is. The Golden Ale is a pleasant enough beer. It is 5 percent ABV, a crisp and relatively full-bodied beer for the style.

Berkley also brews two seasonals, the **Harvest Ale,** available in the fall, and the **Coffee Porter,** available in November. The Harvest Ale is brewed in the Oktoberfest style, but with Berkley's house ale yeast. There's a lot of rich, sweet caramel-like flavors in the beer, with just a hint of alcohol in the finish. The Coffee Porter is brewed with local coffee beans, and has strong coffee flavors and a hint of chocolate.

Berkley Brewing does not offer tours. All of its beers are available in 22-ounce bottles.

**Coffee Porter**
**Style:** Porter
**ABV:** 6 percent
**Availability:** Rotating
The addition of coffee can turn a decent porter into a really good porter. That's the case with Berkley's Coffee Porter. Although the body is a little light, the fabulous coffee flavors, along with the chocolate notes, more than make up for the lighter body.

## BERKSHIRE BREWING COMPANY

12 Railroad St., South Deerfield, MA; (413) 665-6600; www.berkshirebrewingcompany.com
**Founded:** 1994 **Founder:** Gary Bogoff and Chris Lalli **Brewer:** Gary Bogoff **Flagship Beer:** Steel Rail Pale Ale **Year-round Beers:** Berkshire Traditional Pale Ale, Dean's Beans Coffeehouse Porter, Drayman's Porter, Gold Spike German-Style Kolsch, Lost Sailor IPA, River Ale, Russian Imperial Stout, Shabadoo Black & Tan **Seasonals/Special Releases:** Cabin Fever Ale, Czech-Style Pilsner, Hefeweizen, Holidale, Maibock Lager, Oktoberfest Lager, Raspberry Barley Wine-Style Ale **Tours:** Sat, 1 p.m.

For years, Berkshire Brewing Company was western Massachusetts beer. It rarely got east of I-495. Now the secret is out. South Deerfield's Berkshire Brewing Company is available pretty much state-wide and people now know how good their beers are.

From their year-round beers to their seasonal beers, Berkshire does a great job with pretty much everything they brew. The **Steel Rail Pale Ale,** Berkshire's flagship beer, is a New England classic—a hoppy, well-balanced pale ale that is a treat to find on tap. **Dean's Beans Coffeehouse Porter** is a fantastic beer with strong coffee flavor from the use of real coffee beans, making it a perfect after-dinner drink. The **Drayman's Porter** (similar to the Coffeehouse Porter without the coffee) is a really good porter. The **Gold Spike Kolsch,** a year-round beer, is perfect to drink during the summer, and the **Lost Sailor IPA** is a quality IPA. The **Shabadoo Black & Tan** saves you the trouble of getting out a spoon and trying to do your own black and tan at home. The **Russian Imperial Stout** is an underrated beer. Drink this next to some of the nationally respected imperial stouts and it will hold up more than adequately.

Where Berkshire really excels is its seasonal beers. They have the best lineup of seasonal beers in all of New England. The **Czech-Style Pilsner** is excellent—nearly perfect for the style. It is a great summer beer, as is Berkshire's other summer beer, the **Hefeweizen.** The **Maibock Lager** is a German style brewed to be released in May. It's stronger than an average bock and has some heat from the alcohol—it's one of the best maibocks brewed in the US today. The **Oktoberfest Lager** is a

**Coffeehouse Porter**
**Style:** Coffee Porter
**ABV:** 6.2 percent
**Availability:** Year-round
A good porter can be an enjoyable beer to drink, but add real coffee and you have something special. Berkshire's Coffeehouse Porter is one of those special beers. The coffee flavors in this beer are incredible, yet it is still an easy-drinking beer. Great in a bottle, and on nitro draft. It is a perfect after-dinner drink.

slightly stronger version of the popular German style. It's one of the many quality Oktoberfest-style beers brewed in New England. Berkshire also brews three stupendous winter seasonals, the **Cabin Fever Ale, Holidale,** and the **Raspberry Barley Wine-Style Ale.** The Cabin Fever is a malty pale ale. The Holidale is a phenomenal barleywine. The Raspberry Barley Wine-Style Ale is not a traditional barleywine. It is actually a strong ale. Whatever style you call it, the raspberries make this a beer to seek out. Get a bottle of the Coffeehouse Porter and a bottle of the Raspberry Barley Wine-Style Ale. Pour a glass about three quarters full of the porter and then fill the rest with Raspberry. Yum.

Brewery tours are held on Saturday, and there are tastings in the Dick Schatz Tap Room. The tap room is named for a volunteer who died in 2006 and who left to Berkshire his large collection of beer memorabilia, which now adorns the walls at the brewery.



## BIG ELM BREWING

65 Silver St., Sheffield, MA; (413) 229-2348; BigElmBrewery.com
**Founded:** 2012 **Founder:** Christine and Bill Heaton **Brewer:** Christine Heaton **Flagship Beer:** Big Elm IPA **Year-round Beers:** 413 Farmhouse Ale, Gerry Dog Stout **Seasonals/ Special Releases:** Lion's Ale, Dead of Winter, God Save the Queen, Route 7 Rauchbier
**Tours:** Sat, noon to 4 p.m.; free

Christine and Bill Heaton brought a lot of experience with them when they founded Big Elm Brewing in the western Massachusetts town of Sheffield. They had worked together at the popular Pennsylvania brewery Victory Brewing Company (Bill Heaton hired Christine) and then moved to Pittsfield Brew Works in 2005, before selling it in 2012. Now, the husband and wife team have a small production brewery (less than 1,000 barrels of beer a year).

Big Elm brews three year-round beers that are all canned. They also brew several different special releases that are all hand-bottled. The year-round beers include the **Big Elm IPA,** a 7 percent alcohol by volume (ABV) IPA brewed with American hops and a mix of American and German malts. Despite the high alcohol for the style, the beer is balanced. The **413 Farmhouse Ale** is Big Elm's take on a farmhouse ale. It's brewed with honey, chamomile, lemon zest, and Brazilian pink peppercorns. The **Gerry Dog Stout** is a pleasant, roasty, creamy oatmeal stout that comes in at 6.5 percent ABV.

Special releases include the **Lion's Ale,** a 5.3 percent ABV English amber ale; the **Dead of Winter,** a Russian imperial stout that is the brewery's biggest beer at 10.5 percent ABV; **God Save the Queen,** an extra special bitter; and the **Route 7 Rauchbier,** a classic German-style smoked beer.

## Beer Lover's Pick

**The 413 Farmhouse Ale**
**Style:** Saison
**ABV:** 6 percent
**Availability:** Year-round
Massachusetts has become a hotbed for saisons and farmhouse ales. It seems like any brewery that started after 2006 brews one. Big Elms puts a twist on the style, adding several ingredients such as local honey and Brazilian pink peppercorns, which make this a unique beer worth trying.

Big Elm is open for tours on Saturdays from noon to 4 p.m., which are free. Samples of the various beers are also free, and growlers, as well as glasses and shirts, are available for purchase.

### BLATANT BREWERY

Contract brewed by Brewmaster's Brewing Company, Williamsburg, MA; no phone number; BlatantBrewery.com
**Founded:** 2011 **Founder:** Matthew Steinberg **Brewer:** Contract brewed **Flagship Beer:** Blatant Session Ale **Year-round beers:** Blatant IPA, Blatant Imperial Stout **Seasonals/ Special Releases:** None **Tours:** None

Founded by veteran Bay State brewer Matthew Steinberg in 2011, Blatant Brewery is contract brewed by the Brewmaster's Brewing Company in Williamsburg.

Blatant brews three beers—the flagship **Blatant Session Ale,** the **Blatant IPA,** and the **Blatant Imperial Stout.** The Blatant Session Ale is a 3.75 percent alcohol by volume (ABV) blonde ale. A session beer is meant to be a beer you can have during a drinking "session," where you drink several beers over a long period without getting intoxicated. The key is to make the beer tasty enough that you want to keep coming back for more. The Session Ale does it. Blonde ales are mild, but this one has more flavor than many, with just a hint of hops to add some character to it.

**Blatant Imperial Stout**
**Style:** Imperial Stout
**ABV:** 9 percent ABV
**Availability:** Year-round
It seems like every imperial stout coming out today is brewed with coffee or chocolate or vanilla or some other ingredient, or aged in Bourbon barrels. Blatant Imperial Stout is just that, an imperial stout. It's simply a good beer done right.

Blatant describes its IPA as being "heavily hopped," and they are correct. There are major hop flavors and aromas in this 6.5 percent ABV IPA. However, the malts are almost doughy, bread-like, which provides a nice balance, keeping this from being too bitter. The Blatant Imperial Stout is Blatant's biggest beer at 9 percent ABV. All of Blatant's beers are available in bombers and on draft.



## BLUE HILLS BREWERY

1020 Turnpike St., Canton, MA; (781) 821-2337; BlueHillsBrewery.com
**Founded:** 2009 **Founders:** Peter Augis, Martin Grots, Andris Veidis **Brewer:** Andris Veidis **Flagship Beer:** IPA **Year-round Beers:** Black Hops, Comet Ale, Imperial Red IPA, Wampatuck Wheat **Seasonals/Special Releases:** Antimatter, Dunkelweizen Wampatuck Winter Wheat, Oktobrau, Pumpkin, Quarter Mile Double IPA, Watermelon Wampatuck Wheat **Tours:** Mon through Fri, 9 a.m. to 5 p.m.

What's better than spending the day on the slopes at the Blue Hills ski area and ending that day by a warm fire with a nice cup of hot cocoa? Ending the day cozied up to a bar with a good beer in your hand, that's what. And thanks to the nearby Blue Hills Brewery, there is plenty of fresh, locally brewed beer for the skiers and non-skiers alike.

Andris Veidis, a longtime brewer, brings years of experience to the brewery, brewing both traditional and newer styles of beer, giving local beer fans a wide variety to choose from. The **Black Hops** is a black India pale ale, or as some people call it, a Cascadian dark ale. Blue Hills incorporates the same malts into the Black Hops

**OktoBrau**

**Style:** Oktoberfest

**ABV:** 5.8 percent

**Availability:** Fall Seasonal

This is Blue Hill's best beer. The OktoBrau is a German-style Oktoberfest, and it's close to being spot on for the style, with a tad more sweetness than you would expect. There are caramel flavors, as well as the flavors of brown sugar. There is a graininess present, but it does not detract from the beer.

as they would for a German-style black lager. They then use the house ale yeast, and then lager it—fermenting it in the cold rather than at room temperature. This gives it a combination of chocolaty and citrus aroma and flavor. The **Imperial Red IPA** is basically an imperial red ale. It is a big beer (9 percent alcohol by volume). There's a lot of malt in it, typical of a red ale, and it's aggressively hopped like a double IPA. The regular **IPA** is a good, solid IPA. It leans toward the hoppy side, but has enough sweet malt to balance it out. The final year-round beer is the **Wampatuck Wheat,** a refreshing German-style hefeweizen. The Wampatucks were a local American Indian tribe, and Blue Hills honors them by naming several of their beers after them.

Their seasonals include the **Wampatuck Winter Wheat** and the **Watermelon Wampatuck Wheat,** which is a summer beer. The winter wheat is a heartier wheat beer, while the watermelon wheat is the original Wampatuck Wheat flavored with watermelon extract. The **Antimatter** is an interesting series of beers. Several breweries do what are called "single hop" beers. These are typically IPAs, all brewed exactly the same, except with different hops. The Antimatter alternates between being a single hop or single malt beer. It is cool to see how changing one ingredient changes the beer. The fall seasonals consist of the **Pumpkin** and the **OktoBrau.** Pumpkin beer fans will enjoy the pumpkin ale and the OktoBrau is a traditional German-style Oktoberfest.

## BOG IRON BREWING

33 West Main St., Suite 5, Norwood, MA; (508) 952-0555; BogIronBrewing.com
**Founded:** 2013 **Founders:** Matt Menard, Brian Shurtleff, Frank White **Brewers:** All three founders share brewing duties **Flagship Beer:** Burley Blonde **Beers:** Babula, Campout Mild, Cease & Desist, Da Honey Stank, Dunkel Weizen, One Down, Slap Happy, The Stinger
**Taproom hours:** Wed, 4 to 8 p.m.; Sat, 10 a.m. to 2 p.m.

Bog Iron Brewing may be small, but they are prolific. Even though they are a nano-brewery, Bog Iron produces nine very different styles of beer. Founders Matt Menard, Brian Shurtleff, and Frank White, three members of a homebrew club, all share brewing duties for the beers that are available in a few restaurants and bars and in the brewery's taproom.

The brewery specializes in unique beers. Almost all are slightly different from the norm. For example, the **Burley Blonde** is a blonde ale, usually light and sometimes on the bland side but not the Burley Blonde. This is a 7.5 percent alcohol by volume (ABV) blonde ale, a huge beer for the style, with quite a bit of floral and citrus hop flavors. The **Cease & Desist** is a California common (better known as a steam beer, but "steam" is trademarked by the Anchor Brewing Company of California). But it's a California common with a twist. It's brewed with roasted malts, giving it a not typical roasted flavor and a darker color than other California commons. The **Campout Mild** is an English mild, coming in at a very low 3.5 percent ABV, while the **Dunkel Weizen,** one of the more traditional beers, is a 5.5 percent ABV example of the style.

The brewery has also dabbled in barrel aging, releasing the **Babula,** a 4.8 percent ABV lambic aged in Chardonnay barrels. The **One Down** is a 7.15 percent porter that is smoked with cherry wood. **The Stinger** is a typical IPA, except with the addition of locally produced honey.

The other beers are the 5.8 percent ABV **Slap Happy,** a rye lager, and **Da Honey Stank,** a 5.5 percent ABV pale ale brewed with wild yeast to give it a little sourness and barnyard flavor (that's a good thing when done right).

Bog Iron's brewery also serves as a taproom, with pints of beer, as well as food from the nearby Dawg House available. The brewery also offers 33.8-ounce and 16.9-ounce refillable bottles of its beers to go, rather than the typical 64-ounce growlers. Technically, there are no tours, but the taproom is open to the whole brewery and you can see everything from there.

## BOSTON BEER COMPANY

30 Germania St., Jamaica Plain, MA; (617) 368-5080; www.samueladams.com
**Founded:** 1984 **Founder:** Jim Koch **Brewer:** Jim Koch **Flagship Beer:** Samuel Adams Boston Lager **Year-round Beers:** Sam Adams Light, Boston Ale, Pale Ale, Black Lager, Honey Porter, Irish Red, Blackberry Witbier, Latitude 48 **Seasonals/Special Releases:** Bonfire Rauchbier, Chocolate Bock, Cranberry Lambic, Dunkel-weizen, East West Kolsch, Harvest Pumpkin Ale, Holiday Porter, Noble Pils, Octoberfest, Old Fezziwig Ale, Rustic Saison, Summer Ale, White Ale, Winter Lager, Imperial Series, Barrel Room Collection, Infinium, Utopias **Tours:** Six tours daily, Mon through Sat, between 10 a.m. and 3 p.m. There is also a Friday evening tour and several special events at the brewery.

You can't talk about New England beer without talking about the Boston Beer Company. The story has been told numerous times—how Jim Koch, using a mid-nineteenth-century family recipe, brewed the first Samuel Adams Boston Lager in his kitchen, and the rest is history. They are now the largest American-owned brewery. You can find Samuel Adams Boston Lager everywhere in the country, and it is often the better beer lover's only viable option at bars and restaurants.

But Samuel Adams is about more than the Boston Lager. Nearly every Samuel Adams beer is top-notch. The **Latitude 48** is a solid IPA, and the **Octoberfest** is one

### Beer Lover's Pick

**Utopias**
**Style:** Strong Ale
**ABV:** 27 percent or higher
**Availability:** Released every other year
The Utopias is the strongest beer brewed in the US, and the most unique. It is 27 to 28 percent alcohol by volume (ABV). It has no carbonation, and maple syrup is used to help jack up the alcohol. It's also fermented for years in different barrels. And, oh yeah, it'll cost about $160 a bottle. But what you get is something akin to a fine liquor, worth savoring and sharing with friends.

of the best of the style brewed in the US, as is the **Noble Pils.** Other seasonals, such as the **Harvest Pumpkin** and **Winter Lager,** and are all worth trying.

Samuel Adams constantly introduces those new to craft beers to styles not often seen from larger breweries. Case in point, the **Bonfire Rauchbier,** or German smoked beer, is a great introduction to the style, as is the **Rustic Saison** and **East West Kolsch.** The brewery also continues to experiment. The **Imperial Series,** all high-alcohol beers, features four different ales—the **Imperial Stout, Imperial White,** the **Doppelbock,** and the **Wee Heavy.** They also introduced the **Barrel Room Collection** in 2010, which is a series of barrel-aged beers, all using what Jim Koch describes as Kosmic Mother Funk, a blend of wild yeasts and bacteria that gives the beers a unique quality.

After all the success he's had through the years, Koch has not forgotten his roots as a homebrewer. Samuel Adams sponsors two homebrewing contests every year. The largest is the LongShot contest, which is open nationally. Two homebrewers, as well as an employee homebrewer, will have their winning beers released in six-packs. The Patriot Homebrew contest is open to New England residents and the winning beer is put on tap at Gillette Stadium, home of the New England Patriots, all football season.

Tours are available at the Jamaica Plain brewery, and they often offer beers not available outside of the brewery for sampling.



## BREWMASTER JACK

Contract brewed at Paper City Brewing Company, Holyoke, MA; (413) 367-7190; BrewmasterJack.com

**Founded:** 2011 **Founder:** Tyler Guilmette **Brewer:** Contract brewed **Flagship Beer:** Stray Dog Lager **Year-round Beers:** Ambrewsia Imperial IPA, Aquila Pale Ale, Total Eclipse Rye Porter **Seasonals/Special Releases:** James, Soleil, Hop Essence Series **Tours:** None

There is no Jack who works at Brewmaster Jack. Rather, the small contract brewery is named for founder Tyler Guilmette's grandfather, who brewed beer during Prohibition. Brewmaster Jack produces a wide variety of beers, both year-round and special releases, brewed at Holyoke's Paper City Brewing Company.

BREWMASTER JACK

The **Stray Dog Lager** is a 4.5 percent alcohol by volume (ABV) amber lager. It is full-flavored, sweet, but crisp, reminiscent of a lighter Oktoberfest lager. The **Ambrewsia Imperial IPA** is on the lighter side of an imperial IPA at only 7.7 percent ABV. But don't let

## Beer Lover's Pick

**Stray Dog Lager**
**Style:** Golden lager
**ABV:** 4.5 percent
**Availability:** Year-round
Maybe because the craft beer world is dominated by ales, when I get a hold of a great tasting lager, I get excited. This beer is fabulous, a touch sweet, very crisp, and easy drinking. It's a treat.

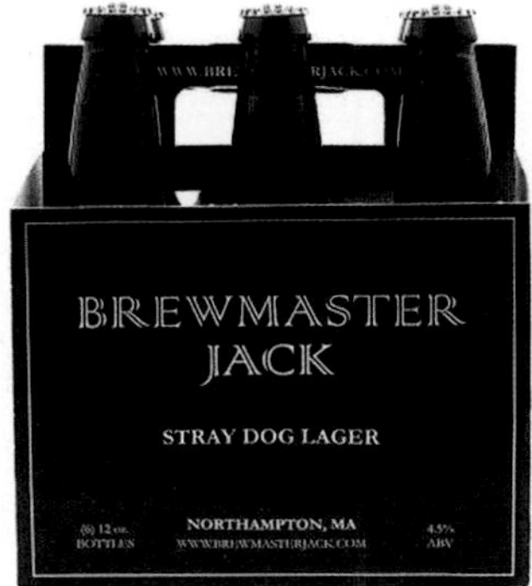


the low alcohol fool you, this beer is packed with hops and will satisfy almost any hophead's cravings. The **Aquila Pale Ale** is pretty much a standard pale ale. If you're a fan of the style, you could do worse. The **Total Eclipse Rye Porter** is a 6.8 percent porter brewed with both rye and chocolate malts. There is just a hint of chocolate, but the spicy rye really comes through. The beer is a little lighter-bodied than you'd expect, but that doesn't take away from the flavors.

Brewmaster Jack also produces what is called the **Hop Essence Series.** It is a series of beers created to showcase a single hop. Unlike many single hop series, where each beer is brewed using the same malt bill, but different hops, each beer is a completely different recipe, designed to showcase whatever hop is being used in that beer. Other beers include **James,** which is a hoppy blonde ale, and the **Soleil,** a French saison.

Brewmaster Jack also strives to use local ingredients whenever it can. In all of its beers, at least 25 percent of the malt comes from Valley Malt, a Hadley maltster. The goal is to reach 100 percent of local hops some day. If you're wondering about food pairings, Brewmaster Jack offers suggestions for each of its beers on its website.

### CAPE ANN BREWING COMPANY

11 Rogers St., Gloucester, MA; (978) 282-7399; CapeAnnBrewing.com
**Founded:** 2002 **Founders:** Jeremy and Michael Goldberg **Brewer:** Jeremy Goldberg
**Flagship Beer:** Fisherman's Brew **Year-round Beers:** Fisherman's Ale, Fisherman's IPA
**Seasonals/Special Releases:** Bavarian Wheat, Pumpkin Stout, Imperial Pumpkin Stout, Fisherman's Navigator **Tours:** Mon through Fri, 11 a.m. to 5 p.m.; free

The Cape Ann Brewing Company has really adopted Gloucester's rich fishing history—all of this small brewery's beers include "Fisherman's" in their titles. The beers aren't fishy, though. Cape Ann produces nothing but solid beers, from its year-round rotation to its seasonal releases.

Brothers Jeremy and Michael Goldberg founded the brewery in 2002. Jeremy Goldberg is a homebrewer who took a 40-day cross-country road-trip with a group of friends that included stops at 38 different breweries. That trip, and Goldberg's concern about his weight gain, can be seen in the documentary *American Beer*, directed by Paul Kermizian. That trip inspired Jeremy Goldberg to open the brewery, and thankfully for us, he did.

Cape Ann offers three year-round beers, the **Fisherman's Brew,** the **Fisherman's Ale,** and the **Fisherman's IPA.** The Fisherman's Ale is a must-have for kolsch lovers. Kolsches are light, refreshing, and delicate beers. They are not easy to brew, and tend to come out either flavorless, or ruined by the addition of too much . . . something, that takes them out of the kolsch realm. The Fisherman's Ale strikes a perfect balance of having enough flavor to make it enjoyable, but not crossing the line into another style. The Fisherman's Brew is an amber/red lager and is an

## Beer Lover's Pick

**Pumpkin Stout**
**Style:** Stout
**ABV:** 7 percent
**Availability:** Fall Seasonal

Cape Ann's Pumpkin Stout is the cure for those who are sick of the number of regular pumpkin beers that flood the market in the fall. Many are overly spicy and taste like liquid pumpkin pie. The Pumpkin Stout, on the other hand, is a stout first and foremost, with the added flavor of real pumpkin. The pumpkin doesn't overwhelm the roasty-coffee flavors from the stout, providing a balance that is the key to this fantastic beer.

easy-drinking beer, perfect after a day out on the boats, or, for most people, walking around Gloucester checking out the sights. The Fisherman's IPA is just what it says, a straightforward IPA.

The seasonals are some of the best out there. The **Fisherman's Navigator,** the winter seasonal, is a wonderfully brewed dopplebock—malty and sweet, just like a good doppelbock should be. Spot on. The **Bavarian Wheat** is a German-style hefeweizen. Like the Fisherman's Ale, this is a great summer beer, good on a hot day. Cape Ann also does a twist on the ever popular style of pumpkin beers. They brew two pumpkin stouts, the **Pumpkin Stout** and the **Imperial Pumpkin Stout.** The Imperial Pumpkin Stout is a big beer, 11 percent ABV, but the roastiness and pumpkin flavors do a good job of hiding the booziness usually present in a beer that big. The Pumpkin Stout is an ideal combination of roastiness and pumpkin, a perfect beer for the fall.

Tours are free, and are offered Mon through Fri from 11 a.m. to 5 p.m. Tours are also available on weekends if an employee is free to give the tour. Samples are also available at the bar. When you make a trip to the Cape Ann Brewery, be sure to stop at the on-site restaurant. Not only do they offer a full menu, but they also offer beers available exclusively at the pub, on draft only and not bottled.

## CAPE COD BEER

1336 Phinney's Ln., Hyannis, MA; (508) 790-4200; CapeCodBeer.com
**Founded:** 2004 **Founders:** Beth and Todd Marcus **Brewer:** Todd Marcus **Flagship Beer:** Cape Cod Red **Year-round Beers:** Cape Cod Blonde Ale, Cape Cod IPA **Seasonals/Special Releases:** Berry Merry Holiday Ale, Dunkel Weizen, Harvest Ale, Old Man Winter, Porter, Summer Ale, Stargazer Stout, Cherry Porter, Hot Blonde, Port-O-Vino, Stock Porter, Vanilla Bean Porter **Tours:** Guided tours on Tues at 11 a.m. and Sat at 1 p.m. Self-guided tour during business hours Mon through Fri, noon to 6 p.m., and Sat from 11 a.m. to 2 p.m.

Cape Cod Beer gives vacationing beer lovers on the Cape a fantastic local option to drink while spending time with the family. The brainchild of husband and wife team Todd and Beth Marcus, Cape Cod Beer is a fabulous little brewery. The beers are not that easy to find outside of the Cape Cod and south shore area, but are worth seeking out if you happen to be vacationing nearby.

The year-round offerings are all pleasant beers to drink. They may not be the most exciting styles, but they are done the right way. The **Cape Cod IPA** is on the bitter side, and the **Cape Cod Blonde Ale** is ultra-refreshing. The flagship beer, the **Cape Cod Red,** is an excellent amber ale.

Where Cape Cod really excels is their seasonals and special releases. The **Old Man Winter** is what is called an old ale. This is a malty beast, which is balanced out with a fair amount of hops. The 8 percent alcohol by volume is perfect to warm you up on a blustery winter night. The **Berry Merry Holiday Ale** is brewed with cranberries, cloves, and orange, and the resulting taste is like Christmas morning in a glass. The **Summer Ale** is a German-style hefeweizen, while the **Harvest Ale** is German-style ale and tastes like an ale version of an Oktoberfest. Cape Cod Beer also does several special releases, including different versions of its porter—the **Cherry Porter** and the **Vanilla Bean Porter.** These beers are not always available, and some are brewery-only releases.

One such brew, the **Port-O-Vino,** is a collaboration with local winery Truro Vineyards. The brewery's porter is aged in fresh Merlot barrels, and the flavors of the chocolate malt and the Merlot work in harmony to create a unique beer. The Port-O-Vino is specially bottled in 750 ml champagne-style bottles and is only available at the brewery.

The brewery tour lasts approximately 45 minutes and includes a description of the brewing process and all of the ingredients, and a history of the brewery is presented. Beer samples are also available. Along with their beer and brewery merchandise, the brewery store also sells locally made products such as Barnstable Bats, candles, honey, soap, potato chips, ice cream, and other items.

**Cape Cod Red**
**Style:** Red Ale
**ABV:** 5.5 percent
**Availability:** Year-round
Red ales are a dime a dozen, and get overlooked because so many are mediocre. The Cape Cod Red is anything but boring. It's a well-done red ale, has flavors of roasted toffee and caramel, and smells sweeter than it is. There is a bit of a hop presence in the background, but this is a malt forward beer.

Massachusetts

### CISCO BREWERS

5 Bartlett Farm Rd., Nantucket, MA; (508) 325-5929; CiscoBrewers.com
**Founded:** 1995 **Founders:** Randy and Wendy Hudson **Brewer:** Jeff Horner **Flagship Beer:** Whale's Tale Pale Ale **Year-round Beers:** Bailey's Blonde Ale, Baggywrinkle Barleywine, Captain Swain's Extra Stout, Grey Lady, Indie Pale Ale, Moor Porter, Sankaty Light **Seasonals/Special Releases:** Celebration Libation, Pumple Drumkin, Summer of Lager, Woods Series, Island Reserve Series **Tours:** Mon through Fri, 4 p.m.; $20

Cisco Brewers has evolved over the years. The Nantucket brewery has always brewed great beers, but a few years ago they started taking advantage of the fact that the Nantucket Vineyard and the Triple Eight Distillery are all on the same grounds. The brewers started to incorporate the barrels used at the vineyard and distillery, and began creating exceptional offerings. At that point, Cisco moved from a solid brewery with a great track record to one of the best breweries in all of New England.

The **Woods Series** beers are, without exception, fabulous. **Cherry Woods** is one of the best beers brewed in Massachusetts, and definitely the best fruit beer. It is a wheat beer aged in Chardonnay oak barrels, brewed with whole sour cherries. The only fruit beer on Cherry Woods level is also from Cisco, the **Monomoy Kriek,** which is a Flemish sour red ale, is also made with whole sour cherries, fermented in oak barrels. The **Winter Woods** is an ambitious beer. It's a Flemish braggot brewed with wild yeast and aged in French oak barrels with Pinot Noir grapes, mulling spices, and cherry-wood-smoked malt. If this does not scream "cold winter night beer," nothing does. The **Lady of the Woods** is a white ale aged in oak Chardonnay barrels, and **Full & By Rye** is aged in rye whisky barrels.

If barrel-aged beers are not for you, there are plenty of other choices. The **Whale's Tale Pale Ale,** the flagship beer, is a solid pale ale. The **Sankaty Light Lager** is a good option for those who are not fans of bigger beers with high ABVs. The **Captain Swain's Extra Stout** is a full-flavored stout full of coffee notes, and the **Baggywrinkle Barleywine** is a big beer, meant to be enjoyed slowly. The **Moor Porter** is a good English-style porter. The **Indie Pale Ale** is a hoppy, west coast IPA, while the **Grey Lady** is an excellent Belgian-style witbier (the same beer becomes Lady of the Woods after aging in oak Chardonnay barrels). The **Bailey's Blonde Ale** is an easy-drinking blonde ale.

If you are on vacation on Nantucket, make sure you take the tour at Cisco Brewers because it is much different than the average brewery tour. For $20, brewer Jeff Horner will lead you through a tour of the brewery, the winery, and distillery. There, you will learn about the various processes for all three, and get a chance to

## Beer Lover's Pick

**Pechish Woods**
**Style:** American Wild Ale
**ABV:** 4.9 percent
**Availability:** Rotating

The Pechish Woods is a fantastic beer—I do not even like peaches, and I like this beer. The Pechish Woods is a wheat beer that incorporates real peaches and is aged in white wine barrels that impart some wine character. Combine that with the use of wild yeast, and the result is a beer that has a nice tartness that makes you want to take one sip after another after another.



try the different products each offers. The tours last about an hour, and are offered daily at 4 p.m. from Memorial Day through Columbus Day. You can also buy beer to go in six-packs of 12-ounce bottles, bombers, and growlers.

### CLOWN SHOES BEER

Contract brewed in Ipswich, MA; ClownShoesBeer.com
**Founded:** 2010 **Founder:** Gregg Berman **Brewer:** n/a **Flagship Beer:** Hoppy Feet **Year-round Beers:** Blaecorn Unidragon, Brown Angel, Clementine, Chocolate Sombrero, Galactica, Hoppy Feet 1.5, Muffin Top, Tramp Stamp, Undead Party Crasher **Seasonals/ Special Releases:** Bombay Berzerker, Crunkle Sam, Ghengis Pecan, Luchador en Fuego, Swagger **Tours:** None

Clown Shoes beers draw a lot of attention, and sometimes not for the right reason. Some of their beer labels and names are on the risqué side. For instance, the **Tramp Stamp** features a close-up drawing of a tattoo on the small of a woman's back who is wearing low-riding jeans, or the **Brown Angel** who features a clown-shoed-wearing angel appearing to do a booty dance.

Even beer lovers who can be easily offended should not let their scruples overshadow the beer. Clown Shoes is responsible for some really high-quality beer. The brewery, which contract brews its beer at Mercury Brewing Company in Ipswich, started off with just one beer, the **Hoppy Feet.** It was one of the first east coast versions of a black IPA. Clown Shoes later introduced Hoppy Feet's big brother, the **Hoppy Feet 1.5,** which is basically the same beer with one and half times the ingredients.

Brown Angel is a quality brown ale, if not traditional for the style. It is packed with malts and is hoppier than a lot of brown ales. It also comes in at a relatively hefty 7 percent alcohol by volume (ABV). The **Clementine Witbier** is another one of the underrated beers from Clown Shoes. This is exactly what a Belgian-style white beer should be and it stands up to any other Belgian wit being brewed today. Like Hoppy Feet and Hoppy Feet 1.5, Tramp Stamp is Clown Shoes' version of a newer beer style, this time a Belgian-style IPA. **Muffin Top** is another Belgian IPA, but higher in alcohol (7 percent ABV to 10 percent ABV), and is the better beer. It is a nicely done beer, and there are still enough hops in there to balance the beer out. It is almost like a black pale ale. Other year-round beers include the **Chocolate Sombrero, Galactica,** and **Undead Party Crasher.**

Clown Shoes also offers several seasonals, including **Bombay Berzerker, Crunkle Sam, Swagger, Genghis Pecan,** and **Luchador en Fuego.**

**Clementine**
**Style:** Belgian wit
**ABV:** 6 percent
**Availability:** Year-round
Clementine is an underrated Belgian witbier, probably one of the best available in all of New England. It is ultra-refreshing, even if it's a little stronger than the typical beer of the style. While it is made with the traditional spices, the addition of Clementines sets this beer apart.

## CODY BREWING COMPANY

36 Main St., Amesbury, MA; (978) 378-3424; CodyBrewing.com
**Founded:** 2006 **Founder:** Sean Cody **Brewer:** Sean Cody **Flagship Beer:** Cody's Pub Ale **Year-round Beers:** Black Hole Stout, Dog Daze, Cody's Original North Shore Amber Ale, Gee Man's Lemon Honey Hypnotic Tonic, No Name IPA, Powwow Golden Ale, SOS, Wheelers Brown **Seasonal/Special Releases:** Too many to list, dozens of beers make occasional appearances **Tours:** None

The Cody Brewing Company may be one of the best kept secrets when it comes to great New England breweries. They do not distribute far outside of the Amesbury area, but their beers are definitely worth seeking out. Founder Sean Cody originally started Cody Brewing as a brew-on-premises business, but he expanded to distributing his own beer in 2006, and he has not looked back since. Cody Brewing Company's beers are available all over the north shore, and have recently expanded to Boston and central Massachusetts.

Cody brews some phenomenal beers, many with Belgian influences, and others that come straight from the founder and brewer's creative imagination. One of those beers is the **Gee Man's Lemon Honey Hypnotic Tonic,** an 8.8 percent strong ale brewed with "obscene amounts of citrus," as well as 1 pound of honey per 1 gallon of beer, which makes for a sweet, but shockingly drinkable beer. The **SOS** is a Belgian/IPA hybrid. The SOS was first brewed before Belgian IPAs became all the rage. It is brewed with a combination of American, Canadian, and German malts; American hops; and Belgian yeast. The combination works—the SOS tastes like the two styles melded perfectly, unlike most Belgian IPAs that taste like two separate styles working against each other. **Cody's Pub Ale** is an American-style pale ale, nicely hopped with a solid malt body. The **No Name IPA** is a well-hopped IPA. It is not overwhelmingly bitter, but a nicely done beer. It is not quite west coast style, but it is too hoppy to be English style—it's Cody style. The **Black Hole Stout** is an Irish stout with more chocolate undertone than the traditional stout. **Cody's Original North Shore Amber Ale** is Cody's first-ever beer. It is a hoppy amber ale and remains a solid beer after all these years. Other year-round beers include the **Wheelers Brown,** which is an oatmeal brown ale, and the **Powwow Golden Ale,** a Belgian-style golden ale named for the Powwow River on which the brewery is located. The **Dog Daze** is a light, refreshing hefeweizen.

The Cody Brewing Company brews many other beers throughout the year, but none are regulars and some may not be brewed every year. These occasional releases include some extremely creative beers. The occasional releases include the **Cookie Puss,** which is an oatmeal raisin stout; **Wasabi Lemongrass Lager; Plum Dubbel;**

## Beer Lover's Pick

**SOS**
**Style:** Belgian IPA
**ABV:** 5.5 percent
**Availability:** Year-round

Belgian IPAs are all the rage now, but Cody Brewing Company's SOS was one of the early pioneers of the style. This beer combines the hoppiness of a nice IPA with the sweetness of Belgian yeast and malt. The result is an extremely complex beer. Belgian IPAs can go awry when one side dominates the other, but this one plays it down the middle, and to delicious effect.

the **Mullet,** a mulled strong ale; **Red Ryder,** a Christmas "fruitcake" ale; and the **Sick Pumpkin,** an imperial pumpkin ale.

## ELEMENT BREWING COMPANY

30 Bridges St., Millers Falls, MA; (413) 835-6340; ElementBeer.com
**Founded:** 2009 **Founders:** Ben Anhalt, Tom Fields, Dan Kramer **Brewer:** Dan Kramer **Flagship Beer:** Extra Special Oak **Year-round Beers:** Red Giant, Dark Element **Seasonals/ Special Releases:** Summer Pilsner Fusion, Altoberfest, Brix, Vernal **Tours:** Thurs through Sat, noon to 6 p.m.

Element Brewing Company is a tiny brewery that brews big beers—all of their offerings tip the scales at 7.75 percent alcohol by volume (ABV) or more. Located in the small town of Millers Falls in Western Massachusetts, Element is the brainchild of friends Ben Anhalt, Tom Fields, and Dan Kramer. Both Anhalt and Kramer have had long brewing careers—Anhalt brewed at Maplewood Farms Restaurant & Brewery, Paper City, and Opa-Opa Brewing; and Kramer brewed at the Commonwealth Brewery, River City Brewing (Florida), Owen O'Leary's, and Opa-Opa Brewing. Fields is a jack of all trades, having worked in sales, construction, and business.

Element's beers stand out on the shelves—they're packaged in 750 ml caged and corked bottles, wrapped in paper. Currently, this nano-brewery (they only brew 200 barrels of beer a year) only brews three year-round beers. If you're a fan of traditional beers, Element Brewing Company may not be for you since style guidelines really do not exist in their world.

The **Extra Special Oak** is a big, malty beer, coming in at 7.75 percent ABV. Light carbonation allows vanilla from the oak to come through. The **Red Giant** is another malty beer, but this one also has a lot of hop bitterness. It's similar to an imperial red, but

## Beer Lover's Pick

**Extra Special Oak (Cask)**
**Style:** English Strong Ale
**ABV:** 7.75 percent
**Availability:** Year-round
Extra Special Oak is an excellent beer, but having it served on cask brings it to another level. It smooths out and becomes creamy, and the vanilla/oak flavors really come through. The caramel malt sweetness blends with that vanilla to make this a decadent after-dinner dessert beer. If you're lucky enough to find this on cask at a bar, get it—you won't be disappointed.

sweeter than one of the typical style. Like the Extra Special Oak, this is a sipping beer, weighing in at 8 percent ABV. The **Dark Element** is described as a "New American Black Ale." It tastes like a combination German-style black lager and an American IPA. Flavors of chocolate and toffee mix in well with the hop bitterness. This is their biggest year-round beer at 8.8 percent ABV.

Element also offers four seasonals, called the **Interval Series.** The **Summer Pilsner Fusion,** brewed with pilsner malt and oatmeal, is available during the summer. The **Altoberfest,** a German-style altbier, is available during the fall. **Brix,** Element's winter seasonal, is similar to an English-style barleywine, but brewed with beet sugars and English hops. **Vernal,** the spring beer, is a dark wheat wine.

Tours are available during the day and are run by one of the owners. Samples of the year-round beers are available during the tour, but not of the Interval or other special releases. Their beer is also available to go at the brewery, either in growlers or in the normal 750 ml bottles.

Massachusetts

### GLASS BOTTOM BREWERY

480 Pleasant St., Lee, MA; (413) 243-6170; GlassBottomBrewery.org
**Founded:** 2012 **Founders:** Erza Bloom, Evan Williams **Brewer:** Erza Bloom **Beers:** TeaSB, Trail Magic, Motte & Bailey, Dark Sails Stout, Parsnipitty, Banana Cream Stout, Prairie Whale Cask Ale, Forest Farmer's Ale **Tours:** No formal tours, but brewers will show people around if it's not too busy during the tasting room's Saturday hours from 1 to 6 p.m.

The Glass Bottom Brewery wants to be Berkshire's own brewery. They use as many local ingredients as possible and they are growing hops on their one acre farm in nearby Great Barrington, with plans on using the mature hops in their beers. The Glass Bottom Brewery is the brainchild of high school friends Erza Bloom, who is the head brewer, and Evan Williams, who is in charge of the farm. (They pretty much do everything else, too).

The brewery produces a series of unique beers. The **TeaSB** is an English-style bitter, but with a twist—it's brewed with Earl Grey tea and lemon zest. The **Trail Magic** celebrates the Appalachian Trail, putting a trail mix worth of ingredients in this nontraditional pale ale. The ingredients include chocolate, nuts, and dried fruits. The **Mottle & Bailey** and **Dark Sails Stout** are probably the most traditional beers for Glass Bottom. The Mottle & Bailey, 5.3 percent alcohol by volume (ABV), is a Scottish ale brewed with peat-smoked malt. The Dark Sails Stout is also 5.3 percent ABV, and it's a smooth and roasty dry stout. The **Parsnipitty** is perhaps the first Belgian-style tripel in the world brewed with parsnips, while the **Banana Cream Stout** is described as "a banana milkshake in a stout glass." The **Prairie Whale Cask**

**Parsnipitty**
**Style:** Belgian tripel
**ABV:** 7.4 percent
**Availability:** Rotating
I'm not sure if I like this beer, but what I will say, it is one of the most unique beers you'll taste. I always give credit for brewers who take chances to create good beers, and using parsnip was a big chance. Give it a try and see what you think.

**Ale** is a hybrid of an American an English IPA. It uses American hops, but the traditional grain bill of and English IPA. The **Forest Farmer's Ale** is probably the closest beer Glass Bottom has to a seasonal. It is brewed with local maple syrup, which is harvested in the spring, as well as spruce nettles and oak chips.

The Glass Bottom Brewery offers samples and growlers of all of its available beers at its Lee brewery. They are open for growler fills from 1 to 6 p.m. on Saturday. Although there are no tour hours, if the employees aren't too busy filling growlers, they are willing to take visitors on an impromptu tour.

## GOODFELLOW'S BREWING COMPANY

8 Race Course Rd., Lakeville, MA; phone number not available; GoodfellowsBrewing.com
**Founded:** 2011 **Founders:** John and Lisa Goodfellow **Brewer:** John Goodfellow **Flagship Beer:** WheneverFest!Ale **Year-round Beers:** Frugal Farm Light, Race Course IPA, The Townsman Stout **Seasonals/Special Releases:** Red Ale, Maple Scottish Ale **Tours:** By appointment, using contact form on website, free

When husband and wife team John and Lisa Goodfellow decided to open Goodfellow's Brewing Company, they set a goal to become Lakeville's brewery and to use as many local ingredients as possible. To get those ingredients, the Goodfellow's formed an agricultural cooperative agreement with Paul and Kim Hunt, owner of Frugal Endeavors Farms, who grow ingredients that the Goodfellows buy and use in their beer. The results, are a portfolio of beers that have a local flare that many New England breweries don't have. Goodfellow's finally began selling its beers in growlers and on draft in 2013.

The brewery features four year-round beers and two seasonals. Goodfellow's most popular beer is the **WheneverFest! Ale,** which is Goodfellow's take on a Marzen, or Oktoberfest (Oktoberfest beers are traditionally lagers, this is an ale). Unlike most Oktoberfest beers, which are only available in September through early November, the WheneverFest! Ale is year-round, giving fans of the malty style pleasure throughout the year. The **Frugal Farm Light** is named for the Goodfellows' partners at the farm. The "Light" part of the name does not mean low alcohol or low flavor, instead, it refers to color. The Frugal Farm Light is a 6 percent alcohol by volume (ABV) blonde ale. The **Race Course IPA** is a 7 percent ABV beer that really falls somewhere between an IPA and an English-style bitter. The beer, brewed with locally grown Cascade hops, is mildly bitter, with fruity notes and a bready malt background. The **Townsman Stout** is a 7 percent ABV American stout. It has the typical roasted and chocolaty flavors you expect from the style, with just a hint of hops in the finish. Goodfellow's fall/winter seasonal is the **Maple Scottish Ale,** a warming 7.2 percent ABV malty beer with locally harvested maple syrup. The spring/summer seasonal is the 7 percent ABV Red Ale, a malt-forward, sweet beer. Actually, it's kind of an unusual summer beer, as most summer beers are lighter, less malty, more effervescent than the typical red ale.

**WheneverFEST! Ale**
**Style:** Oktoberfest-ish
**ABV:** 6.5 percent
**Availability:** Year-round

Each year, I lament the shrinking number of Oktoberfest beers available on liquor store shelves as pumpkin beers have taken over the fall seasonal market. This is a welcome alternative during the year. Although not a traditional Oktoberfest, it has many of the characteristics of one, and will help Oktoberfest lovers bide their time until the German ones are once again available.

Goodfellow's currently only does tours by appointment and its growlers are available in local stores, and the beers are available on draft at local restaurants.

### HARPOON BREWERY

306 Northern Ave., Boston, MA; (617) 574-9551; HarpoonBrewery.com
**Founded:** 1986 **Founders:** Rich Doyle, Dan Kenary, George Ligeti **Brewer:** Al Marzi
**Flagship Beer:** Harpoon IPA **Year-round Beers:** Leviathan Imperial IPA, Munich Dark, UFO Hefeweizen, UFO White Harpoon Cider, Harpoon Honey Cider, Rich & Dan's Rye IPA
**Seasonals/Special Releases:** Bohemian Pilsner, Bronze King, Celtic Ale, Chocolate Stout, Grateful Harvest Cranberry Ale, Imperial Pumpkin Ale, Octoberfest, Summer Beer, UFO Pale Ale, UFO Pumpkin Ale, UFO Raspberry Hefeweizen, Winter Warmer, 100 Barrel Series, Harpoon Pumpkin Cider **Tours:** Mon through Wed, noon to 5 p.m.; Thurs and Fri, noon to 6 p.m.; Sat, 11:20 a.m. through 6 p.m.; and Sun 11:30 a.m. to 5:30 p.m.; $5.The Harpoon Beer Hall is open Sun through Wed 11 a.m. to 7 p.m.; Thurs through Sat, 11 a.m. to 11 p.m.

The Harpoon Brewery has been around since the beginning of the craft beer revolution in the mid-1980s, and they continue to evolve to this day. Founded in 1986 by friends Rich Doyle, Dan Kenary, and George Ligeti, the brewery was inspired

#### Beer Lover's Pick

**Grateful Harvest Cranberry Ale**
**Style:** Fruit Beer
**ABV:** 5.9 percent
**Availability:** Fall Seasonal

Cranberries and beer? It really shouldn't work, but it does in this beer. The cranberry does not overwhelm the other flavors, which so often happens in fruit beers. It's also a perfect accompaniment for Thanksgiving. Much better than that can-shaped pile of cranberry sauce, and with alcohol, which sometimes you need to deal with your family.

by their love of European beer, and their realization that there was nothing up to that standard available locally.

Harpoon's biggest selling beer is the **Harpoon IPA,** which is a perfect example of how the brewing culture has changed over the years. When the IPA was introduced in the late 1980s, it was considered a hoppy, bitter beer. Now, there are pale ales that are hoppier than this beer. That doesn't mean you shouldn't drink it—it's a great, easy-drinking, malty IPA, more along the lines of an English style than an American version.

Nearly as popular as the Harpoon IPA is the **UFO Hefeweizen.** UFO stands for "unfiltered offering." The UFO is based on German-style wheat beers, although it is not the same. It lacks the bubble gum/clove/banana flavors a traditional German hefeweizen typically has. What it does have in common with its German brethren is how refreshing it is. The UFO Hefeweizen's popularity has inspired a whole series of UFO beers—the **UFO Raspberry Hefeweizen,** the **UFO Pale Ale,** the **UFO White,** and the latest series offering, **UFO Pumpkin.** Like the original UFO, these beers are perfect thirst quenchers, with enough flavors to satisfy the discerning palate.

Other year-round beers include the **Munich Dark** (a dunkel weizen), the **Harpoon Cider** (a solid hard cider), and the **Leviathan Imperial IPA.** Harpoon also brews the **100 Barrel Series.** The 100 Barrel Series is just that—100 barrels of a beer are brewed just once (although some have been brought back for encores). Typically, one particular brewer, or a guest brewer from another brewery or country develops the beer. There have been 50 installments of the series. Seasonals also include the **Summer Beer, Octoberfest, Winter Warmer, Chocolate Stout,** and the **Grateful Harvest Cranberry Ale.**

Throughout the year, Harpoon hosts several outdoor festivals that include good beer, good food, and good music, right at the brewery, located in the Seaport District. Harpoon also owns a second brewery in Windsor, Vermont. Both breweries host tours and tastings.

Harpoon in Boston also has the Harpoon Beer Haul, which features Harpoon beers and ciders on tap, often brewery-only releases. They serve pretzels made in-house with the spent grain from the brewing process.

### HIGH & MIGHTY BEER COMPANY

108 Cabot St., Holyoke, MA; (413) 323-8040; HighAndMightyBeer.com
**Founded:** 2006 **Founder:** Will Shelton **Brewer:** n/a **Flagship Beer:** Beer of the Gods **Year-round Beers:** Purity of Essence, Two-Headed Beast, XPA **Seasonal/Specialty Releases:** Fumata Bianca, Fumata Nera, Home for the Holidays, Pas De Deux, Saint Hubbins Ale
**Tours:** None

High & Mighty Beer Company has a high opinion of itself. "We're not just brewers, we're beer-evangelists," they say on their website. "We're the clergy of Zymurgy, the Priests of Yeasts, the Joyful Congregation of High Fermentation." With an introduction like that, High & Mighty sets themselves up for a major fail if their beer does not live up to expectations. Luckily, High & Mighty delivers.

The **Beer of the Gods** is High & Mighty's flagship beer. It is a 4.5 percent ABV, easy-drinking blonde ale with a nice hop kick. It holds a special place in my heart. I fondly remember drinking several of these with friends on the deck of a cabin in Cooperstown, New York, in 2007. The **Purity of Essence** is described as an India pale lager. This is a hoppy lager, but different than other hoppy lagers as it is brewed with all German malts and German hops, giving it a much more subtle flavor than American hops. The **Two-Headed Beast** is an excellent, creamy stout, made with organic cacao and Belgian yeast. The combination works. The yeast gives it an interesting flavor you do not get with many chocolate stouts. The **XPA** is a pale ale brewed with hops and grains from both the United Kingdom and the Pacific northwest. The middle of the "X" in the XPA is Massachusetts.

## Beer Lover's Pick

**Home for the Holidays**
**Style:** American Brown Ale
**ABV:** 7 percent
**Availability:** Winter Seasonal
Home for the Holidays is one of the standout brown ales being brewed anywhere, in New England and beyond. This brown ale has a slightly Belgian character, but it has a lot of nutty and caramel flavors. There are also hints of chocolate. There is very little roasted character and it has some flavors of dark fruits. This may be 7 percent alcohol by volume (ABV), but it so smooth and drinkable, you would never know.

Specialty beers include the **Fumata Bianca** and the **Fumata Nera.** Both of these beers are smoked rye beers. However, the Bianca is a smoked white rye beer while the Nera is a smoked black rye beer. Both are excellent, but if you have to pick one, get the Nera. The **Pas De Deux** is a classic Belgian-style saison brewed with French ale yeast. It is a very dry beer, perfect for pairing with foods, particularly chicken and turkey. The **Home for the Holidays** is a superb brown ale, brewed just for the winter. It is smooth, creamy, and wonderfully nutty. The **Saint Hubbins Abbey Ale** is a traditional Belgian-style abbey ale.

## IDLE HANDS CRAFT ALES LLC

89 Commercial St., Malden, MA; (617) 819-4353; IdleHandsCraftAles.com **Founded:** 2011 **Founders:** Christopher and Grace Tkach **Brewer:** Ben Howe **Flagship Beer:** Pandora **Year-round Beers:** Blanche de Grace, D'Aison, Dubbel Dimples, Triplication **Seasonals/Special Releases:** Absence of Light, Bourbon Barrel-Aged Triplication, Charlton Rogue, Darkness Prevails, Enlightenments Ales line of beers including Brut, Cosmos, Day Trip, Illumination, Rite of Spring **Tours:** Wed through Fri, 5 to 8 p.m., Sat, noon to 5 p.m; $5. Private tours are available by appointment.

Husband and wife team Christopher and Grace Tkach founded their brewery in 2011, but thanks to a licensing issue with the state, Idle Hands Craft Ales LLC did not release its first beer until 2012. Idle Hands is one of the smallest breweries in all of Massachusetts, a true nano brewery. Despite that, they produce a fairly large number of Belgian-inspired ales available in 750 ml caged-and-corked bottles.

Idle Hands' year-round beers include **Pandora, Blanche de Grace, Dubbel Dimples,** the **D'Aison,** and **Triplication.** Pandora is a classic Belgian pale ale, while Blanche de Grace (named after Grace Tkach) is a Belgian-style witbier. The Dubbel Dimples is a Belgian dubbel, while the D'Aison is a non-traditional dark saison, rather than the typical, light-colored, effervescent beer. Other beers include **Absence of Light,** a Belgian-stout, and **Darkness Prevails,** a barrel-aged version of the Abscense of Light. The **Charlton Rogue** is a Flanders red ale.

In January 2014, Idle Hands and a small Lowell brewery named Enlightenment combined. Idle Hands bought the Enlightenment line of beers, and Enlightenment's owner, Ben Howe, joined Idle Hands as the new head brewer. The Enlightenment Ale beers include

## Beer Lover's Pick

**Triplication**
**Style:** Tripel
**ABV:** 9 percent
**Availability:** Year-round
Triplication is Idle Hand's take on a classic Belgian-style tripel. This 9 percent alcohol by volume is spicy and fruity, with just a hint of heat from the alcohol. It is balanced and easy to drink. It's an excellent take on the popular style.

the **Brut,** a Belgian-style Champagne ale, where the beer is aged and fermented similar to a Champagne. The **Illumination** is a unique beer, a blend of a funky, barnhousey (yes, that's a good thing), farmhouse ale, and a hoppy IPA. The **Cosmos** is a Belgian stout, while the **Rite of Spring** is a "rustic saison" brewed with local honey and wild yeast that adds a similar funkiness to it similar to the Illumination. The **Day Trip** is a golden ale with extra hops.

### JACK'S ABBY BREWING

81 Morton St., Framingham, MA; (508) 872-0900; JacksAbbyBrewing.com
**Founded:** 2011 **Founders:** Eric Hendler, Jack Hendler, Sam Hendler **Brewer:** Jack Hendler **Flagship Beer:** Jabby Brau **Year-round Beers:** Hoponius Union, Smoke and Dagger, Mass Rising **Seasonals/Special Releases:** Framinghammer Baltic Porter, Framinghammer Coffee Baltic Porter, Framinghammer Vanilla Baltic Porter, Barrel-Aged Framinghammer, Kiwi's Rising, Copper Legend Octoberfest, Saxonator, Berliner Braun, Smoked Marzen, Numb Swagger, Sunny Ridge Pilsner, Maibock Hurts Like Helles, Babymaker, Lashes, Cascadian Scwharzbier, Leisure Time Lager, Fire in the Ham **Tours:** Sat, 1 to 5 p.m., each hour; free. Tasting room open Wed through Sat, noon to 8 p.m.

Jack's Abby Brewing is a little different than most breweries in New England (or any craft brewery in the US)—they brew only lagers. Lagers take much longer to brew than ales, usually taking up tank space that can be quickly turned around by brewing ales. But Jack's Abby Brewing, one of the newest breweries in Massachusetts, has been inspired by the monastic brewing tradition of Germany, where the best lagers in the world are brewed.

The brewery is a family affair, owned by the Hendler brothers. Jack, the head brewer, is the former brewer of the popular Boston Beer Works brewpub. Sam and Eric handle all of the other duties (marketing, web, sales). The "Abby" in Jack's Abby Brewing is not a typo—it's named for Jack's wife, Abby.

Although inspired by German brewing, not all of the beers are traditional. They brew four very different beers. The brewery's flagship is the **Jabby Brau,** which is described as a "session lager." It is only 4.5 percent alcohol by volume. The beer has some qualities of a pilsner, but is darker than the golden yellow that most pilsners are. The **Smoke and Dagger** is a smoky, black lager. The smokiness goes well with the roastiness. Neither flavor dominates, and neither is so overwhelming that you

**Hoponius Union**
**Style:** India Pale Lager
**ABV:** 6.7 percent
**Availability:** Year-round

There aren't many hoppy lagers like the Hoponius Union. It hits you with big floral notes and grapefruit flavors from the hops. This is the kind of lager even the most hard-core hophead will enjoy. The lager yeast really allows the hops to come through. Not the most balanced beer, but it's not supposed to be. Share a growler of this with friends and everyone will be happy.

can't have more than a glass. An overly smoky beer can be a chore to drink, but the Smoke and Dagger strikes the perfect balance of smokiness and drinkability. The **Hoponius Union** is Jack's Abby Brewing's attempt at an India pale lager. It's hopped like a west coast IPA, but it still has the clean lager taste. They also brew **Mass Rising,** a double India pale lager, which won a gold medal at the Great American Beer Fest in Colorado.

Jack's Abby also brews several seasonals, such as **Maibock Hurts Like Helles, Copper Legend, Leisure Time Lager,** and **Pumpkin Crop Lager.** They also have plans to brew a still-unnamed wet hop lager.

The **Kiwi's Rising** is a double India pale lager. There are no kiwis in this beer. The name comes from the use of New Zealand hops. This may not be a true double IPA, but it is a great beer for hopheads. Other special releases include **Fire in the Ham,** a fantastic smoked beer, and **Framinghammer,** a Baltic Porter. Jack's Abby brews several different versions of Framinghammer, including a coffee and vanilla version.

Since opening in 2011, Jack's Abby has more than doubled their physical space, and increased their brewing capacity by several thousands barrels a year. They have added a taproom, where they serve full pints of beer, as well as several brewery-only releases.

## KRETSCHMANN BREWING COMPANY

294 Thompson Road, Webster, MA; (508) 671-7711; KBCBrewing.com

**Founded:** 2012 **Founder:** Brian Kretchman **Brewer:** Brian Kretchman **Flagship Beer:** Webster Lake Ale **Year-round Beers:** Bock, Double Bock, Dunkel, Lake Lager, Vienna Lager, Copper Pot Ale, Hermann the Great, IPL **Seasonals/Special Releases:** Butternut Ale, Cranberry Snow, Holiday Porter, Roasted Pumpkin, Rooftop Brown Ale **Taproom hours:** Fri 6 to 9 p.m. and Sat noon to 4 p.m.

Kretschmann Brewing Company, which gets its name from founder/brewer Brian Kretchman's family's original last name, is located in tiny Webster, Massachusetts. in a tiny 700-square-foot brewery. Despite the small size, Kretschmann brews many beers that are in rotation throughout the year, as well as numerous seasonals. The beers are available as growlers in the brewery's taproom on Friday from 6 to 9 p.m. and Saturday noon to 4 p.m. There are also free samples.

Kretschmann brews both German-style (in honor of Kretchman's family heritage) and American-style beers. The German styles include the **Lake Lager,** a 4.5 percent alcohol by volume (ABV) Czech-style pilsner, the **Bock** and **Dopplebock,** the **Dunkel** and the **Vienna Lager.** Kretschmann's Amercian styles include the **Copper**

**Pot Ale**, a 6 percent amber ale; **Hermann the Great**, a pale ale named for one of Kretchman's ancestors; the **IPL,** a 5 percent ABV India pale lager; and the flagship **Webster Lake Ale,** a light ale made with local corn.

Kretschmann also brews several seasonals. The **Roast Pumpkin Ale** comes in at 7 percent ABV and is made with pumpkins Kretchman grows himself. The **Butternut Ale** is also made with his own homegrown butternut squash.

They also brew the **Holiday Porter,** which uses cherry and oak, the **Rooftop Brown Ale,** which is made with molasses and aged with Bourbon-soaked oak and the **Cranberry Snow,** made with wheat and Massachusetts cranberries.

Due to the brewery's size, Kretschmann does not offer tours.

### LEFTY'S BREWING COMPANY

301 Wells St., Greenfield, MA; (413) 648-6111; LeftsBrew.com
**Founded:** 2010 **Founder:** Bill Goldfarb **Brewer:** Bill Goldfarb **Flagship Beer:** IPA **Year-round Beers:** Chocolate Oatmeal Stout, Coffee Porter, English-style Porter, Irish-style Stout, Pale Ale, Golden Ale, Imperial Porter, Graham Cracker Porter, Smoked Porter **Seasonals/Special Releases:** Honey Brown Ale, Oktoberfest, Big Brekkie Breakfast Stout, Maple Ale, Maple Oatmeal Stout **Tours:** Sat 2 to 4 p.m.

Like Greenfield, the town that hosts it, Lefty's Brewing Company is not well known outside of the general geographic area. People in Boston have probably never heard of either the town or the brewery. That's okay. The brewery, founded in 2010 by Bill "Lefty" Goldfarb, is a hidden jewel in western Massachusetts.

Goldfarb was a longtime homebrewer who left his roofing job to pursue his dream of brewing professionally. His brewery is tiny: a small two-barrel brew house that includes retrofitted milk tanks. He hand bottles all of the beer. He only brews 320 barrels of beer a year, not a lot, but for a one-man operation, it's impressive.

Currently, Lefty's Brewing Company brews six different beers, **Pale Ale, IPA, English-style Porter, Coffee Porter, Irish-style Stout,** and a **Chocolate Oatmeal Stout.** The Pale Ale is on the hoppier side of the style, which gives it a nice bitter zing when you take that first sip. The IPA is well balanced, leaning toward west coast style with enough hops that a hophead won't be bored by it, but not too

**Chocolate Oatmeal Stout**
**Style:** Oatmeal Stout
**ABV:** 7.2 percent
**Availability:** Year-round

The problem with many chocolate stouts is the chocolate often overshadows the rest of the ingredients. That's not the case with Lefty's Chocolate Oatmeal Stout. This is a lusciously creamy stout, and the chocolate adds to this beer rather than overwhelms it. It is not a huge imperial stout, either, but you do get hints of alcohol, particularly in the finish.

overwhelming to those who aren't hop lovers. The two porters are fantastic. The English-style Porter is spot on for the style. No hop presence, rich and creamy, just like a real porter should be. The Coffee Porter is similar to the English-style Porter, except for the addition of Sumatra coffee beans, hand-roasted by Lefty himself. The two stouts may be Lefty's best beers. The Irish-style Stout is a little stronger than the average Irish stout (6.6 percent alcohol by volume (ABV) to about 4.5 percent ABV), but don't let that scare you. It still has the requisite creaminess. A great after-dinner beer, or maybe to enjoy with some meat loaf or pot roast. The Chocolate Oatmeal Stout is a decadent dessert beer. Not as chocolaty as some imperial stouts that incorporate chocolate, this still provides enough chocolate to be like a liquid dessert, while still retaining its beeriness. The Valrhona cocoa powder adds a bitterness to the beer. The Chocolate Oatmeal Stout is also Lefty's strongest beer, coming in at 7.2 percent ABV. Lefty's Brewing Company's beers are available in 12-ounce bottles, bombers, in Franklin County and parts of central Massachusetts.

## MAYFLOWER BREWING COMPANY

12 Resnik Rd., Plymouth, MA; (508) 746-2674; MayflowerBrewing.com
**Founded:** 2007 **Founder:** Drew Brosseau **Brewers:** Ryan Gwodz and Michael Smith
**Flagship Beer:** Mayflower Pale Ale **Year-round Beers:** Golden Ale, IPA, Porter **Seasonal/Special Releases:** Autumn Wheat Ale, Spring Hop Ale, Summer Rye Ale, Thanksgiving Ale, Winter Oatmeal Stout **Tours:** 11 a.m. to 3 p.m.

Some say the *Mayflower* landed at Plymouth Rock because the Pilgrims got lost on their way to Virginia. But, according to several of the passengers' diaries, they landed because they ran out of ale. Mayflower Brewing Company's founder

**Thanksgiving Ale**
**Style:** Strong Ale
**ABV:** 8 percent
**Availability:** Fall Seasonal

Mayflower's Thanksgiving Ale is a fabulous beer. This is a dark red beer, full of malty sweetness with an herbal hop presence. This is a toasty beer, but not overwhelmingly so, with some notes of toffee and caramel. The beer is aged on white oak, and you get the flavor of oaky vanilla in the beer. A perfect beer to pair with—what else?—a turkey. Gobble, gobble.

Drew Brosseau is the tenth great-grandson of John Alden, beer barrel cooper on the *Mayflower*, and you could say he was destined to open his own brewery in 2007.

Mayflower Brewing Company quickly built up a reputation for brewing good beers that don't cross into the extreme category. They all have moderate alcohol levels, but are full-flavored. The **Mayflower Pale Ale** is a solid pale ale—hoppy and balanced, a real treat to drink. The **Golden Ale** is a lighter-tasting ale, easy to drink with enough flavor to make it worth seeking out. Mayflower's **IPA** is one of the better India pale ales brewed in Massachusetts. It is well-bittered from the hops, and the malt backbone makes this a fantastic beer. It is the biggest of the year-round beers, coming in at 7 percent alcohol by volume (ABV). The **Porter** is a straightforward English-style porter. It is creamy, slightly roasty, and just plain tasty.

Mayflower also does a really good job with its seasonals. The **Autumn Wheat Ale** is a dark wheat beer, with bready malt character and fruity aromas. The **Spring Hop Ale** is a welcome change from most spring beers. Many spring beers are light and bordering on flavorless. This is a full-flavored, hoppy red ale. The caramel malts play off nicely with the hops. It's definitely worth seeking out. The **Summer Rye Ale** is a perfect light beer for summer at only 3.8 percent ABV. It is light-bodied, but has a nice hop zing. The rye adds a pleasant spiciness, so even though this beer is low on alcohol it is not low on flavor. The **Winter Oatmeal Stout** is a full-flavored oatmeal stout, with hints of chocolate and coffee. It is creamy and is sweeter than many oatmeal stouts, a wonderfully done beer. The **Thanksgiving Ale** is a treat. It is a blend of an American strong ale and English old ale, aged in oak barrels. Obviously, a perfect beer to share on Thanksgiving.

The Mayflower Brewing Company offers tours of its brewery and also has a tasting room where beer fans can try the various beers they have on draft. You can buy growlers, or the freshest six-packs, 12-packs, and cases of beer to go.

## MERCURY BREWING COMPANY (IPSWICH ALE BREWERY)

23 Hayward St., Ipswich, MA; (978) 356-3329; IpswichAleBrewery.com

**Founded:** 1991 **Founders:** Jim Beauvais and Paul Sylva **Brewer:** Dan Lipke **Flagship Beer:** Ipswich Ale **Year-round Beers:** Ipswich Dark, Ipswich IPA, Ipswich Oatmeal Stout; Stone Cat line: Blonde, Blueberry, ESB, IPA **Seasonal/Special Releases:** Ipswich Harvest, Ipswich Summer, Ipswich Winter, 5-Mile Stock Ale, Castle Hill Summer Barley Wine, Choate Bridge Imperial Stout, Hosiery Mill Double IPA; Stone Cat line: Hefeweizen, Octoberfest, Pumpkin, Scotch Ale, Winter Lager **Tours:** None

The Ipswich Ale Brewery, technically the Mercury Brewing Company, is one of the most important breweries in Massachusetts. Not only do they brew their own Ipswich beers, they also brew the **Stone Cat** line of beer that owner Rob Martin purchased in the late 1990s, in addition to brewing **Notch Session Ales, Sherwood Forest, Clown Shoes Beers,** and others.

Despite brewing all of those other beers, the Ipswich line certainly doesn't suffer. The **Ipswich Ale** (once named one of the top 10 beers in the world by *Wine Spectator* magazine) is a classic English-style pale ale. It is not too light and not too heavy, malty, and almost creamy, with just a touch of hops. The **Ipswich IPA** is a blend of American hops and English malts. The dry bitter hops and the sweet English malts work well together. The **Ipswich Oatmeal Stout** is a bigger than usual oatmeal stout at 7 percent alcohol by volume. It still retains the creaminess you want in an oatmeal stout, and it has a stronger espresso-like flavor from the roasted malts. The **Ipswich Dark** is an exceptional brown ale with more hops than the usual brown ale.

Ipswich seasonals include the **Summer,** which is a light and refreshing blonde ale; the **Harvest,** which is almost like a lighter-colored black IPA; and the **Winter,** an English-style old ale. Ipswich also brews a series of beers called the **5-Mile Stock Ale.** The beer is made with at least one ingredient, and as many as possible, from within 5 miles of the brewery. This beer changes each time it's brewed, and the

**Ipswich Dark Ale**
**Style:** Brown Ale
**ABV:** 6.3 percent
**Availability:** Year-round

A lot of New England breweries make brown ales, and many of them are kind of boring. The Ipswich Dark Ale is not one of those beers. This is a full-flavored brown ale, with hints of chocolate, molasses, and a little almond nuttiness. There are more hops present than typically seen in the style, and that provides a pleasant fruity flavor. A nicely done beer worth getting your hands on.

style varies. In addition, Ipswich brews a series of bigger beers as limited releases, all inspired by local Ipswich landmarks. Those beers include the wonderful **Choate Bridge Imperial Stout.** Ipswich also brews the Stone Cat line of beers. The beers are all pretty straightforward—the **Blonde** is light and refreshing, the **Blueberry** is a solid blueberry beer, and the **IPA** is a malty English-style IPA.

The seasonals include a really well-done **Octoberfest** lager and a big and malty **Scotch Ale.** Ipswich also makes a series of sodas under the Mercury label, as well as mustards, both of which can be bought at various stores. At the time of this writing, Ipswich does not offer tours at their breweries, but they were working to open a new brewery where they would offer tours. Check their website for more information.

## MYSTIC BREWERY

174 Williams St., Chelsea, MA; (617) 466-2079; Mystic-Brewery.com
**Founded:** 2011 **Founder:** Bryan Greenhagen **Brewer:** Bryan Greenhagen bills himself as head fermenterer **Flagship Beer:** Mystic Saison **Year-round Beers:** Descendant, Saison Renaud **Seasonals/Special Releases:** An Dreoilin, Hazy Jane, Mary of the Gael, Will O' The Wisp, Entropy, Old Powderhouse, Day of Doom, Three Cranes, the Native Series, the Wigglesworth Series **Tours:** Sat, 1 and 2 p.m.; free. Tasting room is also open Wed through Fri 3 to 7 p.m.

Bryan Greenhagen is a scientist, studying fermentation for years in a lab setting, and he has taken that knowledge to the Mystic Brewery, creating one of the most unique breweries in the state. People talk about hops and malts, but without the yeast, beer wouldn't exist. Greenhagen, who calls himself a fermenterer, propagated the yeast used on all of Mystic's beers. Unlike many breweries, Mystic brews its beers off-site before bringing the wort back to its Chelsea brewery, and fermenting the beer for various lengths of time, many of which are Belgian-style saisons. The results are some of the most complex and interesting saisons in New England.

The brewery's flagship is the **Mystic Saison,** a dry, 7 percent alcohol by volume (ABV) saison that is eververvescent with a hint of hops in the finish. Other year-round beers include the **Saison Renaud** (named for the house yeast) and the **Descendant,** called a Suffolk dark ale, it's basically a 7 percent ABV English stout and it's a delight.

Mystic also does several special-release beers throughout the year, including **Old Powderhouse,** an amazing wheat wine, and **Day of Doom,** a Belgian quad. Seasonals include the **An Dreoilin,** a winter

## Beer Lover's Pick

**Mystic Saison**
**Style:** Saison
**ABV:** 7 percent
**Availability:** Year-round
The original beer is still a standout. When I first tried it, I thought it was one of the best first beers by a brewery that I have ever tasted. If you're a fan of saisons, you'll want to try this. Drink it by itself, or pair it with some fish or chicken and you're in for a delight.

saison that is basically the Mystic Saison fermented at cooler temperatures, resulting in a beer that tastes completely different than its original. The **Hazy Jane,** which is the summer ale, is a saison brewed with wheat, along with both American and Japanese hops. The **Mary of the Gael** is a hoppy saison and is available during the summer, while the **Will O' The Wisp,** is the fall seasonal. It is a rye ale made with brown sugar, as well as a combination of American and Slovenian hops.

The **Native Series** is an interesting experiment by Mystic. They gather wild yeast to make the beer. The **Vinland One** used a yeast from a Massachusetts grown plum, while **Vinland Two** is brewed using yeast from wild Maine low bush blueberries. The **Wigglesworth Series** is a series of beers created by assistant Alastair Hewitt, an award-winning homebrewer. Most of these beers are traditional, bottle-condition English ales.

Mystic's **Entropy** may be the brewery's most ambitious beer. It's a 14.2 percent ABV beer that really falls into no beer style category. It's also expensive, it'll run you about $50 for a bottle, but it is expected to be able to be aged and to continue to improve for as long as 20 years.

Mystic's tasting room in Everett is one of the nicest in the state, constructed with many reclaimed materials from area factories and buildings. Tours are available on Saturday at 1 and 2 p.m., and tastings are available the same time, as well as Wednesday through Friday from 3 to 7 p.m. All are free. Items available at the brewery include shirts, glasses, full growlers, and half-growlers of beer. Often, special, barrel-aged beers that are only available at the brewery will be on draft and available for growlers.

## NASHOBA VALLEY WINERY

100 Wattaquadock Hill Rd., Bolton, MA; (978) 779-5521; NashobaWinery.com
**Founded:** Winery, 1978; brewery, 2004 **Founder:** Jack Partridge **Flagship Beer:** Heron Ale **Year-round Beers:** Bolt 117 Lager, IPA, Wattaquadock Wheat **Seasonals/Special Releases:** Belgian Pale Ale, Dunkelweizen, Imperial Stout, Oaktoberfest, Robust Porter, Summer Stout, Watermelon Wheat, Nashoba Special Reserve Series **Tours:** Sat, 11 a.m. to 4 p.m.; $7

The Nashoba Valley Winery is a one-stop bonanza for those who like adult beverages. They produce many phenomenal fruit wines (the Blueberry Merlot is to die for), as well as spirits, such as whiskey, brandy, and vodka. They are also home to a small craft brewery that brews great beers, only available at the winery. The brewery was added to the winery and distillery in 2004, and has been steadily improving its quality of beers throughout the years, adding several interesting seasonals and special releases to the solid lineup of year-round beers.

The **Heron Ale,** the flagship beer, is a traditional English-style bitter. It uses British hops to give it the traditional earthy flavors. Actually slightly stronger than some versions at 5.3 percent alcohol by volume (ABV), it is still an easy-drinking beer. The **Bolt 117 Lager** is a German-influenced Dortmunder lager. It is slightly dark, and it has a strange, but not unpleasant, aftertaste that comes from the use of German noble hop varieties. The **IPA** is a solid New England IPA, meaning it is not full of grapefruit or piney aromas and flavors, but rather more malt-forward. It's definitely worth drinking. The final year-round beer is the **Wattaquadock Wheat,** a German-style hefeweizen with hints of clove and banana, thanks to the use of traditional hefeweizen yeast.

Nashoba's seasonals and special releases are even better than their year-round beers. Nashoba's summer seasonal is an unusual pick for a summer beer, a stout. But the **Summer Stout** is easy drinking and quite light, so it kind of fits. The **Oaktoberfest** is also different than most, if not all, American and German Oktoberfest-style beers. It is aged on oak, giving it some flavors, such as a little vanilla, not found in traditional Oktoberfests. The winter seasonal, the **Imperial Stout,** is a big beer at 8.5 percent alcohol by volume (ABV). This beer has strong flavors and aroma of dark, bitter chocolate, and it is aged on oak, giving it more depth of flavor. Other special releases include the **Belgian Pale Ale,** the **Dunkelweizen,** and the **Watermelon Wheat.**

## Beer Lover's Pick

**Oaktoberfest**
**Style:** Oktoberfest
**ABV:** 5.3 percent
**Availability:** Fall Seasonal
The Oaktoberfest is not the best Oktoberfest you may try, but it may be the most unusual. This is a traditionally brewed Oktoberfest/Marzen lager, but aged on oak chips. The combination of caramel flavors typically found in an American Oktoberfest blend well with the vanilla oak characters to create a unique beer. Try this side-by-side with a beer like Samuel Adams Octoberfest to taste the difference.

Massachusetts

Nashoba Valley also brews what is called the **Special Reserve Series.** These are extra-small batches of beer, and available while supplies last. Some of the Special Reserve beers have been the **Chai Brown,** the **Special Reserve Porter,** and the bourbon-barrel-aged **Vanilla Porter.**

The Nashoba Valley Winery is also family friendly, with apple picking in the huge apple orchards, as well as having a sit-down fine-dining restaurant, J's, that also sells picnic lunches to those who want to take advantage of the beautiful scenery and sit outside.

Tours and tastings are available on Saturday, and the winery store has all the wines, spirits, and beers, as well as glassware and other goods, available for sale. Along with 12-ounce bottles of beer, they also sell growlers of the various beers to go.

### NEWBURYPORT BREWING COMPANY

4 New Pasture Road, Newburyport, MA; (978)463-8700; NbptBrewing.com
**Founded:** 2012 **Founders:** Bill Fisher and Chris Webb **Brewer:** Mike Robinson **Flagship Beer:** Newburyport Pale Ale **Year-round Beers:** Green Head IPA, Joppa Stout, Plum Island White **Seasonals/Special Releases:** 1635 Series **Tours:** Sat, 5 p.m.; free

If you like live music and pints of locally brewed ale, the Newburyport Brewing Company is the place for you. In the brewery's tasting room, from 5 to 8 p.m. on Thursday, Friday, and Saturday, a different live band will play while attendees get a chance to drink the available beers on tap. The brewery was founded in 2012 by friends Bill Fisher and Chris Webb, and they hired award-winning homebrewer Mike Robinson as their head brewer. They are currently the only can- and keg-only brewery in Massachusetts. They do not offer growler fills.

The brewery brews four year-round beers, the **Newburyport Pale Ale, Green Head IPA,** the **Joppa Stout,** and the **Plum Island White.** The Green Head IPA is a 7.2 percent ABV. It has big citrusy aromas, and the citrus continues when you take your first sips. It blends with the sweet malt flavor to taste almost like a citrusy candy-like beer. The Joppa Stout, named for the local Joppa Flats, is a smooth, creamy stout with roasted coffee and dark chocolate flavors. The Plum Island White is a Belgian-style witbier with citrus and coriander flavors.

They also brew the **1635 Series,** which is a series of one-off beers, usually bigger, higher-in-alcohol beers than Newburyport's year-round beers. The Newburyport Pale Ale is the brewery's flagship. It's a 5.5 percent alcohol by volume (ABV) pale ale with citrusy hops and a sweet malt backbone. It falls somewhere between a west coast pale ale and an east coast pale ale.

Along with the music, the Newburyport Brewing Company's tasting room is open from 3 to 8 p.m. on Thursday and Friday and noon to 8 p.m. on Saturday. People can taste samples of the beer or buy pints. The brewery hosts tours on Saturday at

## Beer Lover's Pick

**Plum Island White**
**Style:** Belgian wit
**ABV:** 5.4 percent
**Availability:** Year-round
The Plum Island White is a wonderful Belgian-style witbier. It is a perfect beer for the summer, with citrus and coriander flavors dominating this beer. Steam some clams or a lobster and this is the perfect pairing for it.

5 p.m. with complimentary tastings. There is also a brewery store with several items available for sale.

## NIGHT SHIFT BREWING

87 Santilli Hwy., Everett, MA; (617) 294-4233; NightShiftBrewing.com
**Founded:** 2012 **Founders:** Robert Burns, Michael O'Mara, and Michael Oxton **Brewer:** Robert Burns **Flagship Beer:** None **Year-round Beers:** Bee Tea, JoJo, Viva Habanera **Seasonals/Special Releases:** Fallen Apple, Marblehead, Rose, Seaglass, Taza Stout, Trifecta, Whirlpool, the Sour Weisse Collection, the Nation of Hops Series, the Art Series
**Tours:** Tasting room open Mon through Sat, noon to 9 p.m; tours are free



Since its humble beginnings by three friends in 2012, Night Shift Brewery (the name comes from the fact they all had day jobs and worked at the brewery at night) has quickly become one of the most inventive and prolific breweries in all of New England. The brewery has a constantly changing lineup of beers, with some of the original beers becoming seasonals, experimental beers (Snow, a stout that looked like a pilsner for example) and a series of Berliner weisses, the Everett brewery has become one of the top destinations in the state for beer geeks.

The brewery has three year-round beers, the **Bee Tea,** which is a wheat ale brewed with orange blossom honey and loose green tea leaves; the **JoJo,** a pink IPA infused with hibiscus flowers and the extremely popular **Viva Habanera,** a rye ale brewed with agave nectar and aged on habanera peppers.

However, the beers that really got the attention of better beer drinkers were those in the **Sour Weisse Collection,** a series of Berliner weisses, a German-style wheat ale known for being tart and sour. The **Ever Weisse** is made with strawberries, kiwis, and dried hibiscus flowers. The **Somerweisse** is brewed with lemongrass and ginger. The **Cape Codder** is made with cranberry and orange zest, and the **Maine Weisse** is made with Maine wild blueberries and cinnamon sticks.

But, Night Shift doesn't limit themselves to sour beers. They also do a series of beers called the **Nation of Hops.** The Nation

## Beer Lover's Pick

**Ever Weisse**
**Style:** Berliner Weisse
**ABV:** 5.5 percent
**Availability:** Rotating
The most perfect beer you'll find on a hot summer day. It's light and refreshing and the tartness almost makes you want to take another sip, similar to a lemonade. The kiwi and strawberry blends for a refreshing combo, and even though it's a 750 ml bottle, you'll be left wanting more. This is one to seek out.

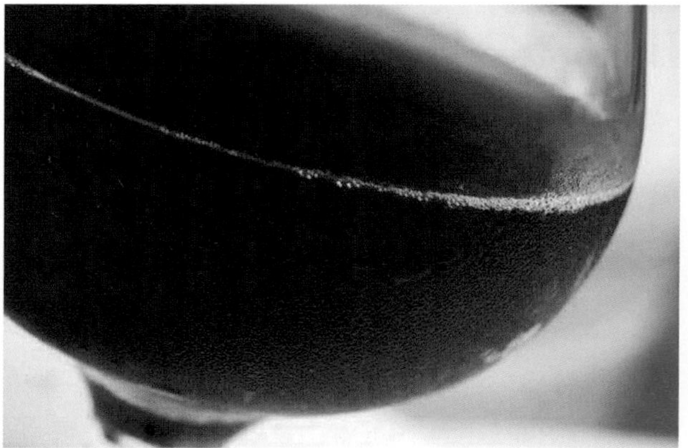

of Hops series is a collection of Belgian double IPAs brewed with a single hop in each beer. Most IPAs are brewed with a mixture of hops, but this really shows drinkers what flavors their favorite hops actually add to the beer. The Nation of Hops beers include **Citranation, Cascaadenation,** and **Motuekanation.**

The **Art Series** is a collection of experimental, test-batch beers and beer blends. At the time of publication, Night Shift had brewed 14 Art Series beers. Seasonals include the **Trifecta,** a Belgian pale ale made with three different types of Trappist yeasts and vanilla beans; the **Taza Stout,** brewed with chicory and aged with locally produced Taza Chocolate cacao nibs; and the **Rose,** a saison brewed with honey, rosemary, rose hips, and aged on crushed pink peppercorns.

Night Shift is also host to one of the largest taprooms in Massachusetts. The 2,500-square-foot taproom has more than a dozen of Night Shift beers on tap, as well as eating areas and food trucks outside if someone gets hungry. Beer is offered in full pours or flights, and tours are also available. Growlers and half growlers as well as other swag are also available for sale at the brewery.

## NOTCH BREWING

Contract brewed at Ipswich Ale Brewery in Ipswich, MA, and Kennebunkport Brewery in Kennebunkport, ME; (978) 853-9138; NotchSession.com

**Founded:** 2010 **Founder:** Chris Lohring **Flagship Beer:** Notch Session Ale **Year-round Beers:** Notch Session Pils, Notch Saison, Left of the Dial **Seasonals/Special Releases:** BSA Harvest, Cerne Pivo, The Mule, Polotmavy, LP India Pale Lager Taffelbier **Tours:** Not available

Most breweries try to enter the market with a big, high-alcohol beer, something that will catch beer geeks' attention right away. Notch Brewing is not like most breweries. They brew nothing but low-alcohol beers, or session beers. A session beer is a low-alcohol ale or lager, 4.5 percent alcohol by volume (ABV) or less. The idea behind session beers is that you can sit at a bar for a few hours and have a few beers without becoming intoxicated.

The key for session beers is to somehow have enough flavor without increasing the alcohol. Notch does this perfectly and dispels the myth that good beers have to have loads of alcohol. All three of Notch's year-round beers are full-flavored. The **Notch Session Ale** is an American pale ale with a big hop presence, and just

**Notch Session Pils**
**Style:** Pilsner
**ABV:** 4 percent
**Availability:** Year-round

Pilsners get a bad rap in the US because nearly all mass-produced beers are based on pilsner. But, those beers have strayed, and the Notch Pils is the real deal. It's light, unfiltered, dry, and crisp and it has enough hops, resulting in a delightful taste. It's a refreshing beer, perfect for a hot summer day, or for sitting at a bar and having a few while sharing stories with good friends. It is a joy to drink. The best thing about it is the low alcohol percentage, making this an all-day type of beer.

enough sweet malt to balance the beer out. It drinks dry and comes in at a low 4.5 percent ABV. The **Notch Session Pils** is a Czech-style pilsner. A pilsner should be light colored, moderately hopped, and delicate on the tongue, but with enough flavor that you want to take another sip. This fits the bill. At 4 percent ABV, this is a perfect beer for a party. You can have a few and not get stupid. The **Notch Saison** is a traditional Belgian-style saison. While American versions have strayed from the original style of low-alcohol beers, Notch Saison strives to be true to the classic style, a low-alcohol beer that is refreshing and goes well with food, such as a roasted chicken or grilled salmon. The **Left of the Dial** is a low-alcohol IPA. Many breweries are attempting these, but most fall flat. Notch's is one of the two or three best on the market.

The seasonals include some hard-to-find styles. The **Notch Cerne** (winter) is a Czech black lager, while the **Notcch Taffelbier** (spring) is a Belgian-style table beer, meant to be an everyday beer. The **Notch BSA Harvest** (fall) is an American-style farmhouse ale, which is similar to a saison.

Notch Brewing also does a series of one-off cask-conditioned beers, so if you're lucky enough to find one on draft, try it as soon as possible because it will never be available again. Notch has done two cask-conditioned beers, the **Notch Mild** and the **Notch Bitter.**

All of Notch Brewing's beers are available in 12-ounce bottles, except for the cask-conditioned beers.

## PAPER CITY BREWING COMPANY

108 Cabot St., Holyoke, MA; (413) 535-1588; PaperCity.com

**Founded:** 1995 **Founder:** Jay Hebert **Brewer:** Ben Anhalt **Flagship Beer:** Holyoke Dam Ale **Year-round Beers:** PC Blueberry Brew, Fogbuster Coffee House Ale, Hop Monster, India'n IPA, One Eared Monkey, Riley Stout **Seasonal/Special Releases:** Summit House Oktoberfest, Nut Brown Ale, Radler Brau, Paper City Spring Beer, Paper City Summer Brew, Winter Palace Wee Heavy **Tours:** Tastings Thurs and Fri nights, 6 to 8 p.m.; $6

The Paper City Brewery is one of the best breweries in which to just kick back and hang out. On Friday nights, head to the Paper City Brewery for the weekly 6 p.m. tasting/open house, and you are in for a good time. The brewery is located in an old warehouse, so make your way to the fifth floor and pay the $6. For that money, you get to drink plenty of good Paper City beers, but you also get to listen to live music from a band that typically plays every Friday night. Food is not served, but feel free to bring in some snacks (as long as you clean up after yourself). Not into live music? The tasting/open house also takes place on Thursday without a band for the same $6.

Besides being a great hangout spot, the Paper City Brewery is one of the oldest breweries in Massachusetts, and they brew many good beers. The **Holyoke Dam Ale** was Paper City's first beer, and it is still the flagship after all these years. It is an English-style pale ale, with sweet malty flavors and just a touch of hops. Other year-round beers include three beers with some of the best names in New England—**Fogbuster Coffee House Ale, Hop Monster,** and **One Eared Monkey.** But, names on the labels do not matter—it's what's inside that counts. All three are superb beers. The Fogbuster Coffee House Porter is strong on big roasted coffee flavors. It is almost like Paper City brewed a porter, brewed coffee, and blended them together. The Hop Monster is a big, 9.5 percent alcohol by volume beer. The One Eared Monkey is a light golden ale with peach flavoring added. The **India'n IPA** (named for Indian motorcycles) is a solid IPA. It may not be a hop bomb, but it is well-balanced and pleasant to drink. The **PC Blueberry Brew** is a typical New England blueberry beer. The **Riley Stout,** meanwhile, is an excellent dry Irish stout, better than any of the stouts brewed in Ireland and available in the US.

**Hop Monster**
**Style:** Double IPA
**ABV:** 9.5 percent
**Availability:** Year-round

Hop Monster combines a mix of piney and citrusy hop aromas, which continue into the taste. The hops almost taste oily, with a lot of bitterness. The malt is sweet, almost to the point of crossing over to cloying, but not quite. That works to keep this beer relatively balanced, despite the amount of hops used. This is one of the better New England double IPAs.

The seasonal beers include the **Radler Brau,** one of the most refreshing summer beers available. A radler is basically a beer and lemonade blended together to create an ultra-refreshing brew. This is no different. The **Summit House Oktoberfest** is also a well-done beer, as is the extremely malty **Winter Palace Wee Heavy Ale.** The **Paper City Spring Beer** is a really nice German-style bock, while the **Summer Brew** is a lighter helles bock.

## PERCIVAL BEER COMPANY

Contract brewed at Paper City Brewing Company; (781) 664-4705; PercivalBeerCompany.com
**Founded:** 2013 **Founder:** Filipe Oliveira **Brewer:** None **Flagship Beer:** None **Year-round Beers:** Dot Ale 1630, Kompadre Lager **Seasonals/Special Releases:** None **Tours:** None

Filipe Oliveira founded Percival Beer Company (named after the street he grew up on in Dorchester) to honor the Boston neighborhood of Dorchester. The Percival beers are brewed at the Paper City Brewing Company in Holyoke, but are available in or near Dorchester exclusively.

Percival produces two beers, the **Dot Ale 1630** and the **Kompadre Lager.** The Dot Ale 1630 is a 5 percent alcohol by volume (ABV) pale ale. It is lightly hopped, with a bit of malt sweetness and just a bit of hop aroma and bitterness. The "Dot" part of the name comes from the nickname for Dorchester, while the 1630 comes from the year Dorchester was founded. The Kompadre Lager is a 5 percent ABV pale lager. It has more flavor than the average mass produced lager, but not as complex or flavorful as the average craft lager. "Kompadre" is a Cape Verdean expression meaning friendship and family. Both beers are available in six packs.

## PIONEER BREWING COMPANY

195 Arnold Rd., Fiskdale, MA; (508) 347-7500; PioneerBrewingCompany.com
**Founded:** 2004 **Founder:** Todd Sullivan **Brewer:** Chris Courtney **Flagship Beer:** American Pale Ale **Year-round Beers:** American IPA, Into the Woods, Path of the Unkown, The New Frontier **Seasonals/Special Releases:** None **Tours:** None

In 2013, the the Pioneer Brewing Company sold its brewery in Fiskdale to Rapscallion, but continues to brew its beers at the facility. It also underewent a major change in its beer portfolio, only keeping two of its original beers, and then adding three high-octane beers to its line-up.

The **American Pale Ale** is still an extremely drinkable beer with a nice touch of hops, while the **IPA** is suitably balanced and hoppy enough to keep hop lovers happy. The three new beers are completely different animals. They are big beers, completely different than anything Pioneer had done before. **Into the Woods** is a double Vienna

**The New Frontier**
**Style:** Double IPA
**ABV:** 11 percent
**Availability:** Year-round
The problem with many double IPAs is when they cross into double digit ABVs, one of two things happen—either the beer is exceedingly bitter or it's overly sweet, neither of which make for a pleasant drinking experience. However, the New Frontier somehow finds a decent balance. Yes, it's a little boozy, but for an 11 percent beer, it's not bad, and it's actually relatively drinkable for such a big beer.

lager, brewed with American-grown, but German-style hops and malts, this is a big, sweet, malty beer, coming in at 9 percent alcohol by volume (ABV). The **Path of the Unknown** is a double brown ale. This beer borders on crossing into cloyingly sweet, but the hop burst in the finish really evens it out and makes it a drinkable beer, even at 10 percent ABV. **The New Frontier** is an 11 percent ABV double California IPA.

With the new agreement, Pioneer's distribution has increased significantly, reaching near the Boston area for the first time in its history.

## PRETTY THINGS BEER & ALE PROJECT

Offices located in Cambridge, beer brewed in Westport; (617) 682-6419; PrettyThingsBeerToday.com

**Founded:** 2008 **Founders:** Dann Paquette, Martha Holly-Paquette **Brewer:** Dann Paquette **Flagship Beer:** Jack D'Or **Year-round Beers:** Baby Tree, Saint Botolph's Town **Seasonals/ Special Releases:** American Darling, Babayaga, Field Mouse's Farewell, Fluffy White Rabbits, Magnifico!, Our Finest Regards, Through the Looking Glass Series **Tours:** None

Pretty Things Beer & Ale Project is what you would call a gypsy brewery. They don't have a home of their own. Instead, Dann Paquette rents space at existing breweries and brews the beer himself. That's why it's called a "project" instead of a "brewery." Whatever the Paquettes want to call it, Pretty Things beers are amazing. Not good, not great, but amazing. Almost without exception, you'd be hard-pressed to find better beers for the styles they're doing.

The styles are American takes on classics. The flagship beer, **Jack D'Or,** is called a "Saison Americain." Again, the styles don't really matter here. What does matter is how good this beer is. There's a lot of spiciness in this beer—pretty amazing for a beer that has no spices added to it. Just oats, barley, yeast, hops, and water. The **Baby Tree,** a Belgian-style quad brewed with dried plums, is one of the best beers ever brewed in Massachusetts. The plum adds interesting notes to this big, sweet beer. It almost tastes like you could pour it on ice cream and use it as a syrup. But, it's not so sweet that you couldn't drink a full glass of it. Like all Pretty Things beers, it comes in a bomber. It's a big beer at 9 percent ABV, so you may want to share it with a friend or special someone, or be selfish like me and drink the whole thing. The third year-round beer from Pretty Things is **Saint Botolph's Town,** described as "a malty northern brown ale." A great beer to drink alone, or pair it with some grilled beef and you have a perfect night.

Pretty Things' seasonal beers are also worth seeking out. **American Darling** is the Paquettes' take on an American lager. Although it looks like your typical mass-produced lager, there are no other similarities. The use of all malt, quality pilsner malt, and handcrafted brewing create a perfect summer beer. The result is a flavorful, refreshing, 7 percent ABV lager. Other seasonals include the **Fluffy White Rabbits** (Belgian-style tripel), **Field Mouse's Farewell** (saison), **Babayaga** ("rustic" stout), **Our Finest Regards** (barleywine) and **Magnifico!** ("robust minimal ale").

The Paquettes also have started an interesting project called **"Once Upon a Time."** They partner with British beer historian Ron Pattinson to find classic beer recipes. The series features offerings based on historical recipes from the 1800s and early 1900s. Each one is named for the date the recipe was written—**February 27, 1832** (mild ale), **November 15, 1901** (Burton ale), and **December 6, 1855** (India porter) are examples.

## Beer Lover's Pick

**Baby Tree**
**Style:** Belgian Quad
**ABV:** 9 percent
**Availability:** Rotating

Not an easy choice—pretty much every beer from Pretty Things is a "must have," but this is the standout. A big beer, meant to be sipped, savored, and enjoyed, rather than pounded back like you're still a frat boy. All the sweet maltiness and Belgian-yeast flavors you want from a quad, with plums added. You can taste the 9 percent alcohol by volume (ABV), but many quads have some alcohol burn, and it does not detract from a beer. This is a perfect nightcap.

## RAPSCALLION

195 Arnold Rd, Fiskdale, MA; (508) 347-7500; DrinkRapscallion.com
**Founded:** 1993 **Founders:** Brett Pacheco (as Concord Junction Brewery) Cedric and Peter Daniel (as Rapscallion Brewry) **Brewer:** Shaun Razuik **Flagship Beer:** Honey Ale **Year-round Beers:** Blonde, Lager, Black IPA **Seasonals/Special Releases:** None **Tours:** Sat, 2 p.m.

The history of the Rapscallion Brewery is like a roller coaster ride. Brett Pacheco founded the small brewery, originally called the Concord Junction Brewery, in 1993. In 2000, then brewer Dann Paquette (now of Pretty Things Beer & Ale Project) created the Rapscallion line of artisan beers. In 2002, new owner Mike Labbe moved

### Beer Lover's Pick

**Lager**
**Style:** American Pale Lager
**ABV:** 4.5 percent
**Availability:** Year-round
Based on the name alone, this might sound like the most boring of Rapscallion's beers, but it is not. If you want to see what our grandfather's grandfathers were drinking, and to see how far American brewers fell, try this beer to see what a real American lager can taste like. This is a flavorful lager that uses all malts, no corn or rice extracts. There is also a touch of hops that you will not find in mass-produced lagers, even those that claim to be "triple hopped."

the brewery from Concord to Shirley, renaming it the Concord Brewery. The following year, he sold the brewery and remained on as the head brewer. Finally, in 2007, brothers Cedric and Peter Daniel bought the brewery with an idea in their minds. They renamed the brewery the Rapscallion Brewery after the popular line of beers. They also decided to go draft only, originally just brewing the **Honey Ale.** And in 2013, they purchased the Pioneer Brewing Company in Fiskdale, operating its own brick-and-morter facility. Pioneer's beers are still brewed at the facility.

Along with the flagship Honey Ale, they brew three other beers and many one-offs that are brewery-only releases. The Honey Ale is an extra pale ale, brewed with real local honey. Some honey beers tend to be overly sweet. Rapscallion's version is certainly sweet, but it keeps the balance and doesn't become cloying. And, at 4.5 percent alcohol by volume (ABV), it is low enough in alcohol that you can have a couple of them without worrying about falling over. The **Lager** is a classic American lager. No, not like the mass-produced beer you see commercials for; it's based on a recipe dating back to the late 1800s, so this is what a lager tasted like before Prohibition. The **Golden Ale,** once known as Premier, is a Belgian-style blonde ale, along the lines of the popular Belgian-style golden ale Duvel. Although it is 7 percent ABV, it still drinks like a lighter beer. It has fruity notes to it, a little bitterness at the end, and a delicate carbonation that tickles the roof of your mouth. The final beer is the **Black IPA,** a 7 percent ABV IPA brewed with all locally grown hops. The roasted flavors and earthy IPAs blend together nicely.

The brewery is open for tours on Saturday, but its tasting room is open Tuesday through Friday, 4 to 9 p.m.; Saturday, noon to 9 p.m, and Sunday, noon to 8 p.m.

Massachusetts

## RIVERWALK BREWING COMPANY

3 Graf Rd., Unit 15, Newburyport, MA; (978)499-2337; RiverWalkBrewing.com
**Founded:** 2011 **Founders:** Steve and Elizabeth Sanderson **Brewer:** Steve Sanderson **Flagship Beer:** RiverWalk IPA **Year-round Beers:** Gnomad, Uncle Bob's Bitter **Seasonals/ Special Releases:** Screen Door, Son of Gnomad, Winter Porter **Tours:** Fri, 3 to 7 p.m.; Sat, noon to 4 p.m.; free

Founded in 2011 by the husband and wife team of Steve and Elizabeth Sanderson, RiverWalk Brewing Company joined what is a growing beer scene in the north

shore region of Massachusetts, joining the Newburyport Brewing Company, Ipswich Brewing Company, and Cape Ann Brewing Company in the area.

RiverWalk is the smallest of the breweries, and owner Steve Sanderson is still the head brewer. Sanderson brews three year-round beers, the **RiverWalk IPA,** the **Gnomad,** and **Uncle Bob's Bitter.** He also brews the **Screen Door,** a summer wheat beer; **Son of Gnomad,** a Belgian wit/saison hybrid, and the **Winter Porter.**

The RiverWalk IPA is brewed with classic American hops such as Cascade, Columbus, and Amarillo, giving the beer those west coast IPA flavors of pine and citrus. The RiverWalk IPA is 6.7 percent alcohol by volume (ABV), just under what would be considered a double IPA. Although there are tons of hops, the beer still has enough sweetness to make this extremely drinkable. Uncle Bob's Bitter is a classic English-style bitter. The 4.5 percent ABV brew is made with English barley and British hops. It gives the beer the classic biscuity flavor from the malts and floral and earthy hoppy flavors. If you're a fan of English ales, this is worth seeking out. The Gnomad is described as an "American farmhouse ale," and it is brewed with barley, wheat, and oats, as well as American hops and Belgian yeast.

For seasonals, RiverWalk offers the Son of Gnomad in the spring—it's a Belgian-style witbier/saison hybrid. The summer ale is the Screen Door, which is a hoppy wheat beer and the Winter Porter is brewed with both vanilla and cinnamon.

RiverWalk offers tours and tastings in its brewery on Friday and Saturday. Samples of whatever beers are on tap are free, as are tours. The brewery also sells growlers and half-growlers of its beers as well as glasses, shirts, hats, and tap handles.

**Gnomad**
**Style:** Saison
**ABV:** 7.5 percent
**Availability:** Year-round
RiverWalk's take on a farmhouse ale is a fantastic beer that blends flavors not normally found in the style. The oat used gives the beer a smoothness and creaminess not typical for farmhouse styles, while the hops add fruity flavors that blend well with the earthy spiciness from the Belgian yeast. At 7.5 percent ABV, this is relatively big beer, but it is phenomenal.

## SCANTIC RIVER BREWERY

25 Mill Rd., Hampden, MA; (413) 204-9163; ScanticRiverBrewery.com
**Founded:** 2012 **Founders/Brewers:** Dave Avery and Dave Buel **Flagship Beer:** Hampden Pale Ale **Year-round Beers:** Billy Goat Ale, North Trail Ale **Seasonals/Special Releases:** Trail Series (series of IPAs named for trails at Minnechaug Mountain land trust) Strawberry Wheat Ale **Tours:** None

After a day of hiking the more than 3 miles of walking trails on the Minnechaug Mountain land trust, you're going to be thirsty. The perfect way to slake that thirst is to stop in at the Veterans of Foreign War's post on Main Street and Hampden and try some of Scantic River Brewery's **Hampden Pale Ale.** This small brewery, founded by longtime homebrewers Dave Avery and Dave Buel in 2012, celebrates the walking trails along the 900 foot Minnechaug Mountain, brewing a series of **Trail Series** beers named for the trails on the mountain.

The Scantic River Brewery brews three year-round beers, the **Billy Goat Ale,** the **North Trail Ale** and its flagship, the Hampden Pale Ale. The Hampden Pale Ale is a 5 percent alcohol by volume (ABV) pale ale made with locally grown hops. It is a classic pale ale with nice hop flavor and aroma, but it doesn't overwhelm the malt backbone, creating a balanced beer. The North Trail Ale is a 6 percent ABV India pale ale. This beer is made with honey malts, which works with the hops to create flavors of grapefruit and tangerine. The Billy Goat Ale, like the North Trail Ale, is named for a trail inside the land trust. It is a 5 percent ABV IPA brewed with both locally grown hops and a yet-to-be named hop from the Southern Hemisphere. The **Algonquin** is another 5 percent ABV IPA, brewed with Amarillo hops, which gives the beer a fruity aroma with a slight burst of orange. The **Old CoachTrail Ale** is available from spring through fall. It is a 6 percent ABV IPA, brewed with eight different hops flavors. The hops give this a classic piney/citrusy west coast IPA flavor. Also available is the **Strawberry Wheat Ale,** a spring/summer seasonal. It is a classic summer beer—light and brewed with wheat, but with locally grown strawberries used to make this a delight for strawberry lovers.

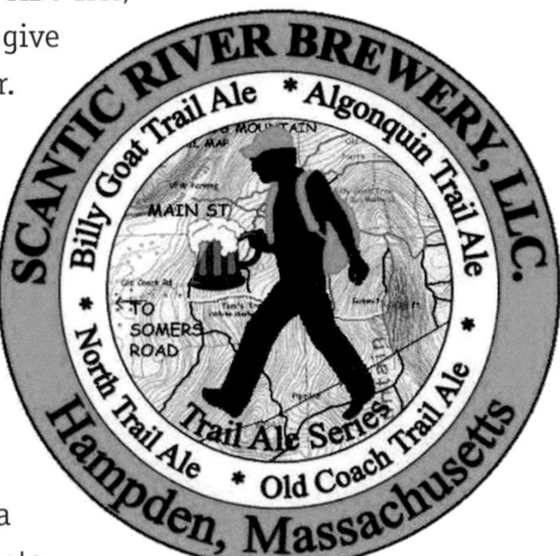


Because the Scantic River Brewery is located in a specially permitted residential area, they aren't allowed to have tours or visitors. The beers are available in 22-ounce bottles at area stores, as well as on draft at local bars and restaurants.

## Beer Lover's Pick

**Hampden Pale Ale**
**Style:** Pale Ale
**ABV:** 5 percent
**Availability:** Year-round

A lot of pale ales have begun to blur the lines between an IPA and a pale ale, but this is a classic pale ale, hoppy but with a dough-like sweet malt body. It is an excellent example of the style.

## SLUMBREW: SOMERVILLE BREWING COMPANY

15 Ward St., Somerville, MA; (800) 428-1150; SlumBrew.com. Beer Garden is located at 310 Canal St., Assembly Row, (617) 764-3790

**Founded:** 2011 **Founders:** Caitlin Jewell, Jeff Leiter **Brewer:** Jeff Leiter **Flagship Beer:** None **Year-round Beers:** Flagraiser Double IPA, Happy Sol, Porter Square Porter, Trekker Trippel **Seasonals/Special Releases:** Attic & Eaves, Lobstah Killah, My Better Half, Naked Hopularity, Sittin' on Hop of the World, Snow Angel, Yankee Swap **Tours:** Yes, see website for details

Somerville Brewing Company is better known under the name of Slumbrew, a homage to Somerville's long-term nickname, Slumerville. Today, Somerville is a bustling destination for culinary delights and the home of hipsters. It is also home to the Slumbrew's taproom.

The taproom features seating for around 100 people and has about 10 to 12 beers on tap at all times. Unlike many taprooms, Slumbrew serves food, such as cheese and meat plates and even deconstructed Fluffernutter. The taproom only brews draft beers. All of Slumbrews' bottled beers are brewed at the Mercury Brewing Company in Ipswich. Slumbrew brews four year-round beers. The **Flagraiser Double IPA** is 7.5 percent alcohol by volume (ABV) beer brewed with Galaxy hops. The **Porter Square Porter** is a wonderful porter, brewed with locally produced Taza Chocolates. The **Trekker Trippel** is a 9.5 percent ABV Belgian trippel, pretty spot on

## Beer Lover's Pick

**Happy Sol**
**Style:** Hefeweizen
**ABV:** 5.5 percent
**Availability:** Year-round

Beer is a happy drink, and Happy Sol makes pretty much everyone who drinks it happy. This is an extremely non-traditional German-style hefeweizen. It has the crispness and ease to drink of a hefeweizen, but the addition of blood oranges makes this one of the most refreshing beers on the market in all of New England. While not specifically a summer beer, this is a summertime favorite that is always in my glass.

for the style. The **Happy Sol** is a German-style hefeweizen made with fresh blood oranges.

Slumbrew also produces several seasonals. **My Better Half** is a 7.5 percent ABV imperial cream ale, which is available in spring. The summer seasonal is the **Sittin' on Hop of the World,** a 6.8 percent ABV white IPA brewed with fresh peaches, and the **Attic & Eaves,** a 7.5 percent ABV toasted brown ale, is available in the fall.

Special releases include the **Snow Angel,** a 9.2 percent ABV, double IPA; **Lobstah Killah,** an 8 percent ABV imperial red ale; **Naked Hopularity,** an 8 percent ABV black India pale ale; and **Yankee Swap,** the brewery's biggest beer at 12 percent ABV. It is a rum barrel–aged strong ale.

The Slumbrew Beer Garden is opened 7 days a week and offers a full menu of food to pair with their beers.

## SPENCER BREWERY

167 North Spencer Rd., Spencer, MA; SpencerBrewery.com
**Founded:** 2014 **Founders:** The monks of the St. Joseph's Abbey **Brewer:** Hubert de Halleux **Beer:** Spencer Abbey Ale **Tours:** None

For 60 years, the monks at the St. Joseph's Abbey, the only Trappist monastery based in the US, made jams and jellies to sell and help support the monks, the property, and all of its charitable endeavors. But, in 2014, after 10 years of research and working with their European brothers, the monks opened their own brewery, the Spencer Brewery, on the monastery's 2,000-acre property. The brewery is a state-of-the-art facility and has the capacity of brewing the third most beer in the entire state. It is only the tenth Trappist brewery in the world and the only one outside of Europe.

However, the monks only brew one beer, the **Spencer Abbey Ale,** a 6.5 percent alcohol by volume (ABV) golden ale, and they only brew about 4,000 barrels (31 gallons equals one barrel) because the goal is only to supplement their income, not to completely take over the monastery. The Spencer Abbey Ale is based on the table beers that Trappist breweries typically brew for the monks themselves, rather than for sale. It's light, dry, slightly fruity, and finishes with a slight hop bitterness.

The Spencer Brewery plans on only brewing this one beer for several years. It is available in four-packs and on draft. The Spencer Brewery also does not allow tours.

## TREE HOUSE BREWING COMPANY

160 East Hill Rd., Monson, MA; (413) 949-1891; TreeHouseBrewing.com
**Founded:** 2011 **Founders:** Damien Goudreau, Dean Rowan, Jonathan Weisbach, Nate Lanier **Brewer:** Nate Lanier **Beers:** Julius, That's What She Said, Sap, Snowtober, Green, Old Man, Eureka, Tornado, Dirty Water, Dirty Berry. **Taproom hours:** Thurs and Fri, 5 to 8 p.m.; Sat, 11 a.m. to 6 p.m.

If you ask the hardcore beer geeks throughout Massachusetts if there is one brewery in the state you had to visit, Tree House Brewing Company is one of the most likely answers you will get. Tree House Brewing Company's collection of world-class beers draws people to tiny Monson in droves, with people waiting in line, no matter the weather, to get their growlers and 750 ml swing-top bottles of whatever beers are available that week. Founded in 2011, Tree House is a draft only brewery. They offer numerous beers on tap at their taproom Thursday through Saturday.

The brewery's most popular beer is **Julius,** a 6.5 percent alcohol by volume (ABV) IPA that is bursting with citrus and mango flavors. It is one of the best IPAs brewed in New England. **That's What She Said,** a 5.6 percent ABV milk stout, has the typical sweetness found in a milk stout, but more roastiness. The **Sap,** originally only available in the winter, is a piney IPA.

Other beers include the **Snowtober,** a robust porter; **Green,** an 8 percent IPA brewed with both American and Australian hops; **Old Man,** an English-style extra special bitter; **Eureka,** a hoppy blonde ale; **Tornado,** an American Pale Ale; **Dirty Water,** a 3.9 percent ABV session beer; and **Dirty Berries,** made with either raspberries or strawberries.

Tree House's tasting room is open Thursday through Saturday. They fill growlers and half-growlers and offer samples of their beers in the tasting room. Also available are shirts and glasses and other Tree House items.



## TRILLIUM BREWING COMPANY

369 Congress St., Boston, MA; (617) 453-8745; TrilliumBrewing.com
**Founded:** 2013 **Founders:** Esther and J.C. Tetreault **Brewer:** J.C. Tetreault **Flagship Beer:** Trillium **Year-round Beers:** Fort Point Pale Ale, Pot & Kettle, Wakerobin **Seasonals/ Special Releases:** Beaver Hat, Broken Halo, Bug Valley, Congress Street IPA, Cuvee De Tetreault, Mettle, Sinister Kid, Sleeper Street, Lineage Rye, Dry Stack series (dozens of other offerings) **Tours:** No tours. Tasting room open Tues through Thurs, 4 to 7:30 p.m.; Fri, noon to 7:30 p.m.; Sat, noon to 6 p.m.

The Trillium Brewing Company is proof that good things come to those who wait. After a nearly four-year process of finding a location, building, and permitting, Trillium Brewing Company became the brewery in the city of Boston proper when it finally opened its doors in 2013. And, they immediately became one of the shining stars of Massachusetts brewing, releasing fabulous beer after fabulous beer.

The brewery's flagship beer is the self-named **Trillium,** a rustic farmhouse ale. This 6.6 percent alcohol by volume (ABV) is brewed with farmhouse yeast and American hops, it's spicy, balanced, dry, and just plain good. Other year-round beers include the **Fort Point Pale Ale** (named for the neighborhood Trillium is in), a 6.5 percent ABV hoppy pale ale, smoothed out with wheat malt. The **Pot & Kettle** is a 7.5 percent oatmeal that is smooth and creamy. The **Wakerobin** is a 7.4 percent ABV red rye farmhouse ale.

Trillium also brews numerous occasional beers (too many to list) that are a mix of Belgian-influenced ales and American classics. The **Beaver Hat** is a

## Beer Lover's Pick

**Trillium**
**Style:** Saison
**ABV:** 6.6 percent
**Availability:** Year-round
When Trillium first came out, I declared it the best first beer by a Massachusetts brewery, and I stand by it. It may have been the first beer Trillium brewed, but it's a standout that any beer lover should seek out and try.

hoppy American Ale, while **Broken Halo** is a Belgian pale ale. The **Bug Valley** is a fantastic sour beer, while the **Congress Street IPA** is a classic, hoppy American IPA. The **Mettle** is a 8.1 percent double IPA, while the **Sleeper Street** is another IPA. The **Sinister Kid** is a strong dark farmhouse ale brewed with candi syrup and raw sugar.

The Trillium Brewing Company does not offer tours, but the tasting room is open Tuesday through Saturday. Visitors can taste samples of the available beers and buy half or full growlers. Shirts and glasses are also available. Bottles of a few of their beers are available at a few local stores.

### WACHUSETT BREWING COMPANY

175 State Rd., Westminster, MA; (978) 874-0065; WachusettBrew.com
**Founded:** 1993 **Founders:** Kevin Buckler, Ned LaFortune, Peter Quinn **Brewer:** Dave Howard **Flagship Beer:** Country Pale Ale **Year-round Beers:** Black Shack Porter, Blueberry Ale, Green Monsta, IPA, Larry, Nut Brown Ale, Ryde Beer, Light IPA **Seasonals/Special Releases:** Milk Stout, Octoberfest Ale, Quinn's Amber Ale, Strawberry White Summer Ale, White Ale, Winter Ale **Tours:** Wed and Thurs, noon to 4 p.m., Fri and Sat, noon to 5 p.m.

For years, the Wachusett Brewing Company was the only central Massachusetts option for good, locally brewed, fresh beers. Although things have changed over the years, Wachusett Brewing Company has continued brewing quality ales, while remaining the local's first choice for craft beer.

Wachusett's most famous beer is the **Blueberry Ale.** Pretty much every bar in the Leominster/Fitchburg area will have this on tap. It is a light, refreshing ale, strong on blueberry flavors. Some bars will actually put a spoonful of fresh blueberries in the beer to give it that added flavor. The **Country Pale Ale,** formerly known as the Country Ale, is a popular beer. For some reason a Country Pale Ale on draft tastes so much better than in a bottle. It is a treat to find this on draft at a local watering hole. Wachusett's **IPA** is a solid, English-style IPA. It does not get the respect that it deserves because it is not a hop monster like a lot of the IPAs being brewed today. Rather, this is a good, balanced beer.

If you like your IPAs a little bit hoppier, Wachusett does offer other options. The Wachusett **Green Monsta,** named for the iconic left-field wall at Fenway Park, is a more straightforward American-style IPA. If you want even more hops, grab a **Larry,** the wildly popular double IPA brewed with David Ciccolo, owner of the Publick House in Brookline. Rye adds a lot of interesting spice notes to beers, but the final result often leans toward being high in alcohol. Wachusett's **Ryde Beer** is a great low-alcohol option.

Wachusett also brews several seasonals. **Quinn's Amber Ale** is an easy-drinking, reddish-hued beer that is available from mid-winter through April. The **Summer Ale**



### Beer Lover's Pick

**Milk Stout**
**Style:** Milk Stout
**ABV:** 5.8 percent
**Availability:** Winter
A well-done milk stout can be incredible. Brewers add lactose, or milk sugar, to the beer. The lactose is not fermentable, so it does not raise the alcohol percentage, but it does result in a fuller beer. Wachusett's Milk Stout is one of the best milk stouts available. Smooth, creamy, and full-bodied, it is appropriately sweet, yet not cloying. There is some roasted character, with hints of chocolate. Overall, just a wonderful beer.

is a light wheat beer, low in alcohol and easy to drink. The **Octoberfest** is available in the fall. It is not a traditional German-style Oktoberfest. Traditionally, Oktoberfests are lagers, while Wachusett's Octoberfest is an ale. That does not take away from the fact that it is a solid beer. The **Winter Ale** is one of the better winter seasonals. It is a Scotch ale, which is a heavier, malty beer perfect for the cold months.

In the past few years, Wachusett has introduced a few beers in bombers for the first time. To go along with Larry, they have the **White Ale,** which is available for half the year, and the **Milk Stout,** which is available the rest of the year.

The Wachusett Brewery also hosts tours led by a brewery employee and they include tastings. Growlers are also available to go.

### WANDERING STAR BREWING COMPANY

11 Gifford St., Pittsfield, MA; (917) 573-3942; WanderingStarBrewing.com
**Founded:** 2011 **Founders:** Chris Cuzme, Alex Hall, Chris Post **Brewer:** Chris Post **Flagship Beer:** Raindrop Pale Ale **Year-round Beer:** Bash-Bish-Bock **Seasonal/Special Releases:** Alpha Pale, Berkshire Hills 01201, Bert's Disqualified Imperial Stout, Mild at Heart, Zingari
**Tours:** Tasting room, no tours

The Wandering Star Brewing Company is the brainchild of three beer-loving friends who realized their dream by opening a brewery. The shared dream by founders Chris Cuzme, Alex Hall, and Chris Post must have included a lot of excellent beers, because the beers Wandering Star Brewing releases are nothing short of excellent.

The brewery only brews two year-round beers, its flagship **Raindrop Pale Ale** and the **Bash-Bish-Bock.** The Raindrop Pale Ale is an American pale ale brewed with west coast hops, as well as hops from New Zealand and England, giving it a more unique taste than many pale ales. The Bash-Bish-Bock is a German-style bock brewed with authentic German hops and yeast. Even at 6.8 percent alcohol by volume (ABV), this is a smooth drinking beer that goes down incredibly easy. It is a tad on the sweet side, but not overly so, so it is easy to enjoy.

**Bert's Disqualified Imperial Stout** is a beer based on a recipe by western Massachusetts homebrewer Bert Holdredge, whose imperial stout was named the winner of a large homebrewing competition in New York, only to be disqualified because he forgot to remove the label from the beer. The **Alpha Pale** is an English-style pale ale—smooth, creamy, and malty, with a nice little hop kick. The **Berkshire Hills 01201** is a Belgian-style saison using the same yeast as Saison Dupont (one of the best saisons). It also uses locally malted wheat, with almost all of the ingredients

**Mild at Heart**
**Style:** English Dark Mild
**ABV:** 4.3 percent
**Availability:** Occasional
The Mild at Heart is the perfect beer for a pub. When you go to a bar, you can buy one or two high-alcohol beers, but you will have to stop at a couple if you plan on staying for a while. But with the Mild at Heart, you can have a few of these low-alcohol beers without sacrificing flavor. It is a dark, creamy beer, with hints of chocolate and dark fruits with a nice hop presence.

for this beer bought in Massachusetts. The **Zingari** is Wandering Star's interpretation of a Belgian witbier. While most witbiers are brewed with coriander and bitter orange peel, this one is brewed with coriander, lemongrass, cardamom, and fenugreek. These added herbs give it a unique, yet refreshing, flavor. The **Mild at Heart** is an English-style dark mild. It is a dark, but light-drinking beer, and it is only 4.3 percent ABV, so it is easily a beer you can drink a few of in one sitting.

Wandering Star does not offer brewery tours, but does have a tasting room where people can come and try the various beers available. They also sell growlers of their beer to go. Growlers are the only way Wandering Star's beers can be enjoyed at home because they are a draft-only brewery. The tasting room is open on Saturday from noon to 3 p.m., unless the brewery is attending a festival.

## WESTFIELD RIVER BREWING COMPANY

707 College Hwy., Southwick, MA; WestfieldRiverBrewing.com
**Founded:** 2012 **Founder:** Sergio Bonavita **Brewer:** Sergio Bonavita **Flagship Beer:** Charlie in the Rye **Year-round Beers:** Pop's Old Fashion Lager, Honey Brown Ale, Black Squirrel Pale Ale, 413 IPA **Seasonals/Special Releases:** Peak Basket Saison, Summer Ale, Midnight Milk Chocolate Stout, Wyben Black IPA, Octoberfest, Test Batch X, Humble Pie **Tours:** Wed through Sat, noon to 8 p.m. and Sun, noon to 4 p.m.

The Westfield River Brewing Company opened this much larger facility in Southwick last year. But, what stayed the same, founder/brewer/majority owner Sergio Bonavita said, are the beers.

**Midnight Milk Chocolate Stout**
**Style:** Milk stout
**ABV:** 5 percent
**Availability:** Winter
Milk stouts are an underrated style. They use lactose sugar to add body to the beer without increasing the alcohol. The Westfield River version also uses chocolate, so it's like an adult chocolate milk.

The brewery's flagship beer is the **Charlie in the Rye,** a 5.8 percent alcohol by volume (ABV) rye IPA, brewed with local honey. That honey adds a sweetness that provides a nice counter to the spiciness the rye adds to the beer. **Pop's Old Fashioned Lager** is a 5.2 percent American pale lager, which is based on a pre-Prohibition lager recipe. Like many of Westfield's beers, the **Honey Brown Ale** uses local ingredients, again, honey, while the spring seasonal, **Peach Basket Saison,** uses local peaches and apricots. The other year-round beers are the **Black Squirrel Pale Ale** (named for the locally abundant black squirrels) and the **413 IPA,** which uses five pounds of hops in each batch.

Some of the seasonals include the **Midnight Milk Chocolate Stout,** a 5 percent ABV chocolaty beer, and the **Wyben Black IPA,** brewed with locally grown Cascade hops.

The Southwick brewery has a full taproom with 12 rotating beers on tap, two patios, full pints, sampler paddles and a large stone fireplace. Tours are available, and local food producers are often on hand providing food. Westfield River also plans on planting a farm on the property and growing local fruit and hops to use in the beers sold in the brewery, which will also have homebrewing supplies.

## WORMTOWN BREWING COMPANY

72 Shrewsbury St., Worcester, MA; (774) 239-1555; WormtownBrewery.com
**Founded:** 2010 **Founders:** Ben Roesch and Tom Oliveri **Brewers:** Ben Roesch and Megan O'Leary Parisi **Flagship Beer:** Seven Hills Pale Ale **Year-round Beers:** Be Hoppy IPA, Turtle Boy Blueberry, Hopulence Double IPA **Seasonals/Special Releases:** O'Connor's Irish Red, Blonde Cougar Summer Ale, Pumpkin, Wintah Brown; O'Fest, Ales for ALS, Hogshead Red, Buddha's Juice, Sweet Tat's Imperial Breakfast Stout, MassHole Hefeweizen, Tennessee Tat's, Be Hoppier **Tours:** Taproom is open Wed, Thurs, and Sun, noon to 8 p.m. and Fri and Sat, noon to 9 p.m.

Wormtown Brewery moved to a larger facility on Shrewsbury Street that allows them to significantly increase the amount of beer they brew.

The brewery brews tons of fabulous beers, including its year-round **Seven Hills Pale Ale,** the excellent **Be Hoppy IPA,** and the well-received **Hopulence Double IPA.** The seasonals range from good (**Blonde Cougar**) to fantastic (**Wintah Brown**).

But the special releases really set Wormtown apart. The **Sweet Tat's Imperial Breakfast Stout** is one of the best beers brewed in New England. The **Hogshead Red,** which is Wormtown's Elm Park Amber fermented in red wine barrels and aged with fresh raspberries, is amazing. Wormtown has also brewed **Norm,** a chocolate-coconut stout named for this author.

Other special releases include the **O'Fest** (an Oktoberfest-style lager), the **Buk** (a rye pale ale), **Foxy Brown Maple Brown Ale, Tennessee Tat's** (Sweet Tat's aged in Jack Daniel's barrels), **Buddha's Juice** (an IPA brewed with Buddha's hand fruit), and **Be Hoppier** (a bigger version of Be Hoppy).

Wormtown Brewery also likes to support other local businesses. Every single beer has at least one ingredient from Massachusetts, and the **MassHole Hefeweizen**

**Norm**

**Style:** Oatmeal Stout

**ABV:** 6.8 percent

**Availability:** Rotating

I've had a dream for years—for someone to brew a chocolate-coconut stout. After months of pestering Ben Roesch, he agreed to brew a small batch and it took off. The beer was later bottled twice and it sold out each time. It will now become an annual release. Is it good? The answer is yes. It is fabulous. A lot of coconut and chocolate flavors, this is a dessert beer for sure. It's almost like a liquid Mounds bar.

is brewed with every single ingredient produced in the Bay State. The brewery is connected to Peppercorn's Grille & Tavern, a popular Worcester restaurant that features American and Italian cuisine. All of the Wormtown beers that are being brewed are always on tap there.

Growlers of Wormtown beers will also be available for sale, and cost between $8 and $11 (plus a $5 deposit for the growler). Wormtown bottles several of its beers, and cans Be Hoppy.

## AMHERST BREWING COMPANY

10 University Dr., Amherst, MA; (413) 253-4400; AmherstBrewing.com
**Draft Beers:** 24 (mix of house and guest taps) and 4 casks

The Amherst Brewing Company is in the midst of the college town of Amherst. Many brewpubs in an area heavy with colleges will often dumb down their beer to cater to college students, but the Amherst Brewing Company is not one of those establishments. They have a full range of house beers, cask beers, and guest beers on tap that will satisfy the most discerning palates.

The standard beers are all good beers. The **Ace in the Hole Pilsner** is a very good pilsner, while the **Honey Pilsner** adds a nice twist on the style. The **Cascade IPA** gets its name from the use of Cascade hops and it is excellent. The **Puffers Smoked Porter** is a tasty porter with smoky flavors. The **North Pleasant Pale Ale** is nicely hopped, and the **Two Sisters Imperial Stout** is absolutely phenomenal.

Amherst Brewing Company also brews a number of seasonal and specialty beers. They include the **Belgian Tripel, Captain Code's Baltic Porter,** the **Chocolate Porter,** the **Heather Ale, Lewmeister Oktoberfest, Pumpkin Ale, Ryeteous Red, Super Stout,** and the **Muddy Brook Maibock.** Along with the house-brewed beers, the Amherst Brewing Company also has a number of guest beers, featuring such breweries as Ballast Point from California, Berkshire Brewing Company in Massachusetts, and Schlenkerla from Germany.

The brewpub also hosts several beer dinners a year, as well as monthly beer tastings. On the first and third Monday of every month, they host the Amherst Jazz Orchestra.

Hungry? Start with the Beer-Battered Fried Pickles or the ABC Beer Bread, which is made with light lager, smoked cheddar, scallions, and a sharp beer and cheese dipping sauce. Next, consider ordering from a variety of ABC Hot Dog Sliders. The options include bratwurst, Chicago-style wieners, cheese-filled hot dogs, and jalapeño hot dogs. Entrees include several sirloin steaks, the Tequila Lime Grilled Chicken and Shrimp, the German Sausage Platter, bangers and mash, Brewers Meatloaf, and shepherd's pie.

Tours are available by appointment. Do not leave empty-handed. You can buy a growler of beer to go, as well as several different T-shirts and an awesome ceramic Amherst Brewing Company mug.

## BARRINGTON BREWERY & RESTAURANT

420 Stockbridge Rd., Great Barrington, MA; (413) 528-8282; BarringtonBrew.net
**Draft Beers:** 9

Take a look at the sky and thank the sun for the beers at the Barrington Brewery & Restaurant. This western Massachusetts brewpub became the first on the east coast to brew their beer using solar panels in 2007. The solar panels heat up the water used in both the brewery and the restaurant.

Maybe it's the sun, or maybe it's just talented brewing (we're going to guess the latter), but the beers at the Barrington Brewery and Restaurant are very good. Barrington always has 9 of their house-brewed beers on tap, and they brew between 20 and 25 beers every year. Beers that are always on tap include the **Hopland Pale Ale, Barrington Brown Ale,** the **Black Bear Stout,** the **Raspberry Ale,** and the **Ice Glenn IPA.**

Like many brewpubs, Barrington really shines with their occasional releases. The Vienna is a lighter German-style lager, while the **Wedded Bliss** is a darker, Dortmunder-style lager. Other German-style beers available include **Alt** and the **Bavarian Wheat.**

Barrington's biggest beer is the **Firecracker Imperial IPA,** which is an 8.5 percent alcohol by volume, west coast–style hoppy beer. The **"R" Hop** is an IPA brewed every year with hops Barrington grows themselves, while the **Yule Fuel** is a popular winter brew and tastes like what Christmas would taste like if you could fit it in a pint glass.

If you're grabbing a beer, why not grab some food? For a starter, the cheddar ale soup is a good choice (see recipe, page 309), as is the mixed sausage sampler, which includes slices of bratwurst, bauernwurst, and kielbasa, all steamed in beer. The Plowman's Lunch is large enough for two, and includes ale bread, dried sausage, brie cheese, chutney, and apples. All hamburgers are made of grass-fed beef, and include a choice of toppings. Where Barrington really excels is their sandwiches. The Chicken Philly Cheese Steak is a traditional Philly cheese steak with one twist—no beef, all grilled chicken. The Mixed N.Y. Grille is a large sandwich that includes corned beef, pastrami, and cheese, served Reuben-style, except with cole slaw instead of sauerkraut. The Steak & Stout Sandwich features sliced sirloin steak that is marinated in Barrington's stout. Don't forget to leave room for dessert; Barrington's offers coconut custard pie and chocolate stout cake, among other dishes.

If you fall in love with a beer at Barrington, buy it to go. You can buy beer in 22-ounce bottles and half-gallon kegs. Of, if you're lucky enough to have a kegerator at home, grab a keg and host a party, sharing your favorite Barrington Brewery & Restaurant beer with all of your friends.

### BEER WORKS

Two locations in Boston. Locations in Framingham, Hingham, Lowell, Salem, and inside Logan Airport; Beerworks.net
**Draft Beers:** 16 to 22

If you have ever been to a Boston Red Sox game, there is a good chance you saw a long line outside of the Boston Beer Works. The Beer Works is a Massachusetts chain of brewpubs. Along with the location outside Fenway Park, there is a second Beer Works outside TD Banknorth Garden, home of both the Bruins and Celtics.

All the beers are solid. They may not be the most complex styles, but they serve their purpose of satisfying large, quick-moving crowds who are coming in for a beer or two before or after a game. The **Back Bay IPA,** named for the Back Bay section of Boston, is a solid IPA worth grabbing. The **Beantown Nut Brown Ale** is a tasty, easy-drinking brown ale, and the **Boston Garden Golden** (say that three times fast) is a light golden ale. The **Boston Victory Bock,** brewed in honor of the Boston sports world's many championship wins, is a good bock beer, and the **Brookline Weizen Bock** is one of Beer Works' best beers.

Other beers include the **Bunker Hill Blueberry Ale,** served with real blueberries in the beer; the **Curley's Irish Stout;** and the **Kenmore Kolsch.** If you happen to be there in the summer, you may see a lot of people drinking the watermelon beer with a slice of watermelon wedged on the side of the glass. There are more complex options, particularly during the off-season. The imperial stout, barleywine, and Belgian-style quads are all standouts.

Beer Works also bottles and distributes three of their more popular beers: the **Bunker Hill Blueberry,** the **Fenway Pale Ale,** and the **Boston Red Ale.** They actually taste better bottled.

At the pubs, there is always a large selection of pub grub. Chicken fingers, wings, and fried mozzarella are all available as appetizers. The menu is also heavy on burgers, sandwiches, and other easy-to-eat food, such as pizza. Growlers of beer are always available, as are six-packs of the bottled beers. If you're going to a sporting event, there are worse options than getting a well-crafted beer at one of the Beer Works.

### CAMBRIDGE BREWING COMPANY

1 Kendall Sq., Building 100, Cambridge, MA; (617) 494-1994; CamBrew.com
**Draft Beers:** 10 to 14

Cambridge Brewing Company is the premier brewpub in Massachusetts, and it just happens to be a pretty good place to grab a meal. Phil Bannatyne founded

Cambridge Brewing Company in 1989, when good beer was hard to find at any restaurant, and brewpubs in Massachusetts were scarce. Brewmaster Will Meyers came to the restaurant in 1993.

Cambridge Brewing maintains 10 to 14 beers on draft at all times—all brewed in house, except for special events. The year-round beers are the **Regatta Golden** (cream ale), **Cambridge Amber, Tall Tale Pale Ale,** and the **Charles River Porter.** Meyers also brews several seasonal beers: **Big Man Ale,** an old stock ale brewed for winter; **Spring Training IPA,** for the spring; the **CBC HefeWeizen** for the summer; and the insanely popular **Great Pumpkin Ale** for the fall.

The Great Pumpkin Ale is so popular that the CBC, as it is often called, hosts a pumpkin beer festival every October, featuring several different house-brewed pumpkin beers, and guest pumpkin beers from around the country. A highlight a few years ago was a cask-conditioned pumpkin beer served out of a giant pumpkin.

The brewery also brews 22 other beers at least once a year, and introduces 10 to 12 totally new beers every year. Some of those beers brewed every year include the **Blunderbuss Barleywine** and the **Arquebus Summer Barleywine.** They are two of the best barleywines brewed in the world. Other standout beers include the **CBC Heather Ale,** one of the rare beers brewed without hops; **Cerise Cassee,** an American sour ale aged in oak barrels and **Om,** an American wild ale aged in chardonnay barrels.

Although beer is the star at the Cambridge Brewing Company, don't forget the food. The menu is a mix of traditional pub foods like burgers and chicken tenders, and more adventurous foods like grilled swordfish and beer-brined half chicken. The menu features several appealing appetizers, including the native corn and clam

### Barleywine Festival

Usually in January, the Cambridge Brewing Company hosts its annual Barleywine Festival, a celebration of its two fantastic barleywines, the Arquebus and the Blunderbuss. There will be several vintages of each of the two barleywines available, as well as versions of each beer aged in different types of barrels. For a barleywine fan, this is the mecca of all events. The beer is world-class, and the Cambridge Brewing Company also offers up a special tapas menu during the event.

hushpuppies and the organic pork pâté. The burgers are cooked well and to order, but the best sandwich on the menu is the slow-cooked pulled pork served with onions, Vermont cheddar, and pale ale–infused barbecue sauce. There is also a brunch, or beerunch, served on Sunday. Locavores and foodies rejoice: Many of the ingredients CBC uses for its dishes come from local farms and the chefs head out to local farmers' markets looking for fresh ingredients daily.

### THE GARDNER ALE HOUSE

74 Parker St., Gardner, MA; (978) 669-0122; GardnerAle.com
**Draft Beers:** 12

North Central Worcester County is not known as a beer haven. But, thanks to the Gardner Ale House, there is a sanctuary for better beer lovers. The Gardner Ale House opened its doors in 2006 with owner Rick Walton, a homebrewer who also liked to cook. Along with head brewer Dave Richardson, Walton has created a brewpub that appeals to anyone and everyone. A craft beer lover? Richardson's beers are excellent. Don't care about craft beer? Go there for a good meal and to listen to the frequent live musical acts playing in the pub.

The bar has a townie feel, but that's not a bad thing. There are always regulars at the bar and the bartenders seem to know everyone. The highlight is the beer. There are always at least five Gardner Ale House beers on tap, a few popular American domestics and a few other guest brews.

Richardson's beers are top-notch. The year-round beers include the **Summer's End Kolsch, Chair City Pale Ale, American Pale Ale, Facelift IPA, Naked Stout,** and the **XSB.** The Gardner Ale House also has a number of special beers and seasonals that seem to be inspired by every major brewing country—Belgium, England, Germany, and, of course, the US. **Belgian Chair** is the Chair City Pale Ale brewed with Belgian yeast, the **Old School Pilsner** is exactly what the name describes, and the **Rocker Red** is a traditional red ale. The **Dunkelweizen** is a German-style dark wheat bear, the **Chocolate Porter** is a wonderful dessert beer, and the **Face-Off Double IPA** is a big, hit-you-in-the-mouth, west coast–inspired double IPA. **Oma's Altbier,** the brewpub's best beer, is spot on for the style, with biscuity flavors and just a hint of grassy hops.

The Gardner Ale House has a full menu of appetizers, sandwiches, salads, pizzas, fish & chips (see recipe, page 312), and entrees. Appetizers include warm crab dip, crab cakes, coconut shrimp, and the best sweet potato fries in central Massachusetts. If you are lucky enough to be at the Gardner Ale House during the summer, do yourself a favor and get the lobster roll—it's as good as any you'll find at the beachside clam shacks.

## HIGH HORSE BREWING

24 North Pleasant St., Amherst, MA; (413) 230-3134; HighHorseBrewing.com
**Draft Beers:** 12+

High Horse Brewing has one of the most well-known and respected brewers behind their beers in Matthew Steinberg. Steinberg is the former head brewer at Offshore Ales and Mayflower Brewing Company and founded Blatant Beer before brewing for High Horse Brewing. The brewpub, located in the former Amherst Brewing Company's location, has several of its own beers on tap, as well as guest beers and cask-conditioned beers.

Some of the beers include **Another Lover IPA** and **Satisfaction IPA.** Other beers include the **Smoked Lager, Lady K** (pale ale), **The Moan** (Belgian pale ale), **Yellow** (kolsch), **Libertine Porter,** the **Business** (Russian imperial coffee stout), **Mr. White** (Belgian wit), **Mr. Pink** (Mr. White with grapefruit juice), **Beastie** (dark rye hoppy beer), and **Pinnacle Saison.**

High Horse also offers a full menu. Appetizers include nachos, chicken wings, meat on a stick (either chicken or beef), several different styles of french fries (regular, garlic, cheese, sweet potatoes, poutine), as well as soups and salads. High Horse also offers several fire-grilled flatbreads. High Horse also has several burger and sandwich options, including the Wake 'n Bake, which features a dark roast coffee-rubbed burger topped with bacon, Munster cheese, and a sunny-side-up egg. Entrees include macaroni and cheese, duck breast, sesame-crusted salmon, steaks, and pulled pork. High Horse also offers a dessert menu, and large gluten-free and vegetarian menus.

High Horse Brewing is open seven days a week from 11 a.m. to 1 a.m. Brunch is served Saturday and Sunday from 11 a.m. to 3 p.m. The second floor of High Horse Brewing, which features several pool tables, is open Monday through Thursday 6 p.m. to 1 am. and Friday through Sunday from 1 p.m. to 1 a.m.

## JOHN HARVARD'S BREW HOUSE

33 Dunster St., Cambridge, MA; (617) 868-3585; JohnHarvards.com
**Draft Beers:** Around 8

John Harvard's Brew House might be a chain, but the beers they brew are better than most chain brewpubs. Though most of the beers are on tap at the three locations, each of the brewers has autonomy to brew beers of their own creations. Most of the time there are also several interesting beers available.

The John Harvard's Brew House in Cambridge is the original pub. It is in the lower level of a building right off of Harvard Square, and it is a slightly dark, older-feeling bar. The John Harvard's in Framingham is located in the Shoppers World mall at 1 Worcester Rd. (508-875-2337). It is a much larger location and is set up more like a family restaurant. The third John Harvard's is located in Hancock at the Jiminy Peak ski area at 37 Corey Rd. (413-738-5500, ext. 3780) and is only open during the winter.

Year-round beers include the **All American Light Lager, Dry Irish Stout, John Harvard's Pale Ale, Nut Brown Ale,** and the **Old Willy IPA.** Their extensive roster of seasonals includes the **Mid-Winter Strong Ale** (Jan), **Celtic Red** (Feb through Mar), **Queen Bee Honey Beer** (Apr through May), **Wheat Beer** (June), **Summer Blonde** (July through Aug), **Oktoberfest** (Sept through Oct), and the **Holiday Red** (Nov through Dec).

If you do go to John Harvard's, expect a few surprises on tap. There are always some goodies available. The **Fade to Black Porter** is an excellent porter, while the **Bavarian Hefeweizen** is a nice, refreshing beer. The **Belgian Quad** is a big sipper of a beer, and the **Blackout IPA** is a solid black IPA. The **Espresso Stout,** brewed using real espresso beans, is top notch. The **Pumpkin Spice Ale** is very popular—get it with or without the rim of the glass dipped in cinnamon—and the **West Coast IPA** is a nicely hopped beer. If you like a particular beer on tap, grab a growler and bring it home.

The appetizer menu includes a huge hummus platter and a plate of nachos, perfect for sharing. The Asian Crispadillas features tortilla triangles with chicken and ginger drizzled with apricot ginger and Asian barbecue sauces, and the fried chicken wings are a step above the average pub wings. Instead of throwing away the grains after the brewers are done, John Harvard's actually uses the spent grain to make the dough for their pizzas. Entrees include the Maple Dijon Salmon, the Ale and Mustard Chicken, meat loaf, ribs, chicken pot pies, and fish and chips with a huge slab of fried cod.

### NORTHAMPTON BREWERY

11 Brewster Court, Northampton, MA; (413) 584-9903; NorthamptonBrewery.com
**Draft Beers:** 10

The Northampton Brewery is part of New England brewing history. It is the oldest existing brewpub in all of New England. The brewery was founded in 1987 by brother and sister team of Peter and Janet Egleston, who later went on to open the Portsmouth Brewery in New Hampshire.

For a brewpub to last this long, they have to brew good beers, and Northampton certainly does just that. The standard beers that can be found at most times include the **(Snow) (Sand) (No) Shovel ESB,** the **Altbier,** the **Byzantine Blonde,** the **Golden Lager,** the **Nontuck IPA,** and the **Red-Headed Stepchild.** If you have ever visited the Portsmouth Brewery, you will notice that some of the same beers, such as **Old Brown Dog** and the **Black Cat Stout,** are available at both locations, even though they are not technically connected anymore.

The Northampton Brewery also offers a number of specialty beers. The **88′ Tor** is a doppelbock, while the **Black Boots** is a black IPA. The **Conundrum,** a German-style schwarz beer, is an excellent black lager. The **Hoppily Ever After** and the **Hopzilla** are both hoppy IPAs, and the **Wild Blue Funk** is a beer brewed with fresh Maine blueberries and then fermented with wild yeast, making this a wonderfully tart/sour beer. The brewpub also offers several seasonals, such as the **Graduation Ale,** a wheat ale brewed with raspberries; the **Octoberfest;** and the **Pumpkin Ale.** Along with its own beer, the Northampton Brewery almost always features several guest beers from other breweries.

The inside bar area is larger than many brewpubs and Northampton also has a rooftop beer garden with a bar so you do not have to worry about going in and out every time you want a drink. There is also a sun room that is open if there are no special events taking place.

Grub-wise, the Northampton Brewery has a large and varied menu. Appetizers include Cajun Catfish Bites, which are fried and dusted with Cajun spices, and Arancini, which is mozzarella encased in Parmesan risotto, panko battered, and deep-fried. The Northampton Brewery has numerous interesting sandwiches, including the Hot Poblano, which features bacon-wrapped poblano-stuffed meat loaf topped with chipotle mayo, black beans, and grilled corn salsa. Another option is Basil's Rathbone, which is a sandwich filled with sliced tomatoes, roasted red pepper, red onions, fresh basil, provolone cheese, and garlic mayonnaise. If you're part of a large group, try one of the brewpub's platters, such as the New England Cheese Platter and the Ploughman's Platter.

## OFFSHORE ALE COMPANY

30 Kennebec Ave., Oak Bluffs, MA; (508) 693-2626; OffshoreAle.com
Draft Beers: 8

Martha's Vineyard is a picturesque summer destination, and the Offshore Ale Company in Oak Bluffs is the best place to grab a beer on the small island. Offshore Ale is a brewpub that serves good beer all year-round.

There are always eight beers on draft, and cask offerings are sometimes available. The standard beers include the **Offshore Amber Ale,** the **Offshore IPA,** and the

**East Chop Light House Ale.** The best of the standard-line beers is the **Menemsha Creek Pale Ale,** which is one of the top pale ales being brewed in New England. It is hoppy, but balanced. Each sip makes you want to take another sip. Get this if it is the only beer you get at Offshore.

Offshore also has a number of occasionally brewed beers. The **Argus** is a nice Belgian ale, while the **Helles Bock** is a great interpretation of the German style. The **Island Double IPA** is a big, hoppy beer, and the **Hop Goddess** is a hoppy Belgian pale ale, almost an IPA. The **Inkwell Stout** is a beer worth seeking out. The alcohol changes each year, and each version of the beer tastes slightly different than past years.

The restaurant has a good mix of food—from simple, down-home cooking to more sophisticated dishes. Starters include some items you might not see on a typical brewpub menu, such as the turkey wings, which includes four wings with honey barbecue sauce. The grilled brie, Parmesan truffle fries, and the Bavarian pretzel spears are other delicious options. Offshore also offers several brick-oven pizzas. Options include the white clam pizza that has a garlic oil base with bacon, onions, mozzarella cheese, and chopped littleneck clams. The portobello pizza and roasted duck pizza are also worth getting. There is also a raw bar that includes littleneck clams and oysters on the half-shell.

Offshore typically has live music every Tuesday and Wednesday. They offer tours during business hours, and have plenty of items for sale, such as golf balls, shirts, hats, glasses, and Frisbees. Can't get to the island? Several of Offshore's beers, including the Offshore Amber Ale, the Menemsha Creek Pale Ale, and the East Chop Light House Ale are available in 12-ounce bottles throughout Massachusetts.

### Oktoberfest

Although Martha's Vineyard is thought of as more of a summer playland, Offshore does host Oktoberfest, which will give you a reason to venture out onto the island during the fall. The event features great beer, German-style food and oompah music, and, of course, tons of Offshore's fresh and fantastic beers. It becomes a big party, and you should go if you get a chance.

### OPA OPA STEAKHOUSE & BREWERY

169 College Hwy., Southampton, MA; (413) 527-0808; OpaOpaSteakhouseBrewery.com
Draft Beers: 20

Put on your 10-gallon hat and grab your cowboy boots—it's time to head to the Opa Opa Steakhouse. Opa Opa is a western-style steakhouse that also happens to brew some pretty good beer.

Opa Opa has a large selection of beers, including the **Opa Opa Light,** the **Kix Beer, Honesty 47 Pale Ale, Buckwheat IPA,** the **Brown Ale,** the **Southampton Porter,** the **King Oak Milk Stout,** and the **Red Rock Ale.** The **A-10 Warthog Double IPA,** a big, hoppy monster of a beer, is also routinely available. Opa Opa also brews several seasonals and fruit beers, including the **Belgian White,** the **Blueberry Lager,** an **Oktoberfest,** and the **Raspberry Wheat.**

Although the beers are quite good, Opa Opa is one of the few brewpubs where the food is the star. Opa Opa is a carnivore's dream. Sure, there are a few veggie options, several salads, as well as a vegetarian pie called the Hey Grazers, which is stuffed with spinach, garlic, carrots, ginger, grilled eggplant, zucchini, squash, tomatoes, mushrooms, fennel, and onions, but it's really all about the meat. Not too hungry? Get the Tenderfoot, which is an 8-ounce filet. Have a bigger appetite? Go for the Trail Hand, a 16-ounce T-bone steak. Or if you're really hungry, the Trail Boss, a 20-ounce porterhouse, is for you. The prime rib is one of the best you'll ever have, and available in three sizes: the Deputy is 8 ounces, the Sheriff is 12 ounces, and the Marshall is 16 ounces.

Several of Opa Opa's beers are available in stores in six-packs or in growlers. They also have brewed several exclusive beers for Julio's Liquors in Westborough, Massachusetts, which are definitely worth seeking out.

### THE PEOPLE'S PINT

24 Federal St., Greenfield, MA; (413) 773-0333; ThePeoplesPint.com
**Draft Beers:** 8

Downtown Greenfield is a place that appears to be about 10 years behind the times, but in a good way. They have neighborhood video stores, family-run pizza places, and a bunch of corner stores. It is also the home of The People's Pint, a popular brewpub that is known just as much for their use of local ingredients in almost all their food as they are for their lineup of freshly brewed beers.

The beers are actually not brewed on-site, but at The People's Pint's nearby brewing facility on Hope Street. There are always eight house beers on draft (and sometimes a guest draft or two). Most of the beers are typically New England styles, but all are done really well. The **Natural Blonde Ale** is a light, refreshing, blonde ale that goes down easy. The **Provider Pale Ale,** a nice, hoppy pale ale, is the People's Pint's most popular beer. The **Pied Piper IPA** tastes like a hoppier version of an English-style IPA. The **Oatmeal Stout,** meanwhile, is the People's Pint's best beer. It is a work of art in a glass; utterly and completely fantastic. Other beers include a few lagers, such as the **Doppelbock, Dark Helmut** (German-style black lager), and the **Oktoberfest.**

The People's Pint also brews some adventurous styles you might not see at any other brewpub. The **Slippery Slope** is a braggot-style ale, extremely heavy on ginger. The **Tap & Die Malt Liquor** is a craft interpretation of those old 40-ounce bottles of cheap, high-alcohol malt liquor like Cobra. Suitably, if you buy a bottle of this beer in a store, it actually comes in a 40-ounce bottle. Also available is the **Midnight Special,** which is an imperial black IPA. The People's Pint also offers locally made meads and hard ciders.

The menu is an interesting mix of traditional pub food and more ambitious fare. Starters include the incredible smoked wings, as well as the housemade pickled eggs. The People's Pint has several sandwiches on the menu, but the one you can't miss is the Squealer; it's made with local, grass-fed beef and housemade bacon ground together into one patty. Their entrees are especially interesting. Case in point, the Green Thai Curry Bowl is made with chicken or tofu in a Thai curry, with local seasonal vegetables and a spicy green Thai curry sauce served over basmati rice. Consider ordering the El Salvadorian Pupusa, which consists of two housemade corn tortillas stuffed with organic beans and cheese, served with black beans, Spanish rice, and salad greens tossed with lemon tahini and salsa.

Beer is also available to go in the form of 22-ounce bombers and growlers. But make sure to bring cash—the People's Pint does not accept credit or debit cards.



### THE TAP BREWPUB

100 Washington St., Haverhill, MA; (978) 374-1117; TapBrewpub.com
**Draft Beers:** 8

The Tap at the Haverhill Brewing Company is one of those underrated brewpubs that is overlooked because of its location; Haverhill is not near anywhere else that is considered a beer destination. But the beers brewer Jon Curtis produces are good enough to make any beer lover make the trek out to Haverhill.

The Tap has a great rotating lineup, heavy on German-style beers, which is not common for brewpubs. Among the German-style beers brewed at the Tap are the **Annie Schwartz Black Lager,** the **Beerstand Berliner Weiss, Dunkel Weizen, GestAlt, Hefe Dampfbier, Helles Belles, Kolsch, Munich Dunkel,** and the **Scapegoat Bock.** The best are the Beerstand Berliner Weiss, a tart German-style wheat bear that has become more popular in New England brewpubs in the past couple of years, and the GestAlt, an excellent altbier. The Tap does not ignore Belgian ales. They have several on tap, including the popular **Whittier White,** as well as the **Ascension Belgian IPA,** the **La Dame De Peronne, Ruby Bruin,** and **Three Graces.** The Ruby Bruin is a solid Flemish Belgian sour ale, and the Ascension Belgian IPA is one of the best of the style.

Then there are the American beers—the **Breakout India Dark Ale,** the **Chocolate Porter,** the **Haver Ale, Homerun APA, Leatherlips IPA,** and **Pumpkin Eater Ale.** The Leatherlips was one of the earliest New England IPAs that abandoned the British tradition and became more hop forward. It may not be as extreme as it used to be, but it is still a very good IPA.

They also bottle several of their beers in six-packs under the Haverhill Brewing Company name. These include their flagship beers—the Leatherlips, the Homerun APA, Whittier White, and the Haver Ale. Haverhill also bottles some of the Tap's other beers, mostly the special releases, in 22-ounce bottles. They are Ascension, GestAlt, **Joshua Norton Imperial Stout,** La Dame De Peronne, **Snowbound, Three Graces,** and **Triskelion.** Beer in growlers, six-packs, and bombers are all for sale to go from the Tap.

If you are at the Tap, you have to order the Portabella Pub Fries. They are thin strips of portabella mushrooms, fried and served like french fries. Other appetizers worth trying include the Witbier Mussels and the Artisan Cheese Plate. Or, grab a potato, leek, and ale soup to whet your appetite for the main meal. The menu features several flatbread pizzas and hamburgers. The Back Deck Burger features an 8-ounce burger rubbed with Jamaican jerk seasoning, topped with lettuce, tomatoes, onions, and banana-mango ketchup. The top entree is the Sea Captain's Platter, which consists of a 4-ounce piece of haddock served with mussels and shrimp.

The Tap is proof that good beer can be found almost anywhere you look, as long as you search it out.

## WATCH CITY BREWING COMPANY [CLOSED]

256 Moody St., Waltham, MA; (781) 647-4000; WatchCityBrew.com
**Draft Beers:** 8 plus 2 casks

People say bacon makes everything better, but did they mean beer, too? Watch City Brewing Company's head brewer, Aaron Mateychuck, thinks so. He brews bacon beer. Let that sink in—beer made with real bacon. Salivating yet?

If not, give this even more thought: In 2011 Watch City held the "14 Degrees of Making Bacon Cask Extravaganza" at the Moody Street brewpub. The event featured 14 different versions of the bacon beer, all cask-conditioned. Every single one of them had bacon essence in the flavor, smokiness, and then some wild and crazy spices. Thai coconut curry and bacon? Hot peppers and bacon? Chocolate and bacon? Yeah, they were all there. Some were great, some not so much, but it was a worthy effort, and sure to make a return to the pub.

But don't get the wrong idea. Watch City is not all about gimmicks. The year-rounds—**Hops Explosion IPA, Moody Street Stout, Shillelagh Irish Red Ale,** and **Titan Ale**—are all great beers. There are also always tons of special beers and seasonals on tap. The **'FNA Imperial IPA** is an excellent beer. The **Monkey Monk Saison** is another winner. The phenomenal **Toasted Ah Ah Pale Ale** is brewed with coconut and hibiscus flowers. If you want a big beer, try **Lunarshine Burleywine,** a 9.8 percent alcohol by volume barleywine. The **Chocolate Thunder Porter,** brewed with local chocolate, is perfect as a nightcap, while the **BitchLoden Wheat Lager** offers a different twist on wheat beers. The **Beejeszus Botanical Ale** is a hopless beer and uses ingredients grown in Mateychuck's own backyard.

Watch City also likes to collaborate with their customers. The **Trident's Old Spearhead IPA** was brewed with homebrewer and frequent patron Mike Johnson of Natick. The brewpub has even started a Patron's Appreciation Society; the first beer brewed is called **Stephanie's Cherry Raspberry Wheat,** brewed with customer Alan Muir.

For the less experimental types, there are plenty of "normal beers," such as the **Bitter and Jaded ESB** (extra special bitter), **Skye High Scotch Ale, Bombed Blondshelle Tripel,** and **Brilliant Brunette,** a Belgian strong ale. For those who like lower alcohol beers, **Wee Light** is a lighter version of a Scottish-style wee heavy.

Watch City's burgers are especially good. The oddest—and most likely to clog your arteries—may be the Tick Tock Burger, which consists of a patty deep-fried in beer batter and then topped with chipotle lime mayonnaise. You can also get some bacon on the burger if you want. Hey, if you are drinking a bacon beer, you might as well go all out.

# Beer Bars

## THE ALE HOUSE

33 Main St., Amesbury, MA; (978) 388-1950; AmesburyAleHouse.com
**Draft Beers:** 30 **Bottled/Canned Beers:** Around 100

Although they do not get as much recognition as other Boston-area bars, the Ale House is one of the best beer bars in all of New England. If you take a look at the draft list and, even more impressive, the bottled list, it would be hard for even the most hard core of beer geeks not to be impressed. Add to the fantastic beer selection a huge and varied food menu, you have a beer destination that everyone should seek out.

The bottled list is simply a thing of beauty. They have one of the largest selections of wild ales and lambics you will ever find. Wild ales, for those who do not know, are typically brewed with wild yeast, which makes the beer sour and/or tart. They have many, including several options from Jolly Pumpkin from Michigan, Cascade Brewing from Washington, and even Haandbryggeriett from Norway. The Ale House also offers several varieties of gueuze, a Belgian ale that is spontaneously fermented with wild yeast and is often sour. The options range from easy to find, like the Lindeman's Framboise, to the harder to find (and expensive) Drie Fonteine Oude Gueuze. Pretty much every other Belgian style of ale is available, including saisons, white ales, dubbels, tripels, and quads.

The draft list has more beers that are meant to turn over quickly, and they are all excellent examples of specific styles. If you like hefeweizens, they typically have Weihenstephan Hefeweiss available. They also have several IPAs, lagers, and seasonals on draft.

The awesomeness that is the Ale House continues to the food side. Starters include Guinness beef stew; Belgian-style frites with a choice of seasonings, toppings, and dipping sauces; fried pickles; lobster corn cakes; and smoked chicken taquitos. Pub food such as American chop suey, a patty melt, and club sandwiches are also available, as are several entrees, which include the lobster quesadilla, which is made with lobster, mozzarella, and guacomole; sesame-crusted tuna; turkey tips; lobster sliders; balsamic braised beef short ribs; and beer-battered fish and chips.

Adding to the Ale House's charm is the location. The bar is located in an old mill, and it still retains a lot of the mill's features, such as the high tin roofs. It also sits on the Powwow River, and the views are amazing. If you're on the north shore for any reason, the Ale House is a place at which any self-respecting beer lover has to stop.

## ARMSBY ABBEY

144 North Main St., Worcester, MA; (508) 795-1012; ArmsbyAbbey.com
**Draft Beers:** 22 **Bottled/Can Beers:** Around 150

The best beer bar in Massachusetts is not in Boston. It is in central Massachusetts, Worcester to be exact, an area that used to be a beer wasteland. The Armsby Abbey, founded in 2008 by Alec Lopez and his wife, Sherri Sadowski, takes everything to another level.

Sure, there is beer, but that is not the only thing that makes the Armsby Abbey special. They make the best food in Worcester, with almost all locally sourced ingredients. They do not carry name brands. The wines are from small wineries. The spirits are from small-batch distillers. The mixed drink menu is put together with care and a sense of artistry. If you want a Pepsi, you are out of luck. You will have to get a Polar Cola, made in Worcester.

Start with the beer selection. The draft list, posted on a large chalkboard, features 22 hand-selected offerings. Heavy on Belgian ales, but with a great selection of American craft ales, it is a well-put-together list. Even though there are only 22 beers on tap, even the most hard-core beer drinkers will not have any trouble finding something they have never had. The bottled list is also incredibly impressive. Not only does it include beers of nearly every style from every craft brewery producing good beers today, it also features some special, and sometimes pricy, selections from Lopez's beer cellar.

If a member of your party is not a beer fan, do not be concerned. The liquor and wine selection is extensive, and the cocktail menu is fantastic, featuring dozens of unique creations made with the small batch liquors.

Food-wise, there are not many beer-centric places, except for the Sierra Grille in Northampton, that can match what the Armsby Abbey does. The menu changes constantly and is based on what Lopez can get locally. Do not go in looking for a quick meal. This is not fast food; it is slow-cooked food, cooked to order, and cooked right. The menu always features various cheese plates, local fruits, house-baked breads, desserts, and soups. Entrees can range from a cold duck sausage sandwich to smoked bone marrow.

The pizzas are incredible. If you have a chance, go to the weekend brunch. There are breakfast pizzas (the harvest pizza with pumpkin puree instead of tomato sauce is to die for), gourmet macaroni and cheese, Belgian waffles, different versions of pancakes, toast, and a breakfast slate featuring fruits, local honey, and other condiments and cheeses.

## Beer Event

### Founder's Breakfast

Each April, the Armsby Abbey hosts a special beer meal. While most beer meals are dinners, this is a breakfast. It makes sense, because at this particular sellout event, Armsby hosts the Founders Brewing Company of Michigan and their collection of excellent breakfast stouts, including the regular Breakfast Stout, the Kentucky Breakfast Stout, and the Canadian Breakfast Stout. These beers are paired with a breakfast prepared by chef/owner Alec Lopez.

There are many events throughout the year. Lopez, who is also the chef, hosts several beer dinners a year, where a brewery's beers are each paired with a different dish. These sell out quickly. The Armsby Abbey is a must for beer lovers, particularly if you are in the Worcester area. Stop in and be amazed.

### BRITISH BEER COMPANY

Ten locations in Cedarville, Danvers, Falmouth, Framingham, Franklin, Hyannis, Manchester, Pembroke, Plymouth, Portsmouth, Sandwich, Walpole, Westford; (508) 888-6610 (corporate number); BritishBeer.com

**Draft Beers:** At least 20 at every location **Bottled/Canned Beers:** Various

The British Beer Company may be a chain (currently with 13 locations and continuing to grow), but the restaurant has never lost its original goal, to provide its beer-loving guests with an experience they won't soon forget.

Modeled after English pubs, most of the bars at the British Beer Company are designed and purchased in England. All of the locations have an extensive beer list, with at least 20 beers on tap. In all, the chain features 290 beers on tap (or draught to keep with the English terminology), and each pub usually features at least 1 cask-conditioned beer. Most of the bars also have a large bottled list of British- and Belgian-imported beers. The beer menu is also arranged in a way that is very helpful to the British Beer Company's customers—they are listed from least complex to most complex.

The British Beer Company also hosts numerous events throughout the year, including tap takeovers, Oktoberfest celebrations, and beer dinners. The Dogfish Head Tap Takeover is always a favorite, especially when the British Beer Company breaks outs some of their Randall the Enamel Animals (a device that runs a draft beer through fresh ingredients right before it hits the glass, adding fresh flavors). They have also recently started hosting scotch and single-batch bourbon tastings. Throughout the week, the British Beer Company restaurants also host live musicians, so there's always something going on.

The baked brie appetizer, featuring warm brie cheese wrapped in a puff pastry with an apple-mango chutney, is excellent. The Royal Pu Pu includes several of the available appetizers on one plate—the shrimp wontons, crispy panko-encrusted green beans, bourbon sauce wings, bourbon BBQ ribs, sweet potato fries, BBC fries, and onion rings. Of course, there are many British favorites on the menu, including beer-battered fish and chips, bangers and mash, and shepherd's pie. They also have several British pasty pies available, including the popular chicken and leek pasty pie. Burgers are bountiful, and entrees include ribs, steaks, pasta, and the Guinness steak pie.

Their pizzas are also top-notch. If you want to be especially adventurous, try the Over 21 Pizza, which is topped with the brewpub's bourbon sauce, cheddar cheese, steak, peppers, onions, and mushrooms. If that wasn't enough, the pizza is also misted with bourbon tableside. Obviously, the pizza can't be shared with youngsters—let them eat off the kids' menu while you enjoy your bourbon pizza and a nice British ale on draft.



## BUKOWSKI'S TAVERN

50 Dalton St., Boston, MA, (617) 437-9909; 1281 Cambridge St., Cambridge, MA, (617) 497-7077; BukowskisTavern.net

**Draft Beers:** Boston, 20; Cambridge, 30 **Bottled/Canned Beers:** Boston, about 100; Cambridge, about 130

Bukowski's Tavern is a Boston classic. If you like good beer and live in the area, odds are you have been there. The Boston and Cambridge locations do have some differences: Boston's Bukowski's is small, a wee bit dingy, and has a limited menu, while the Cambridge location is larger and has a full menu as well as a wine and cocktail list. What they both have in common is great beer, and a rather friendly staff of bartenders.

The draft list features a specially brewed beer by the Wormtown Brewing Company in Worcester called the Buk, which is a rye pale ale. It also features beer from great breweries from around the country, including Brooklyn Brewery, Ithaca Brewing Company, Sierra Nevada, and Brewery Ommegang. They usually feature plenty of New England beers, such as stuff from Pretty Things Beer & Ale Project, Notch Session, Cisco Brewers, and Smuttynose Brewing Company. Cambridge also has a few imported beers on draft. The bottled and canned list features beers from most of the better breweries around the country, as well as local favorites.

As far as food goes, we'll start with the Boston location. Appetizers include sweet potato fries, fried plantains, mini-mozzarella sticks, and a true Bukowski's original, the White Trash Cheese Dip. The dip is made with a mix of American cheese, green chili peppers, jalapeños, diced tomatoes, and diced onions, served with tortilla chips. Other than starters, burgers, hot dogs, and sandwiches dominate the menu. A particular standout is the gourmet grilled cheese sandwich, which is made with Havarti cheese and sliced tomatoes, pressed between slices of sourdough bread. Burgers include the peanut butter burger, which is a grilled 6-ounce burger topped with chunky peanut butter. Another option is the Hangover Helper, which is topped with aged cheddar, bacon, and a fried egg.

The Cambridge food menu is identical save for a few extras, such as PBR onion rings, soup, and even a couple of salads. Entrees include rosemary duck breast served over a smoked gouda risotto; fish and chips; and baked mac and cheese, made with cavatappi pasta and cheddar, Swiss, blue, and mozzarella cheeses. More sophisticated sandwiches, such as the roast beef and brie, are also available.

### The Annual Kung-Fu Christmas

The holidays can be a stressful time. You're forced to visit family members you have not seen all year, and usually after a couple of hours, you remember exactly why you haven't seen them all year. If you need to escape, head to the annual Kung Fu Christmas at Bukowski's in Cambridge. They are open from 5:30 p.m. to 1 a.m. to give you a Christmas free of stress, fruitcakes, and irritating ho, ho, hoing. No Santa hats allowed, and Christmas music will not be blaring in your ear. You will just be drinking a lot of good beer and there will probably be no real kung-fu fighting.

## CAMBRIDGE COMMON RESTAURANT

1667 Massachusetts Ave., Cambridge, MA; (617) 547-1228; CambridgeCommonRestaurant.com
**Draft Beers:** 31 **Bottled/Canned Beers:** 12

The Cambridge Common Restaurant may not have the biggest draft selection in the greater Boston area, but it is one of the most fun places to hang out. There is always something going on at the Cambridge Common and the staff, servers, and bartenders are some of the friendliest in town. It is the kind of place you can go to grab a good meal, watch a game (during the World Cup they open early in the morning to allow people to come in and watch their favorite teams and eat breakfast), or take in a beer event.

The beer selection is nothing to sniff at. The staff has a well-thought-out draft list of 31 beers, heavy on locals, but not ignoring beers from other states. Cambridge Common breaks up the draft list into "Always on Tap" and "Rotating Brews." The beers always available include Allagash White, Berkshire Brewing Company's Coffee House Porter, Ithaca's Flower Power IPA, and Victory Golden Monkey. A recent rotating draft list included Massachusetts beers such as Blue Hill's AntiMatter 2, Cambridge Brewing Company's Biere de Gourde, and Jack's Abby Brewing's Copper Legend Oktoberfest. Other beers from the Brooklyn Brewery and Troegs brewery were also available.

Throughout the year, the Cambridge Common hosts several tap takeovers, including a New England tap takeover during Boston Beer Week in June. They also host several beer dinners throughout the year, as well as beer release parties.

The *Improper Bostonian* magazine once said the Cambridge Common had "Boston's Best Bar Food," and the restaurant tries to live up to those lofty standards. Starters include deviled eggs, tater tots, mac and cheese bites, and the huge Middle Eastern platter. The platter includes roasted garlic hummus, Israeli couscous, feta, kalamata olives, tomatoes, greens, pepperoncini, red onions, and pita bread. Comfort foods such as fish and chips and grilled meat loaf are available as entrees, as is the seafood jambalaya that features cod, calamari, mussels, chicken, and chorizo. Healthier options include fish tacos, tofu curry, and numerous salads. A special brunch menu is served on Saturday and Sunday. You can get French toast, pancakes, numerous types of omelets, and breakfast burritos.

Prices are some of the best in the Boston area, and unlike a lot of bars, they do have an on-site parking lot. Drive down the narrow alleyway next to the pub and it opens into a small lot. So many people do not know about it you can often find a spot even if it is standing room only on the inside.

### DEEP ELLUM

477 Cambridge St., Allston, MA; (617) 787-2337; DeepEllum-Boston.com
Draft Beers: 28 Bottled/Canned Beers: 80

Deep Ellum may not have the sheer number of beers as the most famous beer bar in Allston, the Sunset Grill, but it stands up to any beer bar with a great selection of more than 100 beers between its bottled and draft lists. Located just down the street from the Sunset Grill, Deep Ellum has 28 beers on tap, as well as about 80 bottled and canned beers, with several cask options available.

The draft list typically features several beers from Belgium and Germany, as well as occasional visits from Norway and Spain. It is also heavy on New England craft beers, such as Clown Shoes, Element, Haverhill Brewing Company, Jack's Abby Brewing, Pretty Things Beer & Ale Project, and Smuttynose Brewing Company. Beers from other parts of the country are not ignored. It would not be unusual to find beers from Stone Brewing Company and Green Flash Brewing Company from California, or Stoudts from Pennsylvania, on tap.

The bottled list is also well thought out, and separated into either the ale or lager category. The lager selections include some of the best German varieties available. The ale list is further broken down into styles, so it is easy to find a Belgian ale, such as Cantillon, or a wheat beer, such as Schneider Edel Weiss.

To go along with the great beer selection, Deep Ellum features a full menu. Starters include cheese plates, charcuterie plates, and french fries offered in four different styles—Parmesan, chili and pepper jack, malt vinegar and fleur de sel, and truffled gorgonzola. Other options include deviled eggs and the root-beer-braised pork belly. Burgers are available, as are sandwiches, including the Big Easy, which is a New Orleans' style sandwich made up of cold cuts, provolone cheese, and olives. Another standout is the pork meatball banh mi, which features pork meatballs on French bread, topped with pickled daikon, carrots, srirachi aioli, and cilantro. Other delicious mains include the golden beet and wild mushroom risotto, coffee-braised lamb shank, and chicken schnitzel. Deep Ellum also offers brunch daily. The Fall River French Toast, made with Portuguese sweet bread, and the BBQ Breakfast, which includes braised pork shoulder, cornbread, mustard aioli, and a fried egg, are two of the highlights.

Along with beer, Deep Ellum offers a large selection of cocktails, wines, bourbons, and rye whiskeys. During the summer, make sure to take advantage of the outdoor deck and sit outside while drinking a few beers.

**THE DIVE BAR**

34 Green St., Worcester, MA; (508) 752-5802; TheDiveBarWorcester.com

**Draft Beers:** 16 **Bottled/Canned Beers:** More than 100

The Dive Bar is not a pretty place. When you look at it from the outside, it actually looks more like a place where you would go to have a couple of shots of cheap whiskey and then get into a knock-down drag-out fight. It does get better when you walk inside. The walls are a mishmash of beer signs, old-fashioned diving equipment (think full-head diving helmet), and stickers. It is dark inside, and there are not a lot of seats. In fact, the Dive Bar was so divey that *Stuff* magazine once named it one of the best dive bars in America.

But you soon discover the beauty of the bar when you see all the tap handles and the draft list scrawled out on the giant chalkboard. This is not your father's dive bar. This is Alec Lopez's Dive Bar, a bar with a fantastic draft list. The days of dollar draft nights for college students are gone. Lopez also owns the Armsby Abbey. But, except for great beer and a staff that is knowledgeable about beer, there are not many similarities.

There is no food menu, although during the summer, Lopez opens up an outdoor beer garden and throws food on the grill. If you are hungry, a sausage truck is usually outside. The beer is the star at the Dive Bar, which exclusively features American craft beer on draft. There is a good chance you will find beers from Berkshire Brewing

### Dogfish Head Halloween

Every Halloween, the Dive Bar hosts Dogfish Head Halloween, a tap takeover by the popular Delaware brewery. Every single tap is a Dogfish Head beer, and there are also some Dogfish Head spirits available. Do not even consider driving that night. Get a room and take a cab. This is a party to end all parties. Go to the Dive Bar's sister bar, the Armsby Abbey, the next morning for the Dogfish Head brunch to recover.

Company, Brooklyn Brewery, Sixpoint, and Southern Tier on draft. The beers are affordable and handled correctly. The staff is friendly and the crowd is loud and raucous, but all are having a good time.

Along with the great beer, the Dive Bar is a haven for local live music enthusiasts. Every Thursday is "Dive Thursday," when local musician Duncan Arsenault and a group of various musicians come together and jam the night away with awesome music. It is loud, so conversation may be tough, but the music will make up for that. Monday usually features live music from the Bob & Pop Jazz Organization, and there are often live bands on other nights.

### GREEN STREET GRILLE

280 Green St., Cambridge, MA; (617) 876-1655; GreenStreetGrille.com
**Draft Beers:** 10 **Bottled/Canned Beers:** About 30

The Green Street Grille is a restaurant first, and beer bar second. The draft list is small but impressive, and the bottled list features numerous quality beers.

Let's start with the food. With just a quick look at the menu, you will soon realize that the food is a little different than at the average beer bar. Starters include the grilled octopus stew, confit of duck legs, fried goat cheese salad, and an artisanal cheese plate. Dinner highlights include the baked Gloucester haddock that is served with mustard spaetzle, shaved brussels sprouts, bacon, and vinaigrette. The spicy Wellfleet clam stew is made with borlotti beans, jalapeño, bacon, and local kale. The quality continues through the desserts menu, which features such sweet dishes as English toffee pudding cake, housemade ice-cream sandwich, and a banana upside-down cake.

The beer menu is just as well done as the food menu. The list includes an IPA of the Day, Stout of the Day, and Draught of the Day. Some beers that are often on the draft list include Jolly Pumpkin of Michigan, Left Hand Brewing Company of Colorado, Clipper City Brewing Company of Maryland, and Uinta Brewing Company of Utah. The bottled list is also varied, and often offers little-seen beers, such as Prestige Lager from Haiti and Dragon Stout from Jamaica. There are several American craft beers available, too, such as Butternuts from New York, the Bruery from California, and Arcadia Ales from Michigan. Green Street also has a large brandy and rum menu, as well as wine and cocktails, so there is something for everyone.

## HORSESHOE PUB & RESTAURANT

29 South St., Hudson, MA; (978) 568-1265; HorseshoePub.com

**Draft Beers:** 80 **Bottled/Canned Beers:** 20

The Horseshoe Pub & Restaurant is the kind of neighborhood bar everyone would want. Take a stroll over, grab your favorite seat at the bar, chit-chat with the bartender and the regulars you see there all the time, and enjoy the game on the televisions. Oh, and enjoy a few of the 80 beers they have on tap.

The Horseshoe Pub is located in downtown Hudson, a working class town, not a place you would normally find a craft beer haven. But the Horseshoe Pub reflects its population. It is a no-frills kind of pub. The bar area is set up like a sports bar, and there is a good size dining area on both the first and second floors. In warmer weather the outside deck is a great place to sit and enjoy a few pints.

Many beer bars go out of their way to get the "proper" glassware for various styles of beer. That is fine, but the Horseshoe offers most of its beers in normal pint glasses. Nothing wrong with that. Sometimes it is nice to get a big glass of an IPA that is not served in a tulip or a snifter. The beer list is heavy on American craft beers. The Horseshoe Pub may not have all the beer geek, hard-to-find beers, but they pretty much have nothing but beers. Beers from Bear Republic, Boulder Beer, Saranac, and Victory always seem to be available. The 'Shoe, as the locals call it, always has a lot of Massachusetts beers on tap. Expect to find beers from Berkshire Brewing Company, the Haverhill Brewery, Mayflower Brewing Company, Wachusett Brewing Company, and Wormtown Brewing Company available most of the time. There are also always a few Belgian ales, English ales, and German lagers and wheat beers available as well.

If you happen to be at the Horseshoe Pub, grab dinner. The menu is a good mix of pub and comfort foods, with some twists thrown in. Appetizers include some tasty housemade potato chips and Reuben eggrolls, stuffed with corned beef, sauerkraut, and Swiss cheese. Or try the Irish nachos, which are topped with Mexican cheese sauce, chopped bacon, and scallions. There are plenty of burgers, sandwiches, and salads on the menu, but the strength of the offerings is really in the entrees. The Horseshoe offers meat loaf and country-style shepherd's pie and beef tips, but they also offer General Gao's chicken. Also available is the Sicilian haddock, which is topped with baby spinach, diced tomatoes, oregano, and shredded Parmesan cheese. If pasta is on your mind, the braised short rib ravioli is a strong contender, as is the butternut squash ravioli and maple butternut chicken.

October is also a good time to be at the Horseshoe Pub. They hold a month long Oktoberfest with a German-style food-heavy menu and extra German beers on tap. Prost.

### JACOB WIRTH RESTAURANT

31–37 Stuart St., Boston, MA; (617) 338-8587; JacobWirth.com
**Draft Beers:** 32 **Bottled/Canned Beers:** About 30

Jacob Wirth's Restaurant is a true Boston classic. They've been filling glasses with the good stuff for close to 150 years, and to this day it remains a great place to have a good German-style meal and grab a half-liter of beer.

Jacob Wirth opened the restaurant in 1868. He and his family owned several breweries and were the sole distributors of Budweiser beers, so they wanted a place to sell the beer locally. Today, you can still find Budweiser at Jacob Wirth's, but you can find so much more. The restaurant has 32 beers on draft and around 30 bottles available at all times.

Being a German-style restaurant, Jacob Wirth's has a large number of German beers available, but that is not all they have. German beer is great, but if you want something different, they have a fair amount of American craft beer, Belgian ales, and English-style ales, mostly in bottles. They even have two German non-alcoholic beers available in bottles.

Make sure if you're in town in October to head there for the Oktoberfest celebration. Throughout the month there are special events, such as tap takeovers, so it's not to be missed. Other events throughout the year include brewer's nights where the brewers come in and discuss their beers. They have also hosted a mini-golf tournament inside the restaurant.

The food is amazing. You cannot go to a German restaurant and not at least consider getting wursts, or sausages. Jacob Wirth's has several different options—steamed bratwurst, grilled smoked bratwurst, steamed knockwurst, grilled weissewurst, and Jake's Black Label Sausage. The sausages are done right and should be savored with a big glass of a German lager. The appetizers also feature a couple of German standbys, potato pancakes and a bucket of giant soft pretzels. If those aren't for you, they have nachos, wings, and calamari, which are probably quite popular in Germany. Maybe not. Other German dishes on the menu include the Wiener schnitzel, jaegerschnitzel, and sauerbraten. There are also entree-sized sausage plates.

If German food is not for you, don't worry, there's something for everybody. Non-German entrees include beer-battered fish and chips, vegetable ravioli, and buffalo chicken macaroni and cheese. There are also several salads on the menu, as well as a wide variety of hamburgers. The can't-miss burger is the Bavarian burger, which is topped by red cabbage and cambazola cheese, served with a side of German potato salad.

The atmosphere at Jacob Wirth's is fun. It is set up like a German beer hall with high ceilings and large tables. It gets loud, but it is not annoying. By the time you leave, you'll consider wearing some lederhosen the next time you come in.

### LORD HOBO

92 Hampshire St., Cambridge, MA; (617) 250-8454; LordHobo.com
**Draft Beers:** 40 **Bottled/Canned Beers:** About 50

Lord Hobo is one of the many up-and-coming beer bars that takes as much care with every aspect of its food menu as it does its beer. The beer menu, though, is utterly phenomenal. It is changed almost every day, and there is also always at least one cask beer available.

Lord Hobo serves up a fantastic mix of beers. It always has a few New England options, such as High & Mighty Brewing Company or the Smuttynose Brewing Company. It also features many beers from all of the best breweries, such as Founders Beer in Michigan, Victory Brewing in Pennsylvania, and the Avery Brewing Company from Colorado. Also, there always seems to be at least one fresh-tasting German lager on draft, served in a hefty mug. It just seems right to drink a German beer out of a half, or full-liter mug. There are almost always a few rare Belgian ales on draft.

The bottled list is also varied, heavy on large-format bottles such as bombers and 750 ml, which are perfect for sharing. Belgian ales are the stars on the menu, with several great Cantillon beers available (at big bucks), and beers from Achel and Drie Fonteinen. Top-notch American and German beers round out the bottled list.

Your cocktail-inclined friends have a lot of interesting options to chose from, and all of Lord Hobo's drinks are made with fine liquors. They all have eye-catching names, too, such as the Cat Wagon, which is made with Raid Red grape hibiscus vodka, Clear Creek raspberry, Lillet blonde, and fresh lemon topped with Prosecco. Or, give the Soylent Green (it is not people), the Interloper, or the Sloppy Possum a try.

The food is on the pricey side, but excellent. The appetizers include housemade turkey chili, miso baby clams with Chinese broccoli and sticky rice noodles, grilled cheese with cauliflower soup, chicken lollipops, and a cheese board. Make sure to try the Belgian frites with multiple dipping sauces. If you're not in a mood for an entree, Lord Hobo offers several small plates, such as hummus, a beet salad, roasted asparagus, and scallop ceviche.

The entree menu is not large, but has several good options. The pulled pork sandwich is served with cheddar and cabbage, while the mozzarella sandwich includes eggplant caponta and Peppadew tomato. The mac and cheese is one of the best in the greater Boston area, and it is slathered in cheddar, Parmesan, and mascarpone cheeses. The shaved prime rib sandwich with onion jam and bleu cheese is the best sandwich option. Desserts are also available, but the best choice is to get one of the beers as a dessert—a great end to a great night at Lord Hobo.

### THE MOAN AND DOVE

460 West St., Amherst, MA; (413) 256-1710; MoanAndDove.com
**Draft Beers:** 21 **Bottled/Canned Beers:** Nearly 200

The Moan and Dove is not the average bar you find in the middle of a college town like Amherst. You know the kind of place: plenty of $4 pitchers of cheap beer and not much else to offer. No, the Moan and Dove is one of the most well-known and most respected beer bars in all of New England. The beer list is just fantastic. No bad beers to be found on the chalkboard. High & Mighty Brewing Company is often available, as are beers from Ballast Point, Laughing Dog, De Ranke, Founders Brewing Company, and Stone. The bottled list includes nearly 200 various beers.

The beer menu (more like a book) is broken down into categories, which makes it much easier to search for a beer you want. In the mood for a sour beer? Just look under sours and pick out something like Monk's Cafe Flemish Sour. The Moan and Dove has beers of almost all Belgian styles, such as lambics, saisons, and Belgian stouts. The menu also has a section on "Strange brews," which are beers made with unusual ingredients, or that do not really fit in the typical categories. Several of Dogfish Head's beers are featured, such as Theobroma and Midas Touch. Stouts are broken up into sweet/coffee stouts, imperial stouts, and stouts. They have several fantastic selections, including Dieu Du Ciel's Peche Mortel and Lion Stout from Sri Lanka. The Moan and Dove also offers what they call the "Nostalgia Series," which includes Pabst Blue Ribbon, Narragansett, Old Milwaukee, and Schlitz.

One thing you should not expect at the Moan and Dove is the ability to order a meal. The only food they have is a big barrel of free peanuts. Although they do not serve food, the Moan and Dove does allow customers to bring in their own food.

### MOE'S TAVERN

10 Railroad St., Lee, MA; (413) 243-6637; NoCoorsLight.com
**Draft Beers:** 13 **Bottled/Canned Beers:** More than 100

Moe's Tavern is the winner for the best website name for a beer bar anywhere—Nocoorslight.com. And although the name of the website for this western Massachusetts beer bar is funny, it also sets the tone for the kind of bar that Moe's Tavern is. It is a place for those who love good craft beer. There is no Coors,

### Moezapalouza

Each October, Moe's Tavern celebrates its anniversary with a big blowout. Head to Moe's to party and to drink special beers, both on draft and in bottles. Moe's waits until this day to break out some truly amazing treats, or beers rarely found on draft. At its fifth anniversary in 2011, for example, it tapped Dogfish Head's 120 Minute IPA, which is hard to find in bottles or on draft.

Budweiser, Miller, or even some of the more popular but larger craft beer producers.

No, this is a no-frills bar that offers nothing but some of the best beers brewed in the US. Do not come looking for a beer and a burger—Moe's Tavern does not offer food. Moe's is for beer. And whiskey. Moe's draft list may not be huge, totaling only 13 beers, but the worst beer they have on draft could be as good as the best one at some lesser beer bars. Beers from Brewery Ommegang and Ithaca Brewing Company, both of New York, often find their way onto the menu, as well as the Nebraska Brewing Company and Port Brewing Company. Dogfish Head, Stone Brewing Company, Pretty Things, and Allagash Brewing Company are also usually available.

The bottled and canned beers are truly impressive. Like the draft list, Moe's Tavern's bottled list features all American beer, with the exception of Unibroue from Canada. Almost every great brewery that distributes beers in Massachusetts is available in bottles (or cans) at Moe's Tavern. Breweries often available include Avery, Oskar Blues, and Left Hand from Colorado; Full Sail from Oregon; Goose Island from Illinois; Founders Brewing Company from Michigan; Sixpoint from New York; and Bear Republic, Lagunitas, and Sierra Nevada from California.

Lee might be in the middle of nowhere—about two hours from Boston—but Moe's definitely makes it worth the trip.

### THE PUBLICK HOUSE & MONK'S CELL

1648 Beacon St., Brookline, MA; (617) 277-2880; EatGoodFoodDrinkBetterBeer.com
**Draft Beers:** 34 **Bottled/Canned Beers:** Well over 100

There are a lot of competitors for the best beer bar in the greater Boston area, but one bar that has to be put at the top of that list is the Publick House & Monk's Cell. It is a place where serious beer lovers go to grab fine Belgian ale served in the perfect glass for the style.

The draft list is extremely impressive, and all 34 beers that are on draft are always fantastic offerings. The Publick House is heavy on Belgian ales, with beers from Oud Beersel, St. Feullien, and Bavik. It also usually features some wonderful Belgian-style ales brewed here in the US, such as from Allagash Brewing Company. But not all of the beers are Belgian ales. There are beers from Founders Brewing Company in Michigan, Great Divide Brewing Company in Colorado, and Southampton Publick House in New York. They even have beers from Japan—Hitachino Nest—and Germany. The Monk's Cell, which is right next to the main seating area of the Publick House, serves nothing but Belgian ales.

The bottled list cannot be matched in the Boston area. Just like the draft list, the bottled list is heavy on Belgian beer. They also have all of the Belgian Trappist ales available in the US—Achel, Chimay, Orval, Rochefort, and Westmalle. The Publick House also carries some of the underrated Danish beers, such as Evil

#### Hophead Throwdown

The Publick House hosts an event made for those who love hops every July called the Hophead Throwdown. The event features nothing but ultra-hoppy beers, paired with extremely spicy food. Needless to say, the entire experience is quite an attack on the taste buds. Even better, the Hophead Throwdown benefits the Multiple Sclerosis Society.

Twin Brewing. The menu also features several German beers, including some of the Weihenstephan and Ayinger beers. American beers are well represented, with beers from Ballast Point Brewing Company in California, Jolly Pumpkin in Michigan, and local brewery Pretty Things Beer & Ale Project.

The Publick House also has fantastic food. The menu features delicious pots of mussels with a variety of broth options, such as Echte Kriekenbier and herbed garlic butter or Victory Prima Pils with red curry, coconut milk, lime, and sweet chili. Also available are hand-cut Yukon gold potatoes dusted with sea salt and served with several house-made dunking sauces. Other starters are a selection of artisanal cheeses, cured meats, housemade pate, and housemade hummus. The entrees are just as good, if not better, than the starters. The Belgian stew is made with mixed seafood in a roasted tomato and herb broth. A can't miss meal is the orrechetti pasta (basically gourmet macaroni and cheese), made with a five-cheese sauce and a list of about 10 different additions such as bacon, mushrooms, or truffle sauce.



## SIERRA GRILLE

41 Strong Ave., Northampton, MA; (413) 584-1150; TheSierraGrille.com
**Draft Beers:** 21 **Bottled/Canned Beers:** About 20

Sierra Grille serves up some excellent food. Not just excellent food for a beer bar, but excellent food for any kind of restaurant. They just happen to be a restaurant that has great beer, too. The 21-beer draft list is fantastic, featuring a good mix of American craft and imported beers. The draft list will often feature beers from Green Flash, Great Divide, and Lagunitas, as well as Chimay and Rodenbach. The bottled list is not as big as those at many places featured, but it is well thought out. Many of the beers are perfect to enjoy with meals, such as several versions of Rochefort or Scaldis. They also have several different J.W. Lee's Harvest Ales, aged in different barrels and of different vintages. They also have something a little different—several meads from Qhilia from South Africa. If you have the inclination, it may be worth experimenting with one of these.

The food menu is not huge, but it is fabulous. Starters include spicy nuts, empanadillas, various cheese plates, and slow-cooked pork shank. The most unusual appetizer they have may be the shrimp with chocolate sauce, which is shrimp sautéed in sherry, orange, chiles, and bittersweet chocolate. Other options include steamed mussels and a loaf of locally baked sourdough bread, served with either butter or olive oil for dipping. The entrees are pretty straightforward. You pick a protein, two sides, and a sauce. Meat options include chicken, duck, salmon, shrimp, and filet mignon. Sauces include Thai hot basil coconut, fruit barbecue, and citrus salsa,

### The Big Game and Big Beer Dinner

This is one of the premier food and beer events in all of New England. Each fall, the Sierra Grille prepares a special menu of rarely featured meat, and each course is paired with big, high-alcohol beers. A past Big Game and Big Beer menu included yak, python, antelope, wild boar, and deer. It is a unique meal, which will please an adventurous palate.

and sides include smashed potatoes, basmati rice, and grilled asparagus. Salads and paninis are available, as are desserts, which include Allagash White Crème Brûlée, chocolate truffles (infused with Framboise), and fruit crisp.

## SUNSET GRILL & TAP

130 Brighton Ave., Allston, MA; (617) 254-1331; AllstonsFinest.com
**Draft Beers:** 112 **Bottled/Canned Beers:** 380

If you are a fan of good food and good beer, you can't come to Boston without stopping at the Sunset Grill & Tap in Allston. Founded in 1989 by Marc Kadish, the Sunset Grill was an immediate haven for those looking for an alternative to bland, flavorless American macro lagers, offering up what were then rare imports such as Chimay from Belgium and Samuel Smith's from England.

Today, there are dozens of really good bars throughout the greater Boston area, but the Sunset Grill & Tap is still worth a stop, if for nothing else than the pure volume of beers they have available. The problem with a lot of bars with such a large tap selection is sometimes you run into a dirty line, or a past-its-prime beer. That rarely happens at the Sunset. Every draft line is cleaned every two weeks, and with all the colleges in the area, the kegs are emptied fairly regularly.

The beer menu (about a dozen pages long), is easy to get through. The bottles are split up by beer style, so if you want an IPA, it won't be mixed in with dunkelweizens or oatmeal stouts. If you're interested in drafts, flip to the back of the menu. All the current drafts are listed, along with a manager's choice for each style, on the back page. The selection is fantastic with most every big-name craft brewery from around the country represented, such as Dogfish Head Craft Brewery and Victory Brewing Company, sharing space on the beer menu with local favorites like Pretty Things Beer & Ale Project and Smuttynose Brewing Company. If your eyes begin to cross and you're having trouble deciding which beers you want, get a set of four 4-ounce samples, and pick one to order as a full pint.

As far as food, it's mainly pub style, but done really well. The beer-steamed burgers are some of the best in the area (see recipe on page 311), and the chicken wing appetizers are phenomenal. The nacho plate is large and meant for sharing, and there are ample larger entrees such as steaks and fish, as well as Mexican cuisine. Finish it off with ice cream made with beer. A pizza is also a worthy option.

The bartenders are knowledgeable about beer, so if you have any questions, always feel free to ask. The only problem is parking—if you're driving you're going to have to hope a spot on the street opens up. But once inside, you won't worry about the time it took to find a spot. Enjoy.



### YARD HOUSE

950 Providence Hwy., Space 200, Dedham, MA; (781) 326-4644; YardHouse.com/ma/dedham

**Draft Beers:** 116 **Bottled/Canned Beers:** 5

Located in the midst of Legacy Place, a large mall that features a giant movie theater, expensive stores, a bowling alley, and many other restaurants, is the Yard House. Sure, it might be a chain, but Yard House has more and better beers than a lot of bars, and much better than expected food for a typical chain.

The Yard House always prides itself on having the largest beer selection wherever it is located, and the Dedham Yard House is no different, featuring 116 beers on tap. They may not have the hard-to-find rare beers some other beer bars have, but they have many excellent beers available. The draft list is broken up by style, and has several British beers, including Old Speckled Hen; German beers, such as Franziskaner Hefeweizen; and Belgian ales such as Piraat Ale. Most of the draft beers are from American craft breweries, such as Anderson Valley Brewing Company from California, Atwater Block from Michigan, Boulder Beer from Colorado, Goose Island from Illinois, and Troegs from Pennsylvania. The Yard House also has several beers brewed for them as house beers. The menu features several beer blends, from the traditional black and tan made with the house pale ale and Guinness, to the unique, such as the Youngberry Chocolate, which is a blend of Lindeman's Framboise and Young's Double Chocolate Stout. Yummy.

Not in the mood for a big appetizer? Start with a snack-size dish like the truffle fries or deviled eggs. If you're a little bit hungrier than usual, start with the grilled Korean BBQ beef, the onion ring tower, the shiitake garlic noodles, or the seared ahi sashimi, which are all excellent. The sandwich highlight is the blue crab cake hoagie, which includes applewood-smoked bacon, avocado, Swiss cheese, tomatoes, and Cajun aioli served on garlic-toasted French bread. Entrees include the orange peel chicken, which is crispy chicken breast served with baby corn and bok choy, all mixed together in a spicy and sweet orange glaze. Other options include the miso-glazed sea bass and the ginger-crusted Norwegian salmon. The Garden menu is a specially created menu that substitutes chicken or beef with soy-based substitutes. Vegetarian versions of boneless wings, chicken strips, spicy Thai chicken pizzas, and burgers are all available.

# Maine

Maine people with their ol' Yankee ways know what they like—they like Maine potatoes, they like Maine lobster, and they like Maine-brewed beer. Luckily for them, the beer they brew is quite fantastic.

Maine boasts numerous breweries inspired by those in Old England—Geary's Brewing Company, Gritty McDuff's Brewing Company, and Shipyard Brewing Company (all based in Portland) all brew traditional English-style ales, on traditional English-brewing systems.

But not that far from them you have the Allagash Brewing Company, a brewery that specializes in Belgian-inspired brew. And in Lewiston, you have the first brewery, Baxter Brewing Company, that exclusively packages its beers in cans. And the Marshall Wharf Brewing Company is one of the best brewpubs in New England, even though they are not the most well-known one.

Maine has remained one of the brewing hotspots on the East Coast.

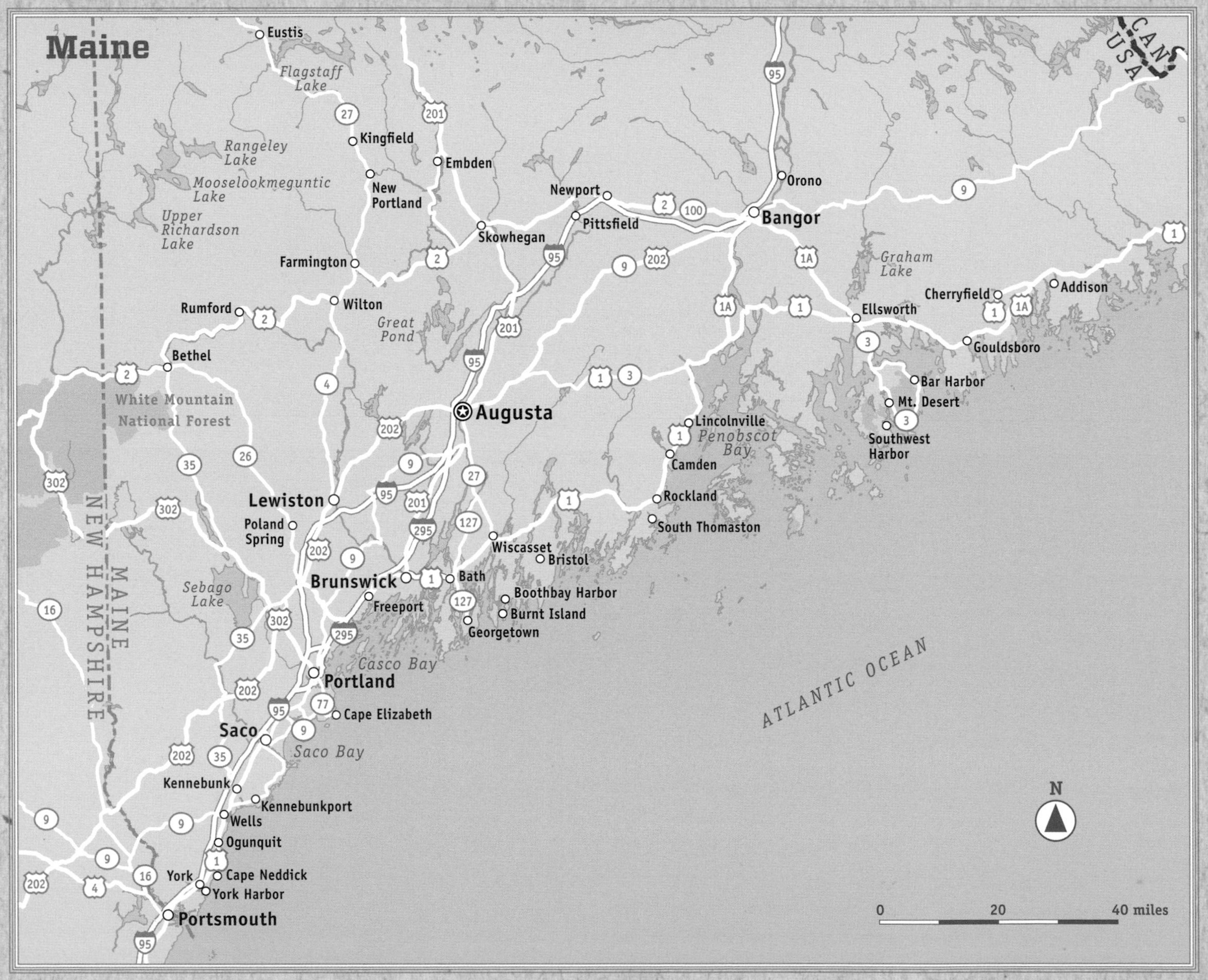

Maine
Eustis
Flagstaff Lake
Kingfield
Embden
Rangeley Lake
Mooselookmeguntic Lake
Upper Richardson Lake
New Portland
Newport
Pittsfield
Orono
Bangor
Skowhegan
Farmington
Wilton
Rumford
Great Pond
Bethel
White Mountain National Forest
Augusta
Lewiston
Poland Spring
Brunswick
Bath
Freeport
Wiscasset
Bristol
Boothbay Harbor
Burnt Island
Georgetown
Sebago Lake
Casco Bay
Portland
Cape Elizabeth
Saco
Saco Bay
Kennebunk
Kennebunkport
Wells
Ogunquit
York
Cape Neddick
York Harbor
Portsmouth
MAINE
NEW HAMPSHIRE
CAN
USA
Graham Lake
Ellsworth
Cherryfield
Addison
Gouldsboro
Bar Harbor
Mt. Desert
Southwest Harbor
Lincolnville
Penobscot Bay
Camden
Rockland
South Thomaston
ATLANTIC OCEAN
N
0
20
40 miles

### ALLAGASH BREWING COMPANY

50 Industrial Way, Portland, ME; (207) 878-5385; Allagash.com
**Founded:** 1995 **Founder:** Rob Tod **Brewers:** Rob Tod, Jason Perkins **Flagship Beer:** Allagash White **Year-round Beers:** Black, Curieux, Dubbel, Four, Tripel, Saison **Seasonals/ Special Releases:** Confluence Ale, Eleventh Anniversary, Interlude, Musette, Odyssey, and Tenth Anniversary, as well as the Tribute Series—Fluxus, Hugh Malone, Victor Ale, Victoria Ale. Other special releases include the Coolship beers **Tours:** Mon through Sat, 10 a.m. to 5 p.m.; free.

Can't get to Belgium and try all the wonderful beers brewed there? Don't worry, look to Portland, Maine, for your Belgian fix. Allagash Brewing Company, founded by Rob Tod, produces some of the best Belgian-style beer brewed, not just here in New England or in the US, but in the whole world. When Tod founded Allagash in 1995, Maine was strictly a place for traditional English-style pale ales, bitters, and other similar beers. Allagash revolutionized brewing in the state, introducing interestingly complex, flavorful beers.

The **Allagash White** is the brewery's best-known beer, and it's easy to see why. It's a Belgian-style witbier, a beer brewed with unmalted wheat, coriander, and bitter orange peel. If you haven't had one, you're missing out. It's the perfect summertime beer, and a great beer to pair with a lobster or steamed clam dinner. The **Dubbel** and **Tripel** are spot on for the styles, and are available in both 12-ounce and 750 ml bottles. The **Four** is a big, appropriately boozy quad, and the **Curieux** is simply amazing. Aged in bourbon barrels, the Curieux picks up some amazing flavors, and is pure bliss.

Allagash's special releases are, well, special. The **Odyssey,** in particular, is a standout. Odyssey is a dark wheat beer aged for ten months, some in oak barrels and the rest in steel barrels. The mix of aging in the two different containers forms a truly unique beer. The **Tribute Series** is perhaps the best group of special releases in New England. The **Fluxus** might change every year, but what doesn't change is the quality. The 2011 Fluxus was French farmhouse style ale, while the 2010 was an imperial chocolate stout.

Also unique (at least here in the US) are the **Coolship** beers. Allagash has built a coolship, basically a giant flat pan that is kept outside where the wort (a portion of the early brewing process) is cooled and inoculated with wild yeast. The next

## Beer Lover's Pick

**Curieux**
**Style:** Tripel
**ABV:** 11 percent
**Availability:** Rotating
The Curieux, aged in bourbon barrels, is one of the best tripels you can get your hands on. It is an exquisite beer. The bourbon flavors really come out in this beer, both in flavor and aroma, and the body has the traditional Belgian-yeast sweetness. It's also full-bodied and malt forward, with fruity flavors and hints of vanilla from the oak barrels. This is a sipping beer, meant to be savored.

morning, the beer is put in wooden barrels to age for however long the brewers think the beer needs. The Coolship beers have yet to be sold but have been poured at special events.

The brewery hosts several tours daily that last approximately 45 minutes. Each starts with a tasting, and then the tour leader will bring the guests through the brewery, explaining the brewing, packaging, and barrel-aging process.

### ANDREW'S BREWING COMPANY

373 High St., Lincolnville, ME; (207) 763-3505
**Founded:** 1992 **Founder:** Andrew Hazer **Brewer:** Andrew Hazer **Flagship Beer:** Andrew's Olde English Ale **Year-round Beers:** Andrew's Northern Brown Ale, St. Nick's Porter **Seasonal:** Summer Golden Ale **Tours:** None

Andrew's Brewing Company cares about brewing beer, and only brewing beer. They don't have a brewery store. They don't have a website (although they can be found on Facebook). They don't even offer tours. But what they do is brew beers, and brew beers well. Andrew's offers three year-round beers and one seasonal. The beers are available only in Maine and a small portion of Vermont.

**Andrew's Olde English Ale** falls somewhere between an American and English pale ale. The hops are present, but not overwhelming. There is a decent malt presence, but the beer is light. It's one of the lighter pale ales, American or English, out there. The **Andrew's Northern Brown Ale** is a more traditional beer. Very little hop presence, which is perfect for the style. This has a nice caramel aroma that carries on into the taste. There is also a pleasant nuttiness to it, and a slight roasted character. Many porters brewed today actually tend to taste like a lighter stout. Not **St. Nick's Porter.** This is a porter, through and through. It has a much lighter body than a stout, but it does not have as much coffee flavor, with just a hint of sweetness. There is a slight smoky character in this beer. People who like a bigger porter may be surprised by how light this one is. The only other beer is the **Summer Golden Ale,** Andrew's Brewing Company's only seasonal beer. The beer is an exceptional blonde ale. Malty, bready aroma dominates, and that carries on into the taste. The Summer Golden Ale is actually creamy, which you never find in a blonde ale.

As said above, Andrew's Brewing Company does not offer tours. However, if you're trying to complete the Maine Beer Trail pamphlet, call ahead and brewer Andrew Hazer will sign it for you. The Maine Beer Trail is a way to earn prizes from the Maine Brewers Guild while visiting all of Maine's breweries. Andrew's Brewing Company beers are available in 12-ounce bottles and on draft at several restaurants.

**Summer Golden Ale**
**Style:** Blonde Ale
**ABV:** Unknown
**Availability:** Summer Seasonal
Compared to other styles, blonde ales can be a bit boring—they're beers brewed to be easy drinking and not much else. Andrew's Brewing Company's Summer Golden Ale is not boring. There is much more malt aroma and flavor in this summer beer than any other beer in this style, and it finishes with a little kiss of citrusy hops at the back end. It's a summer beer definitely worth seeking out.

## ATLANTIC BREWING COMPANY

15 Knox Rd., Bar Harbor, ME; (207) 288-2337; AtlanticBrewing.com
**Founded:** 1991 **Founders:** Doug and Barbara Maffucci **Brewer:** James Taylor **Flagship Beer:** Bar Harbor Real Ale **Year-round Beers:** Blueberry Ale, Coal Porter, Island Ginger **Special Releases:** Brother Adam's Bragget, Scottish Ale, Special Old Bitter, Summer Ale, Manly Man Beer Club Series **Tours:** Available 7 days a week between Memorial Day and Columbus Day at 2, 3, and 4 p.m.

Blueberry beer fans should thank the Atlantic Brewing Company. In 1992, they became the first brewery to brew and distribute a blueberry beer. Now, most New England breweries and brewpubs brew their own versions of this New England classic.

Although the oldest, Atlantic Brewing Company's **Blueberry Ale** is still one of the best. It's light and refreshing, with the taste of real blueberries, not the overwhelming sweetness typical of blueberry beers that use concentrate. The other year-round beers are also very good. The **Bar Harbor Real Ale** is actually Atlantic's most popular beer. A traditional English-style brown ale, the Bar Harbor is an easy drinking, smooth, and malty beer—a New England classic. The **Coal Porter** is a solid beer. It has chocolaty and coffee notes, with just a slight roastiness. Despite how dark it is, it is not too heavy. The **Island Ginger** is a wheat beer with a twist—it's brewed with gingerroot. The root gives it a flavor reminiscent of a good ginger ale, except with a buzz-inducing kick.

Braggots are an ancient style of beer rarely brewed today. Atlantic Brewing Company's **Brother Adam's Bragget** is an excellent beer, brewed with more than 2,000 pounds of local honey. This is a sipping beer, coming in at a hefty 11.8 percent alcohol by volume. The honey gives it a pleasant sweetness, and helps counteract the hotness of the alcohol.

The **Scottish Ale** is a traditional, malty version of the style, while the **Special Old Bitter** is a hoppy, English-style bitter. The **Summer Ale** is a blonde ale, which is an easy-drinking, light, summery style of beer.

Atlantic Brewing Company also brews a special line of more complex, higher alcohol beers, called the **Manly Man Beer Club.** The Manly Man Beer Club beers include the **Blackstrapped Molasses** (a brown ale brewed with molasses), the **El Hefe** (a wheat wine), and the **Sea Smoke** (an English-style barleywine). Unlike the rest of the Atlantic beers (except for the Brother Adam's), all of the Manly Man beers come in 22-ounce bottles instead of 12-ounce bottles.

The Atlantic Brewing Company is located in beautiful Bar Harbor, a popular summer destination. When in Bar Harbor, it is definitely worth stopping at the brewery. Not only are tours available all summer, but they also have an on-site restaurant that

## Beer Lover's Pick

**Brother Adam's Bragget**
**Style:** Braggot
**ABV:** 11.8 percent
**Availability:** Year-round
The Brother Adam's Bragget isn't for everyone because it doesn't taste or drink like your average beer. This beer is similar to a barleywine, but with the addition of tons of honey, which adds body, sweetness, and alcohol. It has some toffee-like flavors, and hints of sugary sweetness. This is a thick beer—even if you wanted to down one glass, it would be hard to. For the craft beer–inclined, this is a brew to be experienced at least once.

serves barbecue. Atlantic Brewing Company also makes its own sodas, so kids can enjoy something locally made on site while mom and dad enjoy an adult beverage.

Make sure to stop in the guest shop before leaving. Not only do they sell all of their beers, sodas, and brewery-made mustards, they also sell other local food products. They also sell their own line of wines, the Bar Harbor Cellars Farm Winery, which the brewery founded in 2004.

### BANDED HORN BREWING COMPANY

13 West Main St., Building 13-W, Biddeford, ME; BandedHorn.com
**Founded:** 2014 **Founder:** Ian McConnell **Brewer:** Ian McConnell **Flagship Beer:** None
**Year-round Beers:** Pepperell Pilsner, Veridian IPA, Norweald Stout, Bineary Double IPA
**Seasonals/Special Releases:** Mo Chara Irish Red Ale, The Mountain **Taproom hours:** Wed, 3 to 8 p.m., Sat, 2 to 6 p.m.

Banded Horn Brewing Company founder and brewmaster Ian McConnell brings some serious brewing experience to the job. Like many brewers at new breweries, McConnell was a homebrewer. But, he turned that into a career, when he became the brewmaster at one of the most-respected craft breweries in the country,

Sixpoint Brewery in New York. McConnell brings the talent he showed that helped grow Sixpoint into the brewery it is today to his small taproom in Biddeford.

Banded Horn brews several year-round beers. The **Pepperell Pilsner,** a 4.6 percent alcohol by volume (ABV) unfiltered pilsner with bready malt and spicy hop flavors that finishes dry. The **Veridian IPA** is a 6 percent ABV IPA with flavors of tropical fruit and lemon. If you want something a little bigger, then try the **Bineary Double IPA,** a big, 9.1 percent ABV IPA with melon flavors. The other year-round beer is the **Norweald Stout,** a 6.5 percent ABV stout with flavors of chocolate, toffee, and caramel.

Banded Horn also brews two special releases. The **Mo Chara Irish Red Ale** is Banded Horn's take on an Irish red ale. There is an untraditional ingredient in this 5 percent ABV beer—it is made with Maine potatoes.

Banded Horn's biggest beer is the **Mountain,** a 12 percent ABV behemoth of a Russian Imperial Stout with big coffee flavors, oak, vanilla, coffee, and more.

Banded Horn's tasting room is open on Wednesday and Saturday, where people can come in and try the beers and buy growlers to go.

## BAR HARBOR BREWING COMPANY

8 Mt. Desert St., Bar Harbor, ME; (207) 288-4592; BarHarborBrewing.com
**Founded:** 1990 **Founders:** Tod and Suzi Foster **Brewer:** James Taylor **Flagship Beer:** Thunder Hole Ale **Year-round Beers:** Cadillac Mountain Stout, Harbor Lighthouse Ale, True Blue Blueberry Ale **Seasonals/Special Releases:** None **Tours:** Mid-May through Columbus Day, daily, 10 a.m. to 7 p.m.

The Bar Harbor Brewing Company was a family-owned brewery until 2009, when fellow Bar Harbor brewery Atlantic Brewing Company purchased it. The purchase meant the consolidation of the breweries into one brewing location, although the Bar Harbor Brewing Company remains open at 8 Mt. Desert St., where there is a tasting room, brewery store, and the pilot brewery.

What didn't change was the four year-round beers that Bar Harbor brews. Atlantic kept the recipes, and the beers remain as good as they have always been. The **Thunder Hole Ale,** Bar Harbor's first beer and its flagship, is a classic English-style brown ale. At 4.7 percent alcohol, you can afford to have a few of these beers, and with how it tastes, you'll definitely want more than one. This brown ale has flavors of toffee and a hint of molasses. The **Cadillac Mountain Stout** is simply one of the best stouts brewed in New England, and maybe the best that is less than 8 percent alcohol by volume (ABV). This American stout is worth seeking out. Buy a bomber if you find one, because you will want more if you only buy a 12-ounce

**Cadillac Mountain Stout**
**Style:** American Stout
**ABV:** 6.7 percent
**Availability:** Year-round
The Cadillac Mountain Stout is a classical version of an American stout. This beer has a lot going on—chocolate and coffee notes in the aroma, blended with some earthy smells. This is an amazingly smooth and creamy beer. There's a pleasant sweetness in the flavor, balancing out the roastiness. Seek this out.

Maine

bottle. The **Harbor Lighthouse Ale** fits the definition of a session beer. A session beer should be low in alcohol (4 percent ABV or less), but full-flavored. It's called a session beer because you can have a few in one session without getting drunk. The Harbor Lighthouse Ale is 3.2 percent ABV, but it's not your average light beer—it's an English dark mild ale that packs a whole lot of flavor. Bar Harbor's only other beer is the **True Blue Blueberry Ale.** If you're a fan of a blueberry beer, you will like this beer—it's a little more mellow than some other berry-filled ales.

The brewery is open from mid-March through Columbus Day. There you can go to the tasting room and try the beers before deciding which ones you want to bring home. You can also go inside the brewery, walk around, and take a look at the brewing equipment. The brewery store sells beer to go, as well as local food and wine. There are also shirts, hats, and glasses available.

## BAXTER BREWING COMPANY

130 Mill St., Lewiston, ME; (207) 333-6769; BaxterBrewing.com
**Founded:** 2010 **Founder:** H. Luke Livingston **Brewer:** Ben Low **Flagship Beer:** Pamola Xtra Pale Ale **Year-round Beers:** Stowaway IPA, Tarnation California-style Lager **Seasonals/ Special Releases:** Hayride Autumn Ale, Phantom Punch Winter Stout, Summer Swelter **Tours:** Wed through Sun 3 p.m.

The Baxter Brewing Company has found itself a niche in the competitive beer market of Maine—they're the first brewery to can all of their beers. This may not seem like a big deal. Why would having a beer in a can make that much of a difference that people would buy it over a bottled beer? The answer is easy: There are a lot of outdoor recreation activities in Maine. Want to go on a hike and have a beer after you reach your destination? Cans are lighter and take up less space than a bottle in your backpack, and will not shatter if you drop your bag. That goes for boating, too. Do you really want to clean up glass while on a lake or the ocean? And a lot of places, such as campgrounds, do not allow bottles. It is also more environmentally friendly than glass bottles. Of course, it wouldn't matter if the beer wasn't any good. But Baxter Brewing Company's beer is quite good, and it would still be worth buying even if they were in bottles.

Baxter offers a handful of beers. The first is the **Pamola Xtra Pale Ale.** This 4.9 percent alcohol by volume (ABV) beer is a light, refreshing pale ale, with just enough of a hop bite to let you know this is a pale ale. It's a crisp, dry-drinking beer. According to a local Native American legend, Pamola is a flying moose with eagle wings that is the god of thunder; no wonder Baxter includes the creature in its brewery logo.

**Stowaway IPA**
**Style:** IPA
**ABV:** 6.9 percent
**Availability:** Year-round
The Stowaway IPA is a west coast IPA without being a huge, high-alcohol beer. This beer is a balanced version of the west coast IPA, with plenty of up-front hops that continue all the way to a relatively dry finish. The malt backbone is present, and you can taste a little sweetness. It is a good, solid IPA that has enough hops to satisfy hopheads and enough balance that those who don't want a tongue-scorching beer will like it.

The **Stowaway IPA** is a west coast–style IPA. It's hop forward, with a mix of grapefruit, citrus, and pine aromas that carry into the flavor. At 6.9 percent ABV, it does not cross into the double IPA and remains extremely drinkable. The **Tarnation California-style Lager** is based on the California common style of beer made famous by Anchor Brewing Company's Steam.

Seasonals include the **Phantom Punch Stout,** the **Summer Swelter,** and the complex **Autumn Hayride,** which is brewed with rye, ginger, black pepper, orange peel, and New Zealand hops and aged with oak.

If you're in the Lewiston area, you'll want to stop in at Baxter Brewing to take the tour, offered Wednesday through Sunday. If you are not interested in a tour, they offer pints and flights of beer for sale to drink in the tasting room. Their store is also one of the better stocked brewery stores around. They have a lot of the usual items, such as T-shirts and glasses. But, they also have embroidered polo shirts and beanie-style winter hats. The best thing—they all sport Pamola the flying moose. Other items for sale include golf balls, Ultimate Frisbees, Stowaway IPA Body Soap, ice six-pack coolers, temporary tattoos, floating key chains, and spicy mustard made with Pamola Xtra Pale Ale.



## BELFAST BAY BREWING COMPANY

100 Searsport Rd., Belfast, ME; (207) 338-2662; BelfastBayBrewing.com
**Founded:** 1996 **Founder:** Pat Mullen **Brewer:** Contract brewed by Shipyard Brewing Company **Flagship Beer:** Lobster Ale **Year-round Beers:** Mack Point IPA, McGovern's Oatmeal Stout **Seasonals/Special Releases:** None **Tours:** None

Maine is known for its Maine lobsters—it's hard to find a restaurant that doesn't have steamed lobster, or lobster rolls, or a number of other lobster dishes. So it makes sense that a brewery would come up with a lobster beer. Don't worry, though, Belfast Bay Brewing Company's **Lobster Ale** doesn't have any lobster in it at all. Rather, it is a beer brewed to go with lobster.

Belfast Bay Brewing Company has gone through a lot of changes throughout the years. It started in 1996 as a brewpub. Now the brewpub is closed, but the beers are being contracted at Shipyard Brewing Company and are available throughout New England. They only sell three beers: the Lobster Ale, the **Mack Point IPA,** and **McGovern's Oatmeal Stout.**

The Lobster Ale is far and away the most popular and easiest of the three beers to find. It's an amber/red ale that's all about the malt. It is sweet, with just a hint of hops. When pairing beer with a lobster, usually some sort of wheat ale, a Belgian-style witbier, or a German-style hefeweizen, seems like the best choice. However,

## Beer Lover's Pick

**Lobster Ale**
**Style:** Amber/Red Ale
**ABV:** 5 percent
**Availability:** Year-round
Sure, red ales might not be the most exciting beers in the world, but this is a really well-made one. There is just a hint of hops, and the caramel and toffee flavors work nicely in this beer. It's also relatively light-bodied, which is perfect for a year-round beer.

the Lobster Ale really does pair well with a lobster. The malty sweetness grabs hold of the succulent lobster meat's flavor and works in harmony. And although this is a malty beer, it is not an overly heavy beer, so it does not overwhelm the taste of the lobster. The Mack Point IPA is a decent IPA that's appropriately hoppy, decently balanced, and easy to drink. If you find it on tap at a bar in Maine, grab a pint and it will not disappoint you. The McGovern's Oatmeal Stout is a great example of the style. It's more chocolaty than most oatmeal stouts, smooth, and creamy, while being full-bodied. It's the perfect beer to pair with your dessert after you finish your lobster (and Lobster Ale).

### BISSELL BROTHERS

1 Industrial Way, Portland, ME; (207) 423-3622; BissellBrothers.com
**Founded:** 2013 **Founders:** Noah Bissell, Peter Bissell **Brewer:** Noah Bissell **Flagship Beer:** Substance Ale **Year-round Beers:** None **Seasonals/Special Releases:** None **Tours:** Tasting room open different hours during different seasons, call ahead for hours.

A key to any brewery's success is for the owners to have a goal, a direction, they want their brewery to take and to make sure the beer is consistent and good. Noah Bissell and big brother Peter Bissell have taken that to another level. The pair, owners of Bissell Brothers in Portland, brew one beer, the **Substance Ale,** a 6.5 percent alcohol by volume IPA.

The beer fits in with the brewery's mantra to brew "Fresh, hoppy beers." Cans and kegs of the Substance Ale are often at stores and in bars and restaurants within one week of being packaged. For those who don't know, that's really quick.

Bissell Brothers have only brewed one other beer, a special one-off called **Heartstrings,** which was brewed for popular Maine beer bar Novare Res' Valentine's Day chocolate pairing event. It was a hoppy red ale.

Instead, the Bissell boys continue to pump out the Substance Ale. The beer is popular and, because of that popularity, it sometimes can be hard to find. Cans are only available at select locations. The Bissell Brothers only have four employees (including the two brothers themselves), so they ask that anyone who visits the brewery only does so on the advertised times (which change) on the website.

## BLACK BEAR MICROBREWERY

19 Mill St., Suite 4, Orono, ME; (207) 949-2880; BlackBearMicrobrew.com
**Founded:** 2008 **Founder:** Tim Gallon **Brewer:** Tim Gallon **Flagship Beer:** Gearhead Ale **Year-round Beers:** Drop Dead Red Ale, Pail Ale, Pirate Bear Ale **Seasonals/Special Releases:** Bad Omen IPA, Black Bear Stout, Blueberry Ale, Liquid Sunshine Ale, Patriot Brown Ale, Tree Tugger Barleywine, Voodoo Porter **Tours:** By appointment only

Tim Gallon likes to talk beer. So, if you happen to be in Orono, Maine, you should stop at his Black Bear Brewery, where he will lead you through a tour of his small brewery, telling you about his beers and the history of Black Bear.

The passion Gallon has for beer really comes out in his product. The brewery, which started brewing in 2008, features four year-round and several seasonal and rotating beers. The year-round beers are the **Gearhead, Drop Dead Red, Pail Ale,** and the **Pirate Bear Ale.** The Gearhead Ale is a malty, easy-drinking dark amber ale, while the Drop Dead Red is another malty beer, which is what you want in a red ale. The Pail Ale has the hops the other two beers are missing. It has a nice hop bite for a pale ale. The Pirate Bear Ale is another hoppy pale ale.

Black Bear brews two winter seasonals and two summer seasonals. The winter seasonals are the **Stout** and the **Voodoo Porter.** The Stout is a smooth, creamy, and slightly bitter (from the roasted malts, not from the hops) stout. The Voodoo Porter is robust, well-balanced, and a great cold night beer. The summer seasonals are the **Blueberry Ale** and **Liquid Sunshine.** Most New England breweries brew a blueberry beer, and the Blueberry Ale is another solid entry into a long line of such beers. The Liquid Sunshine is a Bavarian-style hefeweizen. It has the traditional clove-like flavors, and little lemon notes. The flavors come directly from the yeast, which Gallon brought over from Germany to use in this beer.

## Beer Lover's Pick

**Black Bear Stout**
**Style:** American Stout
**ABV:** 6.3 percent
**Availability:** Winter

The Black Bear Stout falls somewhere between a traditional stout and an imperial stout. It comes in at a solid 6.3 percent alcohol by volume (ABV). The beer has big roasty flavors, with espresso-like coffee flavors, mixed well with cocoa. The beer has a nice head, and it is full-bodied and creamy. It is a really easy-drinking beer, and perfect for a cold Maine night.

Other beers include the **Bad Omen IPA** and the **Patriot Brown Ale**, two beers that have some similarities—hops. The Bad Omen IPA is brewed with hopheads in mind. It's definitely leaning toward west coast style, and it is a strong beer, coming in at more than 7 percent ABV. It's also flirting with being a black IPA—it's an extremely dark IPA, which gives it some chocolaty notes from the malts. The Patriot Brown Ale is a hoppier than the usual brown ale. The combination of the dark and caramel malts used in a brown ale works nicely with the hops, making it a pleasantly unusual interpretation of the style. Black Bear also brews an annual anniversary beer that comes out in October.

Tours are available as long as Gallon and his assistant have time for them. The tour also includes a tasting, which is always a good thing. In the brewery store, you can buy growlers of any of the beers they have available.

## BOOTHBAY CRAFT BREWERY

301 Adams Pond Rd., Boothbay, ME; (207) 633-6314; BoothbayCraftBrewery.com
**Founded:** 2011 **Founders:** Lori and Win Mitchell **Brewer:** Win Mitchell **Flagship Beer:** "633" American Pale Ale **Year-round Beers:** Boothbay Common Ale, Dexter "Rippa" Red IPA, Black Rocks Stout, South-Porter **Seasonals/Special Releases:** Ken Brown Ale, Fisherman's Memori-Ale, Steganos, Devil's Thumbprint Black IPA, Gentia Dementia Copper Ale **Tours:** Seven days a week during summer, check website for hours; $10

You're on vacation during the summer. You've spent your day swimming in the pool, playing bocce, and just relaxing. But, the one thing that always seems to be missing when you go to a resort is good beer. You're trapped with good mixed drinks and poor beer options. The Boothbay Resorts owners Lori and Win Mitchell, however, have that covered. In 2011, they started the Boothbay Craft Brewery on the grounds of their cottage resort, brewing a host of beers for their guests, as well as anyone who wants to stop in for beers. Win Mitchell attended the Siebel's Institute of Brewing Technology in Chicago, Illinois, before starting the brewery. The brewery, along with the adjacent Watershed Tavern, gives guests options for beer and wood-fired pizza.

Boothbay Craft Brewery's flagship beer is the **"633" American Pale Ale,** a 6.33 percent alcohol by volume (ABV) pale ale named for Boothbay's telephone exchange. Other year-round beers include the **Boothbay Common Ale,** the **Dexter "Rippa" Red IPA,** the **Black Rocks Stout,** and the **South-Porter.** Seasonals include **Ken's Brown Ale,** a 5.6 percent ABV brown ale named for a local town celebrity, and the **Fisherman's Memori-Ale,** imperial pale ale.

The brewery's most renowned beer may be the **Steganos,** a 12 percent imperial stout aged in Kentucky Bourbon barrels for 6 months. It is sold in 12-ounce, wax-dipped bottles. Other special releases include the **Devil's Thumbprint Black IPA** and the **Gentia Dementia Copper Ale.**

The brewery has different hours depending if it's on-season or off-season, so check the website before going. They do offer a tour that features samples. The tours are $10 each, but each person will receive a wooden nickel worth $5 toward any purchase in the brewery store or in the Watershed Tavern.

## BUNKER BREWING COMPANY

122 Anderson St., Portland, ME; (207) 450-5014; BunkerBrewing.com
**Founded:** 2011 **Founders:** Chresten Svenson, Jay Villani **Brewer:** Chresten Svenson **Flagship Beer:** Machine Czech Pils **Beers:** 122 Coffee IPA, Beast Coast IPA, Munjoy Mild, Unfiltered IPA, Peninsula Pale Ale **Taproom hours:** Thurs and Fri, 5 to 8 p.m., Sat, noon to 5 p.m.

Beer and food have a lot in common—they both use several ingredients to help create the perfect combination of flavors to come out with the perfect taste. Bunker Brewing Company founders Jay Villani and Chresten Svenson come from a food background. Villani owns several Portland, Maine, restaurants, while Cresten Svenson baked for Villani.

They take that background to help create the Bunker Line of beers, such as the **122 Coffee IPA,** the 6 percent alcohol by volume (ABV) IPA brewed with local coffee. Many beers use coffee, but most of those beers are either stouts or porters, dark beers with roasted notes already in them. But, IPAs are often fruity, with tropical fruit, pineapple, or sometimes piney flavors, so coffee does not seem to be the perfect fit. However, Bunker makes it work. Bunker's Flagship beer is the **Machine Czech Pils,** a traditional German-style pilsner hopped with Saaz hops.

Other Bunker beers include more IPAs, such as the **Beast Coast IPA** and the **Unfiltered IPA.** They also brew the **Peninsula Pale Ale** and the **Munjoy Mild,** an English-style mild ale, which is a style that has seemingly and sadly fallen out of favor with American craft brewers.

Bunker Brewing beers are only available on draft, and in growlers at the brewery. The brewery has tastings, samples, and growler fills Thursday through Friday.

## D.L. GEARY BREWING COMPANY

38 Evergreen Dr., Portland, ME; (207) 878-2337; GearyBrewing.com

**Founded:** 1986 **Founders:** David and Karen Geary **Brewer:** David Geary **Flagship Beer:** Hampshire Special Ale **Year-round Beers:** Imperial IPA, London Porter, Pale Ale, Wee Heavy **Seasonals/Special Releases:** Autumn Ale, Summer Ale, Winter Ale **Tours:** By appointment

The D.L. Geary Brewing Company is one of the oldest craft breweries in all of New England, and helped to form the early brewing tradition in the region. David and Karen Geary actually incorporated the brewery in 1983, when there were only thirteen other microbreweries in the country. But the brewery did not distribute its first beer until 1986, after David Geary went to Scotland and England to learn and research the art of brewing in those two countries.

Geary was a good learner. The D.L. Geary Brewing Company's beers reflect what Geary learned, with high-quality English- and Scottish-style ales throughout their portfolio. Geary's first beer was the **Pale Ale,** and it is still one of the best English-style pale ales being brewed today. It makes use of traditional English-style hops to give it a mild, earthy flavor, with a great malt body. The **Hampshire Special Ale** is a stronger beer, at 7 percent alcohol by volume (ABV). It's an English strong ale, and it

## Beer Lover's Pick

**Wee Heavy**
**Style:** Scottish Ale
**ABV:** 8 percent
**Availability:** Year-round

Hoppy beers are awesome, but sometimes a big malty beer is called for. This Wee Heavy is a wonderfully malty beer, sweet and full-bodied. You can taste the alcohol and flavors of molasses, and there's a woody character even though it is not barrel aged. There are also hints of chocolate. Do not expect to taste any hops—this is all about the malts.

has a big malty body, with great balance from the earthy hop flavors. The **Imperial IPA** is Geary's newest beer, and its most American. It is also the brewery's strongest beer at 8.2 percent ABV. It definitely uses American hops, and you get the citrusy aroma and flavors from them. The caramel malt flavors works well in this beer. The **London Porter** is a classic English-style porter, and the **Wee Heavy** is a perfect example of the Scottish-style ale—robust and malty.

Geary also does a good job with their seasonals beers. The **Autumn Ale** is an excellent nut brown ale, a perfect fall style. The **Winter Ale** is an English-style IPA, much milder than the American version of the style. The **Summer Ale** is closest to a kolsch beer. It is actually a little stronger in alcohol than most summer beers at 6 percent ABV, and a nice change to the numerous bland summer beers being brewed today.

Tours are typically available daily in the afternoon, but by appointment only. Make sure to call ahead before going, because if it is a busy brewing day, tours will not be available. The tour is led by one of the brewery employees, and it ends with a tasting of all the beers they currently have available.

## FOUNDATION BREWING COMPANY

1 Industrial Way, Portland, ME; (207) 370-8187; FoundationBrew.com

**Founded:** 2014 **Founders:** John Bonney, Joel Mahaffey **Brewer:** Joel Mahaffey **Flagship Beer:** None **Year-round Beers:** Blaze, Eddie **Seasonals/Special Releases:** Wanderlust, Burnside, Zuurzing, and Epiphany **Taproom hours:** Fri, 3 to 6 p.m., Sat, 2 to 5 p.m., Sun, noon to 2 p.m.

Founded by friends and homebrewers, the Foundation Brewing Company is located along what a lot of people call Brewers Row, Industrial Way. Several Maine brewers either are located there or got their start there before moving to a larger facility.

The brewery only brews two beers (at the time of this book)—two very different versions of a saison. **Eddie** is a classic saison, spicy, dry, with floral and herbal hoppy notes and light in color. It is only 5 percent alcohol by volume (ABV), which is a little less than many American saisons, but in line with the original Belgian farmhouse ales. **Blaze,** on the other hand, is a completely different type of saison. It is brewed with many of the classic west coast hops used in IPAs, such as Cascade, Centennial, Chinook, and Nugget hops. However, the beer still has the Belgian saison yeast. The result is somewhere between a saison and an IPA. It's almost like a SaisIPA. Basically, it's a 6.5 percent ABV hybrid beer.

Foundation beers are draft only, and available at the brewery for growler fills. The brewery hosts tours, tastings, and growler fills Friday through Sunday.

## FRIAR'S BREWHOUSE

35 Orcutt Mountain Rd., Bucksport, ME; (207) 469-0882; Facebook.com/Friars.Brewhouse

**Founded:** 2013 **Founders:** Franciscan Brothers of St. Elizabeth of Hungary **Brewer:** Brother Donald Paul **Flagship Beer:** None **Year-round Beers:** Traditional Monastery Ale, St. Francis Brown Ale, Whoopie Pie Porter **Seasonals/Special Releases:** None **Tours:** None

The Trappist order of monks is well-known for making some of the most sought after and best beers brewed in the world, but why should they have all the fun. In 2013, the tiny Franciscan Brothers of St. Elizabeth of Hungary, located in Bucksport, Maine, began brewing its own beers commercially, according to the *Bangor Daily News*. The brothers were known for their baked goods, and decided to help defray the costs of their monastery, by taking that baking knowledge and

**Whoopie Pie Porter**
**Style:** Porter
**ABV:** 7 percent
**Availability:** Year-round
Whoopie pies are one of my all-time favorite snacks. But you know what's better? A Whoopie Pie Porter. You don't get as full, you get most of the same flavors, and it has alcohol. It's a great after dinner adult treat.

applying it to brewing their own beers. Brother Donald Paul is the head brewer, the *Daily News* said.

Friar's Brewhouse brews three beers. The first two are traditional styles. The **Traditional Monastery Ale** is a Belgian saison, brewed with bitter orange peel, coriander, and juniper. It is a dry beer meant to be paired with food. The **St. Francis Brown** is a hoppy English-style brown ale. It has the traditional sweetness from the caramel and chocolate malts found in many brown ales, but it has a nice hop kick in the finish you normally don't find in a brown ale, particularly ones modeled after English brown ales. The third beer is not what you would expect from a monastic beer—it's the **Whoopie Pie Porter.** It is brewed with lacto sugar and has notes of chocolate, vanilla, and butter—the perfect dessert beer. Friar's Brewhouse beers are packaged in 750 ml caged and corked bottles and are only available at limited stores in the Bangor area. They cost about $12 per bottle.



### THE FUNKY BOW BREWERY AND BEER COMPANY

21 Ledgewood Ln., Lyman, ME; (207) 409-6814; FunkyBowBeerCompany.com
**Founded:** 2013 **Founders:** Abraham and Paul Lorrain **Brewer:** Paul Lorrain **Beers:** End of the Line Pale Ale, So Folkin' Hoppy IPA, Five String Oatmeal Stout, Five String Vanilla Oatmeal Stout, Panama Red, F-Hole Autumn Rye, Dobro Double Brown **Taproom hours:** Growler nights are Fri 4 to 7 p.m.

Many breweries are in an industrial setting—you go in, taste a couple of beers, fill a growler, and leave. The Funky Bow Brewery and Beer Company, founded by Abraham and Paul Lorrain, do things a little different. On Friday, on the Lorrain family farm, they fill growlers, grill some food, sometimes have live music, and light a bonfire.

The Funky Bow Brewery and Beer Company brews relatively strong beers—almost all of them are more than 6 percent alcohol by volume (ABV). The **End of the Line Pale Ale** is the brewery's most poplar beer, it is a 7.2 percent pale ale, hoppier and maltier than many pale ales. Most breweries would probably call this beer an IPA. The **So Folkin' Hoppy IPA** is an 8.5 percent ABV double IPA. The beer is loaded with citrusy and piney hops, but the caramel malts provide a nice sweetness to it so the hops don't overwhelm you. There are different versions of the **Five String Oatmeal Stout,** the plain, coffee, and vanilla. All three versions are made with chocolate and roasted malts and made with vanilla beans. Other beers include the **Panama Red,** which is a relatively standard red ale; the **Dobro Double Brown Ale;** and the **F-Hole Autumn Rye.** Cans of the End of the Line Pale Ale and So Folkin' Hoppy IPA are widely available, and other beers are available in growlers at growler night and in stores and restaurants.

## GNEISS BREWING COMPANY

94 Patterson Rd., Limerick, ME; (207) 793-0046; GneissBeer.com
**Founded:** 2013 **Founders:** Dustin Johnson, Tim Bissel **Brewer:** Dustin Johnson **Flagship Beer:** Gneiss Weiss **Year-round Beers:** Gabbro, Obsius, Tweiss **Seasonals/Special Releases:** Cenozoic, Single Hop White IPAs **Tours:** Fri, 2 to 7 p.m.; Sat, noon to 6 p.m.; Sun, noon to 4 p.m.; free

The Gneiss (pronounced Nice) Brewing Company does not call itself a brewery—it calls itself an "agrogeobrewery," to represent its efforts in agriculture, its respect of geology (many of the names are geological terms) and, of course, brewing. Gneiss owns its own farm. The goal of the farm is to feed the farm animals the spent grain from the brewing process. The animals then fertilize the land where the Gneiss folks hope to grow hops, wheat, and local produce to sell at its Patterson Road brewery sometime in the future.

However, until then, the Gneiss Brewing Company continues to brew its line of German-influenced wheat beers. All of the beers Gneiss brews features at least 50 percent wheat malt and they all use the house hefeweizen yeast. The flagship is the **Gneiss Weiss,** a 4.8 percent alcohol by volume (ABV) American interpretation of a German weiss beer. The difference is, unlike German wheat beers, the Gneiss Weiss features American hops. The **Gabbro** is a 4.9 percent ABV dunkelweizen, creamy with hints of banana and clove. The **Obsius** is a weizen stout. At 5.9 percent ABV, you get a hint of banana and chocolate, making this a good dessert beer. The **Tweiss** is a 7 percent ABV weizenbock, which is a stronger, heftier version of a hefeweizen. Gneiss also brews a winter seasonal, **Cenozac,** which is a wheat porter (possibly the

Beer Lover's Pick

**Tweiss**
**Style:** Weizenbock
**ABV:** 7 percent
Availabilty: Year-round

With strong flavors of banana, cloves and bubble gum, the Tweiss is a class German-style weizenbock. It is stronger, sweeter and much more full-bodied than a hefeweizen. This is a wheat beer that can be enjoyed through the cold winter months, or by a campfire at night during the summer.

only one in New England) made with fresh ginger. They also brew a series of single hop white IPAs, which are wheat-based IPAs brewed with one individual hop, not the hop medly found in most IPAs.

Gneiss is open for tours and samples, as well as growler and howler (half-growler) fills, on Friday from 2 to 7 p.m., Saturday from noon to 6 p.m., and Sunday from noon to 4 p.m. There are typically four beers available at all times. Tours are free.

## GRITTY MCDUFF'S BREWERY

396 Fore St., Portland, ME; (207) 772-BREW; Grittys.com
**Founded:** 1988 **Founders:** Richard Pfeffer, Ed Stebbins **Brewer:** Ed Stebbins **Flagship Beer:** Original Pub Style **Year-round Beers:** Best Bitter, Black Fly Stout, Red Claws Ale **Seasonals/Special Releases:** Christmas Ale, Halloween Ale, Scottish Ale, Vacationland Summer Ale, 21 IPA **Tours:** None

The Gritty McDuff's Brewery is one of the old school New England breweries that brews traditional English-style ales, but still flourishes in the modern beer world. The reason is easy to figure out—Gritty McDuff's brews good beer and people like to drink good beer.

Gritty McDuff's is a combination brewpub/brewery. Many of their beers are bottled and distributed throughout New England. In addition to the original brewpub

## Beer Lover's Pick

**Halloween Ale**
**Style:** Extra Special Bitter
**ABV:** 6 percent
**Availability:** Fall Seasonal
This is basically a stronger and more flavorful version of Gritty's Best Bitter. This extra special bitter is an excellent example of the style. It has a great malt body, with a sharp hop balance and great carbonation that dances on your tongue. There are flavors of dark fruits, a little alcohol, and even some grassy, herbal hops in this beer. Definitely a nice change of pace from an Oktoberfest or pumpkin beer for a fall seasonal.

in Portland (the above address), they also have brewpubs in Freeport and Auburn, Maine. Most of Gritty's bottled beers are actually brewed at the Shipyard Brewing Company, also in Portland. However, they do brew and bottle their own 22-ounce bombers at their Freeport brewery. They also brew all of their own beers on-site at all three brewpubs.

The beers, for the most part, are straight-up English style. Gritty's flagship is the **Original Pub Style,** a classic English pale ale with a nice hop presence that's extremely easy to drink. The **Best Bitter** is a wonderful English-style bitter, perfect for an afternoon drinking session with friends. The **Black Fly Stout** is an Irish dry stout. If your only experience with an Irish stout is Guinness, you will be surprised by how different this beer is. It is creamy and roasty and tasty. The **Red Claws Ale** was brewed in honor of the local NBA Developmental League team that started in Maine. Gritty McDuff's also brews several seasonals worth trying. The **Christmas Ale** and the **Halloween Ale** are both extra special bitters. Although they are both the same style, these are not the same beer, so seek them both out to see how one brewery can make two of the same style beers taste so different. The **Scottish Ale** is a robust, malty beer, sweet with very little noticeable hops. The **Vacationland Summer Ale** is one of the few non-British beers brewed by Gritty McDuff's. It is a blonde ale, fine for the style—light and easy drinking. The other non-British beer is the **21 IPA,** an American-style IPA originally brewed for Gritty's twenty-first anniversary.

If you are in Portland, the Gritty McDuff's brewpub is a can't miss. They have all their beers on tap, and several on cask, which is a treat. It's also great place to grab lunch; the burgers are excellent and the sweet potato fries are otherworldly.

### MAINE BEER COMPANY

525 U.S. 1, Freeport, ME; (207) 221-5711; MaineBeerCompany.com
**Founded:** 2009 **Founders:** Daniel and David Kleban **Brewer:** Daniel Kleban **Flagship Beer:** Peeper Ale **Year-round Beers:** Lunch IPA, Mean Old Tom Stout, Zoe, Moe **Seasonals/ Special Releases:** King Titus, Lil One, Another One, Weez, Red Wheelbarrow, A Tiny Beautiful Something Dinner **Tours:** no tours, tasting room open Tues through Sat, noon to 7 p.m.; Sun, noon to 5 p.m.

Maine

The Maine Beer Company's motto is "Do What's Right," and they take that motto seriously—there is a lot right with this tiny brewery's beers. MBC's beers are gaining notice very quickly and for good reason—they're fantastic. The **Peeper Ale,** which originally started as a spring-only beer but was so popular the Kleban brothers had to make it year-round, is a must-buy beer. The ale falls somewhere between a pale ale and an IPA, but what sets it apart is the aroma. You will never find a hoppy beer that smells this good. One whiff and you want to drink this beer. And, oh, is it good, so refreshing and flavorful. **Lunch IPA** is the best India pale ale brewed in New England, and stands up to any IPA brewed anywhere in the country, including the land of hoppy beers, the west coast. Fruity and floral hop aromas carry on into the taste, perfectly balanced with the sweetness from the malts to form a world-class beer. **Zoe** is an amber ale, but not the typical malty amber ale. Sure, it still has the dark malts to provide caramel sweetness, but this is hopped like an IPA. The mix of an amber ale and IPA form a beer that hopheads will enjoy. Another beer, **Mean Old Tom Stout,** is the only beer that doesn't feature hops as a dominant ingredient. The use of dark roasted malts provides this beer with flavors of chocolate and coffee—a perfect after-dinner beer.

With the move to its larger facility, Maine Beer added many occasional releases, such as **Another One** and **Weez,** two beers brewed with the same exact hops, but

## Beer Lover's Pick

**Peeper Ale**
**Style:** Pale Ale
**ABV:** 5.5 percent
**Availability:** Year-round
A pale ale should not be as exciting as Peeper Ale. From the first whiff of the beer in your glass, you'll want to down it immediately, but stop. This is a beer that should be savored. It smells of citrus and grass from the hops. The flavor is fabulous as well, with a light graininess, as well as the ever-present hops.

different malt bills; **Lil One,** a 9.1 percent alcohol by volume double IPA; a **Tiny Beautiful Something,** a single hop pale ale; and **Dinner,** another double IPA.

Maine Beer Company packages of all of its beers in 500 ml, or half-liter, bottles, which is a popular size in Europe, but not in the US. Sometimes two 12-ounce bottles are not enough, but three are too many. The half-liter solves that problem—two beers, you're done, and you didn't drink too much.

Maine Beer Company does more than brew good beer; they care about the environment. They are a member of 1% for the Planet, a group of businesses that commit financially to help the planet. They donate 1 percent of all sales to environmental nonprofit organizations. Maine Brewing Company is 100 percent wind powered, and all the leftover yeast, grains, and grain bags are donated to local farmers.

Although no tours are offered in the new brewery, the tasting room has large windows so visitors can watch the whole brewing process while enjoying pints of beer.

## OAK POND BREWING COMPANY

101 Oak Pond Rd., Skowhegan, ME; (207) 474-3233; OakPondBrewery.com

**Founded:** 1996 **Founders:** Trevor and Pat Lawton **Brewer:** Don Chandler **Flagship Beer:** Dooryard Ale **Year-round Beers:** Oktoberfest Lager, Nut Brown Ale, Somerset Lager, White Fox Ale **Seasonals:** Laughing Loon Lager, Storyteller Doppelbock **Tours:** Mon through Fri, 3 to 5:30 p.m.; Sat, 12:30 to 5:30 p.m.; free

The Oak Pond Brewing Company is housed in a former chicken barn and has a small staff, consisting of owners Don Chandler (brewer) and his wife, Nancy Chandler. But, despite the modest location and staff, the Oak Pond Brewing Company brews several well-done beers. They are also a standout brewer of lagers, perhaps the best at brewing lagers in Maine.

Oak Pond offers five year-round beers: three ales and two lagers. They also offer two seasonals, both lagers. The flagship beer is the **Dooryard Ale.** This is an American pale ale, but on the lighter side for the style. The hops are present, and the malts provide some balance. What makes this lighter than most pale ales is the use of a little wheat malt to make the body lighter. This is almost like a summer pale ale, perfect for when you want a quick, refreshing beer after spending the day mowing the lawn. The **Nut Brown Ale** is a spot-on take on the popular British and New England style. A lively head and hints of chocolate and caramel from the roasted malts make this a pleasure to drink. The **White Fox Ale** is a solid IPA, reminiscent of the old-school New England IPA style before brewers started adopting the west coast, hop-forward version of the style. If you are a fan of IPAs on the mellow side, this is the one for you. Oak Pond may be the only brewery that has an **Oktoberfest Lager** as a year-round style, which is fantastic. There is always room for more good lagers, and this is just that. A lot of caramel, sweet, and bready flavors from the malts, with just a hint of hops, make this a perfect beer to enjoy in January, July, or October. The **Somerset Lager** is a traditional German-style pilsner.

The seasonals are both tasty. The **Storyteller Doppelbock** is a traditional German-style beer. It takes 10 weeks of aging for this beer to be ready, but it is worth it. This is a malt bomb of a beer, and the 6 percent alcohol by volume is hidden well. The **Laughing Loon Lager** is an excellent Munich dunkel lager.

Oak Pond Brewing Company hosts tours throughout the week. There is no set time. If they are open and not too busy brewing, one of the employees will give you the tour. The tour itself is heavy on brewing education, with a thorough explanation of the brewing process, and the role each ingredient—hops, malts, water, and yeast—plays in the beer. It is concluded with a tasting of the five year-round beers and whichever seasonal is on tap. The tasting is the perfect way to determine which

**Laughing Loon Lager**
**Style:** Munich Dunkel Lager
**ABV:** 6 percent
**Availability:** Summer Seasonal
A good Munich dunkel lager is a treat. Even though this is a dark beer, it still fits in as a summer seasonal because it is easy drinking and extremely refreshing. The roasted malts give this beer a slight chocolaty flavor, complemented by some doughy, yeasty taste. The hops provide balance and not much else, exactly what you want for the style.

beer to bring home to drink. You can buy growlers of the beer to go at the brewery. Oak Pond Brewing Company beers are also available in bombers and kegs, and are sold at area stores.

## OXBOW BREWING COMPANY

274 Jones Woods Rd., Newcastle, ME; (207) 315-5962; OxbowBeer.com
**Founded:** 2010 **Founders:** Tim Adams, Geoff Marshland **Brewer:** Tim Adams **Flagship Beer:** Farmhouse Pale Ale **Year-round Beer:** None **Seasonal/Special Releases:** Freestyle Series, Oxtoberfest, Saison Noel, Space Cowboy, Grizacca, Loretta, Sasuga, Funkhouse, Bandolier **Tours:** Tasting room open Wed through Sat, noon to 7 p.m.

The Oxbow Brewing Company calls itself an American farmhouse brewery, and not just because of its location on an 18-acre farm. They brew saisons, which are known as farmhouse beers. Saisons can be beautifully brewed beers. If done right, these are dry, go fantastically with many foods, and are light tasting, even if the alcohol is high. They have a quality that beer lovers enjoy, and they seem to be one of the styles that wine drinkers adopt as their own.

Oxbow only does a few beers, but they are fabulous American takes on the classic Belgian style. The flagship beer, the **Farmhouse Pale Ale,** is a combination of a saison and a pale ale. It looks like a saison, golden and unfiltered, and it has the typical yeasty flavors found in a good saison. It also has the hops and citrusy aromas you do not usually find in a saison. The **Oxtoberfest** is not the typical fall Oktoberfest lager. This is another saison, but completely different than the Farmhouse Pale Ale. This is more malty and creamy, but still retains its dryness. The use of smooth, subtle German hops gives this an interesting flavor not usually associated with saisons. The **Saison Noel** is a heftier saison brewed to help keep people warm during the cold Maine winters.

Other rotating releases include the **Grizaaca,** an "estoteric farmhouse ale"; the **Sasuga,** a rice ale brewed with both brettanomyces and saison yeast; and **Funkhouse,** a farmhouse IPA brewd with brettanyomyces.

Oxbow also brews several beers as part of the **Freestyle Series.** These beers allow the brewers to stretch their creativity and brew beers not often found, such as a smoked chocolate stout and imperial saison. These are planned as one-time releases, but they could return in the future on a limited basis.

Oxbow beers are available only on draft at a few restaurants and bars throughout Maine. The beers are also available in the brewery's tasting room in growlers. While at the brewery, people get a chance to sample the beer and hear the brewing process explained by the founders Tim Adams and Geoff Marshland. Oxbow is also aging several of its beers in oak barrels, and plans on offering some of those beers in 750 ml corked and caged bottles.

**Farmhouse Pale Ale**
**Style:** Saison
**ABV:** 6 percent
**Availability:** Year-round

Saisons are typically dry, often complex beers, but lightly hopped. A west coast IPA can be as hoppy as some mild IPAs. What do you get when you blend the two styles? Oxbow's Farmhouse Pale Ale. This is an extremely interesting beer. The saison and pale ale characteristics actually work together instead of clashing. This would be a great beer to pair with many different foods, particularly duck or even a spicy chicken dish.

## PEAK ORGANIC BREWING COMPANY

110 Marginal Way, #802, Portland, ME; (207) 586-5586; PeakBrewing.com
**Founded:** 2006 **Founder:** John Cadoux **Brewer:** John Cadoux and contract brewing **Flagship Beer:** Pale Ale **Year-round Beer:** Amber Ale, Espresso Amber Ale, Hop Noir, IPA, Nut Brown Ale, Pomegranate Wheat Ale **Seasonals/Special Releases:** Fall Summit Ale, King Crimson, Maple Collaboration, Simcoe Spring, Summer Session, Winter Session, Local Series **Tours:** None

The organic food industry is exploding because more and more people care about how their food is treated before they put it in their bodies. But there are not a lot of options when it comes to organic beers. The Peak Organic Brewing Company gives those who care about organics an excellent option of fantastic beer.

The **Peak IPA** is a wonderfully hopped beer. At 7.2 percent alcohol by volume (ABV), there are more than enough hops to balance the combination of piney and citrusy tastes. This is an underrated IPA, and any hophead should make sure to give this one a try. The **Amber Ale** is a really solid amber with toasty flavors. The **Espresso Amber** is that rare coffee beer that is not a stout or porter. Strong flavors of espresso dominate this beer, but it is lighter than many coffee beers so it does not sit heavy in the stomach. The **Nut Brown Ale** is excellent. The **Pale Ale,** Peak's flagship beer, has big hop flavor when you first take a sip, but then mellows into a slight sweetness. The **Pomegranate Wheat Ale** is not as sweet as a lot of fruit beers,

### Beer Lover's Pick

**Nut Brown Ale**
**Style:** Brown Ale
**ABV:** 4.7 percent
**Availability:** Year-Round
Peak Organic's Brown Ale is a treat of a beer. Although it's hard to mess up a brown ale, it's even harder to make an exceptional one like this. There are flavors of caramel and chocolate, and the use of German Hallertau hops, which are more earthy than fruity, helps bring out the nuttiness in this beer. Have this with a grilled piece of beef and you will be so happy.

and the pomegranate is subtle, rather than dominating. The **Hop Noir** is a black IPA and one of Peak Organic's biggest beers at 8.2 percent ABV. The huge amounts of hops used in this beer and the chocolate malts blend fabulously.

The seasonals include four single-hop beers. Each beer is different, but all share the similarity of only one hop being used in each beer, meant to showcase the different hops. Single-hop beers are interesting, because you get to see exactly what flavor each hop adds to a beer. The four single-hop beers are the **Fall Summit Ale** (Summit hops), **Simcoe Spring** (Simcoe hops), **Summer Session** (Amarillo hops), and **Winter Session Ale** (Citra hops).

Special release beers include **King Crimson,** a true imperial red. Many imperial reds taste like a slightly maltier imperial IPA, but this really tastes like a big red ale—huge caramel and toffee-like malt flavors—with a lot of hops added. The **Maple Collaboration** is not a collaboration with another brewery, but with local businesses. Maine oats and fresh Maine maple are used in the ingredients. The **Local Series** also takes advantage of using local ingredients. There are four beers in the series, and each one is brewed with ingredients specifically from one state (Maine, Massachusetts, New Hampshire, and Vermont) to highlight the local products in each state.



## PENOBSCOT BAY BREWERY

279 South Main St., Winterport, ME; (207) 223-4500; WinterportWinery.com
**Founded:** 2009 **Founder:** Mike Anderson **Brewer:** Mike Anderson **Flagship Beer:** Whig Street Blonde Ale **Year-round Beers:** Half Moon Stout, Humble B, Meadow Road Wheat, Old Factory Whistle **Seasonals/Special Releases:** Red Flannel Ale, Wildfire **Tours:** Mar through Apr, Fri and Sat, 11 a.m. to 5 p.m.; May through Dec, Tues through Sat, 11 a.m. to 5 p.m. Closed Jan and Feb.

The Penobscot Bay Brewery is an arm of the Winterport Winery, a popular Maine winery. Beer and wine deserve equal billing, and at the Winterport Winery and Penobscot Bay Brewery, they get it.

The brewery brews five year-round beers, the **Old Factory Whistle,** the **Whig Street Blonde Ale,** the **Meadow Road Wheat,** the **Half Moon Stout,** and **Humble B.** The Old Factory Whistle is a Scottish ale, a full-bodied, malty style of beer, which is perfect for cold Maine nights. The Whig Street Blonde Ale is just what the name says, a blonde ale, light and refreshing, good for a summertime day of drinking on the porch. The Meadow Road Wheat is brewed like a traditional German-style beer, unfiltered. So, when you pour this beer, do not be concerned if you see something floating in the beer. It is yeast, and it is supposed to be there. The Half Moon Stout

## Beer Lover's Pick

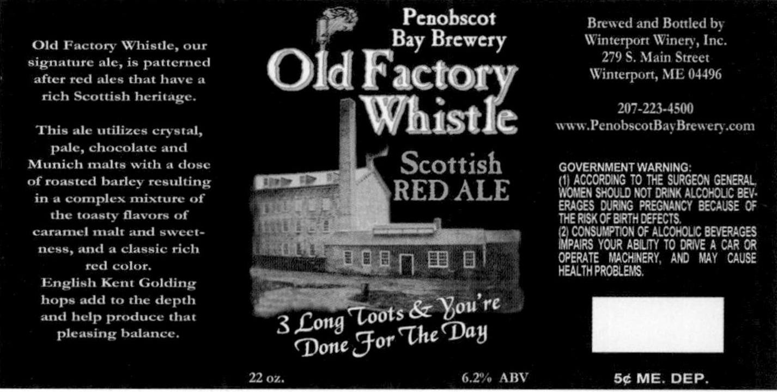


**The Old Factory Whistle**
**Style:** Scottish Ale
**ABV:** 6.2 percent
**Availability:** Year-round

Scottish ales are the perfect beer for a cold New England winter. They are hefty, malty brews that will stick to your bones and warm you up. The Old Factory Whistle is spot on for the style. It is full-bodied, and it has a nice, warming alcohol feel to it. This is a sweet beer, with a hint of burnt sugar. It feels thick in your mouth, but it is not such a high-alcohol beer that you couldn't afford to have more than one.

is based on a historic porter recipe, or a stout porter. Stouts were originally called stout porters, and the porter portion of the name dropped off over the years. The Humble B is Penobscot's newest beer. It is a lager brewed with local Winterport honey and ginger. Those two flavors combine to form an easy-drinking beer.

The Penobscot Bay Brewery also brews two seasonals, the **Red Flannel Ale** and the **Wildfire.** The Red Flannel Ale is a big brown ale brewed for winter. This beer is perfect to drink fresh, or to cellar for the following winter to let it mellow out a bit. The Wildfire is a rauchbier, or a German-style smoked beer. Smoked beers may not seem like warm-weather beers, but imagine barbecuing some smoked meat all day, and then pairing it with the Wildfire. The flavors will meld with each other into a beautiful marriage of smoky goodness.

Penobscot Bay Brewery also offers tours, usually led by a brewer, that end with a tasting of the various beers. If you are there, take the time to tour the winery and learn about the differences and similarities of the two beverages. You may be surprised to learn how much they have in common. Beer is also available to go in 22-ounce bombers and growlers.

## RISING TIDE BREWING COMPANY

103 Fox St., Portland, ME; (207) 370-2337; RisingTideBrewing.com
**Founded:** 2010 **Founder:** Nathan Sanborn **Brewer:** Nathan Sanborn **Flagship Beer:** Atlantis **Year-round Beers:** Daymark, Ishmael, Zephyr **Seasonals/Special Releases:** Calcutta Cutter, Ursa Minor, Spinnaker, Atlantis, Maine Island Trail Ale, Polaris **Tours:** Fri and Sat, 12:30 and 2:30 p.m.

The Rising Tide Brewing Company is growing rapidly, and owner/brewer Nathan Sanborn brews very creative beers, not one beer in Rising Tide's portfolio is boring. All the beers are twists on traditional styles, and every one of them works.

The flagship beer is **Atlantis,** which is a 5.3 percent alcohol by volume (ABV) black ale. Although many dark beers are heavy, thick beers, this one is relatively easy to drink with a fair amount of hops giving a passion-fruit flavor and a hint of a applewood smokiness from the smoked malts used. The **Daymark** is an American pale ale with an addition: rye. The rye malts add a spiciness that plays off the fruity hops nicely. Brewing with rye is not easy (it is thick and gums up the brewing

**Daymark**
**Style:** Rye Pale Ale
**ABV:** 5.1 percent
**Availability:** Year-Round

A west coast pale ale and rye blended together? That is what Daymark is. A lot of brewers seem to use rye in high-alcohol beers, which hides the spiciness associated with rye. Not the Daymark. This is a standard 5.1 percent ABV pale ale, and the spiciness is in the forefront. The rye does not overwhelm the hops, and vice versa. Good job by Rising Tide.

equipment), but when it works right, it can make a beer a pleasure to drink. This is one of those beers that works right. The **Ishmael** is a 5.1 percent alcohol by volume German-style altbier. It is copper in color, and thanks to the American hops used in this beer it has some citrusy fruit aromas and flavors. It is quite good. The **Ursa Minor,** named for the constellation, is a dark, black-as-night American stout. What's different about this stout is that Rising Tide uses wheat malt in this beer. The malts create flavors of dark fruits, chocolate, and coffee, but the wheat adds a decidedly wheaty, yeasty flavor not found in many stouts. Another really well-done beer. Rising Tide has also brewed **Polaris.** The Polaris is the Ursa Minor aged in Jim Beam barrels. You get a lot of booze in the flavor. Other occasional beers are **Spinnaker, Atlantis, Maine Island Trail Ale,** and the **Calucutta Cutter.**

All of Rising Tide's beers are available in 22-ounce bombers.The beers are in finer liquor stores, as well as on draft in some of the better beer bars in southern Maine. Rising Tide Brewing Company offers tours on Friday and Saturday. The tasting room is also open Tuesday and Thursday from 4 to 7 p.m. and Friday and Saturday from noon to 5 p.m.

## SEBAGO BREWING COMPANY

Production brewery, 48 Sanford Dr., Gorham, ME; Brewpubs located Gorham, Kennebunk, Portland, Scarborough; (207) 856-2537; SebagoBrewing.com

**Founded:** 1998 **Founders:** Kai Adams, Brad Monarch, Tim Haines **Brewers:** Kai Adams, Tom Abercrombie **Flagship Beer:** Runabout Red Ale **Year-round Beers:** Boathouse Brown Ale, Frye's Leap India Pale Ale, Lake Trout Stout, Saddleback Ale **Seasonals/Special Releases:** Bass Ackwards Berry Blue Ale, Hefeweizen, Midnight Porter, Slick Nick Winter Ale, Local Harvest Ale, Full Throttle Double IPA, Single Batch Series **Tours:** Mon through Fri, 2 p.m., call ahead; free

Sebago Brewing Company started as a small brewpub in 1998, and now they have taken over the world. Well, not the world, but now Sebago has four brewpubs throughout Maine, and a production brewery that brews and bottles beers for beer lovers throughout New England.

Based in Gorham, Maine, Sebago brews some phenomenal beers, none better than their two IPAs, the **Frye's Leap India Pale Ale** and the **Full Throttle Double IPA.** The Frye's Leap India Pale Ale is one of the better regular-strength IPAs brewed in New England. It is 6.2 percent alcohol by volume (ABV), and is fully packed with hops and caramel malts. The Full Throttle Double IPA is a straight-ahead west coast double IPA, packed with juicy hops, with citrusy and piney flavors from the American hops. There are enough malts to balance out this beer, but this is a hop lover's kind

## Beer Lover's Pick

**Frye's Leap India Pale Ale**
**Style:** IPA
**ABV:** 6.2 percent
**Availability:** Year-round

When introduced in 1998, Sebago's Frye's Leap India Pale Ale was one of the few west coast–style IPAs brewed in New England. All these years later, it still holds up. This is a hop lover's IPA, with strong, fruity hop flavors that are suitably bitter. The use of caramel malts gives it a nice sweetness on the back end of flavor. At 6.2 percent ABV, this is a dangerously drinkable beer.

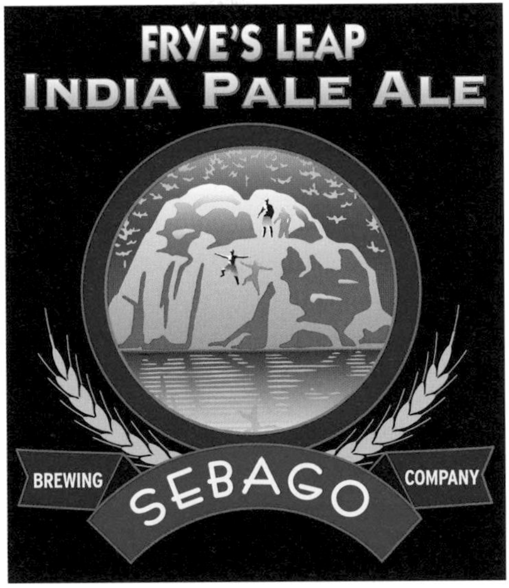


of beer. Sebago's flagship beer, the **Runabout Red Ale,** and the **Boathouse Brown Ale** are both solid versions of their respective styles. The **Lake Trout Stout** is an oatmeal stout with some extra hops added, and the **Saddleback Ale** is a lighter beer for those with delicate taste buds.

The seasonals are pretty tasty, too. The **Bass Ackwards Berry Blue Ale** is one of the better blueberry beers available. The use of real blueberries instead of flavoring gives it a dryness, instead of the sticky-sweet flavor a lot of blueberry ales have. The **Hefeweizen** is a solid summer beer, and the **Midnight Porter** is a good, English-style porter. The **Local Harvest Ale** is an American pale ale brewed with malted barley and hops grown in Maine. The **Slick Nick Winter Ale** is a personal winter favorite of mine. Unlike many winter warmers, this has no spices added. Instead, caramel malts give it a sweet flavor, with caramel and molasses flavors coming through. Throughout the year, Sebago also brews a **Single Batch Series,** which are various styles only available for a limited time and in limited locations.

Even though you can get Sebago beers in stores, don't forget to stop at one of their brewpubs if you are in the area. They have pubs in Gorham, Kennebunk,

Portland, and Scarborough. The pubs are great places to stop to get a Sebago beer on draft and to grab a meal. They all have full menus, and the food is good, so you will not be disappointed.

### SHEEPSCOT VALLEY BREWING COMPANY

74 Hollywood Blvd., Whitefield, ME; (207) 549-5330; SheepscotBrewing.com
**Founded:** 1995 **Founder:** Steve Gorrill **Brewer:** Steve Gorrill **Flagship Beer:** Pemaquid Ale **Year-round Beers:** Boothbay Special Bitter, Damariscotta Double Brown, New Harbor Lager **Seasonals/Special Releases:** Sheepscot Valley Stout, Tinky Winky Double IPA **Tours:** Tours are available, but call ahead.

Hollywood Boulevard in Whitefield, Maine, is a much different place than the Hollywood Boulevard out in California. Sure, in LA you may run into celebrities being followed by camera-toting paparazzi, but Whitefield's Hollywood Boulevard has something going for it that its more famous counterpart does not—it is home to the Sheepscot Valley Brewing Company. Win goes to Maine in this contest.

The Sheepscot Valley Brewing Company is a brewery that has quietly been going about its business brewing good, solid beers since 1995. It is one of those places in Maine that is popular in its general geographic area, but not easy to find in other areas. The **Pemaquid Ale** is the flagship, a full-bodied Scottish ale. This is a beer that is heavy on the malts and reflects the cold Maine climate. This is a perfect beer to have on a cold night while you are warming up with a big bowl of beef stew;

**Damariscotta Double Brown**
**Style:** Brown Ale
**ABV:** 6.8 percent
**Availability:** Year-Round
Brown ales often border on session ale alcohol levels, but not the Damariscotta Double Brown (named for the town of Damariscotta, Maine). This beer is loaded with more malts than the typical brown ale, raising the alcohol to nearly 7 percent alcohol by volume (ABV). Although it is a sweet beer, it is not too sweet, and this beer has an excellent body and great carbonation. Its extremely pleasant caramel flavors round out this excellent offering.

it's a hearty beer meant to go with hearty food. The **Boothbay Special Bitter** is a traditional English-style bitter. It is mild, nicely carbonated with a nice bitterness that plays nicely on your tongue. This beer is often available on cask at better beer bars, and it tastes even better than when served normally. The **Damariscotta Double Brown** is a bigger than average brown ale, while the **New Harbor Lager** is a typical pale lager.

Occasionally brewed beers include the **Sheepscot Valley Stout.** It is a lighter stout, but it has nice chocolate and coffee notes. The **Tinky Winky Double IPA** is Sheepscot Valley's biggest beer at 9.5 percent ABV. This is probably the most American of the beers, and worth seeking out.

Sheepscot founder and brewer Steve Gorrill offers tours at his brewery, but make sure to call ahead before going because if he is busy, he will not have time to give you the tour. Growlers of the beers are also available. Other items sold at the brewery are several different Pemaquid Ale T-shirts, including one that features a T. rex on the front. I guess even the most ferocious dinosaur appreciates a nice Scottish ale.



### SHIPYARD BREWING COMPANY

86 Newbury St., Portland, ME; 800-BREW-ALE; Shipyard.com

**Founded:** 1994 **Founders:** Fred Forsley and Alan Pugsley **Brewer:** Alan Pugsley **Flagship Beer:** Old Thumper **Year-round Beers:** Blue Fin Stout, Chamberlain Pale Ale, Export Ale, Shipyard IPA, Shipyard Light Ale **Seasonals/Special Releases:** Applehead Ale, Summer Ale, Prelude Special Ale, Pumpkinhead Ale, Longfellow Winter Ale, Double Old Thumper, Pugsley Signature Series **Tours:** Guided tours Tues from 5:30 to 7 p.m. (several weeks advance notice needed); video tour daily, every hour between 11 a.m. and 4 p.m.

There is not a more influential brewery in Maine, maybe in all of New England, than Portland's Shipyard Brewing Company. Owner/brewmaster Alan Pugsley came from England and brought over the Peter Austin brewing system. He helped set up the signature system at more than 60 breweries across the country, including several other Maine breweries, such as Gritty McDuff's and D.L Geary's. He also brought over Ringwood yeast, from Austin's Ringwood brewery in England. Some beer lovers love it, and some beer lovers hate it. Whatever people think about it, Shipyard makes it work for them, and the brewery has become one of the largest in the country.

Shipyard actually started as the Federal Jack's Restaurant and Brew Pub in Kennebunk (which still exists) in 1992 until it expanded to a full brewery in 1994. The Shipyard Brewing Company specializes in English-style ales. Almost all the year-round beers are British-inspired ales. They include the **Export Ale, Old Thumper,**

## Beer Lover's Pick

**Pugsley Signature Series Imperial Porter**
**Style:** Imperial Porter
**ABV:** 7.1 percent
**Availability:** Rotating

The Pugsley Signature Series Imperial Porter is the best beer brewed by the Shipyard Brewing Company. There are a lot of flavors going on in this beer, roasted black coffee, dark fruit, maybe even some raisins and figs, as well as a hint of chocolate. This is not an overly sweet beer, and there is a hint of booze in there, but it is most definitely a winner.

**Shipyard IPA,** and the **Chamberlain Pale Ale.** The other two year-round offerings are not English ales; the **Blue Fin Stout** is an Irish stout, and the **Shipyard Light Ale** is a light American blonde ale.

Shipyard is most well-known for one of its three seasonals—the **Pumpkinhead Ale.** For many, the arrival of Pumpkinhead Ale in stores in August means summer is coming to a close and fall is on the way. This is easily the most popular pumpkin ale being brewed today. Shipyard also brews a typical American wheat beer as their **Summer Ale,** and the **Prelude Special Ale** is a suitably malty winter beer. The **Longfellow Winter Ale** is a hybrid beer, a blend of a Scotch ale and a porter.

In the past few years, Shipyard has introduced the **Pugsley Signature Series,** a collection of higher alcohol, less traditional beers. The Pugsley Signature Series includes the **Barley Wine, Imperial Porter, Smashed Blueberry, Smashed Pumpkin,** and **XXXX IPA.** These beers are quite good. The Barley Wine and Imperial Porter, in particular, are the two best beers being brewed at Shipyard today.

Shipyard also brews beers under several other labels; they own the **Kennebunkport Brewing Company,** which brews Shipyard beers to put on draft at Federal Jack's. They also own the **Sea Dog Brewing Company.** Sea Dog has several restaurants in Maine and two in Massachusetts. They also release several fruit beers under the Sea Dog label, including the popular **Bluepaw Blueberry Wheat Ale,** that are easy to find in many liquor stores. Shipyard is also a popular place for other breweries to contract-brew beers. Gritty McDuff's, Geary's, and Peak Organic all bottle their 12-ounce bottled beers there.

Full brewery tours are offered on Tuesday, and are often booked weeks ahead of time, so you have to reserve a space online. If you cannot make it for a full brewery tour, they offer daily video tours and beer tastings at the brewery. Shipyard is part of brewing history, so if you're a beer lover, make a stop there while in Portland.

## SOME BREWING COMPANY

1 York St., Unit 3, York, Maine; (215) 718-3541; SoMeBrewingCo.com
**Founded:** 2013 **Founder:** David (father) and Dave (son) Rowland **Brewer:** Dave Rowland (the younger) **Flagship Beer:** Crystal Persuasion **Year-round Beers:** Box the Compass, Whoopie Pie Stout, York Gold **Seasonals/Special Releases:** Black the Sky Rye, Foghorn Coffee Stout, Cinnamon Toast Ale, Ocie's Island Wheat, Snow Day, Snowball Earth **Taproom hours:** Thurs and Fri, 4 to 8 p.m.; Sat, 1 to 7 p.m.; Sun, 1 to 5 p.m.

SoMe Brewing Company was founded by the father and son team of David and Dave Rowland. After the younger Dave was laid off from his teaching job, he decided to turn his home brewing hobby into a full brewery, opening the brewery in 2013.

SoMe Brewing Company brews four year-round beers, as well as a host of special releases that are available on a rotating basis. The brewery's flagship beer is the **Crystal Persuasion,** a double pale ale (not double IPA), that comes in at 8 percent alcohol by volume (ABV). Ask me the difference between a double pale ale and a double IPA and I will not know. Either way, it's a beer hopheads will enjoy, but balanced enough so it's not a palate scorcher. Also available throughout the year is the **Whoopie Pie Stout** (whoopie pie beers are popular in Maine). This milk stout is aged on both cocoa nibs and vanilla beans to create the flavors of this popular dessert. The other year-round beers are the **Box Compass,** a 6.6 percent ABV American IPA, and the **York Gold,** a rye golden ale. Rotating beers include the **Black the Sky Rye** hoppy black rye ale, the **Foghorn Coffee Stout,** the **Cinnamon Toast Ale, Ocie's Island Wheat, Snow Day** winter warmer, and the **Snowball Earth** double IPA.

SoMe Brewing Company's tasting room is open Thursday through Sunday for growler fills and samples. Twenty-two ounce bottles are also available in limited stores.

## STRONG BREWING COMPANY

7 Rope Ferry Rd., Sedgwick, ME; (207) 359-8722; StrongBrewing.com
**Founded:** 2013 **Founders:** Al and Mia Strong **Brewer:** Al Strong **Flagship Beer:** Localmotion **Year-round Beers:** The Maineiac **Seasonals/Special Releases:** Soul Patch Porter, Blue Barren, 5 Star Peach Ale, Black Strap Marzen, Sante Noel, Bloody Valentine, Hot Chocolate Stout **Taproom hours:** change seasonally, call ahead or check the website

Community supported agriculture is growing in popularity, where people buy into the farm or garden in exchange for the share of fruits, vegetables, and even meat. The Strong Brewing Company in Sedgwick, Maine, has taken that model to the brewing world, creating the "Community Supported Brewery."

How it works is someone buys a "share" of the brewery. People can buy 64-ounce or 32-ounce growler plans, in either a full-share or a half-share. For $458 for the full-share 64-ounce plan, a person will receive 48 growler fills throughout the year, or for $205 they can get 48 32-ounce growler fills. The half-shares are slightly more than half of the cost of the full-share, and people will get 24 fills of either 64-ounce or 32-ounce growlers. This works for both founders Al and Mia Strong and those who purchase the shares. The Strongs get the money up front to help expand their small brewery, while the shareholders get many growler fills for a good price.

As for the beers, Strong Brewing uses many local and organic ingredients in each of their beers. The flagship is the **Localmotion,** a hoppier version of a California Common. The only other year-round beer is the **Maineiac,** a huge, 10 percent alcohol by volume (ABV) 100 international bittering units (a measurement of how bitter something is), double IPA. Strong releases new beers throughout the year, typically only having them available for a month at a time. The **Blue Barren** is a tart, 3 percent ABV Berliner weisse brewed with local wild blueberries, available in August. The **5 Star Peach Ale,** available in September, is made with local honey and peaches. The **Black Strap Marzen,** a liberal interpretation of an Oktoberfest available in October, is brewed with 6 pounds of organic molasses and 12 pounds of organic brown sugar. The **Hot Chocolate Stout,** available in January, is with organic Fair Trade chocolate, vanilla beans, and other spices. Other beers include the **Sante Noel** (Belgian strong ale), **Bloody Valentine** (hefeweizen with blood oranges), and the **Soul Patch Porter.**

Strong Brewing beers are only available on draft at a few establishments and by growler at the brewery (located in a garage). Call ahead or check the website for seasonal hours.

### THE BAG & KETTLE BREWPUB

9004 Main St., Carrabasett Valley, ME; 207-237-2451; TheBagAndKettle.com
**Draft Beers:** 8

After a day skiing and snowboarding on the slopes of Sugarloaf, you could always grab a nice mug of hot chocolate. But, what would even be better would be a pint of house-brewed beer at the Bag & Kettle Brewpub, located on the Sugarloaf Mountain.

The Bag & Kettle Brewpub is open during the skiing season, and offers visitors eight beers on tap, as well as the typical mass-produced beers in bottles. The available beers include the **Trout Brook Gold,** a light golden ale; the **Pick Pole Pale Ale,** which uses the popular Cascade hops; the **Bag Brown Ale,** which is an English Brown Ale; and **Uncle's Winter Ale,** a hoppy, dark beer, perfect for winter.

Other beers include the chocolaty **Half Pipe Porter;** the **Alpine Red Raspberry,** which is a lighter beer with raspberry; the **Joe Stout,** which is made with local espresso beans; and the popular **Bags Potato Ale,** which, you guessed it, is made with potatoes.

As for food, the Bag & Kettle pretty much offers your standard pub fare. Appetizers include potato skins and Mexi-skins, which are the potato skins with jalapeno peppers added. There are also nachos, shrimp cocktail, and chili. Burgers are a big part of the Bag & Kettle's menu. The most interesting is the Gucci, which is a burger covered with crispy, spicy bacon. Other sandwiches include a Reuben and the Triple Fromage Melt, which is a grilled cheese sandwich with American, mozzarella, and provolone cheese. They also have a large pizza menu, including the Bag's Fiery Cool Blue. The typical red tomato sauce is replaced by bleu cheese. It also has buffalo chicken, bacon, and celery as toppings. Entrees like grilled chicken and New York sirloins are also available.

During ski season, the Bag & Kettle is open seven days a week from 11:30 a.m. to 9:30 p.m.

## BOON ISLAND ALE HOUSE

1677 Post Rd., Wells, ME; (207) 641-8489; BoonIslandAle.com
**Draft Beers:** 4

The Boon Island Ale House is a restaurant first and a brewpub second. There's nothing wrong with that. The problem with many good restaurants is they take great care preparing food, developing a nice wine list, and selecting spirits, but then only offer easy-to-get, boring beers. The Boon Island Ale House, on the other hand, has four of its own beers on draft at all times, giving beer lovers something good to drink while they enjoy their meals.

The four Boon Island Ales are not particularly complex beers. They are meant to be good, easy-drinking beers you can enjoy with a meal. The **Nut Brown Ale** is a traditional English-style brown ale. It has a lot of nutty flavors, along with strong caramel notes and even a touch of chocolate in the finish. The **India Pale Ale** leans toward the English style. The earthy hop and the strong malt base actually work well with seafood because they will not overwhelm it. It is a perfect beer for a Maine restaurant with a lot of seafood. The **Boon Island Light** is the perfect beer for those who are not into craft beer. The **Lager** is Boon Island's best beer; a traditional Czech-style pilsner, it's a clean, easy drink with a frothy head. Again, a good pairing for seafood because it will not overwhelm the delicate flavors.

The real attraction of Boon Island is the food. The appetizers are heavy on seafood-related items, such as the Shark Bites, which are actually deep-fried haddock chunks. The fried calamari and the crab cakes are also available, as are the Boon Island Wings, which are made with a honey lager barbecue sauce (available for purchase). Cheese sticks, a pile of fried mozzarella sticks, are always a crowd pleaser. Or maybe you want something a little heartier. Boon Island offers three different chowder options. You can get the clam chowder, the lobster chowder, or the Boon Island's 1940s Original Fish Chowder, based on a recipe developed by a local housewife in the 1940s.

After the chowder, move on to a burger. The burgers are half-pound patties and feature several topping options. The Harbor Master is topped with roasted red peppers, provolone cheese, caramelized onions, and Boon Island's Special Sauce. Entrees include the lobster mac and cheese, which is macaroni smothered in a special blend of cheeses with chunks of lobster mixed in. Another highlight, the Diver Down, is a dish of pan-seared sea scallops served with a chipotle maple drizzle.

## BRAY'S BREWPUB & EATERY

678 Roosevelt Tr., Naples, ME; (207) 693-6806; BraysBrewpub.com
**Draft Beers:** 6 house beers, 26 in all

Maine is full of hidden beer jewels—small breweries and brewpubs no one outside of the general area knows, but which serve some wonderful beer. Bray's Brewpub & Eatery in tiny Naples is one of those places. The brewpub isn't far from Portland, where the brewpubs, breweries, and beer bars in the large port city overshadow other worthy beer establishments on the outskirts. But Bray's is an exceptional brewpub; they brew some great beers, have a lot of really good guest taps, and sport a large and varied food menu. It's a worthy destination in its own right.

The draft list is an impressive mix of Bray's own beers, usually 6 of them on draft at one time, along with 20 guest taps. The guest taps feature local beers such as those from Allagash Brewing Company and Sebago Brewing Company, both from Maine, as well as beers from breweries in other parts of the country, such as Victory Brewing Company in Pennsylvania, and some from as far away as Europe, like St. Bernardus from Belgium.

The house-brewed beers stand up well to these well-known beer heavyweights. Bray's offers two different IPAs, one dark and one light, both coming in at a solid 7 percent alcohol by volume. The **Mt. Olympus Special Ale** is the dark IPA while the **Epicurean IPA** is the light IPA. The **Yammityville Horror** gets extra points by channeling one of the best horror movies of the 1970s, the *Amityville Horror.* Bray's also gets points for brewing this fall beer with yams rather than pumpkin. Other beers include the **Brandy Pond Blonde** (wheat ale), the **Pleasant Mountain Porter,** and the **Muddy River Bog Brown Ale.** Also available throughout the year is the **Songo Lock Scotch Ale,** a 9.4 percent malty monster of a beer, the **Caseway Cream Ale, Graveyard Coffee Stout, Burnt Meadow Mountain Peated Porter,** and the **Viciously Vivacious Vanilla Porter.**

If you make the trip to Naples, you might as well stay for a meal. Bray's offers five different nacho options for appetizers, as well as housemade hummus and grilled shrimp skewers. Or grab the lobster stew for a starter, which features hunks of lobster in a cream sauce with scallions and bacon. If you are not into meat, you may want to skip the pub menu. Except for the veggie burger, the pub menu is designed for those who enjoy meat. It features baby back ribs, the Barbecue Smoked Beef Brisket & Pulled Pork Plate, a sausage platter, sausage sub, and half-pound burgers. The dinner menu is heavy on seafood. You can get baked or fried scallops; baked haddock; or the Broiled Seafood Combo, which features haddock, shrimp, and scallops, panko-encrusted and served in a white wine butter sauce. The mixed grill

### One Night Stand

Every August, for one night, Bray's clears its taps of all guest beers and puts all the beers they brew on tap at one time. This is the only night of the year that you can get any of the Bray's beers you want. Order a sample platter to make the job of trying all of their offerings a little more manageable.

comes with a 6-ounce sirloin steak, two jumbo shrimp, and some sausage. Bray's also has a fairly large dessert menu that features freshly made pies, cheesecake, and even a Toll House cookie pie.

Bray's also has live music several nights a week, so there is always something going on there.

## FEDERAL JACK'S RESTAURANT & BREW PUB

8 Western Ave., Kennebunk, ME; (207) 967-4322; www.federaljacks.com
**Draft Beers:** 7

Federal Jack's Restaurant & Brew Pub is the birthplace of one of the oldest and most well-known New England breweries, the Shipyard Brewing Company. Fred Forsley and Alan Pugsley, who went on to found Shipyard Brewing Company in 1994, founded Federal Jack's in 1992. Many of Shipyard's most popular beers were first brewed, and are still available, at Federal Jack's.

Like Shipyard, Federal Jack's concentrates on brewing English-style ales. In fact, most of the beers available at Federal Jack's are members of the Shipyard standard line of beer. The year-round beers include the **Shipyard Blue Fin Stout, Brown Ale, Export Ale, Fuggles IPA,** and **Old Thumper.** The other year-round beers not part of Shipyard's normal rotation include the **Goat Island Light Ale** and the **'Taint Town Pale Ale.**

Federal Jack's also rotates in popular seasonal ales such as the **Longfellow, Prelude,** and **Pumpkinhead** ales. Other seasonals that are not Shipyard beers include the **Sunfish Wheat Ale,** as well as a series of oak-aged beers. The brewpub also often has beers available on cask. Although many of these beers are Shipyard beers, they are as fresh as can be, being brewed in the Kennebunkport Brewery, located right beneath Federal Jack's.

Federal Jack's has a large menu that should have something for everyone. Full meals include sandwiches, burgers, steaks, and turkey, but like many Maine restaurants, Federal Jack's is heavy on seafood options, including crab-stuffed Atlantic haddock, fish and chips, fried clams, Maine shrimp, and potato-encrusted haddock. And, of course, there is lobster. Get a regular steamed lobster, or get the Federal Jack's Feast. The Feast comes with a cup of New England clam chowder, Goat Island mussels, a steamed Maine lobster (twin lobsters are available), fries, cole slaw, and either a pint of beer or homemade root beer.

If you happen to fall in love with a beer while at Federal Jack's, grab a half-gallon growler and bring it home so you can enjoy it again in the privacy of your own living room. It will help to bring back all of those memories of great lobster you ate at Federal Jack's.



## GEAGHAN'S RESTAURANT & PUB

50 Main St., Bangor, ME; (207) 945-3730; GeaghansPub.com
**Draft Beers:** 8

Geaghan's Restaurant & Pub has been around since the 1970s, but became home to Geaghan's Brother's Brewery in 2013, when brothers Larry and Peter added a small brewery to the restaurant.

The restaurant typically has about eight beers on tap. The beers include the **Bangor Brown,** a dry, malty brown ale that ends with citrusy hops; the **Smiling Irish Bastard;** an **American Strong Pale Ale,** which is a misnomer because it's only 6 percent alcohol by volume (ABV), but it is excellent with big, bold flavors; the **Refueler,** which is an American wheat ale; the **Roundhouse Porter,** a robust porter available during the winter; **Hose 5,** an American Amber Ale; **Bangor Tiger,** a 6.5 percent ABV IPA; and **Dad's Oatmeal Stout.** The beers are available to go in growlers and half growlers, and on draft at the restaurant.

Geaghan's is one of the few brewpubs open for breakfast in New England. The breakfast menu includes the Whole in the Wall, which is a fried egg placed in the center of homemade bread, topped with ham and cheese and served with toast and hash browns. The Geaghan's Steak & Eggs is served with a 7-ounce rib eye. There are also several omelet's available, including one made with hunks of boneless Buffalo chicken wings.

The lunch menu includes typical bar-type apps, such as fried mozzarella sticks, fried mushrooms and nachos. There are also several soups and salads available. Sandwiches and burgers make up most of the lunch menu, including the Cajon rib eye steak sandwich, which features a whole rib eye on the sandwich. Also available are choices of several melts. The Porky Cheese Melt is made with ham, bacon, and Swiss cheese.

The dinner menu includes all of the above items, but adds steak dinners and fish entrees. One of the standouts is the Broiled Pub Cheese Haddock, which is an 8-ounce serving of haddock, broiled and topped with Geaghan's housemade pub cheese.

Geaghan's is open Sunday through Thursday 7 a.m. to 11 p.m.; and Friday and Saturday from 7 to 12:45 a.m.

## KENNEBEC RIVER PUB & BREWERY

1771 US 201, The Forks, ME; 800-765-7238; NorthernOutdoors.com
**Draft Beers:** 6

After a long day of rafting on the Dead River, you will probably be in need of a beer (or three) and some food. The Kennebec River Pub & Brewery at the Northern Outdoors Resort, located at The Forks, Maine, is exactly the kind of place you need to go. They serve good, simple, filling pub food, and brew better-than-expected beers for a brewpub at a resort.

The Kennebec River Pub & Brewery always has at least six of its beers on tap at all times, and they also distribute three of their beers—**IPA, Sledhead Red,** and the **Summer Ale**—in six-packs throughout New England. Along with those three beers, Kennebec has another 10 beers that they rotate throughout the year. The **Deer-in-the-Head Lite** is Kennebec's version of a mass-produced lager. The **Whitewater Wheat** is a Belgian-style witbier brewed with coriander and orange peel, and the **Kennebec Logger** is a well-made pilsner, while the **Big Mama Blueberry Ale** is your typical blueberry ale. If you like blueberry beers, you'll like Big Mama; if you don't, she won't change your mind. The **Octoberfest** is a solid interpretation of the popular fall seasonal, while the **Hazelnut Brown** is fantastic. The use of hazelnuts in a brown ale is almost always excellent, and this is no exception. The other beers

## Spring Raft 'n Brews

Each spring, the Kennebec River Pub & Brewery holds the Raft 'n Brews event. It starts with a day of canoeing on the Dead River, and then continues into the Northern Resort Community Center for a barbecue and tours of the brewery. Different beers are available at special prices and there are live bands to keep the party going all day and into the night.



include the **Penobscot Porter** and the **Class V Stout.** They are both really well-done dark beers, perfect to warm you up after you have fallen out of your raft and gotten soaked several times throughout the day.

Kennebec's burgers are huge, a half-pound each, and can come with a variety of toppings. Other sandwiches include a fried fish sandwich and a grilled meat loaf sandwich. Several different shrimp dishes are available as entrees, but the meal you really should get is the Tornadoes of Beef, which features two 5-ounce filet mignons, char-grilled and topped with homemade herb butter. Desserts are made daily and are different each day. Breakfast is also available in the pub.

## LIBERAL CUP PUBLIC HOUSE AND BREWERY

115 Water St., Hallowell, ME; (207) 623-2739; TheLiberalCup.com
**Draft Beers:** 6

The Liberal Cup Public House and Brewery is what an old-time New England bar should be—a little small, a little dark, nothing but dark wood furniture and beer signs and posters on the wall. It's the kind of place that will make you feel like you belong. The Liberal Cup is located in downtown Hallowell, Maine, fitting into the old-time New England charm that the town gives off with antiques shops and other small establishments.

The beer selection may be small, but it's always rotating, so you should be able to find a beer you like every time you go in there. The beers include a good mix of British styles, with a few others thrown in. The **Alewife Ale** is a red ale, while the **Ex-Wife Extra Bitter** (sounds a little personal) is a 6.7 percent alcohol by volume ESB. The **Backhouse Bitter** is also another good British option, as is the **Summer Bitter Summer Not.** Another good choice would be the **For Richer or Poorter,** a solid beer. Other beers include the **Oatmeal Stout, Old Hallow Ale IPA,** and the **Tarbox Stout.** The two standouts, though, are the **Chazmo Altbier,** a solid spot-on German-style alt, and the **Bug Zapper Super Lager,** which is a red or amber lager, full of malty sweetness and flavor. Liberal Cup also offers the **Bug Lager,** which is their interpretation of a mass-produced lager. The Liberal Cup also typically has a beer on cask.

Food-wise, the Liberal Cup offers mainly pub-style food, trying to mimic the English pub culture of simple food with good beer. Appetizer highlights include the Mills Mussels (a recipe stolen from their sister pub, the Run of the Mill) and the Creole Quesadillas. The quesadillas are made with grilled sun-dried tomato tortillas filled with Andouille and chorizo sausages with pepper jack cheese, topped with cilantro-lime sour cream and remoulade for dipping. Starting your meal off with the Liberal Cup's beer cheese soup may be the best decision you'll ever make. Each day a different beer and a different cheese is used, so check with your server before ordering.

Larger meals include the Ale Bird, which is a roasted free-range chicken that has been brewed in Alehouse Ale, served with garlic smashed potatoes. The Drunken Pot Roast is a classic pot roast, slow-roasted in beer. The Haddock Napoleon is beer-battered haddock, served with garlic smashed potatoes, applewood-smoked bacon, and spinach, topped with a mornay cheese sauce. The most unique offering on the menu is the Not Your Mama's Meat Loaf, which is a meat loaf stuffed with spinach and mozzarella, then wrapped in applewood-smoked bacon and covered in homemade gravy.

The Liberal Cup is also a great place to hang out to listen to live music. They host bands of all genres most nights of the week, so grab a pint (actually 20-ounce glass) of your favorite beer and relax to some good music.

## MAINE COAST BREWING COMPANY

102 Eden St., Bar Harbor, ME; (207) 288-4914; BHMaine.com
**Draft Beers:** 6

The Maine Coast Brewing Company is the house brewery for Jack Russell's Steakhouse and Brewpub. Maine Coast brews a number of beers, year-round and seasonals alike. The beers include the **Bar Harbor Espresso Stout,** which is a perfect after-dinner beer instead of having a coffee. Additional offerings include **Jack Russell's Best Brown Ale,** which is a traditional brown ale and the beer you really should get with all of the beef offered on this menu. The **Wild Blueberry Ale** is the obligatory blueberry ale most Maine breweries brew. The **Precipice Pale Ale** is a solid pale ale, while the **Jordan Pond Ale** is a decent IPA. Other beers include the **Black Irish Stout** and the **Eden Porter.**

But more than any other brewpub in Maine, Maine Coast Brewing Company/Jack Russell's Steakhouse is all about the food. As the name implies, steak is the star at Jack Russell's. Options include the Jack Russell's Filet Mignon that comes in a variety of sizes, from the Ladies' Cut that weighs 6 ounces to the Butcher's Cut, which comes in at 12 ounces. Jack Russell's Maine Maple N.Y. Strip comes with a homemade maple steak sauce, while the prime rib is served as large as 21 ounces. The tenderloin tips are served on skewers, and there are also pork tenderloins on the menu. Not a meat eater or steak lover? No worries—they have you covered with the Vegetarian Platter, which includes roasted veggies, an eggplant cutlet, the vegetable of the day, and a side of hummus with pita bread.

## MARSHALL WHARF BREWING COMPANY/THREE TIDES RESTAURANT

2 Pinchy Ln., Belfast, ME; (207) 338-1707; MarshallWharf.com and 3Tides.com
**Draft Beers:** 17

The Marshall Wharf Brewing Company is Maine's best kept secret. Marshall Wharf, which is the house brewery for the Three Tides Restaurant, is easily one of the top 10 beer producers in New England, but because they are only available in a few places, they fly under the radar.

Marshall Wharf does not know how to brew bad beers, and has a rotation of more than 30 beers; it's nearly impossible to pick a favorite. Like hoppy beers? Marshall Wharf brews several IPAs/double IPAs. The **Toughcats IPA** is a single-hop IPA, brewed with Palisade hops, which give it a peachy, apricot-like flavor. The **Big Twitch** is a big, west coast double IPA, coming in at 9 percent alcohol by volume (ABV). Then there's the **Cant Dog,** a 10 percent ABV beer. Do you like German-style beers? Go with the **Wiener,** a German-style Vienna lager, or maybe the **Deep Purple,** a smoked ale, or even the **Attenuator Doppelbock,** or maybe the **Illegal Ale-ian,** a kolsch-wheat beer hybrid. Oh, and don't forget about the stouts. There's the **Danny McGovern's Oatmeal Stout.** Marshall Wharf also brews two great imperial stouts. The first is the **Chaos Chaos Russian Imperial Stout,** a big beast of a beer coming in at a hefty 11.2 percent ABV. The second is the vanilla bean and oak-aged version of the Chaos Chaos, called **Sexy Chaos.** It is a decadent treat. Another stout is the **Pemaquid Oyster Stout,** a traditional style of British stout brewed with 10 dozen oysters. Other beers available include the **Ace Hole Pale Ale, 42 Cream Ale, Bitty** (a Belgian take on the Illegal Ale-ian), **Cornholio** (blonde ale), **Happy Dock Coffee Porter, Maximillian Imperial Red Ale,** and the **Phil Brown Ale.**

But before going to Marshall Wharf, stop inside Three Tides for some food and to try several of these beers on draft. Not many brewpubs have 17 beers on tap, let alone 17 awesome beers. Three Tides offers a tapas menu that includes garlic pita chips and salsa, a small dish of olives, baked mozzarella sticks, Swedish meatballs, Maine crabmeat or chicken quesadillas, Pemaquid oysters, and rope-grown mussels.

The best part, though, is you can try several of the Marshall Wharf beers before you go inside the brewery portion of the restaurant and pick out which growler of

### The Beer and Pemaquid Mussel Fest

Each year, this outside festival is held on the Three Tides Restaurant property. The event features three different bar areas outside, serving more than 30 different Marshall Wharf beers. For the $25 fee, you get a glass and 10 tickets to get beer. All the food, including Pemaquid mussels, is pay as you go. The four-hour event occurs rain or shine.



beer you want to take home. Trust me, you will want to take at least one, if not more, home. If you can't make it to Belfast, Marshall Wharf beers are available on draft at several bars in Portland.

## THE RUN OF THE MILL

100 Main St., Saco, ME; (207) 571-9652; TheRunOfTheMill.net
**Draft Beers:** 7

Despite its name, the Run of the Mill is anything but another run-of-the-mill brewpub. As the sister brewpub of the Liberal Cup Public House & Brewery in Hallowell, it's an exceptional beer destination, with some really good beer and a full menu of tasty food.

Many of the beers available at the Run of the Mill are the same ones available at the Liberal Cup, such as the **Bug Lager, Alewife Ale,** and the **Ex-Wife Extra Bitter,** but there are some different offerings. Some of those beers include the **Tented Kilt Scottish Ale** (the name makes me giggle), the **Smelt Cap Strong Ale,** the **Mud Flap Spring Bock,** and the **What's Hoppenin' IPA.** The beers are all solid. There are a variety of styles available, seven, and there should be something for all different beer tastes.

### The Brewer's Dinner

Every May, the Run of the Mill brewers and chefs get together to create a six-course beer dinner. Each course of food is developed especially for the beer dinner and uses their house brew as an ingredient. Then each dish is paired with a Run of the Mill beer, showing the harmony beer and food can have if paired correctly.

The Run of the Mill's menu also shares several items with the Liberal Cup, but there isn't too much overlap. Start with the croquettes, which are made of potatoes, bacon, and cheddar cheese and then deep-fried. The Maine crab cakes are also delicious, as are the Mussels Dijon, which are sautéed with garlic, onion, red peppers, white wine, and butter and served in a Dijon cream sauce. There are loads of salads available, and Run of the Mill's special house dressing makes them stand out from the usual salad fare. If you're in the mood for a sandwich, there are two standouts. The Indian Island Chicken Sandwich is a grilled chicken breast covered in bacon and cheddar—simple but great. The Grilled Salmon Focaccia features a quarter pound of salmon, a grilled portobello mushroom, tomatoes, and greens, all stacked on focaccia bread and served open faced with a lemon dill aioli.

The menu also offers several comfort food items, such as shepherd's pie and a home-style turkey dinner (perfect if you want to have a taste of Thanksgiving in July). The standout dish, though, is the Mac & Beer Cheese. It is made with macaroni and a triple cheese sauce made with Bug Lager and topped with a blend of pretzels and crackers and a crispy Parmesan cheese wheel.

## SEA DOG BREWING COMPANY

Three locations: 26 Front St., Bangor, ME; 125 Western Ave., South Portland, ME; 1 Bowdoin Mill Island, Suite 100, Topsham, ME; SeaDogBrewing.com
Bangor: (207) 947-8720; South Portland: (207) 871-7000; Topsham: (207) 725-0162
**Draft Beers:** Various

The Sea Dog Brewing Company is a chain of brewpubs owned by the Shipyard Brewing Company. There are also several Sea Dog restaurants in Massachusetts that do not brew beer. The Sea Dog Brewing Company is most famous for its fruit beers, none more than the **Bluepaw Blueberry Wheat Ale,** a blueberry ale. Their other fruit beers are the **Apricot Wheat Ale** and the **Raspberry Wheat Ale,** both light fruit beers, popular among those who like sweet, light beers.

Other Sea Dog offerings include the **Old East India Pale Ale,** the **Old Golly Wobbler Brown Ale,** the **Owls Head Light Ale,** the **Sea Dog Pale Ale,** and the **Sea Dog Stout.** But Sea Dog's best beer is the **Riverdriver Hazelnut Porter.** The hazelnut works fantastically in this beer.

Sea Dog's menu is full of excellent pub fare. Appetizers include the Windjammer Mussels and Frites, which are steamed in Sea Dog's Windjammer Ale. Also available are fried calamari, tuna sashimi, and a cheese plate of local cheeses. The most unusual of the appetizers is the Mexicali Wontons, which are deep-fried wontons filled with blackened chicken, green chili, and cream cheese. They also have tons of sandwiches, including a lobster roll, a grilled crab cake and Havarti sandwich, and the Firecracker Shrimp Roll, made with spicy Maine shrimp, shaved lettuce, and Cajun remoulade.

As can be expected of the location, entrees are heavy on seafood, such as fish and chips and the potato chip–encrusted haddock. There are also fried clams and steamed lobsters, as well as jambalaya. Non-seafood options include fried chicken and mashed potatoes, and wild mushroom and goat cheese ravioli. Another highlight is the Barbecue Bluepaw Short Ribs (recipe on page 316), which is made with a marinade that uses the popular Bluepaw Blueberry Wheat beer.

The Sea Dog is also a great option if you're looking for a family restaurant in the area, so if you have the little ones with you, this may be a better option than other brewpubs and beer bars.



### SUNDAY RIVER BREWING COMPANY

1 Sunday River Rd., Bethel, ME; (207) 824-3541; SundayRiverBrewpub.com
**Draft Beers:** 7

The Sunday River Brewing Company has a special place in my heart—they're the only establishment where you can get beers from the now defunct Stone Coast Brewing Company, the brewery that introduced me to craft beer.

The brewery, located near the Sunday River Ski Resort, offers seven beers on draft, food, and a place to relax after a long day on the slopes. The Stone Coast beers are the **420 IPA, 840 IPA, Jamaican Stout, Black Bear Porter,** and the **Redstone**

**Ale.** They also brew beers under the Sunday River name, including the **Sunday River Alt, Sunday River Lager,** and the **Sunsplash Golden Ale.**

The 420 IPA is a good, solid American-style IPA. It smells of freshly cut grass, and packs a little citrusy punch when you take a sip. If the 420 IPA isn't hoppy enough for you, try its big brother, the 840 IPA. This is a big, hoppy double IPA. It is also on the sweet side as tons of malts are used to provide balance. At 8.5 percent alcohol by volume (ABV), you can feel the burn as it travels down your throat. The Jamaican Stout is a traditional foreign export stout, typically brewed for tropical regions. This has huge roasted coffee characters, almost like fresh espresso grounds. It also has some caramel notes, and some bitterness. It's another big beer at 8 percent ABV, however, unlike the 840 IPA, you will not notice the alcohol. Meanwhile, the Redstone Ale is a good, solid red ale, malty and sweet, with few hops.

The Sunday River beers are solid. The Alt is tasty, if not up to the standards of the top beers in the style. The Sunday River Lager is an easy-drinking, flavorful lager, and the Sunsplash Golden Ale is a light, refreshing beer and is good for those who are intimidated by heavier beers.

Sunday River's menu mainly consists of tasty pub standards, such as chicken wings, nachos, and onion ring starters. You can also grab a bowl of onion soup to whet your appetite for the main course. Sunday River offers salads, sandwiches such as pastrami and burgers, and fish and chips, as well as lobster; the Memphis-style pulled pork sandwich is a standout, which makes sense because where Sunday River really excels is their barbecue. The meat is slow cooked, and is slathered in tasty sauce. You can get brisket, ribs, and barbecue chicken, or you can get a mixed plate of brisket and ribs, along with fresh corn bread and a baked potato.

If you can only make it to Sunday River one day, try to make it on Wednesday, when the brewery offers $1.50 pints from 3 to 7 p.m. And before you leave, pick up a growler of your favorite beer and save it for the next time you go skiing.

### THE BADGER CAFE & PUB

289 Common Rd., Union, ME; (207) 785-3336; BadgerCafeAndPub.com
**Draft Beers:** 6 **Bottled/Canned Beers:** 50

Most beer bars in Maine are heavy on finely brewed beers from the immediate area. The Badger Cafe & Pub, though, has a beer list that is heavy on import beer, often only having one or two Maine beers available. Sometimes you just need a bottle of St. Louis Frambois from Belgium, rather than a blueberry ale.

Where the Badger Cafe really excels is their bottled list. There are about 50 bottled options, and there is not one beer on the list that is anything less than stellar. The list features beer from all of the great beer countries—Belgium, England, Germany, and the US, as well as other countries you might not think of when you think about quality beer, like Italy. Some breweries frequently represented include Orval from Belgium, Harvieston and Meantime from England, Unibroue from Canada, Amaracorde from Italy, Schneider from German, and Dogfish Head Craft Brewers and North Coast Brewing Company from the US.

As far as food, the Badger Cafe is a mix of typical pub fare, plus some dishes that you wouldn't expect to see in a pub. Sandwiches include the homemade falafel burger, chicken cordon bleu, and two sandwiches that are pretty much total opposites—the All Veggie and the Barnyard Burger. The All Veggie is made with grilled eggplant, roasted sweet peppers, onions, and fresh greens with garlic and herb cream cheese, while the Barnyard is made with local beef, pork, and lamb. Other entree options include the buttermilk fried chicken, the turkey tetrazzini, and the pork chop Normandy, which is a thick-cut chop served with sautéed apples and a creamy mustard sauce. If you are in Union on Saturday or Sunday, make sure to stop at the Badger Cafe for brunch.

### EBENEZER'S PUB

44 Allen Rd., Lovell, ME; (207) 925-3200; EbenezersPub.com
**Draft Beers:** 35 **Bottled/Canned Beers:** More than 1,000

If you were just to look at Ebenezer's Pub from the outside—it's in half of an old farmhouse—you may pass it up and go to a different bar. That would be your loss. Once inside, Ebenezer's is beer heaven, a bar that people travel from around the country to visit. It's regarded on many beer review websites as one of the best,

### Ebenezer's Belgian Beer Dinner

In August, Ebenezer's hosts a week-long Belgian Beer Festival, with people camping on site and enjoying some of the best beers in the world. The highlight of the week is the Belgian Beer Dinner, an 8- to 10-course dinner of gourmet food with Belgian influences. Each dish is paired with a rare, or vintage, beer. The dinner costs well over $200, but it's well worth it.

if not the best, craft beer bars in the world. It's a designation Ebenezer's deserves and has earned.

Owned by Chris Lively and his wife Jen, Ebenezer's Pub has one of the most mind-blowing beer lists ever seen. There are rare Belgian ales on draft and in bottles. If an American brewery brews a beer just once and it cannot be found anywhere, there is a good chance Ebenezer's will have it. There are 35 beers on tap and more than 1,000 bottles available. Do you like vintage beers? How about Thomas Hardy ales from England dating back to the late 1960s and early 1970s, or multiple years of Belgium's Cantillon lambics and gueuzes? Although Belgian ales are the specialty, Lively does not skimp on American craft beer. Offerings from breweries such as Rogue Brewery from Oregon and Sierra Nevada Brewing Company from California are also available in bottles.

If Lively is working when you stop in, make sure to try to get a few minutes of his time. There are a lot of beer lovers out there, but he is one of the most passionate people about beer there is. You can hear the passion in his voice when he talks about beers, particularly those he loves. And, if you're lucky, maybe he'll give you a tour of his beer cellar, where some of the rarest of the world's rare beers are stored. It really should be some kind of beer museum; he should charge admission to go down there.

Lovell is a small town, and Ebenezer's is one of the few restaurants, so it gets pretty full during the summer. If you want a seat, you may have to call ahead for reservations, or plan on waiting for a while. Beer is obviously what brings people to Ebenezer's, but the food is nothing to ignore. One of the best meal options is the Caesar salad—order it with lobster on top, and you get nearly a whole lobster. Pizza is always available, and there are plenty of burgers. The star burger is the Chimay Burger, topped with both provolone and Stilton garlic cream cheese, and goes perfectly with a Chimay Red. Entrees include sirloin tips and the Sausage Fest, which includes two foot-long, char-broiled sausages. Fish choices include the Fish 'n Frites and the seafood scampi, which includes lobster, mussels, scallops, and shrimp.

### THE GREAT LOST BEAR

540 Forest Ave., Portland, ME; (207) 772-0300; GreatLostBear.com
**Draft Beers:** 69 **Bottled/Can Beers:** Macros and retro beers only

You can't talk about the Portland beer scene without mentioning the Great Lost Bear, the granddaddy of New England beer bars. Founded in 1979, the brewery jumped on the craft beer revolution of the mid-1980s and has never looked back.

The Great Lost Bear, which has one of the best bars (a giant horse shoe), features 69 beers on tap, mostly beers from the northeast, heavy on local Maine breweries. They're big fans of the Allagash Brewing Company, also located in Portland. They always have at least five rare Allagash beers on tap as part of "Allagash Alley," and several hand-pumped beers, mainly local beers, served on cask. The Great Lost Bear also has a rotating selection of Belgian beers and extreme beers. Draft beer is the star, but they do have some canned and bottled beers, mainly mainstream beers, or retro cans such as Ballantine, Schlitz, and Narragansett. The beers are rotated often, and whenever a Maine brewery releases a new seasonal or a new beer, there's a good chance you'll be able to find it on tap at the Great Lost Bear.

Although they don't host beer dinners, the Great Lost Bear hosts a Brewer's Showcase. The featured brewery's beers will be available at a discounted price, and often the brewers themselves attend the event. The Great Lost Bear also likes to party, and every year they host numerous events. In October they host the Gritty McDuff's Halloween Party and in December they host a "12 Beers of Christmas" event with winter beers available at discounted prices. The first Wednesday of every month is the Shipyard Ale Society night, with all Shipyard pints available for $2.99 each from 5 to 7 p.m. And if you like a game of chance, spin the "Wheel of Destiny." You have to buy whatever beer the wheel ends on.

There's a large menu with mostly typical pub fare, kind of what you'd expect from an old-time bar in Maine. The teriyaki grilled mushrooms and Yippie Thai Yi Yi, fried tortilla chips with Thai dipping sauce, are the stars of the starter portion

### Maine Brew Pub Cup

January is an exciting time for Maine breweries. The Great Lost Bear hosts the Maine Brew Pub Cup, where Maine breweries contend against each other to see which brewery sells the most beer during the competition. The best thing about the event for beer fans: The pints are cheap, at $2.99 each for participating breweries. Each pint of the various breweries is tallied, and at the end of the event, a winner is named.

of the menu. Nachos are offered in nine different styles, from plain cheese to the works. There are plenty of salads and even a vegetarian menu for the non-carnivores.

If in Maine, make sure to stop in at the Great Lost Bear and experience some New England beer history.

### JIMMY THE GREEK'S

215 Saco Ave., Old Orchard Beach, ME; (207) 934-7499; JimmyGreeks.com
**Draft Beers:** 50 **Bottled/Canned Beers:** About 60

Old Orchard Beach is a summer destination that attracts people from all over New England and a large number of Canadians and bikers. During the summer (and any time of year, really), Jimmy the Greek's is the place for beer lovers to go for craft beer. It's a fun little beer bar, and it has a solid draft list and bottle selection that stands out among the competition.

Jimmy's draft list is heavy on Maine beers, such as Allagash, Baxter, D.L. Geary's, Gritty McDuff's, Sebago, and Shipyard. It also typically has beers from other areas' breweries, such as the Abita Brewing Company in Louisiana and Dogfish Head from Delaware. Imports such as Erdinger from Germany and Delirium Tremens from Belgium are often available. The bottled list also has some more popular mainstays, such as Budweiser and Coors. However, if you're looking for a little more craft in your bottled beer list, Jimmy's has offerings such as Monty Python's Holy Grail Ale and Young's Double Chocolate Stout, both from England, as well as beers from North

Coast Brewing Company in California and Victory Brewing Company in Pennsylvania. The bottled list also includes several Belgian ales, such as Kasteel and Chimay. There is also a section for rare beers that includes Samichlaus from Austria and Porterhouse Oyster Stout (made with real oysters) from Ireland. There are also several different meads available, as well as some ciders.

With a name like Jimmy the Greek's, you bet the menu is heavy on delicious Greek food. Appetizers include feta bread sticks, spanakopita, and saganaki. The menu also offers salads, including a strawberry salad that is made up of mixed greens, strawberries, toasted walnuts, goat cheese, and champagne vinaigrette. Main courses include several flat iron steaks, jambalaya, butternut squash ravioli, and fish and chips. Burgers are also available, including the Opa! Burger, which is an 8-ounce patty with tzatziki sauce and zesty spices. Think your stomach is up for a food challenge? Order the King Leonidas Calzone, which is triple the size of a regular calzone. Pick two meats and two veggies and if you can finish it, it's free. If not, you're out about 20 bucks.

It's never a slow night at Jimmy's. Of particular interest to beer lovers, a Brewer's Night is held every Wednesday from 6 to 9 p.m., where patrons get a chance to meet a brewer, drink a lot of good beer, and win some prizes. There's a second Jimmy the Greek's location in South Portland at 115 Philbrook Rd., with a similar menu, similar beer list, and many different daily events, just like the original location.



### NOVARE RES BIER CAFE

4 Canal Plaza, Portland, ME; (207) 761-2437; NovareResBierCafe.com
**Draft Beers:** 25 **Bottled/Canned Beers:** 500

If you're a beer lover and you don't take the time to go to Novare Res Bier Cafe, you've done yourself a huge disservice. It's a destination bar, to be sure. The bar features 25 hand-selected tap lines, as well as two hand-pumps for casks. There is never a bad beer available.

Novare Res brings together the influences of many different pub and beer cultures. It has the traditional dart boards of the English pubs and always has a couple of cask beers available. It has a somewhat German beer garden feel, with its long tables and excellent German-style beers available, and like a Belgian beer cafe, the draft list is heavy on the Belgians, all served in proper glassware and with a food menu developed to go perfectly with what you have in your glass. So what is Novare Res? It's a uniquely American bar, perfect for nearly anybody.

Whoever chooses the draft list knows their beer. American breweries, such as Rogue from Oregon and Victory from Pennsylvania, share space with Monchshof of Germany and De Struisse from Belgium. There are also plenty of local beers from

### Roguepalooza

Every August, Novare Res hosts this event that celebrates the greatness of the Rogue Brewery in Oregon. Rogue brews dozens of excellent beers, and they take over all the taps during Roguepalooza. There you will find some of their rarer or more expensive beers, all available in one location.

Allagash and Marshall Wharf available. The bottled list is incredible, and easy to navigate. The menu is organized by style and by country of origin, and then further by individual styles. For example, IPAs are listed under the American/U.K. Styles, while pilsners are under German Style and lambics are listed under Belgian Style.

On nice days, sit outside in Novare Res's outdoor beer garden. There's nothing better than having a great beer on a wonderful Maine summer day. Well, having some good food with it would probably make it a little better. Novare Res has a small food menu, but it's all tasty. There are plenty of sandwiches, as well as smaller meals, such as fish tacos or the Mediterranean plates. The highlight of the menu is the meat and cheese bar, which has 1-ounce portions of excellent cheeses and meats served with bread and garnishes.

One of the things that sets Novare Res apart from other beer bars is the staff. Every staff member, from bartenders to the wait staff, is a beer geek. They know their beer, and they don't mind helping those having trouble negotiating the beer menu to try to find something perfect for their personal tastes.

## POST ROAD TAVERN

705 Main St., Ogunquit, ME; (207) 641-0640; PostRoadTavern.com
**Draft Beers:** 15 **Bottled/Canned Beers:** About 20

At the time of this printing, Post Road Tavern recently began serving house-brewed Rocky Coast Brewery beers, made with a small onsite brewing system.

By the time you read this, the Post Road Tavern may be a brewpub. The tavern plans to open the Rocky Coast Brewery by the spring of 2012, which will be housed in, and will brew house beers for, the Post Road Tavern.

The Post Road Tavern is definitely a beer destination worth seeking out in Ogunquit, Maine. They offer 15 different beers on draft and have about 20 different bottle choices and a solid food menu. The draft list at the Post Road Tavern features some excellent beers, such as beers from Allagash, Abita Brewing Company from Louisiana, and Rock Art Brewery from Vermont, as well as beers from England like Fuller's London Pride and Old Speckled Hen. The bottled list is mainly mass-produced stuff you can get in nearly every bar in every state, with some exceptions, such as Samuel Adams, Shipyard, and even more Abita.

The appetizers for the Post Road Tavern are some of the best around. It's all pub food, but excellent pub food. The pub crisps are house-made potato chips, smothered in melted cheddar, bacon, lettuce, tomatoes, sour cream, and scallions. The Disco Fries are covered with melted cheese, house-smoked pulled pork, sour cream, scallions, and barbecue sauce. Scotch Eggs, which are boiled eggs wrapped in sausage, coated with panko bread crumbs, and then deep-fried, are an awesome choice (but not for the faint of heart!).

The tavern also offers wings in several styles, including the Chipotle Maple and Moroccan Harissa, which is a north African red sauce made with dried chili peppers, garlic, and spices. Have enough room for a wing challenge? Post Road offers wings in varying degrees of heat from "Atomic" through "Toxic Waste." If you can finish 12 Toxic Waste wings without assistance from others, any drinks, any other food, or any dipping sauces, you will receive a $25 gift certificate, a T-shirt, and a pint glass, all for free. Personally, I would have no shot—plain black pepper is my limitation on the hot stuff.

Burgers, sandwiches, and lobster rolls are available, and Post Road also serves several comfort food options, such as shepherd's pie and chicken pot pie, or you can get a steak and kidney pie. The Post Road Tavern also hosts monthly beer dinners, which are six-course meals, each course paired with a different beer.

### THREE DOLLAR DEWEY'S

241 Commercial St., Portland, ME; (207) 772-3310; ThreeDollarDeweys.com
**Draft Beers:** 36 **Bottled/Canned Beers:** More than 50

Three Dollar Dewey's is a classic Maine pub, originally founded as a haven for those seeking imported beers. Now, while still having several imported beers on draft and in bottles, it has become the best place to buy locally brewed beers.

The draft list itself is impressive. It features many Maine-brewed beers, including Allagash, Bar Harbor, D.L. Geary, and Shipyard. Other beers on tap include offerings from Harpoon Brewery, Long Trail Brewing Company, Samuel Adams, and Victory Brewing Company. There are also a few imported beers on tap, such as Newcastle Brown, Smithwick's, and Stella Artois. Three Dollar Dewey's also frequently keeps at least seven or eight different rotating seasonal beers on draft. The bottled list features a lot of mass-produced beers, but also includes brew from Baxter Brewing Company and Sebago Brewing Company. Old Speckled Hen and Boddingtons represent imported beers in the bottles. Although the beers are no longer $3 like they were more than 30 years ago, Three Dollar Dewey's does have a daily Happy Hour Special with a different $3 draft available every day from 4 to 8 p.m.

Hungry for a good burger? At Three Dollar Dewey's, you can choose from nine different variations. The highlight is the Cajun Burger, made with "Louisiana" spices and gouda cheese. The menu also features several sandwiches, such as the pastrami sandwich, a Philly cheese steak, Dewey's Gyros, and the traditional Maine falafel sandwich. Okay, maybe not traditional, but tasty. The sandwich is made with a grilled chick pea sesame patty rolled in a tortilla with spinach, tomatoes, cucumbers, and feta garlic dressing. Entrees are strictly seafood—fried clams, clam cakes, fish and chips, beer-battered shrimp, and a real Maine classic, the lobster roll.

# Vermont

There is hardly a corner of Vermont that does not have a brewery or a brewpub. From the heavy hitters such as Magic Hat Brewing Company in South Burlington to tiny McNeill's Brewery in Brattleboro, the state has you covered. Heck, if you need a place to stay, some breweries, like Jasper Murdock's Alehouse in Norwich, are located in hotels and inns. There are small hidden jewels hidden throughout the state, such as Lawson's Finest Liquids, which brews some of the hardest-to-find beers in New England, or Hill Farmstead, the hottest brewery in the country.

The state's beer bars are fiercely loyal to Vermont-brewed beers, so you're almost always guaranteed to end up with a good beer when you go out for a night in almost any town. Burlington is also home to one of the best pub crawl locations in New England. All three brewpubs—Three Needs Brewery & Taproom, the Vermont Pub & Brewery, and Zero Gravity Brewpub at American Flatbread—are located within a three-minute walk of each other.

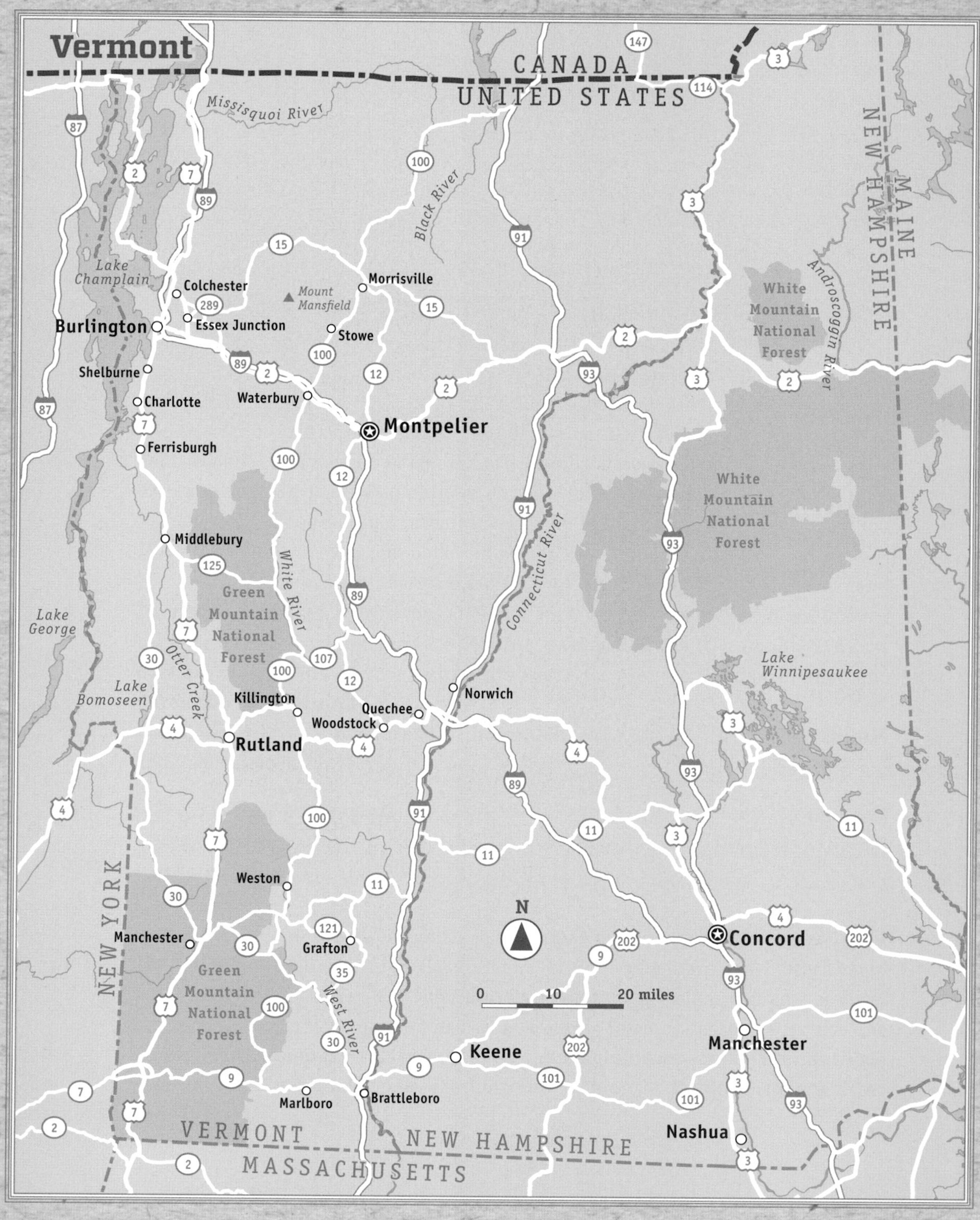

Vermont
CANADA
UNITED STATES
Missisquoi River
Black River
Lake Champlain
Colchester
Essex Junction
Burlington
Shelburne
Charlotte
Ferrisburgh
Morrisville
Mount Mansfield
Stowe
Waterbury
Montpelier
Middlebury
Green Mountain National Forest
White River
Lake George
Otter Creek
Lake Bomoseen
Killington
Quechee
Woodstock
Rutland
Norwich
Connecticut River
White Mountain National Forest
Androscoggin River
Lake Winnipesaukee
MAINE
NEW HAMPSHIRE
NEW YORK
Weston
Manchester
Grafton
West River
Marlboro
Brattleboro
Keene
Concord
Manchester
Nashua
N
0
10
20 miles
VERMONT
NEW HAMPSHIRE
MASSACHUSETTS

## DROP-IN BREWERY

610 Route 7 South, Middlebury, VT; (802)-989-7414; DropinBrewery.com
**Founded:** 2013 **Founders:** Steve Parkes, Chrstine McKeever-Parkes **Brewer:** Steve Parks **Flagship Beer:** Sunshine & Hoppiness **Year-round Beers:** Heart of Lothian, Red Dwarf, Supernova IPA **Seasonals/Special Releases:** River Song, Solar Storm, Dude are you OK?, Lights Out **Taproom hours:** Mon through Sat, 11 a.m. to 7 p.m.; Sun, noon to 5 p.m.

Steve Parkes and his wife Christine purchased the American Brewer's Guild (based in Salisbury, Vermont) in the late 1990s, taking over one of the country's better known brewing schools. Finally, in 2013, the couple realized a long-time dream when they opened up their own brewery, the Drop-in Brewery in Middlebury. The brewery produces only draft beers, and is relatively small. The tasting room is open seven days a week. The brewery is small enough that if you're in the tasting room, you can see every piece of equipment.

Parkes, a native of Scotland, where he attended brewing school, is the head brewer at the Drop-in Brewery. He brews several year-round beers, including his take on a Belgian golden ale, the **Sunshine & Hoppiness.** It is brewed with Belgian yeast, German malts and American hops, a unique take on the style. Other year-round beers include a shout out to his home country with the **Heart of Lothian,** a Scottish ale; the **Red Dwarf,** an amber ale; and the **Supernova IPA,** an ever-changing IPA based on what aroma hops are currently available.

Other rotating beers include the **River Song,** which is a kristal weizen; the **Solar Storm,** a Belgian IPA; **Dude are you OK?,** an IPA; and **Lights Out,** a porter.

The Drop-in Brewing Company is open seven days a week. They offer samples of beer, as well as beer to go in three different sizes—the traditional 64-ounce growler, the 32-ounce mini-growlers they call Squealers, and the mega-growlers they call Grumblers, that hold a whopping 128-ounces of beer.

## FIDDLEHEAD BREWING COMPANY

6305 Shelburne Rd., Shelburne, VT; (802) 399-2994; FiddleheadBrewing.com
**Founded:** 2011 **Founder:** Matthew Cohen **Brewer:** Matthew Cohen **Flagship Beer:** Fiddlehead IPA **Beers:** Hodad Porter, Mad River Lager, Amarillo Getaway, Altbier, Dog Eat Dog, Ruby Claire, Mastermind Double IPA (just an example of dozens of beers, some may be released again, some may not) **Taproom hours:** Sun through Thurs, noon to 8 p.m.; Fri and Sat, noon to 9 p.m.

There aren't many breweries in Vermont founded by a brewer with the pedigree of Matthew Cohen. Cohen was the longtime head brewer at the Magic Hat Brewing Company, the largest craft brewery in Vermont and one of the largest in the whole US. At his own brewery, Cohen has stepped it up, brewing dozens of excellent beers, which are always rotating. Some may only be brewed once, others may be brewed repeatedly.

Fiddlehead's flagship beer is the **Fiddlehead IPA,** a 6.2 percent alcohol by volume IPA. It is brewed with three different hops that provide a burst of citrus as you're drinking it. Despite the amount of hops, the beer has enough malt backbone for balance, making this one of the better New England IPAs you can try. The **Hodad Porter** is a decadent treat. It's a porter brewed with coconut, chocolate, and vanilla and it is pure awesomeness in a glass. It is also the one beer that is packaged for sale in cans. All of the rest of the beers are draft only or by growlers. It is a dessert beer that should be enjoyed by everyone.

Other beers include the **Amarillo Getaway,** an American pale ale brewed and dry-hopped with Amarillo hops; the **Altbier,** a traditional take on the German-style; the **Mad River Lager,** a pilsner brewed as the house beer for the Mad River Glen ski area; and **Ruby Claire,** a red ale dry-hopped with Simcoe.

Fiddlehead has also brewed numerous double IPAs, including the **Mastermind Double IPA, 2nd Fiddle** and a double IPA designed just for the hopheads, the **Dog Eat Dog,** which comes in at a palate blistering 120 international bittering units (the international standard to measure how bitter something is).

Fiddlehead Brewing Company is open seven days a week for free samples, as well as fills of growlers and growlettes (32-ounce version of the 64-ounce growler).

## FOLEY BROTHERS BREWING

79 Stone Mill Dam Rd., Brandon, VT; (802) 247-8102; Facebook.com/FoleyBrothersBrewing

**Founded:** 2012 **Founders:** Patrick Foley, Dan Foley **Brewer:** Dan Foley **Beers:** Native Brown Ale, Native Ginger Wheat, Native IPA, Black Beard's Porter, Red Beard's Ale

**Taproom hours:** Wed through Sat, 11 a.m. to 5 p.m., May through Nov

Foley Brothers Brewing is located on the grounds of the Neshobe River Winery in Brandon, making it a destination for beer lovers and wine lovers alike. Patrick and Dan Foley are part of the Foley family, which owns both facilities. While working on making wine, they also brew the beer, which is available at the brewery/winery, as well as at local farmer markets and in a few select stores.

The brewery uses local ingredients in many of its beers. The **Native Brown Ale** uses maple syrup, which gives the beer a sweeter flavor than even the typically sweet brown ales. There are also some vanilla notes in the beer. The **Native Ginger Wheat** uses fresh ginger in its ingredients, making this a thirst-quenching beer perfect for a hot summer day. The **Native IPA** is a 7 percent alcohol by volume (ABV) west coast IPA full of orange and piney flavors and aroma.

The brewery's two biggest beers are **Black Beard's Porter,** an 8 percent ABV Baltic porter, and **Red Beard's Ale,** a 9 percent ABV red ale. The Baltic Porter has some fairly strong roasted flavors with hints of chocolate. Red Beard's Ale is both bitter and sweet.

Foley Brothers is open seasonal from May through November and typically Wednesday through Saturday, although check its Facebook page for updated times because they sometimes close if participating in events. At the brewery, people can sample the beers and buy growlers and bombers to go.



### FOUR QUARTERS BREWING

150 West Central St., Suite 1, Winooski, VT; FourQuartersBrewing.com
**Founded:** 2014 **Founder:** Brian Eckert **Brewer:** Brian Eckert **Beers:** Opus Dei, Opus Humulus, Chrysalis, Fleu de Lis, Horn of the Moon, Janus 1, Janus 2, Opus Ferum, Le Lion Couchant, Vermont Maple Red Ale, Funky Monkey **Taproom hours:** Fri, 4 to 10 p.m.; Sat, noon to 10 p.m.; Sun, noon to 3 p.m.

Four Quarters Brewing may be small, but they brew an impressive line of creative and unique beers, mostly Belgian influenced and many that use local ingredients. The brewery was founded by Brian Eckert, and started selling its beers in the spring of 2014.

The **Vermont Maple Red Ale** is brewed with 100 percent Vermont maple sap and aged in Sapling Maple Liqueur barrels. **Le Lion Couchant** uses several unique ingredients. Described as an "Alpine Saison," it is brewed with red spruce tips and Labrador tea and aged on alpine bilberries, lingonberries, and mountain cranberries. Four Quarters also experiments brewing the same beer, but with different yeasts. The **Janus 1** is a "rustic farmhouse ale," brewed with Vermont-grown white wine grapes and chamomile and fermented with a house saison yeast. The **Janus 2** is the same beer, except fermented with red wine yeast.

Other beers include the **Opus Dei** (means the works of God) and it's a Belgian paters beer, or table beer. The **Opus Humulus** (means the works of Hops) is also a table beer, but brewed with many more hops. The **Opus Ferum** is the Opus Dei brewed with wild yeast.

The beer that may stand out the most for Four Quarters is the **Funky Monkey.** The Funky Monkey is a wheat beer aged on bananas and dry-hopped with Pacific northwest hops, and fermented with the wild yeast called brettanomyces.

The Four Quarters brewery is open Friday through Sunday. Along with samples and growler fills, visitors can by brewery-related merchandise, as well as local honey, syrup, cheese, and eggs from a nearby farm, to which they provide the spent grains to feed the farm animals.

## 14TH STAR BREWERY

81 Lower Newton St., St. Albans, VT; (802) 393-1459; 14thStarBrewing.com
**Founded:** 2013 **Founder:** Steve Gagner **Brewer:** Steve Gagner **Flagship Beer:** Valor Ale
**Beers:** 1493, Golden Wheat, Harvest Brew, Honey IPA, Double IPA, Maple Breakfast Stout, Maple IPA, Maple Wheat, Roasted Porter, Star Trapp IPA, Year One **Tours:** Thurs and Fri, 5 p.m. to 9 p.m.; Sun 9 a.m. to noon

The 14th Star Brewery is the dream of US Army veteran Steve Gagner. While serving in Afghanistan, he dreamed of opening a brewery in Vermont when he could retire from the Army. In 2013, that dream became a reality, when Gagner opened the 14th Star Brewery in St. Albans.

The brewery's flagship beer, the **Valor Ale,** is a hoppy amber ale. Even more important than the taste, however, is the good deed you'll be doing when you buy the beer. A portion of each 14th Star Valor Ale purchased will be donated to the Purple Hearts Reunited Foundation, which helps reunite veterans with their lost or stolen metals. That's a darn good cause that should inspire anyone to at least give the beer a try.

**Valor Ale**
**Style:** American Amber/Red Ale
**ABV:** 5.4 percent
**Availability:** Year Round
It raises money to help veterans get the medals they earned in service to this country to protect our way of life. Buy the beer and help. It's good, but it tastes better knowing where the money is going to.

Other beers include the **Maple Series** of beers, the **Maple Breakfast Stout, Maple IPA,** and **Maple Wheat.** All three of these beers are brewed with locally produced maple. Additional beers include the **1493,** an American pale Ale; the **Double IPA,** which is on the lower end of the style at 7.8 percent alcohol by volume (ABV); and the **Year One,** an anniversary stout that comes in at 8.5 percent ABV.

The 14th Star Brewery hosts tours and free tastings on Thursday and Friday, as well as Sunday. Along with the samples and the tours, people can buy growlers and bombers of the beers, as well as 14th Star shirts, glasses, and other swag.

### HILL FARMSTEAD BREWERY

403 Hill Rd., Greensboro Bend, VT; (802) 533-7450; HillFarmstead.com
**Founded:** 2010 **Founder:** Shaun E. Hill **Brewer:** Shaun E. Hill **Flagship Beer:** Edward
**Seasonals/Special Releases:** Ancestor Series, Single Hop Series, Collaboration Series Grassroots Brewing beer **Tours:** None

Brewer Shaun E. Hill may be the most prolific brewer in New England. Since the first brew day in March 2010, Hill Farmstead has brewed about 50 different beers. Some breweries that have been around for decades have not come close to that number. Hill's love of hops shines through in most of his beers. Many of his beers are 85 international bittering units (the unit used to measure how bitter a beer is; double IPAs are usually in the seventies) or higher. He proves brewing hoppy beers is not the exclusive domain of west coast breweries.

Most of Hill Farmstead's beers can be called special releases. Almost none are brewed more than once or twice a year, except for **Edward,** an IPA. Edward is named for Hill's grandfather, on whose land the brewery now resides. Many of the beers are named for Hill's ancestors. **Abner,** named for Hill's great grandfather, is a 170 IBU, double IPA. That level of IBUs is unheard of, and almost insane. At least that's what it looks like, until you see the IBUs for **Ephraim,** named for Hill's great-great grandfather. The beer is listed at 280 IBUs. It would be impossible for a human to detect that level of bitterness. Other beers named for ancestors include **Anna** (saison), **Earl** (stout), **Edith** (wheat beer), and **Clara** (a traditional ale). Hill Farmstead also brews several single-hop IPAs—they include the **Citra IPA, Galaxy IPA, Nelson Sauvin IPA,** and **Pacifica IPA.**

Not a hophead? Hill Farmstead does brew beers that are not hop monsters. Some of those include **Civil Disobedience** (saison), **Genealogy** (imperial stout),

**Iced Coffee Stout (Iced Earl)**
**Style:** Imperial Stout
**ABV:** 15 percent
**Availability:** Rotating

The Iced Coffee Stout is one of the most impressive beers I have ever tried. It might be packing 15 percent alcohol by volume, but you'd never know it. There is no boozy taste, which you'd get with similar higher-alcohol offerings, and faithful to its name, it tastes exactly like an iced coffee. A stunning beer.

**Phenomena** (saison), and **Twilight of the Idols** (winter porter brewed with coffee and cinnamon and aged on vanilla beans). Hill Farmstead also has done several collaboration beers, including a series of beers with Danish brewer Anders Kissmeyer. The Kissmeyer collaboration beer is called **Fear and Trembling** and it is a Baltic porter. There are three versions, all aged in different barrels—bourbon barrels, French oak barrels, and a Cabernet and bourbon barrel blend. The beer is the same, but the three different barrels add different flavors. Barrel-aging beer is not uncommon at Hill Farmstead. Several of the beers are barrel-aged, mostly in French oak barrels. Some of the beers are released in two versions, barrel-aged and non-barrel-aged.

Hill Farmstead also brews special release beers under the **Grassroots Brewing** labels. These are usually collaborations brewed once with a well-respected brewer from around the world.

Tours are not available at the brewery, but Hill Farmstead does have a tasting room and retail showroom that is open Wednesday through Saturday from noon to 5 p.m. You can try the beers, including limited releases, that are available in bottles and growlers.



## KINGDOM BREWING

1784 VT 105, Newport, VT; (802) 334-7096; KingdomBrewingVT.com

**Founded:** 2012 **Founders:** Brian and Jenn Cook **Brewer:** Jenn Cook **Flagship Beer:** Round Barn Red, **Year-round Beers:** Bear Mountain Blackberry Chocolate Milk Stout, Clyde River Brown, Out-of-Bounds, the 19th Hole, unnamed session beer **Seasonals/Special Releases:** Cha Cha, unnamed blueberry amber, Fall Harvest Spice **Taproom hours:** Thurs through Sat, 3:30 to 6:30 p.m.

Kingdom Brewing is the northern most brewery in all of Vermont. Because of that, many people may not know about the brewery's own ecosystem that the husband and wife team of Brian and Jenn Cook created there. Kingdom Brewing sits on a farm. There, the Cooks have a large greenhouse where they grow fruits, vegetables, and hops that they use in their beer.

After the beer is brewed, they then feed the spent hops to their herd of Black Angus cow (as well as their chickens). They then collect the manure and use it as fertilizer to grow the fruits, vegetables, and hops they use. It's a circle that keeps Kingdom Brewing going.

Kingdom Brewing's flagship beer is the **Round Barn Red,** named for the oldest barn in Vermont. It's a hoppier than normal brown ale. The **Bear Mountain Blackberry Chocolate Milk Stout** is a milk stout made with Kingdom's greenhouse-grown blackberries, as well as chocolate. The **Out-of-Bounds** is an 8.3 percent alcohol by volume (ABV) double IPA. It originally started as a regular IPA, but fans called for bigger and hoppier, so Kingdom obliged. Kingdom also brews two versions of the **Clyde River Brown**—one is a traditional brown ale while the other is the same beer with a yeast to make it a sour brown.

They also brew a low-alcohol session beer that comes in at 3.1 percent ABV. It was originally named Skinny Bitch, but the name has been retired and the beer has not returned. They also brew a summer version of the beer that is made with blueberries. Another summer beer is the **Cha Cha,** which is the same beer as the **19th Hole** (a hoppy amber ale), but brewed with lemons or limes. The brewery also brews the **Fall Harvest Spice,** which tastes like a liquid apple pie.

Although the brewery does not offer regular tours, the tasting room is set up so that visitors can see the whole brewery. Along with samples of the beer, people can buy growlers and bottles of the available beers. Chicken eggs from the on-site farm are also available, as well as shirts and glasses and the occasional half or quarter of a farm-grown cow (so bring several coolers).

### LAWSON'S FINEST LIQUIDS

Warren, VT (not open to the public); (802) 272-8436; LawsonsFinest.com
**Founded:** 2008 **Founder:** Sean Lawson **Brewer:** Sean Lawson **Flagship Beer:** None **Year-round Beers:** None **Seasonals/Special Releases:** More than 40 beers; for example, Big Hapi, Chinnoker'd IPA, Crooked Cabin Ale, Fayston Maple Imperial Stout, Gonzie, Hopzilla Double IPA, Farmhouse Ale, Maple Nipple Ale, Papelblonde Ale, Weiss-K **Tours:** None

The beers from Lawson's Finest Liquids may be the most sought after in all of New England, and they may be the hardest to find. This small artisan brewery, "located high in the hills," only sells its beers in a few stores. Owner Sean Lawson delivers a different beer once a week, on Friday. Just one type of beer.

You can drink Lawson's Finest Liquids beers on draft at the Common Man and the Pitcher Inn in Warren, American Flatbread in Waitsfield, Mad River Glen in Fayston, and the Village Porch in Rochester. The fun thing is, you'll never know what beer is available. Lawson delivers a different beer to each place every week. So one week you may get the **Maple Nipple Ale** at Mad River Glen, while American Flatbread may have the **Red Spruce Bitter.**

But the real question is: Is the beer worth it? Most definitely. Lawson may brew beer on a small scale, but it is phenomenal. Many of his beers, such as the Maple Nipple Ale, feature local maple syrup. Also brewed with maple are the **Fayston Maple Imperial Stout** and the **Maple Tripple.** Lawson's also brews several IPAs, including the **Chinnoker'd IPA, Big Happi India Black IPA, Hopzilla Double IPA,**

## Beer Lover's Pick

**Gonzie**
**Style:** Pale Ale
**ABV:** 4 percent
**Availability:** Rotating
It's easy to brew a hoppy beer with a lot of alcohol in it: Load up on the malt, which increases the alcohol and balances out the bitterness of the hops. What isn't easy is making a balanced low-alcohol beer packed with hops, especially one as tasty as Gonzie. Lawson worked his magic and hopped the Gonzie like a higher-alcohol brew, but found a way to maintain the balance with a lower ABV for the style.

and the **Fistful-o-Hop IPA.** Other beers include the **Crooked Cabin Ale** (English brown ale), **Equinox Extra XPA** (a big, high-alcohol pale ale), **Weiss-K** (German-style wheat beer), **292 Ale** (a "Hoptoberfest" Ale), and the **Permagin Rye Pale Ale** (a pale ale brewed with rye malt).

Keeping his brewery so small allows Lawson to spend as much time as he feels he needs on each beer, and the quality shows. Not one of the beers is anything less than stellar. Want a tour of Lawson's Finest Liquids? Not going to happen. Due to the limited space and hours, Lawson does not open his brewery to tours or tastings and there is no store. Instead, make the trek to the Warren Store, buy the beer there, and enjoy it in the privacy of your own home.

### LONG TRAIL BREWING COMPANY

5520 US 4, Bridgewater Corners, VT; (802) 672-5011; Longtrail.com
**Founded:** 1989 **Founder:** Andy Pherson **Brewer:** David Hartmann **Flagship Beer:** Long Trail Ale **Year-round Beers:** Blackbeary Wheat, Double Bag Ale, Pale Ale, Traditional IPA, Limbo Double IPA **Seasonals/Special Releases:** Belgian White Ale, Harvest Ale, Hibernator, Pollinator, Brewmaster Series **Tours:** Daily, 10 a.m. to 7 p.m.

The Long Trail Brewing Company is about more than just brewing good beer; they are about brewing good beer while helping the environment. Long Trail uses thermal energy to use less power at its Bridgewater Corners brewery. It also has cut down on water use, only using two gallons of water to brew one gallon of beer, down from the six gallons of water to one gallon of beer that is the industry standard. They also use a system that turns cow waste into methane gas, which is used to help power the brewery; in turn, they donate the nearly eight tons of spent mash they produce every day to local dairy farms to feed the cows.

Most important—at least for beer lovers—Long Trail manages to do all this without sacrificing the taste of their beers. Long Trail has been around for more than 20 years, and they continue to brew several fantastic beers. The year-round lineup has a good mix of beers you typically do not see as year-round beers. The **Long Trail Ale** is a German-style altbier, a light-tasting brown ale. The **Double Bag Ale** is basically an imperial version of the Long Trail Ale, and is the strongest of the year-round beers at more than 7 percent alcohol by volume. The **Traditional IPA** and **Pale Ale** are typical of their styles, and are both very solid beers, while the **Blackbeary Wheat** is a light, refreshing beer, perfect for a hot summer day.

Long Trail also brews four seasonals. The **Pollinator** is a slightly hoppy pale ale, and is available during the spring. The **Belgian White Ale** is a traditional Belgian

## Beer Lover's Pick

**Long Trail Ale**
**Style:** Altbier
**ABV:** 4.6 percent
**Availability:** Year-Round
Sure this is the brewery's flagship beer, and one of its oldest, but it is still worth trying. Not enough authentic German alts make it to this side of the Atlantic, so when you can find a well-made alt, take advantage. The Long Trail Ale is brownish in color, and there is a mild fruitiness to it, as well as a yeasty flavor. It is a smooth drinking beer. Perfect whenever you want to drink it.

## Harpoon Brewery in Vermont

The Harpoon Brewery is one of the oldest breweries in New England, and a Boston classic. But, they also have a brewery in Windsor, Vermont. In 2000, the brewery purchased the former Catamount Brewing Company and moved some of its production to the Green Mountain State.

Today, the Harpoon Brewery brews beer in the large facility, including much of its Leviathan Series, which are Harpoon's high-octane beers. The Windsor facility is also home to an on-site pub. The pub features a dozen fresh Harpoon beers on tap—year-round, seasonals, Leviathan, and the 100-Barrel Series.

The pub also has seats overlooking the brewery, so as you are enjoying your burger, wrap, panini, or appetizers, you can watch the beer you will soon be drinking being brewed and bottled. They also host tours and tastings, and there is a large brewery store.



witbier and comes out during the summer. The **Harvest Ale** is a wonderful brown ale, and a welcome non-pumpkin fall seasonal. The **Hibernator** is a nice and malty Scotch ale and comes out when fall turns to winter. Long Trail also has the **Brewmaster series,** which features stronger beers, available in 22-ounce bombers instead of the usual 12-ounce bottles. The Brewmaster Series includes the **Centennial Red,** the **Double IPA,** and the **Imperial Porter.** It also includes the wonderful **Coffee Stout,** which tastes exactly like a well-brewed cup of joe.

Long Trail also has a pub on-site at the brewery and it features mainly pub food like chicken fingers, hot dogs, burgers, and other sandwiches. Several of the dishes do use beer, such as the Long Trail Cheddar Ale Soup and the Double Bag Chili. They also use ingredients from several local farms, and serve Long Trail Tap Water, which was named Vermont's Best Drinking Water by the Green Mountain Water Environment Association.

### LOST NATION BREWING

254 Wilkins St., Morristown, VT; (802) 851-8041; LostNationBrewing.com
**Founded:** 2013 **Founders:** Allen Van Anda, James Griffith **Brewer:** Allen Van Anda, James Griffith **Flagship Beer:** None **Year-round Beers:** Gose, Petite Ardennes, Pitch Black, Rustic Ale, Saison Lamoille, Vermont Pilsner **Seasonals/Special Releases:** Oktoberfest **Taproom hours:** open Wed through Sun, 11:30 a.m. to 9 p.m.

Lost Nation Brewing is rare among craft brewers—of all the beers they brew they don't brew one IPA, which is the most popular style of craft beer there is. Instead, they brew styles that may not be as popular or well-known, but they do them well, providing a standout lineup of beers at their Morristown taproom.

Lost Nation brews six year-round beers. The **Gose** is a German-style of beer that is just starting to get some attention in the US. It is brewed with salt and coriander. This wheat beer is also light, coming in at 4.5 percent alcohol by volume (ABV). The **Rustic Ale** may be Lost Nation's hoppiest beer, but it's not close to an IPA. The Rustic Ale is a hoppy red ale. The **Pitch Black** is a creamy black ale with hints of smoke and roastiness. The **Vermont Pilsner** is a traditional version of the style, clean, easy drinking, slightly bready with grassy hop flavors. The other two year-round beers are Belgian-influenced. The first is the **Petite Ardennes,** a 4.2 percent ABV light Belgian golden ale. The **Saison Lamoille** is a 5.9 percent ABV saison, filled with slightly spicy notes and a little barnyard funk. Lost Nation's only seasonal is a German-style **Oktoberfest.**

Unlike many taprooms, Lost Nation offers food. They have a small rotating menu that will feature meat and cheese plates, some soups and appetizers, and a few sandwiches. Lost Nation's taproom is open Wednesday through Sunday. Along with pints of beer and food, people can buy growlers to go, as well as T-shirts and other Lost Nation items.

## MAGIC HAT BREWING COMPANY

5 Bartlett Bay Rd., South Burlington, VT; (802) 658-2739; MagicHat.net
**Founded:** 1993 **Founder:** Alan Newman **Brewer:** Justin McCarthy **Flagship Beer:** #9
**Year-round Beers:** Circus Boy, Single Chair **Seasonal/Special Releases:** Hex, Howl, Vinyl, Wacko, IPA on Tour, Flavor Flashbacks, Heart of Darkness **Tours:** Tues through Wed, 3 and 4 p.m.; Thurs through Fri, 2, 3, 4, and 5 p.m.; Sat, 1, 2, 3, 4, and 5 p.m.; Sun, 2 and 3 p.m.

It's safe to say the Magic Hat Brewing Company is a little different than most other breweries. Founded by Alan Newman, the brewery reflects his personality of peace and love, and oddness. After all, his title is Conductor of Cosmic Symphonies. Whatever the title means, Magic Hat has grown to become one of the largest craft breweries in the country, and their flagship beer, **#9,** can be found in many bars that do not cater to craft beer lovers.

The #9, described as a "Not Quite Pale Ale" and flavored with apricots, is also available in every one of the many seasonal mixed 12-packs Magic Hat releases throughout the year. Other year-round beers are the **Circus Boy,** which is a typical American wheat beer, and **Single Chair,** a golden ale that is available year-round, only in Vermont. Magic Hat also brews several seasonals. **Vinyl,** an easy-drinking, refreshing amber lager, is the beer of choice for the spring. The summer seasonal is **Wacko,** which has one of the most wacko beer ingredients ever—beets. The beer pours slightly red, and, shockingly, the beets actually work in the beer. Fall brings you Magic Hat's interpretation of an Oktoberfest-style beer, **Hex.** It is not a typical Oktoberfest since it is brewed with ale yeast, but it is still a nice fall beer. **Howl,** the fall seasonal, is a wonderful black lager.

Magic Hat has an interesting way of releasing their four IPAs. Instead of just having them all out at once, they release one every season as part of the **IPA on Tour series. Demo,** a black IPA, comes out in the spring; **Blind Faith,** an English-style IPA, is the summer offering; **hI.P.A.,** a straightforward American IPA, is released in the fall; and the winter IPA is **Encore,** which is more of a California west coast–style IPA. Throughout the year, Magic Hat also has **Flavor Flashbacks,** which are special releases of two of their early beers. **Humble Patience,** an Irish red ale and the brewery's first beer, is available from August 1 through October 15. **Ravell,** an English-style porter, takes over from there and remains on the shelves through January. **Heart of Darkness,** a nice oatmeal stout, is released only occasionally.



## Beer Lover's Pick

**Heart of Darkness**
**Style:** Oatmeal Stout
**ABV:** 5.7 percent
**Availability:** Winter Seasonal

Heart of Darrkness is Magic Hat's winter seasonal and it is a wonderfully done oatmeal stout. In the earlier days of craft brewing, it was a sought out beer, and it's still tasty. It is smooth, creamy, has some roasted, coffee bitterness, with hints of chocolate and vanilla. It's a perfect beer for a cold winter night.

There are brewery tours daily, either guided or unguided. Growler fills are also available in the brewery store that features a 30-tap growler bar. The bar features year-round beers, seasonals, and sometimes rare, brewery only, or experimental beers. Magic Hat also hosts several events throughout the year, including small concerts and album release parties for new bands. They also host the largest northeast Mardi Gras celebration.

### NORTHSHIRE BREWERY

108 County St., Bennington, VT; (802) 681-0201; NorthshireBrewery.com
**Founded:** 2009 **Founders:** Chris Mayne, Earl McGoff **Brewer:** Chris Mayne **Flagship Beer:** Equinox Pilsner **Year-round Beers:** Battenkill Ale, Chocolate Stout **Seasonals/Special Releases:** Summer Lager **Tours:** Tues through Thurs, 3 to 6 p.m.; Sat, 11 a.m. to 1 p.m.

The Northshire Brewery is the brainchild of homebrewers Chris Mayne and Earl McGoff, who made the successful transition from brewing small batches of homebrew to brewing professionally. Their brewery may be small, but they certainly put out a quality product in their three year-round beers and their lone seasonal offering.

**Equinox Pilsner**
**Style:** Czech Pilsner
**ABV:** 4.2 percent
**Availability:** Year-Round
Sometimes fizzy, yellow beers are looked down upon in the craft beer world. The Equinox Pilsner is one of those beers that proves beer snobs wrong. This is a full-flavored, low-alcohol, Czech-style pilsner. The malts provide a malty and bready flavor, while the hops are grassy and floral. This is an easy-drinking, quality beer even for the most discerning of beer lovers.

The **Equinox Pilsner,** Northshire's flagship beer, is a classic Czech-style pilsner. It is only 4.2 percent alcohol by volume (ABV), but it packs tons of flavor. It's a fizzy yellow beer with a classic bready/yeasty taste and a nice touch of grassy hops. The **Battenkill Ale,** named for a local river, is a really solid amber ale, although darker than some amber ales. It is also a little hoppier than expected, with grassy hops and a sweet malt balance. The beer has slight diacetyl tastes, giving it hints of butter in the flavor. The body is a little thin, but not offensively so. The **Chocolate Stout** is Northshire's biggest beer at a modest 6 percent ABV. It is nice and full-bodied, with a full and creamy head. Flavorwise, the chocolate is not overpowering. Instead, the roasted flavors come out first, and the chocolate is more on the finish, which is a nice change from all the in-your-face chocolate stouts that are on the market today. Northshire also brews one seasonal, a light lager called **Summer Lager.** The Summer Lager is light beer with a bready aroma, but has a nice biscuity flavor with just a hint of hops—a perfect beer to enjoy at a cookout. It is similar to the Equinox Pilsner, but with less hops.

Northshire also hosts tours and tastings during the week. The tours of the brewery, led by one of the two owners, are free. Tastings are $3 each, but you get to keep the Northshire sample pint glass. Northshire also brews several house beers for the Mount Snow ski area, so skiers have something good to warm up with after a day on the slopes.



### OTTER CREEK BREWING/WOLAVER'S

793 Exchange St., Middlebury, VT; (802) 388-0727; OtterCreekBrewing.com
**Founded:** 1991 **Founder:** Lawrence Miller **Brewer:** Mike Gerhart **Flagship Beer:** Copper Ale **Year-round Beers:** Otter Creek: Black IPA, Stovepipe Porter. Wolaver's: Brown Ale, IPA, Oatmeal Stout **Seasonal/Special Releases:** Otter Creek: Otter Summer, Oktoberfest, Winter Red Ale, the Shed Mountain Ale, the Shed IPA. Wolaver's: Alta Gracia Porter, Pumpkin Ale, Wildflower Wheat **Tours:** Self-guided tours, daily, 11 a.m. to 6 p.m.

Otter Creek Brewing and Wolaver's Brewing Company are two breweries in one location in Middlebury, Vermont. Wolaver's purchased Otter Creek in 2002, and kept the Otter Creek line of beers separate from their own. That means there are two separate and distict lines of beer.

The Otter Creek Brewing Company is one of the most well-known names in Vermont brewing. They brew three year-round beers, as well as three seasonals. The **Otter Creek Copper Ale** is a German-style alt, a great choice for a flagship beer. The beer is grainy and has some caramel flavors. It is an easy-drinking beer, yet still has a full body. The **Stovepipe Porter** is an excellent porter and smells of burnt molasses,

## Beer Lover's Pick

**Otter Creek Black IPA**
**Style:** Black IPA
**ABV:** 6 percent
**Availability:** Year-Round
I held a blind tasting with a dozen of the best black IPAs brewed in the US with several other beer lovers. The Otter Creek Black IPA won easily. This is a phenomenal beer. It has the hoppiness of a good, solid IPA, yet has the chocolate and roasted malts of a darker beer. The flavors all meld together into near perfection.

with some sweet aromas wafting up from the glass. This might be a dark beer, but it drinks very light. The **Otter Creek Black IPA** originally started as a seasonal, but it became so popular, they made it a year-round offering. That was the smart choice, considering it is an excellent beer. Seasonals include the **Otter Summer,** which is a light, refreshing wheat beer. The **Oktoberfest** is a non-traditional Oktoberfest beer, mainly because it is an ale instead of a lager, while the **Winter Red Ale** is a hoppy red ale. Otter Creek also purchased the iconic Shed Brewery lineup of beers in 2011 when the brewpub closed. They brew the popular **Shed Mountain Ale** and **Shed IPA.**

Wolaver's brews nothing but organic beers. Their **Brown Ale, IPA,** and **Oatmeal Stout** are all really well-done beers. The brown is nutty and malty, while the IPA is a solid, hoppy beer that does not overwhelm the palate. The Oatmeal Stout is suitably creamy and full-bodied. Wolaver's also brews three seasonals. The **Alta Gracia Porter** is a fantastic coffee beer with huge black coffee flavors, a perfect pick-me-up type of brew. The **Pumpkin Ale** is brewed with locally grown and organic pumpkins, and the **Wildflower Wheat** is a nicely done wheat ale brewed with honey, which provides sweetness and smoothness, resulting in a light, refreshing beer.

Otter Creek offers daily self-guided tours, and has a tasting room where you can sample many of the Otter Creek, Wolaver's, and the Shed's beers.

## ROCK ART BREWERY

632 Laporte Rd., Morrisville, VT; (802) 888-9400; RockArtBrewery.com
**Founded:** 1997 **Founders:** Matt and Renee Nadeau **Brewer:** Matt Nadeau **Flagship Beer:** Whitetail Ale **Year-round Beers:** American Red Ale, Black Moon, IPA, Magnumus Ete Tomahawkus, Ridge Runner, Stock Ale, The Vermonster **Seasonals/Special Releases:** Belgian IPA, Belvidere Big IPA, Jasmine Pale Ale, IPA (II), Pumpkin Imperial Spruce Stout, Double Porter, Hell's Bock, Stump Jumper, Midnight Madness Smoked Porter, Mountain Holidays in Vermont, American-Belgo Style IPA, Infusco, Golden Tripple, The Riddler, Sunny and 75 **Tours:** Fri through Sat, 2 and 4 p.m.

In 2009, Rock Art Brewery played David to Monster Energy Drink's Goliath, when Monster tried to force Rock Art to rename one of its beers—the **Vermonster.** However, like David, Rock Art prevailed, and Vermonster remains on liquor store shelves unchanged today.

Besides its name, the best thing about Vermonster, a big, hoppy barleywine, is that it is an excellent beer. That is not unusual for the Rock Art Brewery, which is one of the best breweries in Vermont and all of New England. They have a large lineup of year-round, seasonal, and specialty beers that even the most hard-core beer fan should be able to enjoy. The **Whitetail Ale,** the brewery's flagship, is a fantastic American pale ale. The **American Red Ale** and the **IPA** are both spot on for their respective styles.

Rock Art is one of the better brewers of hoppy beers in New England. Along with the Vermonster, they also brew a huge black IPA, the **Black Moon,** which is extremely hoppy. The summer seasonal, the **Belvidere Big IPA,** and the winter seasonal, **IPA (II),** are both beers designed for the hop lovers. They also brew a fantastic Belgian-style IPA as part of their Belgian series of beer, the **American-Belgo Style IPA.**

But Rock Art is about more than just the hops. The **Ridge Runner** is a fantastic barleywine, almost on the mild side at only 7 percent alcohol by volume. They also brew two porters as seasonals, the **Double Porter** and the **Midnight Madness Smoked Porter.** The **Mountain Holidays in Vermont** is one of the best bocks brewed anywhere. It is an exquisite beer. Rock Art also brews one of the most interesting pumpkin beers on the market in the **Pumpkin Imperial Spruce Stout.** It is a pumpkin stout, of which there are few, and it is also an imperial stout, of which there are even fewer. Some people may not like the spruce flavor, but most beer lovers should enjoy it. Belgian beer fans rejoice—Rock Art also produces a **Belgian series.** Along with **Belgian IPA,** there is **Infusco** (a dream for those who like the flavor of anise), **Golden Tripple** (a Belgian triple), **The Riddler** (Belgian dubbel), and **Sunny and 75** (Belgian-style witbier).

## Beer Lover's Pick

**Vermonster**
**Style:** Barleywine
**ABV:** 10 percent
**Availability:** Year-round

This was not an easy beer to pick. There are at least five beers that could have been chosen for this spot, but hey, Vermonster won out because it was part of a national news story. But most important, it is a fantastically hoppy barleywine. This is an American barleywine all the way, with 100 IBUs. But, it is also more balanced than you would think. The sweet malt backbone is needed to balance out this monster of a beer, and it works to great effect.

Rock Art hosts tours on Friday and Saturday. They also host daily tastings at the brewery, which cost $3 (the cost of the sample glass you get to keep), and sell beer to go, from singles to cases to kegs, as well as other Rock Art gear.

### STONE CORRAL BREWERY

830 Taft Rd., Huntington, VT; (802) 434-6318; StoneCorral.com
**Founded:** 2013 **Founder:** Bret and Melissa Hamilton **Brewer:** Brett Hamilton **Beers:** Bourbon Mash Amber Ale, Palomino Pale, Latigo, Black Beer, Stone Corral Beer, XX Chocolate Maple Porter, Butternut Brown, Dark Wheat, Wild Red, Stout **Taproom hours:** hours vary, call ahead

Vermont is known as one of the top destination for hoppy IPAs in the US, but the Stone Corral Brewery in Huntington strives more toward balanced and malty beers. Founded by long-time homebrewer Bret Hamilton and his horse-farm-running wife Melissa Hamilton, the Stone Corral Brewery brews numerous beers throughout the year, available in 22-ounce bottles in their taproom.

While several breweries age beers in bourbon barrels, Stone Corral has created a beer that uses the typical ingredients of bourbon called the **Bourbon Mash Amber Ale.** It is made with corn, rye, and barley malt, but instead of being distilled, it is fermented and hopped. This malt forward, spicy beer is a sturdy 7 percent alcohol by volume (ABV). The **Stone Corral Beer** is a pleasant 5 percent ABV blonde ale, while the **Palomino Pale,** its hoppier big brother, comes in at 6.4 percent ABV. The **Black Beer,** which is a cross between a German black ale and a porter, is the brewery's most popular beer, while the **Latigo** is a 6.6 percent Scottish-inspired malt bomb of a red ale. The **Butternut Brown** is a brown ale brewed with locally grown butternut squash, while the **Chocolate Maple Porter** uses local maple and Guatemalan cacao nuts purchased from a local chocolate makers. The other beers are the **Dark Wheat,** which is a traditional German dunkelweisse is flavors of clove and banana; the **Wild Red,** which is a funky Belgian red, and the **Stout,** which is a traditional Irish dry stout.

The brewery's taproom hours change constantly, so it's best to call before heading there.



## SWITCHBACK BREWING COMPANY

160 Flynn Ave., Burlington, VT; (802) 651-4114; Facebook.com/SwitchbackBrewingCompany
**Founded:** 2002 **Founders:** Bill Cherry, Ash Roesch **Brewer:** Ash Roesch **Flagship Beer:** Switchback Ale **Seasonals/Special Releases:** Roasted Red Ale, Slow-Fermented Brown Ale, Switchback Porter **Tours:** Sat, 1 and 2 p.m.; free

Ask someone in Burlington what beer you should try while you are in town, and they are likely to say you have to try a Switchback Ale. Locals love their hometown brewery because Switchback brews quality, tasty, easy-drinking beers. You won't find wild and crazy experimentation going on here, but you will find finely crafted beers.

The **Switchback Ale** is the brewery's flagship beer, and the only beer Switchback brewed for the first five years of its existence. It really does not fit into any particular style—the closest may be an amber or red ale. This beer is brewed with five different malts and yeast the brewery cultivates itself, which creates some unique fruity flavors. The **Roasted Red Ale** is a wonderfully brewed red ale. A combination of caramel and roasted malts with a bigger-than-expected hop kick all comes together to form this excellent beer. It also ends with a taste of chocolate, which is a nice surprise for the style. The **Switchback Porter** is not a traditional English-style porter. The porter is brewed with several different types of malts, as well as flaked barley, which gives the beer a deeper malt presence. But this beer is not all about the malts. Switchback

## Beer Lover's Pick

**Switchback Ale**
**Style:** Pale Ale
**ABV:** 5 percent
**Availability:** Year-Round
The original is still the best. This unique tasting beer brewed with a house yeast is just so drinkable that you will want more than one or two. It is flavorful, easy-drinking, and just plain good. The hops are nice and mild, which allows the malt to come through. This is an amazingly balanced beer, which is exactly what you want while spending a night at the bar.

uses Simcoe hops, a very American hop not found in many British beers, which adds both aroma and bitter flavors, creating a tasty porter. The final beer, introduced in 2010, is the **Slow-Fermented Brown Ale.** Like the porter, this is not a traditional brown ale. Switchback ferments the beer at a much colder temperature than most ales, allowing the yeast to ferment slower, creating a brown ale that has the clean-drinking taste of a lager, but retains the creaminess of a good brown ale.

All of Switchback's beers are available only on draft. Do not get concerned if you get a pint and the beer is cloudy, because all of Switchback beers are unfiltered. Switchback Brewing Company offers tours on Saturday at 1 and 2 p.m. The tours are free, but they do recommend calling ahead to reserve a spot. Participants will get a chance to sample all the beer that is currently available. But do not expect to get beer to go. Switchback does not offer growlers because they feel the beer loses its quality when transferred from keg to growler.

### TROUT RIVER BREWING COMPANY

645 Broad St., Lyndonville, VT; (802) 626-9396; TroutRiverBrewing.com
**Founded:** 1996 **Founders:** Dan and Laura Gates **Brewer:** Dan Gates **Flagship Beer:** Rainbow Red Ale **Year-round Beers:** Chocolate Oatmeal Stout, Hoppin' Mad Trout, Scottish Ale **Seasonals/Special Releases:** Boneyard Barley Wine, Caramel Porter, Dominator Doppelbock, Knight Slayer **Tours:** On-site pub open Fri and Sat, 4 to 9 p.m.

Dan and Laura Gates opened their small brewery in 1996 with the goal of providing good, fresh, and local beer to their customers. All these years later, Trout River Brewing Company is still cranking out those fresh beers, although you now can find them in states other than Vermont.

The brewery only brews four year-round beers. With the exception of one (Chocolate Oatmeal Stout), they are all traditional British styles of beer. The **Rainbow Red Ale,** named for the tastiest of all trouts, is a nicely done red ale. It is slightly toasty, very malty, and full-bodied. The **Hoppin' Mad Trout** is a light pale ale that comes in at 4.7 percent alcohol by volume (ABV). This is not a west coast pale ale with a dominant hop flavor, but it is a well-balanced pale ale, where the hops actually come on more in the finish. The **Scottish Ale** is the strongest of the year-round beers at 5.9 percent ABV. As the style should be, this is a malt dominated beer. There is even a hint of peat smokiness, which adds a little something extra to this beer. The **Chocolate Oatmeal Stout** is on the light side for a stout, but this does not take away from the flavor.

**Chocolate Oatmeal Stout**
**Style:** Oatmeal Stout
**ABV:** 4.9 percent
**Availability:** Year-round

Oatmeal stouts are often creamy, have hints of chocolate and coffee from roasted malt, and are on the low end of the ABV spectrum for stouts. Trout River's Chocolate Oatmeal Stout ratchets up the chocolate flavors by actually adding real chocolate. It is one of the lighter stouts you will ever have, but the chocolate creaminess will more than make up for the lack of body. It is by far the best beer currently being brewed by Trout River.

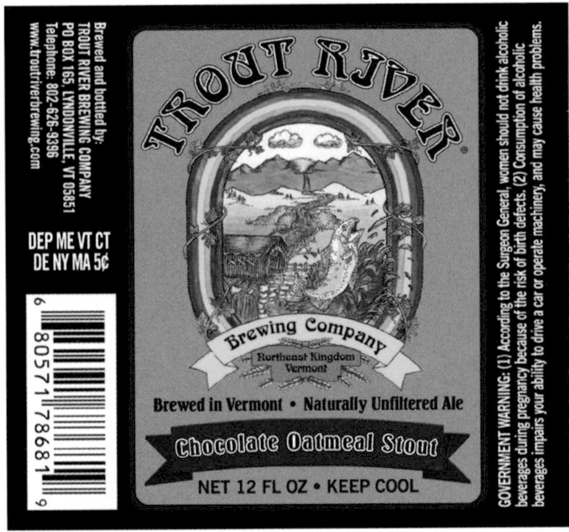

Trout River also brews several beers that are never available outside the brewery, such as the **Boneyard Barley Wine** and the **Knight Slayer,** which is an imperial stout. Those beers are available at the brewery on Friday and Saturday from 4 to 9 p.m., when Trout River's pub is open to the public. Beer lovers can come in and get their growlers filled, as well as sample between 6 and 10 Trout River beers, many only availlable at the brewery. Sourdough pizzas, hand-tossed and made with Dan Gates's own sourdough yeast culture—aged more than a decade—are also available.

## BOBCAT CAFE & BREWERY

5 Main St., Bristol, VT; (802) 453-3311; BobcatCafe.com
**Draft Beers:** 12

The Bobcat Cafe & Brewery is the place to go in Bristol to get good, locally sourced meals and fresh, house-brewed beer. The brewpub prides itself on fresh food and fresh beer, and the quality of both shines through.

Beer-wise, the Bobcat Cafe offers a mix of traditional and not-so-traditional beers. The **Kolsch** is a traditional interpretation with one twist—it is aged for six weeks on French oak. The **Strawberries & Cream** is brewed with both ale and lager yeast, which is different than most beers. The strawberries are added during fermentation for flavor, and the Bobcat Cafe serves the beer on nitro, giving it a creamier head and body. Another unusual beer is the **Unrepentant,** which is a Belgian-style stout, again with a twist: It is brewed with chocolate and pepper. Many beers brewed with the same ingredients usually tip the scales at a higher percent of alcohol by volume (ABV), but the Unrepentant comes in at a modest 5.1 percent ABV.

And then there are the traditional beers, which are exciting in their own way just because they are so good. The **Prayer Rock Pale Ale** is a traditional, west coast pale ale packed with a lot of hop flavor and aroma, but not overwhelming for those not into hoppy beers. The **Pocock Pilsner** is a light and refreshing pilsner with just a little hop bite. The **Dauntaun Braun** is a German-style dunkel weizen with hints of banana and chocolate in the flavor. The **Brickwall** is a big double IPA, brewed with hops grown on the side of the Bobcat Cafe, while the **Lil Brick** is a quality black IPA.

The food is top notch and heavy on local ingredients. Appetizers include butternut squash bisque, Vermont venison stew, and braised duck spring rolls. A different daily flatbread is also an option. The entrees include ginger tofu tempura, which is fermented black bean and sweet potato cake served with curried coconut broth and sautéed bok choy. The maple-brined grilled pork chop is yet another standout, made with wild rice bread pudding, cider-braised red cabbage, and Vermont apple and Riesling pan sauce. If you are not in the mood for such a large meal, order from the pub menu, which features burgers, sandwiches, and nachos.

Oh, make sure to leave room for one of the incredible desserts, such as the chocolate silk pie served in a graham cracker crust with a toasted marshmallow topping; the lavender honey walnut baklava, served with Ben and Jerry's vanilla ice cream; or the maple crème brûlée, made with Hillsboro Sugarworks Maple Syrup.

## BREWSTER RIVER PUB & BREWERY

4087 VT 108 South, Jeffersonville, VT; (802) 644-6366, BrewsterRiverPubNBrewery.com
**Draft Beer:** 14

Usually, when talking about a brewpub, the first thing that is discussed is the beer. But, Godzilla changes those plans. Godzilla is the most incredible, decadent and borderline murderous burger offered in all of New England, and it's exclusive at the Brewster River Pub & Brewery.

Sure, it's a burger. How exciting can it be, really? Well, read these toppings: pastrami, pulled pork, beef brisket, pork roll, smoked bacon, fried egg, hash brown, pepper jack cheese, and cheddar cheese. It is the burger that will make vegetarians run. It'll also run you $17.95, but, seriously, re-read that and say it's not worth it.

If that's a little intimidating (wimp), there are plenty of other burgers and sandwiches, such as the Vermont Grilled Cheese, which is made with local cheddar cheese, bacon, Granny Smith apples, and maple mustard. As for appetizers, you can get cocoanut curry mussels or chicken wings with various sauces, or go a little larger with the Teriyaki Duck Wings. There are also salads and soups available. Entrees include the Seafood Alfredo, made with salmon, shrimp, and mussels, and the BBQ Mixed Grill, with smoked pull pork, grilled chicken, and beef brisket.

Oh, and there is beer. There are typically 14 beers on tap, mostly local Vermont offerings, as well as at least two Brewster River brewed beers. The house-brewed beers include the **Aztec Chocolate Stout,** the **Irish Red Ale,** the **Double IPA,** the **Graham Cracker Brown,** the **Sailing the Seven C's Ale,** the **Belgian Dubbel,** and **Shred the Gnar Red Ale.**

Brewster River is open Monday through Friday, 2 p.m. to 2 a.m. and Saturday and Sunday, noon to 2 a.m.

## CROP BISTRO & BREWERY

1859 Mountain Rd., Stowe, VT; (802) 253-4763, CropVT.com
**Draft Beer:** 10 to 12

The Crop Bistro & Brewery prides itself on providing its guests with many local options as well as a draft list of brews, both of which are constantly changing. They typically have 10 of their own beers on tap, as well as a couple of guest taps, typically Vermont brewers and cider makers. Some of the beers include the **Helles Brook Lager,** the **Maerzen Lager,** the **Belgian Amber,** the **Vermont Pale Ale,** the **Idletyme Double IPA,** the **Crop Brown Ale,** the **Dunkel Lager,** and the **Weizenbock.**

## The Alchemist: Weathering the Storm

### The Alchemist: Weathering the Storm

The Alchemist Pub and Brewery in Waterbury, Vermont, was one of the best brewpubs in the state, respected for its wide selection of world-class beers, from its flagship double IPA, the Heady Topper, to its number of other beers including sours, stouts, and daily drinking beers.

But in August 2011, Hurricane Irene hit Vermont hard. It caused flooding, destroying homes, roads, and even small bridges. It also destroyed the Alchemist, with several feet of water filling up the basement, where all the brewing equipment was located. The Alchemist immediately had to close its doors, and later announced they would not be reopening.

However, this story has a happy ending. Long before Hurricane Irene's assault on Vermont, the Alchemist's founders, John and Jennifer Kimmich, had already started building a cannery, also in Waterbury. Shortly after the brewpub was destroyed, the Alchemist Cannery, located at 35 Crossroad Rd., opened. The one initial beer they brewed, Heady Topper, quickly became the highest rated beer on Beer Advocate's website and one of the most sought after beers in the whole country. So many people began visiting the brewery to buy Heady Topper by the case, they had to shut down the brewery's store, distributing all of its Heady Topper to area stores. Beer geeks staked out stores to get the fabulous double IPA as often as possible. The Alchemist has also brewed a few other beers, and sold them as part of "Truck sales," where they drove the Alchemist truck to various stores, sold the beer in the parking lot, and then moved on to other stores.

They also feature bottle and canned beer from Vermont, Belgium, and Germany, as well as a small selection of mass-produced beers for their customers who don't care about beer and are there for the food.

The menu is constantly changing, based on the whims of the chef and what ingredients are available at any given time. Soups and appetizers include a Cheddar Lager Soup, Beer Battered Fried Pickles, chicken wings, and Pork Shoulder Egg Rolls. There is also a selection of salads. Entrees include the Flat Iron steak with blue cheese, bacon, potato tart, and asparagus; Roast Duck Breast, Stealhead Trout (Beer Lover's note: a personal favorite fish), which is served with sunflower seed risotto. Crop Bistro also offers a meat and cheese menu that offers a selection of locally produced food.

Along with the beer, the Crop Bistro offers both large cocktail and wine menus. The Crop Bistro is open seven days a week at 11:30 a.m. Closing time varies throughout the year, so call ahead to make sure you're not going too late.

### JASPER MURDOCK'S ALEHOUSE

325 Main St., Norwich, VT; (802) 649-1143; NorwichInn.com
**Draft Beers:** 4

The Norwich Inn is a beautiful little inn in picturesque Norwich, Vermont. It is also the home of Jasper Murdock's Pub, a small English-style brewpub. The brewpub is named for the original owner of the Norwich Inn, Jasper Murdock. The inn itself was built in 1797, and President James Monroe was a guest in 1817.

Jasper Murdock's mainly brews finely crafted English-style ales, and the only beer available at all times is the **Whistling Pig Red Ale,** which is an Irish red ale with a little more hops. The brewpub only has four beers on tap, but they are rotated often. Other British-style beers include the **J & R's Birthday Brown Ale,** the **Stackpole Porter, Oh Be Joyful** (English mild), **Second Wind Oatmeal Stout,** the **Old Slippery Skin IPA, ESB, Another Ale** (English best bitter), **Famous Sidekick** (dark mild), **Ma Walker's Double Strength Stout, 70 Shilling Ale, 90 Shilling Pale Ale,** and **Fuggles & Barleycorn** (English golden ale).

Jasper Murdock's also offers several German-style beers, including the **NORweizINN** (German-style weizen), **Oktoberfest, Bock from the Trail** (Maibock), **Munich Dunkel,** and the **Scwarzpils.** Also offered are a few Belgian-style ales, including **Light Humour** and **Dark Humour.** The Light Humour is a traditional Belgian-style witibier, while Dark Humour is also a Belgian-style witbier, except it is dark, not light like a traditional beer. The Norwich Abbey is a strong dark Belgian ale.

The Norwich Inn has two areas for eating—the more rowdy and casual brewpub and then the dining room, which takes reservations and is a little quieter. They offer the same menu, so whatever atmosphere you like, the quality food will be there. And don't worry if there is someone in your party who does not like beer. The Norwich Inn has a wine cellar that includes 2,000 bottles.

Start with the Autumn Salad, which is made of baby romaine lettuce, toasted pecans, lardons, fried brie, and dried cranberries topped with sherry rosemary vinaigrette. Appetizers include duck confit egg rolls and the Charcuterie Plate, which includes venison sausage, country pate, pork rillette, cherry sage chutney, and grilled flatbread. Entrees include cashew-encrusted trout filets, the rack of lamb, and chicken roulade. The seasonal menu changes throughout the year—be sure to sample the pumpkin risotto, which includes caramelized apples, gorgonzola, and toasted pumpkin seeds, in the fall.

Unfortunately, if you do fall in love with a Jasper Murdock's beer, you will not be able to bring it home with you—the only place their beers are available is at the brewpub. In that case, you might want to stay an extra night or two.



## MADISON BREWING COMPANY

428 Main St., Bennington, VT; (802) 442-7397; MadisonBrewingCo.com
**Draft Beers:** 8

The Madison Brewing Company bills itself as the place where "Fermentation & Civilization are Inseparable." Loosely translated, I think that means it is a brewpub where people like to go eat, drink, and be merry. The brewpub is a Bennington mainstay and they brew several excellent beers that have a full and varied nature.

The Madison Brewing Company features eight beers on tap, six year-round beers and a rotation of two seasonals available at a time. The year-round beers include the **Sucker Pond Blonde,** a beer for those who want something easy to drink, and the **Old 76 Strong Ale,** which is basically the opposite, a stronger, full-flavored, malt-dominated English-style strong ale. The **Buck's Honey Wheat** is a wheat beer brewed with local honey. The rest of the year-round beers include **Willoughy's Scottish Ale,** the **Crowtown Pale Ale,** and **Wassick's White Ale.** The seasonals include the **American Honey Brown Ale,** the **Strawberry Hefeweizen,** and the **Octoberfest.** During the year, you may find a homebrew beer on tap; the Madison Brewing Company takes part in a local homebrewing competition where the winning beer is on brewed and put on tap at the pub.

If you cannot decide what beer to order, order a sampler and get six of them at once in 5-ounce glasses.

Appetizers are straight-up pub classics—chicken tenders, nachos, mussels, and calamari. If you'd rather have something on the lighter side, try the You Had Me at

Brie salad, which includes grilled eggplant and brie cheese, stacked with caramelized shallots, wild field greens, diced tomatoes, shredded carrots, and roasted red pepper dressing. Meat lovers will want to order the Brewmaster's Sausage Dinner, which includes bratwurst, knockwurst, and Irish sausage, served with apple chutney, beer sauerkraut, and garlic mashed potatoes.

Once you're done digesting, consider grabbing a growler of one of Madison's beers to bring home.

## MCNEILL'S BREWERY

90 Elliot St., Brattleboro, VT; (802) 254-2553; McNeillsBrewery.com
**Draft Beers:** 10 to 12

McNeill's Brewery is an institution. Founded in 1992 by Ray McNeill, this brewpub is one of the most well-known brewpubs in all of New England. They brew tons of award-winning beers in their small Brattleboro pub.

Their beers, more than 30 to choose from, are all pretty much spot-on for their styles. The **Big Nose Blonde** is an aromatic blonde ale, while the **Dead Horse IPA** is one of the best English-style IPAs being brewed in New England. The **Champ Ale** is a fantastic pale ale. McNeill's **Firehouse Amber Ale** is a wonderful amber ale—very easy to drink, with just enough body to make it a step above the average amber ale. The **Duck Breath Bitter** is a really good English-style bitter, the **Ruby Ale** is a quality red ale, and the **Pullman's Porter** is a better-than-average porter. McNeill's also brews several seasonals. They include the **Octoberfest,** the **Maibock,** and the **Summer Brown Ale.** The brewpub also produces a couple of really good, higher octane beers. The **Warlord Double IPA** is a big, hoppy monster of a west coast IPA. Their biggest beer is the **Dark Angel Imperial Stout;** it is 10 percent alcohol by volume, malty, with a lot of chocolate flavors in the beer.

McNeill's also bottles several of its beers, which are brewed and bottled at its nearby production facility. The bottled beers are the **Blond Bombshell Ale, Champ Ale, Dark Angel, Dead Horse IPA, Extra Special Bitter, Exterminator** (doppelbock), **Firehouse Amber Ale, Oatmeal Stout, Octoberfest, Old Ringwood, Professor Brewhead's Brown Ale, Pullmans' Porter, Sunshine IPA, Tartan Ale,** and **Warlord Double IPA.**

McNeill's does offer some food, but it is a very limited menu that includes a few pub items, such as pizza, chili, nachos, and the like. People are welcome to bring in food from other restaurants if they want. The pub is cash-only, so stock up that wallet before you arrive.

## THREE NEEDS BREWERY & TAPROOM

185 Pearl St., Burlington, VT; (802) 658-0889
**Draft Beers:** 12

There are three brewpubs in downtown Burlington, and each one is completely different. The Three Needs Brewery & Taproom is the place where the younger locals head out to grab a cold beer for cheap. Despite all the bar options in downtown Burlington, Three Needs will often be the only one with a line outside the door on a weekend night. The inside is small, dark, loud, and packed. This is a dive bar. But they have some tasty beer, so if you're a bit of a bar snob, you might want to make an exception. Make sure to get food before you go there, though, because they do not serve food. It is all about the beer and loud music.

You will be hard pressed to find cheaper beer at a brewpub. You can get some pints for $3.50. However, do not mistake cheap for bad; Three Needs' beers are very good. The draft list changes quite often. On any given night, you may find Belgian styles, lagers, IPAs, or numerous other styles. Some of the beers include the **Belgian Chocolate Stout** and the **Chocolate Thunder Porter.** They also brew a very good **Belgian Triple.** Three Needs, which brews its beers in the basement, also brews some sour beers, such as the **Sour Red** and the **Wild Blonde.** A standout is the **Ich Bin Ein Berliner Weisse,** while the **Dortmonder-style Lager** is a solid lager. Three Needs also brews a solid koslch.

Three Needs usually has one of its several IPAs on tap. They brew four different IPAs, as well as several different stouts. Other styles brewed include Scottish ale, a rye beer, wheat beers, a honey ale, and a smoked ESB. Often only about half of the taps are Three Needs beers, and the rest of the tap list is made up of guest brewers, mostly other Vermont breweries, although sometimes beers from as far away as California will find their way on tap.

## TRAPP FAMILY LODGE BREWERY

700 Trapp Hill Rd., Stowe, VT; (802) 243-7509; TrappFamily.com
**Draft Beers:** 4

Does the "Trapp" name sound familiar? This is the same von Trapp family featured in one of the most famous movies of all time, *The Sound of Music.* The Trapp Family Brewery is in the Trapp Family Lodge in the mountains of Stowe. The all-lager brewery was opened in 2010 after family patriarch Johannes von Trapp decided to pursue his dream of brewing beer like he remembered from his formative years growing up in Austria.

The brewery, which is a really a brewpub with all of its beer served at the on-site DeliBakery at the resort, brews three year-round beers and one seasonal at a time. The **Golden Helles,** a German-style helles bock, is the flagship. It is also available at bars and restaurants throughout the state. Helles bocks are light and refreshing beers, and the Golden Helles is exactly that—it has a nice malty flavor, with just a hint of hops. The **Vienna Amber** is a darker lager, malt forward and still relatively light. The beer is fuller-bodied than the Golden Helles, and it has a sweeter finish. The sweetness is balanced by just a touch of hops on the tongue. The **Dunkel Lager** is a dark lager, with hints of chocolate. This is an extremely malty beer, with barely any hops present.

Throughout the year, the Trapp Family Lodge Brewery offers several different seasonal beers. The **Summer Lager** is the most American of the beers, a pale lager that tastes like a more flavorful mass-produced beer. The **Oktoberfest** is excellent, extremely traditional for the style. The **Winter Geist** is a stronger, maltier, and bigger beer than the year-round Dunkel Lager.

The DeliBakery has an interesting mix of food. There's a different pizza served daily, as well as meat and vegetarian quiches. Go authentic and order something from the von Trapp family's homeland, like the Austrian bratwurst. Several sandwiches are also available in addition to the main courses, and freshly baked pastries and breads are available every day. If the DeliBakery isn't your thing, order a couple of beers and then go to one of the other on-site dining areas, which include the Lounge and the Main Dining Room.

## VERMONT PUB & BREWERY

144 College St., Burlington, VT; (802) 865-0500; VermontBrewery.com
**Draft Beers:** 12

The Vermont Pub & Brewery is the oldest brewery in Vermont, founded by the late Greg Noonan in 1988. The beers and the pub are both Vermont classics, and many of the beers originally created during the early days of the brewery are still being produced today. Located within walking distance of two other Burlington brewpubs, the Vermont Pub & Brewery is a must-visit.

The brewpub has a good mix of 12 different beers on tap at all times (including two casks). They do a good job of mixing up their styles so they appeal to people of all tastes. In all, they may brew up to 30 different beers in any given year. Like fruit beers? Grab a pint of the **Forbidden Fruit,** a refreshing 6.2 percent alcohol by volume ale brewed with 500 pounds of fresh raspberries. Like stouts? Get the **Handsome Mick's Irish Stout.** The **Tulack Leis,** a Flemish sour red, or the **Saison d'Automne** are some options if you consider yourself a bit of a Belgian ale fan. Other beers include the **Bombay Grab IPA,** the **Dog Bite Bitter, Milk Stout,** and the **Blue**

**Nile Lotus Gruit.** The Vermont Pub & Brewery also brews several seasonals, including the **Ocktoberfest** and the **Rocktoberfest,** two different versions of a German-style Oktoberfest beer.

As far as food, the Vermont Pub & Brewery has a solid menu of pub fare. The appetizers are heavy on fried seafood such as oysters, calamari, and clam strips. There are tons of sandwiches available, including the Chicken Rolli Polli, which is grilled chicken with jack cheese, sweet and sour jalapeño sauce, lettuce, tomatoes, and onions on a wrap. Want a larger meal? Grab a pulled pork pie, which is a pie full of southern-style barbecued pulled pork, topped with corn and mashed potatoes. The Ploughman's Lunch features hunks of both Vermont cheddar and smoked cheddar, with a house-baked loaf of bread, apple chutney, and honey mustard. The pecan-encrusted trout filet is excellent, and the tequila-honey chicken, which is a chicken breast basted in honey and tequila, is also worth exploring as a dinner option.

Before you leave, make sure to pick up a growler of your favorite beer, as well as tie-dye shirts, glassware, or even some of Noonan's books on brewing.



## WHETSTONE STATION RESTAURANT & BREWERY

36 Bridge St., Brattleboro, Vt., (802) 490-2354, WhetStation.com
**Draft Beers:** 14

The Whetstone Station Restaurant & Brewery takes the word "experimental" to a new level. While many breweries and brewpubs will brew a lot of beers and often brew them only once, Whetstone never brews the same beer twice. So, if you like a beer a lot when you visit the Brattleboro brewpub, drink it while you can, because you will never, ever see it again.

Whetstone typically has 14 beers on tap, usually three of its own singular creations, and then 11 guest taps, which are a mix of local and national craft beer standouts. They also have a large bottled list, a list of cellared beers (a little pricey, but not out of the realm of what they should cost) and then a collection of super special beers that may run you more than $30 a bottle. Whetstone also carries a number of gluten-free beers and ciders.

As for food, it is a seasonal menu that constantly changes. Some of the "Small Scale" menu items are the Station Fries, which are hand cut, fried, and seasoned with chives and parmesan cheese; crispy Brie, and pierogies. Brewpub favorites include burgers; a chicken sandwich; Whetstone Tacos, made with mahi mahi; and the Duck Nachos, which are corn chips smothered in roasted duck tossed in hoisin sauce, pico de gallo, olives, jalapenos, cheddar cheese, and feta cheese. Entrees include the spiced cider ribs, chicken schnitzel, and the pub meatloaf served over cheddar mashed potatoes, which is seared shrimp and scallops, steamed mussels, and clams in a spicy tomato, white wine sauce with pasta, and the Cowboy steak with cheesy mashed potatoes. And, unlike a lot of brewpubs, Whetstone has a children's menu, which will come in handy for parents with little ones.

Whetstone Station is open Sunday through Thursday, 11:30 a.m. to 10 p.m. and Friday and Saturday from 11:30 a.m. to 11 p.m.

### ZERO GRAVITY CRAFT BREWERY @ AMERICAN FLATBREAD

115 St. Paul St., Burlington, VT; (802) 861-2999; AmericanFlatbread.com
**Draft Beers:** 12 house-brewed beers, 8 guest taps, 2 casks

American Flatbread, host of the Zero Gravity Craft Brewery, is the best at a lot of things in Burlington: They make the best pizzas, they are the best brewpub, and they boast the best beer bar in Burlington, with eight guest taps and around 50 excellent selections in craft bottled beers, which does not include the large selection of ciders and meads.

Zero Gravity's brewers produce some excellent beers. Throughout the year they may brew more than 50 beers, with a rotating selection of seasonals. In fall, for example, they brew the **St. Pauli Boy,** a Munich-style Oktoberfest lager. Zero Gravity also brews beers that represent all of the major brewing countries—Belgium, England, Germany, and the US. They brew some experimental beers, such as the **Deus Aqua,** which is a Belgian-style saison brewed with honey and pink and black peppercorns, or the **Gruit,** which is an ancient style of beer brewed with local herbs.

The guest drafts are usually other beers from Vermont (Long Trail) or from other New England states (Smuttynose Brewing Company). Brewery Ommegang from New York is also frequently available. The bottled list includes several beers from Vermont breweries, such as Rock Art Brewery, Trout River Brewing Company, and Wolaver's. American Flatbread also carries numerous beers from the Allagash Brewing Company in Maine, as well as beers from Dieu du Ciel and Unibroue in Canada. There is always a small selection of vintage bottled ales available. These are typically large-format bottles, bombers, and 750 ml, perfect for sharing.

It is strange to say, but even though the beer is excellent, American Flatbread's flatbread pizzas are actually the star at this brewpub. They are stunningly good. They are all made without tomato sauce (unless requested) and are made with fresh, locally grown ingredients and cooked in the large, wood-fire stove located in the middle of the restaurant. There are several different options—the New Vermont Sausage, the Medicine Wheel, and the Revolution Flatbread are just a few of them. Even the plain herb and cheese pizza is great. You can also pick all your own toppings ranging from the normal pepperoni to salsa, corn, goat cheese, and black beans.

## BLACKBACK PUB & FLYSHOP

1 Stowe St., Waterbury, VT; (802) 505-5115; BlackbackPub.com
**Draft Beers:** 25 **Bottled/Canned Beers:** Small selection of special beers

There may not be a more unique beer bar in the world than the Blackback Pub & Flyshop. After all, have you ever heard of a bar with 25 world-class beers on tap that also sells fishing flies and other fly-fishing equipment and serves sushi a few nights a week?

Owner Rick Binet takes a lot of care picking his beer. The beers on tap are not easy-to-find beers like Samuel Adams or Long Trail. Instead, he said there are no "half-assed craft beers," and he seeks out beers from Hill Farmstead, or some of the more complex offerings from the Allagash Brewing Company. Stoudt's and beers from Stillwater Artisanal Ales from Baltimore, Maryland, were also some recent offerings. Blackback Pub also has some rare German beers on draft, as well as options from Belgium and other American breweries. The bottled list is minimal, with a few rare beers.

There is more than just beer at the Blackback Pub. They also have a huge selection of wonderful (and sometimes expensive) whiskeys and bourbons. Some of the whiskeys include Laphroaig Quarter Cask, Balvenie Double Wood 12 Year, Macallan Cask Strength, Glenlivet Nadurra 16 Year, and Ardbeg 10 Year.

The menu is not large but it is eclectic. Blackback Pub serves panini sandwiches and a couple of cheese plates. The pub has also recently added Back Country Flat Breads and calzones from local restaurant La Strada. A sushi chef prepares sushi Wednesday through Friday, with some Saturday specials.

If you are not into the beer, whiskey, sushi, or pizza, this still could be the place to go if you are into fly fishing. Binet is a Vermont fly-fishing guide. At the pub, he sells flies designed for those who are on the hunt for trout in local streams and ponds. The pub also gets its name from the local moniker given to the brook trout that live in the mountain brooks that flow into local streams and rivers, blackbacks. Also available for sale are bamboo fly fishing rods and classic fly reels. These rods and reels are not something you buy as a memory of your stop at Blackback. The rods and reels cost up to $2,600.

The pub is small, but a great place to have a conversation. The bar seats about 25 and there are several small tables. There are TVs for watching games. If you find yourself in Waterbury, the Blackback Pub is a must-stop. Heck, while grabbing a beer and some eel sushi, get the fly-fishing report for an early fishing trip the next morning.

### DAS BIERHAUS

175 Church St., Burlington, VT; (802) 881-0600; DasBierHausVt.com
**Draft Beers:** 8 **Bottled/Canned Beers:** More than 60

Das Bierhaus takes its love of the German beer culture to higher levels than any other German-inspired pub in New England. The menu is huge on German food, and the beer list is heavy on German beers. All draft beers are always German beers. Not German-style beers, but beers directly imported from Germany.

Das Bierhaus always has classic German styles—pilsners, lagers, hefeweizens—on draft. They also change beers for the seasons, putting on Oktoberfest beers in the fall and doppelbocks in the winter. Most of the best German breweries are represented on draft, such as Ayinger, Weihenstephan, Frankziskaner, and Warsteiner. Draft beers are also available in three different sizes: 0.3 liters, 0.4 liters, and 0.5 liters. The bottled list is also heavy into German beers, with about another 15 to 20 German beers available in bottles. They also have several American beers, such as Rock Art, and beers from other countries, such as Samuel Smith's from England. Das Bierhaus also always has some large-format bombers and 750 ml bottles available, and they are typically Belgian ales, or higher-alcohol American beers.

To go along with all of that German beer, Das Bierhaus has a menu heavily inspired by German food. Appetizers include soft Bavarian pretzels and Schnitz on a Stick. You could also order the Kasespatzle, which is made in-house with dill and onion, as well as Swiss, cheddar, and gruyère cheeses. The Jager Sandwich, an open-faced pork schnitzel sandwich with sauteed mushrooms, onions, jager sauce, and a house, or haus, cheese blend, is a sandwich worth trying. Entrees include three types of schnitzel. You can get the classic Wiener Schnitzel, which is made from a hand-pounded veal cutlet and then pan fried; the Schnitzel vom Schwein, a pork loin butchered on-site and pan fried; or the Jager "Hunter" Schnitzel, which is the Schnitzel vom Schwein, but topped with a housemade (or hausmade) mushroom gravy sauce. Of course, a German restaurant would not be complete without wurst. Das Bierhaus offers five different types of sausage: The Bockwurst is mildly spiced pork and veal sausage; knackwurst is spiced, smoked pork and beef sausages; bratwurst is seasoned veal sausage; bauernwurst is a sausage made with mustard seeds and marjoram, making it spicy; and finally the rauchwurst is a smoked sauasge.

## THE FARMHOUSE TAP & GRILL

160 Bank St., Burlington, VT; (802) 859-0888; FarmhouseTG.com
**Draft Beers:** 24 **Bottled/Canned Beers:** About 120

The Farmhouse Tap & Grill bills itself as a farm-to-table gastropub, where almost all the food is made from locally sourced ingredients. Many of its beers are also local. They have 24 beers on tap, and have a huge bottle list of about 120 selections.

The draft list usually features Hill Farmstead beers, as well as those from Allagash Brewing Company from Maine. They have a couple of imported beers available, too. They typically have two beers on cask. The bottled list is varied and it is broken up by country. American bottles usually include both Allagash and Hill Farmstead, but also beers from Maine Beer Company and Stillwater Artisanal Ales. They also have one canned beer, the Alchemist's Heady Topper, which is delivered fresh from the Waterbury cannery every week. The Belgian ales are broken up into two categories—Belgian and Trappist. They have a huge selection of Trappist ales, and the "normal" Belgian list is impressive. The Farmhouse Tap has a large Canadian beer menu, made up mostly of Unibroue and Dieu du Ciel—there is no Molson here. There are plenty of British and German beers on the list, too. Unlike a lot of bars, the Farmhouse Tap & Grill has a cellared beer list that sports many different aged beers, such as Chimay and other Belgian ales.

The menu is not huge at the Farmhouse Tap & Grill, but the food they do serve is delicious. You can start with one of the Tap Room Snacks, which include buttermilk



*Beer Event*

### Allagash Abduction

Every November, the Farmhouse Tap & Grill hosts a special night when Allagash takes over the tap handles, with 17 of Allagash's best beers on draft all at once in one place. Some of the beers are rarer offerings rarely seen on tap, while others are some of their more well-known but still fantastic beers. No matter what, it is a night of Allagash, and that is a night you want to be a part of.

biscuits, Nitty Gritty Corn Bread, and maple-rosemary bar nuts. Entrees include the chicken and biscuits made from local chickens, meat loaf made with both beef and pork, and macaroni and cheese made with carmelized onions and local cheeses. The burgers are all made with local grass-fed beef, and the Winding Brook Farm Pasture-Raised Pork is a sandwich made with local pork, eggs, Grafton cheddar, fennel slaw, and a root beer barbecue sauce.

### PARKER PIE COMPANY

161 County Rd., West Glover, VT; (802) 525-3366; ParkerPie.com
**Draft Beers:** 13 **Bottled/Canned Beers:** 40

Not enough pizza places embrace good beer. It really doesn't make much sense—what goes better together than a good slice and a great glass of craft beer? The Parker Pie Company in tiny West Glover gets it right. They make great pizzas, and have a top-notch beer selection to wash it all down.

The draft list includes 13 excellent beers from a mix of local breweries, such as the Rock Art Brewery, Hill Farmstead, and Wolaver's, and from other parts of the country, such as the Brooklyn Brewery, Rogue Brewery, and Stone Brewing Company. The bottled list is even more impressive. Whoever is in charge of the beer list is obviously a fan of Stone and Rogue, with several beers from both breweries available. There are also several Belgian ales available, such as A'Chouffe, Cantillon, Monk's Cafe, and Bosteels. Beer Here from Denmark, rarely seen at any place except the best beer bars, is also available. The beer menu also features several mass-produced lagers for an affordable $2.75, so even if you are with someone who's not a craft beer lover, he or she will have options. Parker Pie also has a good-size wine menu.

The beer selection alone may be worth making the trip out to Parker Pie, but the real star is the pizza. They offer different sauce choices—tomato sauce, crushed plum tomatoes, pesto, or garlic white sauce. All the typical toppings are available (although many of the toppings are made locally), but Parker Pie specializes in some truly unique pizzas. The Scott's Revenge is slathered in Scott's Oil, a hot housemade oil used on many of the pizzas, and crushed plum tomatoes, topped with mozzarella cheese, spicy shrimp, scallions, and roasted red peppers. Another unique pizza is the Bangkok Disco, which is covered with Scott's Oil, crushed plum tomatoes, mozzarella and cheddar cheese, zesty chicken breast, red onions, and light bleu cheese and dusted with curry powder. Make sure to have a hoppy beer to complement the heat of these pies.

### THREE PENNY TAPROOM

108 Main St., Montpelier, VT; (802) 223-TAPS; ThreePennyTaproom.com
**Draft Beers:** 24 **Bottled/Canned Beers:** 60

The Three Penny Taproom is the best place to seek out beer in Vermont's capital city. There are 24 rotating beers on tap, as well as an ever-changing selection of 60 bottled varieties. The Three Penny Taproom also has fantastic food, using as many local ingredients as possible in its dishes.

The draft list is impressive. There are always numerous great beers on tap. They are also one of the few places to occasionally get Lawson's Finest Liquids beers on draft. There are plenty of other good beers, such as Hill Farmstead, also from Vermont, and the Alchemist Heady Topper, Dogfish Head, Stone Brewing Company, and Allagash Brewing Company.

The bottled list is also good, with a strong mix of imported beers and craft beers from New England and other parts of the US.

A sign of a really good pub, or a gastropub, is if the food is as good as the beer, and vice versa. The Three Penny Taproom is pretty darn close. The use of local, fresh ingredients makes for a fantastic menu. Most of the cheeses, poultry, vegetables, and other meats come from local farms.

Starters include horseradish pickled beets and the dilly deviled eggs with pea greens. If you want a hearty soup, get the chicken borscht. Salads include the winter wheat berry salad with gold raisins and mint. Larger items include sandwiches, such as the maple roasted pork belly with sauerkraut and grain mustard and the raclette with pickled sun-dried plums. Another sandwich to consider is the Namaste (a wonderful beer from Dogfish Head), which is braised rabbit served on pumpkernickel bread with spring greens. The Three Penny Taproom also has an impressive selection of artisan cheeses, mostly from local producers.

Note: The menu changes frequently, almost every other week, based on the availability of local ingredients.

Closing hours are not set. The Three Penny Taproom is always open until at least midnight, but sometimes it remains open until 2 a.m., depending on how busy it is.

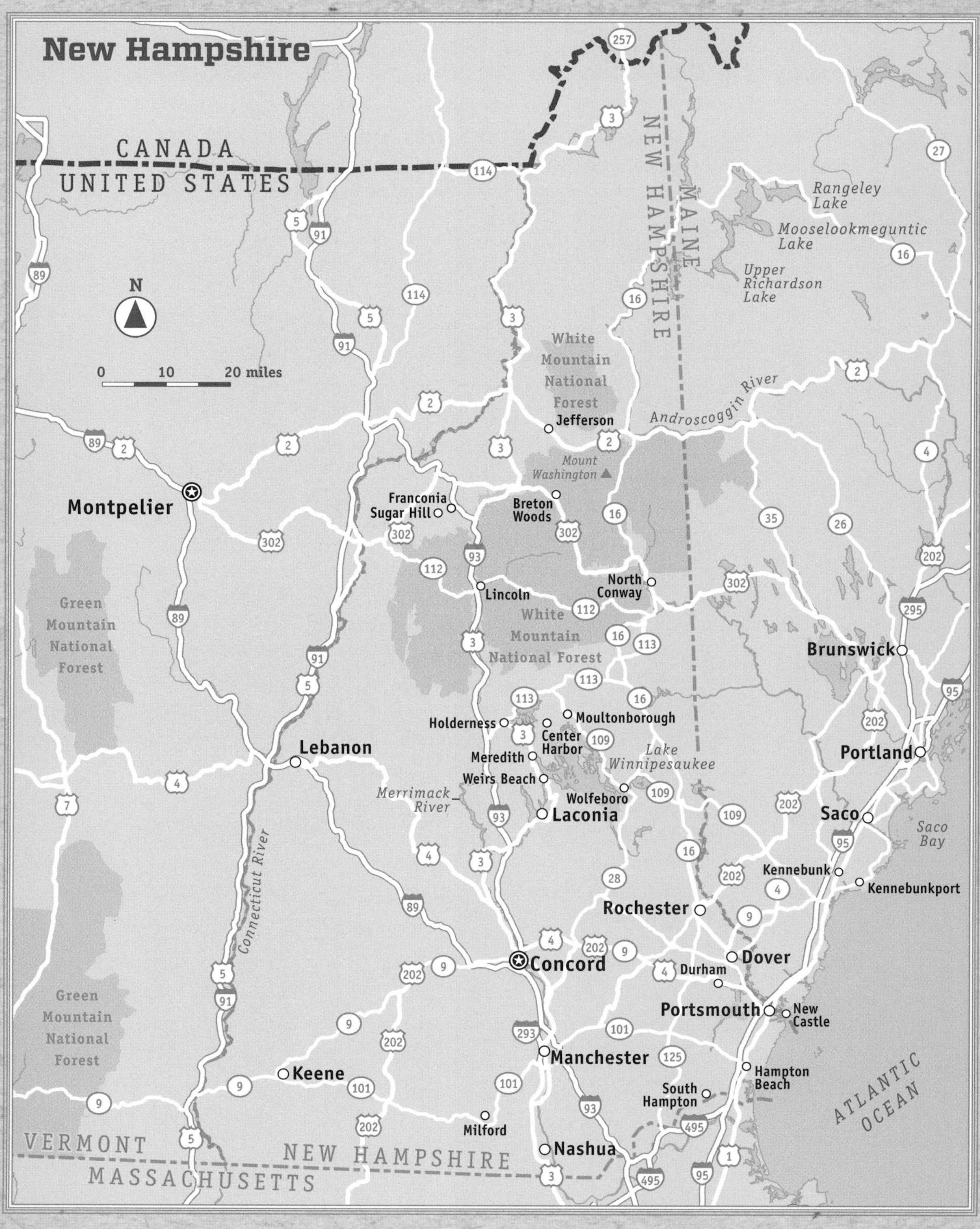

New Hampshire
CANADA
UNITED STATES
N
0
10
20 miles
White Mountain National Forest
Rangeley Lake
Mooselookmeguntic Lake
Upper Richardson Lake
NEW HAMPSHIRE
MAINE
Androscoggin River
Jefferson
Mount Washington
Montpelier
Franconia
Sugar Hill
Breton Woods
North Conway
Lincoln
White Mountain National Forest
Green Mountain National Forest
Brunswick
Holderness
Moultonborough
Center Harbor
Meredith
Lake Winnipesaukee
Weirs Beach
Wolfeboro
Lebanon
Portland
Merrimack River
Laconia
Saco
Saco Bay
Kennebunk
Kennebunkport
Rochester
Connecticut River
Concord
Dover
Durham
Portsmouth
New Castle
Green Mountain National Forest
Manchester
Keene
Hampton Beach
South Hampton
ATLANTIC OCEAN
Milford
Nashua
VERMONT
NEW HAMPSHIRE
MASSACHUSETTS

# New Hampshire

Portsmouth is the center of the brewing world in the Granite State: The Smuttynose Brewing Company, Red Hook Brewing Company, the Portsmouth Brewery, and even Anheuser-Busch are all in the city. But there are other places to get good beer. Manchester has Milly's Tavern, a fun brewpub. The Squam Brewing Company is making good beer in the lakes region, and the White Birch Brewing Company in Hooksett is making some of the most unique beers being brewed today.

There are also some cool little beer bars, such as the Barley Pub in Dover, or if you want a place to stay, drink beer, or even brew beer, spend the weekend at the Woodstock Inn. New Hampshire is on the upswing as far as beer is concerned, and it will only get better.

New Hampshire's breweries are also on the forefront of "green brewing," with many of them leading the way when it comes to using recycled materials and using as many local and organic ingredients as possible.

## AGNER & WOLF BREWERY CORPORATION

4 Bud Way, Unit 16-18, Nashua, NH; (617) 319-9957; AgnerWolfBeer.com
**Founded:** 2013 **Founders:** Erwin Agner, Nataly Agner, Dennis Wolf **Brewer:** Dennis Wolf **Flagship Beer:** None **Year-round Beers:** Altbier, Hefeweizen, Marzen, Schwarzbier **Seasonals/Special Releases:** None **Tours:** None

The Agner & Wolf Brewery Corporation seeks to bring a little bit of Germany to the US. Agner and Wolf specializes in traditional German-style beers, while brewing all beers to the German beer purity law known as Reinheitsgebot (bans the use of anything other than malt, water, and hops).

**Schwarzbier**
**Style:** Schwarzbier
**ABV:** 6 percent
**Availability:** Year-round
This is the creamiest black lager this author has ever tried. It has some of the traditional roasted notes you'd expect from the style, but the creaminess is out-of-this-world. It almost feels strangely pleasant as it slips down your throat.

The brewery only brews four styles—**Altbier, Hefeweizen, Marzen,** and the **Schwarzbier.** The Altbier is a traditional German-style brown ale. This 4.9 percent alcohol by volume (ABV) beer has some toasted barley flavors, a slight sweetness and is balanced out by some herbal hops. The Hefeweizen, which is 5.4 percent ABV, is a traditional German hefeweizen. It has a big, frothy head, and flavors of banana and clove from the hefeweizen yeast. The Marzen is actually an Oktoberfest-style lager, typically only available during the fall. However, Agner & Wolf brews their Marzen year-round. It's a tad sweet for the style, but if someone is an Oktoberfest lager fan, and is craving one in April, this is a good alternative. The final beer is the Schwarzbier, which is a German black lager.

Agner & Wolf does not offer brewery tours.



## CANDIA ROAD BREWING COMPANY

840 Candia Rd., Manchester, NH, (603) 935-8123, CandiaRoad.com
**Founded:** 2012 **Founders:** Thomas Neel **Brewer:** Thomas Neel **Flagship Beer:** East Coast Pale Ale **Year-round Beers:** Hop-Ful IPA, Nut Brown Ale, The Shire, Lotus Eater Double IPA, Whimsical Wheat **Seasonals/Special Releases:** Solo-Springer, New Hampshire Harvest Ale **Tours:** None

The Candia Road Brewing Company is home to the **Nepenthe** line of ales. The brewery is actually housed inside the Candia Road store, a convenience store with a deli that has been a craft beer destination for better beer lovers in New Hampshire for years.

Oh, and a homebrew shop is also located within the store. So, if you want a bomber of Nepenthe beer, an egg salad sandwich and 3 pounds of cascade hops for your homebrew, 840 Candia Road is the place for you.

Candia Road brews six year-round beers and two seasonals, and most of the Nepenthe beers are on the higher side when it comes to alcohol percentage. The flagship beer is the **East Coast Pale Ale,** a 7.4 ABV pale ale. This is a very high alcohol percentage for a pale ale and it has the hop flavor and aroma as some of the more moderate IPAs out there. The **Hop-Ful IPA** is a 9.2 percent ABV double IPA with the classic piney aroma and flavor. The malt backbone is on the sweet side, making sure this beer does not become a palate wrecker. The **Lotus Eater Double IPA** is an 8.2 percent beer. The malts aren't quite as sweet in this beer, and it has more flavors

**The Shire**
**Style:** American Stout
**ABV:** 7.2 percent
**Availability:** Year-round
This beer is almost like drinking a coffee. There are a lot of roasted notes and hints of chocolate. The beer is creamy and relatively dry. At 7.2 percent alcohol by volume (ABV), it does not quite reach the level of an imperial stout, but it is still has a full-body and is hearty enough to satisfy on a cold, New England night.

of tropical fruit, rather than pine. The **Nut Brown Ale** comes in at a hefty 9.5 percent ABV. It has strong flavors of black licorice and candy, with just enough hops in the finish to keep it from being too sweet. The **Shire Stout** is a 7.2 percent ABV American Stout, while the final year-round beer is the **Whimsical Wheat,** which has strong flavors of banana and cloves.

The seasonals are the **Solo-Springer,** a 7.4 percent pale ale with grapefruit and citrus flavors available in the spring and summer, and the **New Hampshire Harvest,** a fall seasonal that is made with fresh hops. The style is not the same all of the time.

## CANTERBURY ALEWORKS

305 Baptist Hill Rd., Canterbury, NH; (603) 491-4539; CanterburyAleWorks.com
**Founded:** 2012 **Founder:** Steve Allman **Brewer:** Steve Allman **Beers:** Be Hoppy IPA, Canterbury Ale, Old Darn Bard, Val-Halla Weizen, Granite Ledge Stout, Light Ale, davESBeer, Smoke House Porter, Alter Ego **Tours:** Sat and Sun, 3 to 6 p.m.

Canterbury AleWorks has one of the most unique brewing set ups in all of New England. The one-barrel brewing system is powered by water and fire. Founder/brewer Steve Allman specially designed a wood-fired stove to boil the water during the brewing process, while a waterwheel provides all of the electricity needed to keep the small brewery running.

From those two alternative energy sources, Canterbury AleWorks brews nine different beers. The **Be Hoppy IPA** falls between a west coast IPA and an east coast IPA. The malt profile seems decidedly east coast, while the citrus/grapefruit-like hops are more west coast. The **Canterbury Ale** is an old school pale ale, more on the malty side, while the **Old Darn Bard** is a brown session ale (a beer of which you can drink several in one sitting without getting intoxicated), coming in at a very mild 3.8 percent alcohol by volume (ABV). The **Granite Ledge Stout** is the rare stout that adds coffee without raising the alcohol. The espresso oatmeal stout is only 4.5 percent ABV. The **Smoke House Porter** is a smoky, robust porter, and at 5.8 percent ABV, it's actually light for the style.

Canterbury also brews several German-inspired beers, the **Val-Halla Weizen,** which is a Bavarian hefeweizen; the **Light Ale,** which is actually a kolsch; and the **Alter Ego,** which is an altbier.

**Granite Ledge Stout**
**Style:** Stout
**ABV:** 4.5 percent
**Availability:** Year-round
Coffee can add some amazing flavors to beers, particularly stouts. But the problem is brewers often make their coffee stout high alcohol so the coffee does not overwhelm the flavor of the beer. The Granite Ledge Stout manages the flavor balance well, despite the relatively low alcohol.

Canterbury AleWorks is open Saturday and Sunday from 3 to 6 p.m. for tours, samples, growler sales and bottle sales. One-ounce samples are free, while a 4-ounce sample will cost $1.

### GREAT RHYTHM BREWING COMPANY

Based in Portsmouth, NH, contract brewed at Mercury Brewing Company in Ipswich, MA; (603) 300-8588, GreatRhythmBrewing.com
**Founded:** 2013 **Founders:** Scott and Kristen Thornton **Brewer:** None **Flagship Beer:** Resonation Ale **Year-round Beers:** Amplified Amber Ale, Resonation Pale Ale, and Hopstock IPA **Seasonals/Special Releases:** Grateful Stout, Doublestop Double IPA
**Tours:** None

The Great Rhythm Brewing Company was founded in 2013 by husband and wife Scott and Kristen Thornton in an effort to combine their love of music and craft beer. Although the couple have a goal of opening their own brewery some day, Great Rhythm currently brews its beer at the Mercury Brewing Company in Ipswich, Massachusetts.

Great Rhythm's one beer is the **Resonation Ale.** It's a hoppy pale ale, obviously inspired by the west coast version of the style like Sierra Nevada's Pale Ale. The Resonation Ale is 5.2 percent alcohol by volume, full of citrusy and floral hops and a hint of pine notes. The malt backbone is just there enough to provide some balance. Great Rhythm's beer is only available in New Hampshire.

### HENNIKER BREWING COMPANY

129 Centervale Rd., Henniker, NH; (603) 428-3579; HennikerBrewing.com
**Founded:** 2011 **Founder:** Dave Currier **Brewer:** Chris Shea **Flagship Beer:** None **Year-round Beers:** Amber Apparition Ale, Hopslinger IPA, Whipple's Wheat Ale, Working Man's Porter **Seasonals/Special Releases:** D.H. IPA, The Roast **Tours:** Sat, noon to 4 p.m.; free. Tap room is also open Mon to Fri, 3 to 6 p.m.

Founded in 2011 by former long-time New Hampshire state representative Dave Currier (and eight partners), Henniker Brewing Company started with the goal to be the local brewery for Henniker and the surrounding communities.

Henniker brews four year-round beers—**Amber Apparition Ale,** the **Hopslinger IPA, Whipple's Wheat Ale,** and **Working Man's Porter.** The Amber

### Beer Lover's Pick

**Working Man's Porter**
**Style:** English porter
**ABV:** 5.2 percent
**Availability:** Year-round
Porters started as a beer for the working men in England, and Henniker's is a classic example of the style. It has flavors of coffee, molasses, and dark fruit. It goes down really smooth. It's an excellent beer for porter lovers.

Apparition Ale is a 5.2 percent alcohol by volume (ABV) amber ale. It has nice sweet caramel notes from the malts. It also has more citrus hop flavors than you would expect from an amber ale. It is one of the more full-flavored amber ales you'll find in New England. The Whipple's Wheat is a hoppy take on an American wheat ale. It combines the traditional flavors of a wheat beer with nice hop flavors and aromas that aren't in a lot of wheat beers. The hops make this beer stand out from the crowd of an often boring style. The Hop Slinger IPA is a classic take on an American IPA. It is 6.5 percent ABV and 65 IBUs (international bittering units, which measures the bitterness of a beer). The hops add flavors of grapefruit and pine. The Working Man's Porter is a 5.2 percent ABV traditional English-style interpretation of the style.

Henniker also does two seasonals, the **D.H. IPA,** a double IPA available in the spring, and the **Roast,** a coffee stout available in the winter.

Henniker's tap room is open Monday through Friday, 3 to 6 p.m. Visitors can sample all the beers, and can buy bombers and growlers of the available beers. T-shirts, coasters, glassware and other local products are also available at the brewery. Tours are available Saturday, noon to 4 p.m. and are free.

## KELSEN BREWING COMPANY

80 North High St., Unit 3, Derry, NH; (603) 965-3708; KelsenBrewing.com
**Founded:** 2014 **Founders:** Paul Kelly, Erik Olsen **Brewer:** Paul Kelly **Flagship Beer:** None **Year-round Beers:** Battle Axe IPA, Paradigm Brown Ale **Seasonals/Special Releases:** None **Tours:** Tasting room hours are Sat, 2 to 6 p.m.

Kelsen Brewing Company is one of several small breweries that took advantage of the state adding a nano-brewery license in 2013. Friends Paul Kelly (the "Kel" part of the name) and Erik Olsen (the "Sen" part of the name) took advantage to open its small, three-barrel brewery in Derry in 2014.

Kelsen Brewing Company only brews two beers—the **Battle Axe IPA** and the **Paradigm Brown Ale.** The Battle Axe IPA is a 7.3 percent alcohol by volume (ABV) IPA. The Battle Axe, Kelsen explains, was one of the most balanced weapons used by the Vikings. And that balance is represented in the Battle Axe IPA. It starts with a strong hop punch, but then gives in to some sweet malt flavors, before ending with a floral burst of hops in the finish.

The Paradigm Brown Ale, on the other hand, does not live up to its name. Paradigm means a "Typical example" of something, according to the Merriam-Webster dictionary. But, Kelsen's Paradigm is not your typical brown ale. This is a hoppy, American take on the British style. The typical, caramel, chocolaty flavors of a brown ale are there, then you get hit with the floral, citrusy hops you rarely find in a traditional brown ale. And, the 7.2 percent ABV is much higher than a typical brown ale.

Kelsen's beers stand out on the shelf thanks to their stunning artwork. The Battle Axe IPA features what looks like a Norse warrior swinging an axe in battle, while the Paradigm Brown Ale features what looks like a dwarf from *The Lord of the Rings,* ready to drink a tankard of ale.

Kelsen's is open Saturday 2 to 6 p.m. for tastings, tours, growler sales, and bottle sales.

### OUT.HAUS ALES

49 Lucas Pond Rd., Northwood, NH; (603) 548-2151; OutHausAles.com

**Founded:** 2014 **Founder:** Tom Albright **Brewer:** Tom Albright **Flagship Beer:** None **Year-round Beers:** American Brown Ale, American Stout, India Pale Ale, Pale Ale. **Seasonals/ Special Releases:** None **Tours:** None

Northwood is in the middle of nowhere, and the only sound you'll usually hear is that of the birds chirping and, if you listen closely, the sound of the boiling water at Out.Haus Ales, on Lucas Pond Road. Out.Haus Ales is perhaps the smallest

## Beer Lover's Pick

**American Brown Ale**
**Style:** Brown ale
**ABV:** 5.7 percent
**Availability:** Year-round

Although a brewery named Out.Haus brewing a brown ale made me giggle like I was a middle schooler, this is a solid beer. Brown ales have historically been a popular style in New England, and this is a good representation of the style. It is sweet, and has a slight roastiness and even a little chocolate from the malts.

brewery in New England, brewing one barrel (31 gallons at a time). Owner/brewer Tom Albright began selling his beers in bombers in 2014.

Out.Haus Ales brews four beers. The **American Stout** is a 5.6 percent alcohol by volume (ABV) stout. Although lower in alcohol than many American stouts, this beer has nice roasted flavors, and is dark as night. The **Pale Ale** is an old school version of the east coast style of pale ale, which relies more on earthy hops than the citrus/pine/flowery flavored hops found in most west coast IPAs. It is more of a showcase for the caramel, toffee malt flavors. The **IPA,** like the Pale Ale, leans more toward the east coast style (which makes sense since New Hampshire is on the east coast), rather than the west coast. This beer has a lot of earthy hops, but the sweet, biscuity malts are the real star here. Out.Haus also brews the **American Brown Ale,** a 5.7 percent ABV version of the style.

Out.Haus does not offer tours. Its beers are available in several New Hampshire stores in bombers.

## PRODIGAL BREWERY AT MISTY MOUNTAIN FARM

Effingham, NH (closed to public); (603) 539-2210
**Founded:** 2010 **Founder:** Paul Davis **Brewer:** Paul Davis **Flagship Beer:** Effinghamburgherbrau **Year-round Beer:** Sacopee Pils **Seasonals/Special Releases:** Rev. Potter Baltic Porter, Curse of the Rye-Wolf, Effinghammer Weiss, Chocorua Kolsh, Progonsticator Doppelbock, Oktoberfest **Tours:** None

The Prodigal Brewery is a true farmhouse brewery. Owner/founder Paul Davis bought a 20-acre farm to raise his kids and start his own brewery. A professional brewer for years, Davis wanted to brew the beers he wanted to brew, no exceptions. He uses his own hops in the beer, and he grows other ingredients on the farm. His wife is a beekeeper, and they use their own honey in some of their beers. His brewery, so far, has only brewed lagers because his well water has low mineral content, which is perfect for lager beers.

His **Effinghamburgherbrau**—say that three times fast—is a golden lager. It is a clean tasting, easy beer to drink. For those who say they do not enjoy "fizzy yellow beers," this is the beer to change their minds. The **Sacopee Pils** was originally introduced to be a half-year beer, but it became so popular, Davis has decided to make it a year-round beer. It is a classic German-style pilsner. Prodigal also brews the **Rev. Potter Baltic Porter** (porters are typically ales, but Baltic porters are lagers). It is available for half the year. Davis plans to introduce a second beer that will be available for the other half of the year. Other beers include the **Curse of the Rye-Wolf,** a rare rye style beer called a roggen; the **Effinghammer Weiss,** a Berlinner weiss; the **Chocorua Kolsh;** the **Progonsticator Doppelbock;** and a traditional **Oktoberfest** lager.

**Effinghamburgherbrau**
**Style:** Lager
**ABV:** Unknown
**Availability:** Year-round
This was an easy choice. The Effinghamburgherbrau is an excellent beer, with biscuity notes and a doughy flavor. It also has some grassy, herbal hops. The beer is extremely easy to drink, and if you happen to see it on tap, don't hesitate to order it.

## REDHOOK ALE BREWERY

1 Redhook Way, Pease International Tpke., Portsmouth, NH; (603) 501-3940; Redhook.com

**Founded:** Portsmouth location, 1996 **Founders:** Gordon Bowker, Paul Shipman **Brewer:** Andy Swartz **Flagship Beer:** ESB **Year-round Beers:** Copperhead, Long Hammer IPA, Pilsner **Seasonals/Special Releases:** Late Harvest, Mudslinger, Winterhook, Wit, Double Black Stout, Treblehook **Tours:** Mon, 3, 4, and 5 p.m.; Tues, 1 and 2 p.m.; Wed and Thurs, 1, 3, 5 p.m.; Fri and Sat, noon to 6 p.m., hourly; Sun, 1 to 5 p.m., hourly; $1 per person

The Redhook Brewery was already one of the most successful breweries on the west coast when they decided to open up a second brewery on the east coast, which would provide fresh Redhook beers to people on this side of the US. In 1996, they opened up the Redhook Brewery in Portsmouth, and it is nearly a mirror image of the Seattle original.

Redhook's **ESB** is a phenomenal English-style beer full of malty goodness. The **Copperhead** is a really well-done copper ale. The **Long Hammer IPA** is a solid IPA, along the lines of a Harpoon or Longtrail IPA. The hoppiness will not blow you away,

**Double Black Stout**

**Style:** American Double Stout

**ABV:** 7 percent

**Availability:** Special Release, draft only at Redhook pub

The Double Black Stout is an excellent stout brewed with real coffee. While many stouts have a roasty, coffee-like flavor, this beer is made with real coffee, which makes a big difference. The beer is full-bodied, dark as night, and with hints of chocolate from the malts. The roasted malts provide just a hint of bitterness. At 7 percent, it is not a big imperial stout, but it is bigger than a regular stout.

but it is still a great representation of the style. The best of Redhook's year-round beers is the **Pilsner.** It used to be a seasonal, but thankfully they listened to their fans and made it year-round. This is the kind of pilsner that I wish big breweries brewed—flavorful, light, with a nice touch of hops on the tongue.

Seasonals include the **Mudslinger,** which is a nut brown ale, a spring beer. The **Wit** is Redhook's summer seasonal, and it is exactly what you want in a Belgian-style wit. Light, but spiced with coriander and bitter orange peel. The **Winterhook** is a spicy winter warmer, and the **Late Harvest Ale** is a nice, malty red ale. Two of Redhook's beers are special releases. The **Treblehook** is a 10.9 percent alcohol by volume, American-style barleywine. It packs a punch with plenty of malts and hops, and is good to drink on a cold winter night. The **Double Black Stout** is an excellent, coffee-flavored stout. It is easy to drink, despite being 7 percent alcohol.

Redhook is also home to a really good on-site brewpub. They have all the typical beers on draft, but it is also where the brewers can experiment with some beers. If you are in the area, definitely stop in for a meal and try the special offerings.

The tour is one of the best in New England. It lasts for almost an hour and includes an in-depth description of the brewing and bottling process. You also get three to four samples of various beers at the end. Redhook hosts several events throughout the year, including concerts and a road race. The best is Redhook Fest in August that features a full day of outdoor music and fun, as well as food and beer.

## 603 BREWERY

12 Liberty Dr. #7, Londonderry, NH; (603) 634-7745; 603Brewery.com
**Founded:** 2012 **Founders:** Geoff Hewes, Dan Leonard **Brewers:** Ben Miller, Matt Neff **Flagship Beer:** Winni Ale **Year-round Beers:** 18-Mile, Cogway IPA, Granite Stout, 9th State, White Peaks **Seasonals/Special Releases:** Ice Out, Summatime, Toasted Pumpkin Ale **Tours:** Thurs through Fri, 4 to 7 p.m.; Sat, 1 to 5 p.m.

The 603 Brewery was founded in 2012 by college friends Geoff Hewes and Dan Leonard, who created a brewery to celebrate its home state of New Hampshire. Nearly all of its year-round beers are named for something in New Hampshire. For example, the **Winni Ale** is named for Lake Winnipesauke, a large lake located in the Lakes Region of New Hampshire, and the **Granite Stout** is named for the state's nickname, the Granite State.

The Winni Ale is 603 Brewery's flagship beer. It's a 6.5 percent alcohol by volume (ABV) amber ale. Amber ales are usually boring beers, but this one has a little more caramel malt flavor and a touch of a hop bite on the finish, making it more interesting than many of the same style. Another year-round beer is the **White Peaks,** a

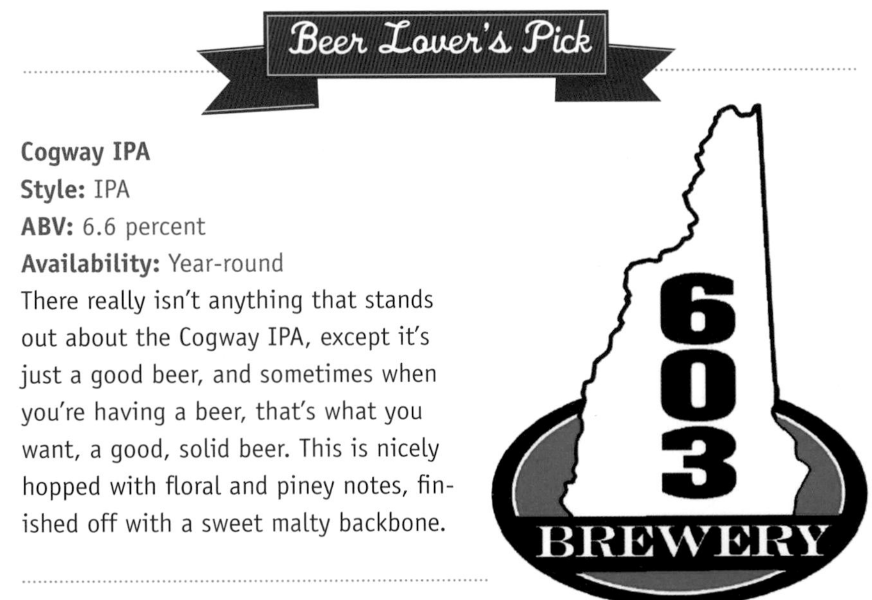


**Cogway IPA**
**Style:** IPA
**ABV:** 6.6 percent
**Availability:** Year-round
There really isn't anything that stands out about the Cogway IPA, except it's just a good beer, and sometimes when you're having a beer, that's what you want, a good, solid beer. This is nicely hopped with floral and piney notes, finished off with a sweet malty backbone.

6.6 percent ABV white IPA. White IPAs continue to grow in popularity. A white IPA basically combines the attributes of an IPA and a Belgian white into a completely new beer, and this is no exception. Other year-round beers include the **Cogway IPA** (American IPA), **9th State** (red IPA), **18-Mile** (Rye pale ale), and the Granite Stout (Irish dry stout).

The 603 Brewery also offers three seasonals—the **Ice-Out,** a spring blonde ale; **Summatime,** described as an "American ale," (not really a style, but we'll go with it); and the **Toasted Pumpkin Ale,** which is the brewery's strongest beer at 8.2 percent ABV.

The brewery is open Thursday and Friday from 4 to 7 p.m. and Saturday from 1 to 5 p.m. Tours are free if anyone is available to give them. Tastings are also available, as are growlers, bombers of 603's beers, and other 603-branded items.

## SMUTTYNOSE BREWING COMPANY

105 Towle Farm Rd., Hampton, NH; (603) 436-4026; Smuttynose.com
**Founded:** 1994 **Founder:** Peter Egleston **Brewer:** David Yarrington **Flagship Beer:** Shoal's Pale Ale **Year-round Beers:** Big A IPA, "Finestkind" IPA, Old Brown Dog Ale, Robust Porter, Bouncy House, Vundebar Pilsner **Seasonals/Special Releases:** Pumpkin Ale, Summer Weizen, Winter Ale, Durty, Big Beer Series, Short Batch Series **Tours:** Fri, 3 p.m.; Sat, 11 a.m.

The Smuttynose Brewing Company sometimes gets overlooked when people are discussing great New England breweries. People always talk about the new, up-and-coming, hot brewery of the month. Smuttynose has quietly been chugging along since Peter Egleston founded the brewery in 1994. More than just chugging along, they've been brewing excellent beers since the mid-'90s, and when other breweries peak, they stay at the same even level, brewing those excellent beers.

Smuttynose brews six different year-round beers. The **Shoal's Pale Ale** and **Old Brown Dog Ale** are New England classics. The **"Finestkind" IPA** is a nice, hoppy IPA; if "Finestkind" is not enough for your inner hophead, grab a bottle of the **Big A IPA.** The **Bouncy House** is one of the growing number of "session" or low-alcohol IPAs, while the **Vunderbar Pilsner** is a well-done German-style pilsner. The **Robust Porter** is just that, big and robust.

The seasonals include the **Pumpkin Ale,** the **Winter Ale,** and the **Summer Weizen,** one of the better New England–brewed wheat beers. Smuttynose also has the **Big Beer Series,** for which a different high-alcohol beer is released each month. These beers are packaged in 22-ounce bombers instead of the usual 12-ounce bottles. The **Baltic Porter** (November release) is absolutely amazing, a beer worth seeking out. The **Maibock** (April) is better than any other maibock brewed anywhere, here in

## Beer Lover's Pick

**The S'Muttonator**
**Style:** Doppelbock
**ABV:** 8.5 percent
**Availability:** Rotating

This entry in the Big Beer Series is a German-style doppelbock. This is pretty much the opposite of a hophead's dream. It's all malt, full-flavored, with a thick mouthfeel. There are strong toffee notes, with caramel, coffee, and the flavor of raisins. It is also very smooth and smells incredible, with an almost freshly baked bread quality to it.

the US or in Germany. Other entries in the Big Beer Series are the **Barleywine Ale,** the **Farmhouse Ale, Gravitation, Homunculus, Imperial Stout, Really Old Brown Dog Ale, Scotch Ale, S'Muttonator,** and the **Wheat Wine Ale.** Smuttynose also does a **Short Batch Series,** which consists of anywhere from 20 to 30 barrels of beer available on draft only. If a Short Batch Series beer is popular and well-received, it may be added to the regular lineup of beers. The Homunculus was the first Short Batch Series beer, when it was known as the Gnome.

The Smuttynose Brewing Company also offers tours on Friday and Saturday and, to top it off, there is a tasting of various beers they have available on draft. Although all the Smuttynose beers are easy to find, you should check out the beers available for sale in the brewery. Oftentimes they have some vintage Big Beer Series beers available.



## SQUAM BREWING COMPANY

118 Perch Pond Rd., Holderness, NH; (603) 236-9705; SquamBrewing.com
**Founded:** 2009 **Founder:** John Glidden **Brewer:** John Glidden **Flagship Beer:** Asquam Amber Ale **Year-round Beers:** Golden IPA, Rattlesnake Rye Pale Ale **Seasonals/Special Releases:** Bobhouse Bitter, No Wake Wheat, Winter Wheat **Tours:** By appointment only

The lakes region of New Hampshire is a great place to go for camping, fun on the water, and good times. And now, thanks to Squam Brewing Company, it's a great place to get a beer. Squam Brewing Company, founded in 2009 by John L. Glidden Jr., bottled its first beer in August 2010, and has produced some fantastic beer from this nano-brewery. How small is Squam Brewing Company? Squam brews about 45 to 50 gallons of beer at a time. That's about one and a half kegs. In his first year, Glidden brewed about 180 gallons. To put that in perspective, that's less than a normal batch of beer brewed at a brewpub at one time.

But what Squam lacks in size, it makes up in the quality of its beer. Currently, Squam brews three year-round beers, the **Asquam Amber Ale,** the **Golden IPA,** and the **Rattlesnake Rye Pale Ale.** The Golden IPA is one of the best imperial IPAs brewed in New England. The Asquam Amber Ale is a solid amber. It is nearly red in color, with a nice, bready malt flavor and just a touch of hops. The Rattlesnake Rye Pale Ale is your standard pale ale with a twist—rye malt. Rye malts add a nice, spicy character to a beer, and that sets it apart from a typical pale ale. Squam also brews three seasonals, the **Bobhouse Bitter** and **Winter Wheat** for the cold months and the **No Wake Wheat** for the warm months. The No Wake Wheat, in particular, is a standout, it's a perfectly light summer beer, great for those hot summer weekends spent grilling with friends or sitting poolside.

## Beer Lover's Pick

**Golden IPA**
**Style:** Double IPA
**ABV:** 8.5 percent
**Availability:** Year-Round

There are a lot of good double, or imperial, IPAs being brewed in New England, but there are few that are this good. The Golden IPA has a lot of fruity aroma (grapefruit, citrus) that continues into the taste, along with a lot of bittering hops. This beer is not super balanced, but it does not want to be. This is a beer for the hopheads, and the color is much lighter than many double IPAs.

Glidden hosts brewery tours by appointment at his brewery, which is also his home. Those taking the tour can try samples of any of the beers Glidden has on hand at the time. Bombers of Squam beers are available at the store, or in liquor stores from Concord north. Do yourself a favor and seek these beers out.

### STONEFACE BREWING COMPANY

436 Shattuck Way, Newington, NH; (603) 498-0211; StonefaceBrewing.com
**Founded:** 2014 **Founder:** Peter Beauregard **Brewer:** Peter Beauregard **Beers:** IPA, Pale Ale
**Taproom hours:** Hours are not set, usually Fri, 5 to 7 p.m. and Sat, noon to 4 p.m.

The Stoneface Brewing Company is the culmination of long-time homebrewer Peter Beauregard's dream to start his own brewery. The brewery only brews two beers, the **IPA** (which was an award-winning homebrew) and the **Pale Ale.**

The IPA is a 7.2 percent alcohol by volume (ABV) take on the style. It has citrusy, flowery flavors, and an almost sweet finish thanks to the malt. The Pale Ale is a 5.6 percent ABV with a ton of hop flavor for the style. The floral notes hit you right away, and it is followed with just a hint of bitterness before the bready malts take over.

Stoneface sells growlers, 4-ounce samples, glasses, T-shirts, and other items at its brewery stores.

### THROWBACK BREWERY

121 Lafayette Rd., Unit 3, North Hampton, NH; (603) 379-2317; ThrowbackBrewery.com
**Founded:** 2011 **Founders:** Nicole Carrier, Annette Lee **Brewer:** Annette Lee **Flagship Beer:** None **Year-round Beers:** Hog Happy Hefeweizen, Dippity-Do, Maple-Kissed Wheat Porter, Campfire **Seasonals/Special Releases:** Love Me Long Time Bohemian Pilsner, Fat Alberta, Hopstruck IPA, Spicy Bohemian, Stout #3 **Tours:** Thurs and Fri, 4 to 6 p.m.; Sat, 1 to 4 p.m.

Before Prohibition, many small local breweries used local ingredients because they were easy to acquire. The Throwback Brewery wants to take you back to those days (hence the name Throwback), purchasing as many of its ingredients from local sources within 100 miles of the North Hampton brewery as they possibly can. They then donate the spent grains used in the beer to local farms to be used to feed animals such as cows and pigs. Of course, the best part of Throwback Brewery is the beer. Brewer Annette Lee and her partner, Nicole Carrier, brew an excellent portfolio of creative beers.

The **Dippity-Do** looks like a regular brown ale, but it tastes nothing like it. It is unusually hopped like a pale ale. The sweetness is still the dominant flavor, but the hops come through, particularly in the finish. The **Maple-Kissed Wheat Porter** is different than most porters in several ways. First, wheat malt is used, which is highly unusual in a porter. This gives the beer a lighter, almost smoother taste. And locally produced maple is used during the brewing to give this a pleasant sweetness. It is a really nicely brewed beer. The **Campfire** is another porter, but this one is smoked. It is not as smoky as a German-style rauchbier, but the smoke is ever present. This is the best beer to drink while barbecuing. The **Hog Happy Hefeweizen** is a really well-done German-style wheat beer, and it features flavors of cloves and banana from the yeast. **Fat Alberta** is a big beer, at 9.5 percent alcohol by volume. Do not let that scare you away because you would be missing an extremely good stout. It is a chocolate and peanut butter stout. Let that sink in. It is like a liquid, alcoholic, peanut butter cup. The **Love Me Long Time Bohemian Pilsner** is a traditional pilsner, but the **Spicy Bohemian** is anything but traditional—it's the Love Me Long Time Bohemian Pilsner, but with roasted jalapeños added. Expect a burn in the back of your throat when you drink this. The **Hopstruck IPA** is a red IPA, and

## Beer Lover's Pick

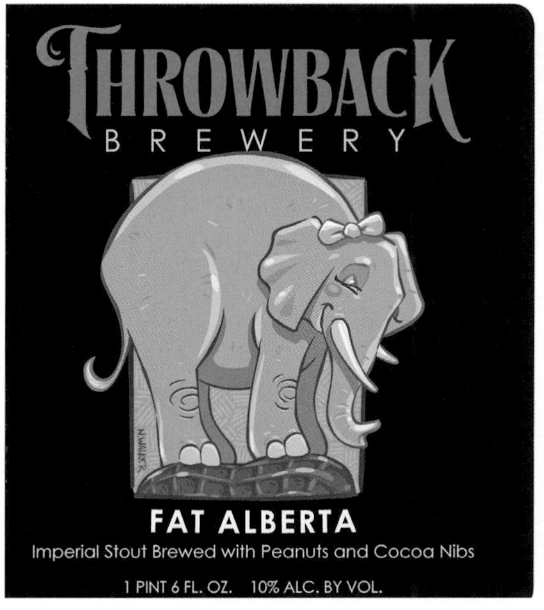


**Fat Alberta**
**Style:** Imperial Stout
**ABV:** 9.5 percent
**Availability:** Year-Round
A peanut butter and chocolate stout is creative and brewing genius. The flavors go together like, well, peanut butter and chocolate. This is a big beer, and the roasted malts and hops used in this beer stand up to these flavors. Many beers that use unusual flavors almost lose their beer-like quality. This does not. This is a phenomenal beer.

the **Stout #3** is an American stout with hints of cocoa and coffee.

Throwback hosts tastings and tours Thursday through Saturday. They also sell beer to go at the brewery, including the coolest-looking growlers ever seen. They are curvy, have a swing top, and, best of all, hold more than 67 ounces, compared to the normal growler that holds 64 ounces. Throwback also sells 22-ounce bombers of some of its beers. They also occasionally sell what they call growlettes, which are 32-ounce bottles of beer.

Throwback Brewery beers, keeping with the goal of being part of the local canvas, are only available in New Hampshire, so if you are driving through, do your best to seek them out.

## TUCKERMAN BREWING COMPANY

64 Hobbs St., Conway, NH; (603) 447-5400; TuckermanBrewing.com
**Founded:** 1998 **Founders:** Kristen Neves, Nik Stanciu **Brewer:** Allan Arnold **Flagship Beer:** Tuckerman's Pale Ale **Year-round Beer:** Headwall Alt **Seasonals/Special Releases:** ALTitude, 6288 Stout **Tours:** Sat, 3 p.m.; free

Tuckerman Brewing Company has been quietly brewing excellent beers for more than a decade and building up a dedicated following. The brewery was founded in 1998 by then-24-year-olds Kristen Neves and Nik Stanciu. Their first beer was the **Tuckerman's Pale Ale,** and for the first six years of Tuckerman's existence, this was the only beer they brewed.

The Pale Ale is a nice beer. It has a huge head, and it is easy to drink. It has a pleasant bitterness, with slight citrusy aroma and flavors. The malt is sweet and a tad biscuity. The **Headwall Alt** is a German-style alt, which is a brown ale. It has a fluffy head and it is dark, almost a reddish-brown. Flavor-wise, this is a traditional alt, big on the malt backbone, but with enough hops to offer a nice balance. The **6288 Stout** is named for the height of New Hampshire's Mt. Washington's peak. It is also a wonderful American stout. It is similar to an Irish dry stout, but a little stronger at 5.5 percent alcohol by volume (ABV). It still has the creaminess that you want in a stout, and a bitterness from the roast, not the hops. Tuckerman's only other beer

**Headwall Alt**
**Style:** Alt
**ABV:** 4.75 percent
**Availability:** Year-round

Alts are the most refreshing dark beer there is, and the Headwall Alt is an exceptional example of the style. The dark malts do not add a roasted character. Rather, this is a light-tasting beer, creamy and malt-forward, with sweet caramel flavors and a slight bready taste. The hops are there, but just enough to provide balance to prevent the Headwall Alt from becoming too sweet. It is an exceptional beer.

is the **ALTitude,** which is Headwall Alt's bigger brother. It is 7.5 percent ABV, and is actually closer to being a German-style sticke alt, which is basically an imperial alt.

Tuckerman takes pride in having a "green" company, getting many of its ingredients and other supplies locally, cutting down on transportation costs and gas consumption. The six-pack holders are manufactured in nearby Hooksett, New Hampshire. The case boxes are made in Maine and use sustainable forest inactivates. Most of the malts come from Maine and Canada, which are the closest locations that grow enough malt for Tuckerman's to brew their beers, and the water is local Conway water that comes from the Swift River.

Tuckerman Brewing Company hosts tours every Saturday at 3 p.m. The tour starts with a tasting of Tuckerman's beer, and follows with a tour of the brewery led by a brewer, who will explain the brewing process and all the ingredients. The tour then ends with another tasting so you can get a full appreciation of the beers after learning how they are brewed.

## WHITE BIRCH BREWING

1339 Hooksett Rd., Hooksett, NH; (603) 244-8593; WhiteBirchBrewing.com
**Founded:** 2009 **Founders:** Bill and Ellen Herlicka **Brewer:** Bill Herlicka **Flagship Beer:** Hooksett Ale **Year-round Beers:** Belgian Style Pale Ale, Hop Session **Seasonals/Special Releases:** Barley Wine Ale, Berliner Weisse, Bohemian Edition Tripel, Cherry Quad, Dubbel, Espresso Stout, Harvest Ale, Indomitus, Indulgence, Night Falls, Quad, Rye Four, Saison, Tavern Ale, Tripel, Wild Ale, Winter Warmer Wrigian, Apprentice Series, Barrel Aged Series, Oak Aged Series **Tours:** Mon and Tues, 10 a.m. to 5 p.m.; Wed through Fri, 10 a.m. to 7 p.m.; Sat, noon to 5 p.m.

There are few breweries as eclectic as White Birch Brewing Company. Founder/brewer Bill Herlicka likes to give a twist to his beers—almost none are traditional. An avid homebrewer, Herlicka and his wife, Ellen, founded the brewery in 2009, and immediately hit the ground running with a great mix of beers.

White Birch brews three year-round beers—the **Belgian Style Pale Ale,** the **Hooksett Ale,** and the **Hop Session.** The Belgian Style Pale Ale may be the closest to traditional that White Birch does. The Hooksett Ale blends Herlicka's love of west coast hoppy beers and his love of Belgian ales into a Belgian-style IPA, while the Hop Session is a hoppy, west coast–style IPA.

But where White Birch really excels, and where Herlicka's creativity really shows through, is in their rotating releases. The **Cherry Quad** is just that, a Belgian-style quad brewed with cherries. The flavors blend together perfectly. The **Espresso Stout** is a stout brewed with espresso beans, and the **Barley Wine Ale** is a big, burly beer, meant to be sipped, not gulped. The rotating releases also feature beers with some of the most unusual names. The **Indomitus** is a Belgian-style wild ale brewed with both White Birch's house yeast and wild yeast. It forms a tart, fruity beer. The **Indulgence** is brewed with huge amounts of chocolate malts. That's not uncommon in some stouts, but this isn't a stout or a porter, just a dark ale with tons of chocolate malts. The **Night Falls** is a dark wild ale, while the Wrigian is a Belgian-style ale brewed with rye.

White Birch also runs an apprentice program. After the program is complete, the apprentice has a chance to brew his or her own beer, which is released in the **Apprentice Series.** Herlicka also brews a **Barrel Aged Series** of beers. The **Oak Aged Series** of beers are brewed with oak chips or oak spirals in the fermenting stage to impart the oaky, vanilla-like flavors often associated with barrel-aging.

White Birch offers tours Monday through Saturday, led by one of the four employees and featuring a tour of the brewery and education about the history of the brewery and the brewing process. There are also tastings, typically limited to the year-round beers. The brewery store has beer to go in bombers and growlers.

**Berliner Weisse**
**Style:** Berliner Weisse
**ABV:** 6.4 percent
**Availability:** Rotating

There aren't many Berliner weisses brewed in the US, so when you see one, you should grab it. This is an excellent Berliner weisse, although much stronger than the typical version. It has a heftier body than the traditional beer, but what it does have is the tartness, which tastes a bit like lemonade. You just want to take a sip.

## WOODSTOCK INN BREWERY

135 Main St., North Woodstock, NH; (800) 321-3985; WoodstockInnBrewery.com
**Founded:** 1995 **Founder:** Scott Rice **Brewer:** Butch Evans **Flagship Beer:** Pig's Ear Brown Ale **Year-round Beers:** Loon Golden Ale, Old Man Oatmeal Stout, Pemi Pale Ale, Red Rack Ale, Through Hiker Double Rye Pale Ale, Scottish Ale, White Mountain Weasel Wheat Ale **Seasonals/Special Releases:** Autumn Brew, Cogsman Ale, Kanc Country Maple Porter, Raspberry Weasel Wheat, Wassail Winter Ale **Tours:** Daily at noon

If you ever want to get away for a weekend, find a nice inn with a nice restaurant, and maybe even enjoy a few good beers, North Woodstock should be one of your top destinations. The Woodstock Station Inn, a 33-room inn spread over five buildings, is also host to the Woodstock Inn Brewery, a small craft brewery that brews some very good beers.

The brewery's most popular beer is the **Pig's Ear Brown Ale,** a traditional English-style nut brown ale. It has a nice nutty flavor, and sweet caramel flavors from the malts. It is an easy beer to savor. The **Red Rack Ale,** like the Pig's Ear, is a traditional brewed beer. This Irish red ale is heavy on the malts, just like most of Woodstock's beers. The **Scottish Ale** is a malty beer, but feels much fuller-bodied than a beer that is only 4.75 percent alcohol by volume (ABV), while the **White Mountain Weasel Wheat Ale** and the **Loon Golden Ale** are two easy-drinking, light, and refreshing brews. The **Old Man Oatmeal Stout** is smooth and creamy, just as an oatmeal stout should be. The **Pemi Pale Ale** leans toward the English version of the style, with a malt-forward base. However it finishes with a nice hop bite. The **Through Hiker Double Rye Pale Ale** is the biggest of the year-round beers at 7.9 percent ABV. It is a hoppy IPA brewed with rye, giving this beer a nice spicy character.

Where Woodstock really shines is its seasonals. The **Autumn Brew** is brewed with apples and cinnamon and just tastes like fall. The **Raspberry Weasel Wheat** is the same beer as the White Mountain Weasel Wheat, except with raspberries added. The **Kanc Country Maple Porter** is a really well-done porter, brewed with local maple syrup. The maple flavor really comes through, making this a cold weather treat. The **Cogsman Ale** is an English-style IPA with just a touch of English hops pushing through. The brewery's biggest beer is the **Wassail Winter Ale,** which comes in at 8 percent ABV. This is a full-bodied beer loaded with a lot of sweet malt. It smells boozy, and that continues on into the taste.

The Woodstock Inn Brewery hosts daily tours that includes an introduction to the brewing process, as well as a sampling of some of their beers. But if you really want to get your hands dirty, you will want to reserve a spot on a Brewer's Weekend. The weekend begins with a welcome reception in the Woodstock Station

## Beer Lover's Pick

**Kanc Country Maple Porter**
**Style:** Porter
**ABV:** 6 percent
**Availability:** Winter Seasonal

The Kanc Country Maple Porter is a wonderful English-style porter, with a twist: the addition of local maple syrup. The porter is malty and has a nice roasty character, with hints of coffee and chocolate. The maple syrup really comes through in this beer, with a pleasant sweetness. If a great breakfast beer ever existed, the Kanc Country Maple Porter would be it.

Inn's restaurant. Work begins on Saturday morning. After a quick breakfast, you will head out to the brewery and help brew beer with brewer Butch Evans. You better be ready to sweat as you start lugging bags of malt and hops around. Top it all off with a nice beer dinner.

## EARTH EAGLE BREWINGS

165 High St., Portsmouth, NH; (603) 817-2773; EarthEagleBrewings.com
**Founded:** 2013 **Founders:** Butch Heilshorn, Alex McDonald **Brewers:** Butch Heilshorn, Alex McDonald **Flagship Beers:** New England Gangsta' Beers: (only an example) Mary of the Marsh, Citra, Hanuman Tripel, Witching Hour, Shepherds Creek, St. Corbian's Red, Antoinette **Taproom hours:** Mon through Fri, 4 to 9 p.m.; Sat, 3 to 9 p.m.; Sun, 1 to 4 p.m.

Earth Eagle Brewings is the most unique brewery in all of New England, possibly the US. While many breweries specialize in a specific style of beer, Earth Eagle Brewings, founded by brothers-in-law Butch Heilshorn and Alex McDonald in 2013, focus on an ancient style of ale called gruits.

Gruits were a medieval beer, which used a mix of herbs and flowers instead of the hops used in today's beers. Very few breweries brew gruits—there are probably only one or two bottled gruits available on liquor store shelves—and Earth Eagle specializes in them. The brewing is split between the two men. Heilshorn handles the gruit brewing and some of their more "unusual beers," (more on that later) while McDonald does the hoppy and more traditional beers. Not all gruits are for everyone. Even though they are the same style, the use of different herbs can change the beer completely. For example, **Antoinette** uses catnip, while **Hanuman Tripel** brews with garcinia fruit and chrysanthemum flowers.

Earth Eagle also brews the **Porter Cochon** and **St. Corbian's Red,** which have extremely unusual ingredients. The Porter Cochon is a porter brewed with green bullet hops, lavender, and four hog heads. You read that right—pig heads are used in the Porter Cochon. The St. Corbian's Red is a sour gruit. One of its key ingredients is bear meat. There are a lot of bears in New Hampshire, but brewing with the meat of one is not common.

Non-gruits include a series of single hop blonde ales, **Shepherd's Creek,** which is a hybrid pale ale brewed with 50 percent barley malt and 50 percent wheat malt, and the extremely popular **New England Gangsta',** a 6.5 percent alcohol by volume (ABV) west coast IPA, which usually sells out in a week.

The Earth Eagle tasting room is small, but one of the cooler beer spots in New Hampshire. Earth Eagle is the only place where you'll find its beers. They sell pints, half pints and 4-ounce samplers, as well as 32-ounce and 64-ounce growlers to go. It is open seven days a week.

### ELM CITY BREWING COMPANY

Colony Mill Market Place, 22 West St., Unit 46, Keene, NH; (603) 355-3335; ElmCityBrewery.com

**Draft Beers:** 9

Keene is one of those small New England towns that you can imagine pictured on a postcard. Not far from Keene State College, in the historic Colony Mill Market Place, is the Elm City Brewing Company. This wonderful little brewpub brews as many as 20 different beers throughout the year and they have 9 beers on draft.

Elm City brews two versions of its kolsch. The regular kolsch is the **Keene Kolsch,** and the second is the **Peachy Keene Kolsch,** which has peaches added. Another fruit beer is the **Raspberry Wheat.** Another interesting beer is the **Oatmeal Pale Ale.** Oatmeal is often used in stouts, but it provides a different depth of character when used in other styles that gives a nice contrast to barley malt that is used in most styles. Other beers include the **Brickhouse ESB, No Name IPA,** the **Porthole Porter, Irish Stout, Monadnock Mt. Ale** (pale ale), and **Vanilla Stout.** Elm City also brews one of the few roggenbiers in New England. Roggenbiers are German-style rye beers, which are hard to find even in Germany! Seasonals include the **Mai Bock, Oktoberfest,** and **Nor'Easter** (wee heavy).

Elm City has a large dining area, as well as a sunny atrium to sit in, and an outdoor seating area during the summer. Elm City offers many sandwiches, including grilled cheese and tomato, pastrami, BLT, a tuna wrap, and the Spinach and Herb Cheese Sandwich, which is made with spinach, tomato, mushrooms, red onions, bean

### Oktoberfest

Elm City Brewing Company hosts their annual Oktoberfest celebration every September. The outdoor event goes from 1 to 5 p.m. and features German food; German music, games, and prizes; and the official first tapping of Elm City's Oktoberfest for the fall season. Grab your lederhosen and head on over.

sprouts, and herb cheese. Entrees include beer-battered fish and chips, vegetable lasagna, and the Brewmaster's Dinner, which includes grilled knockwurst and bratwurst, served with sauerkraut and a potato pancake. Elm City also offers growlers of its beers to go, as well as glasses, mugs, and T-shirts.

### FLYING GOOSE BREW PUB & GRILL

40 Andover Rd., New London, NH; (603) 526-6899; FlyingGoose.com
**Draft Beers:** 17

On a road trip through New England, you are bound to drive through some little towns you may never have heard of and come across a little brewpub. That is the case with the Flying Goose Brew Pub & Grill. It is one of those brewpubs people outside of the area may not know, but they will definitely be happy if they stumble across it. The pub has won awards for being environmentally friendly and self-sustaining. They are solar powered, and they use almost all recycled products in the pub.

Flying Goose always has 17 of its beers on tap. The beers include lighter beers like the excellent **Pleasant Lake Pilsner, Heidelberg Hefeweizen, Split Rock Golden Ale,** and the **Wildflower Honey Ale,** which is made with local wildflower honey. Other beers typically available include **Alexandria Alt,** a traditional German-style altbier, the **Hedgehog Brown Ale, Long Brother's Strong Ale,** and **Crockett's Corner Oatmeal Stout.** Other beers occasionally available include the **Berliner Weisse,** a wonderfully tart and refreshing wheat beer, **Mikey's Vyce Black IPA,** the **Rauchbier Lager,** and the **Isle of Pines Barleywine** (definitely get this if you are a hophead).

The food menu is large and varied at the Flying Goose. Starters include the Goose Bread, which is garlic Italian bread topped with parmesan, mozzarella, and blue cheeses, and the Beer Skins, which are potato skins baked in a Hedgehog Brown Ale and butter sauce. Sandwiches include an open-faced prime rib sandwich, steak and cheese paninis, and Emily's Wrap, which features crispy chicken, cheddar and jack cheeses, tomatoes, and barbecue ranch dressing served in a flour tortilla. The burger to get is the New Englander, which is covered in smoked bacon, sautéed onions, and Vermont cheddar cheese.

The entrees are on the creative side, and include pork risotto, country meat loaf, and the Flying Goose Paella, which is made with mussels, shrimp, chicken, and chorizo sausage. The Devonshire Delmonico is also worth trying. It is a lightly smoked, hand-cut rib eye steak, dusted in Cajun seasoning, pan baked, and finished with bacon mélange butter.

## MARTHA'S EXCHANGE

185 Main St., Nashua, NH; (603) 883-8781; Marthas-Exchange.com
**Draft Beers:** 8

Nashua is the place where Massachusetts residents go shopping so they can avoid paying sales tax. It is also the home of Martha's Exchange, giving beer lovers a reason to go to Nashua, too. Martha's Exchange brewpub is a historic business. It originally opened in 1932 as Martha's Sweet Shop, where it sold handmade candies. It has also hosted nearly every presidential candidate who has come to Nashua during the campaign every four years.

Martha's Exchange still sells handmade candy in the on-site candy store, but they also sell handmade beer and food in what is now one of New Hampshire's premier brewpubs. Throughout the year, Martha's Exchange will have anywhere between 20 and 25 different beers on tap. The only beer on tap at all times is the **Volstead '33,** a lighter, easy-drinking beer. The beer you have to get if available is the **Velvet Elvis Vanilla Bean Stout.** This is an absolutely amazing beer, and if it happens to be on cask, it would almost be a crime to not get it.

Other beers include **Another Ale** (pale ale), **Biscuit City Pale Ale,** the **Dark Rasputin Stout, Indian Head Red, McGann's London Ale** (English pale ale), **Steeplechase Porter,** and the **Vow of Silence Belgian Stout.** Martha's Exchange also brews several seasonals, including the **Hefeweizen, Magi Winter Warmer,** and **Oktoberfest.** Martha's also brews what they call the **Reserve Series,** which are beers typically only brewed once. Once the keg is tapped, it is gone for good.

If you do not want to eat handmade chocolate for dinner (nothing wrong if you do), grab some food. Appetizers include the pulled pork quesadilla, sweet potato wedges, lemon cilantro mussels, beef tenderloin crostinis, and the Tapas Trio Dip, which includes smoked salmon dip, olive tapenade dip, and a red pepper hummus served with blue and yellow corn chips, carrots, cucumbers, and red peppers for dipping. Also available is a large selection of flatbread pizzas, including the Mexican Fiesta. The Mexican Fiesta is topped with pico de gallo, avocadoes, jalapeños, cheddar and jack cheeses, and a zesty salsa. Salads include two standouts: The lobster salad is lobster with dill mayo over red greens with pita, tomatoes, cucumbers, and roasted red peppers, while the lamb salad is made up of grilled lamb, mixed greens, red onions, tomatoes, pita, kalamata olives, pepperoncinis, and feta cheese. Entrees include the mango haddock, which is fresh haddock sautéed with a mango/pineapple salsa sauce, served over pasta; and the ginger wasabi steak, a 12-ounce sirloin steak topped with fresh ginger and soy sauce and served with wasabi mashed potatoes.

If you happen to be there on Friday or Saturday, Martha's Exchange turns into a nightclub at 10 p.m. with drink specials and a DJ playing dance music. And if you stop in, make sure to take a look at the bar itself. It was once in one of Al Capone's speakeasies in Chicago.

### MILLY'S TAVERN

500 Commercial St., Manchester, NH; (603) 625-4444; MillysTavern.com
**Draft Beers:** 18

Milly's Tavern is one of the best brewpubs in the Granite State. The beers are phenomenal, and the food is excellent. It is a combination that cannot be beat, particularly when you throw in the abundant live entertainment at this Manchester brewpub.

Their year-round beers are fantastic. The **Fisher Cat Ale** is a light (3.8 percent alcohol by volume [ABV]) ale made with pale malt, named for the New Hampshire Fisher Cat baseball team located near the brewpub. The **Mt. Uncanoonuc Golden Cream Ale** is a really good cream ale, a style more breweries should brew. **Tasha's Red Tail Ale** is a nicely brewed red ale, with just a hint of a hop kick. Other year-round beers include the **General John Stark Dark Porter,** an exceptional porter, **Milly's Oatmeal Stout,** the **Manch-Vegas IPA,** and **Bo's Scotch Ale,** a type of big beer you usually don't see as a year-round brewpub offering, at 9.5 percent ABV.

The specialty beers are also worth seeking out. Milly's Tavern brews two beers based on the **General John Stark Dark Porter.** They brew the **Chocolate Porter,** made with Van Otis chocolate, and the **Cherry Porter,** brewed with real cherries. The **Coffee Espresso Stout** is a winner, as is the **Burton Ale** (a classic English-style IPA) and **Hopzilla** (a double IPA). **Milly's Famous Pumpkin Ale** is much sought after by pumpkin beer fans.

But the two beers you have to try are the **Blueberry Lambic** and **Raspberry Lambic.** These are not your typical fruit beers, which are usually lighter ales with either fruit flavor or real fruit added. These are traditional Belgian-style lambics. They have a champagne-like carbonation, are extremely tart, and are brewed with a Belgian strain of yeast. Superb beers, both of them.

Food-wise, Milly's Tavern really stands out, particularly for the price. You would be hard-pressed to find better food for a better price. Milly's nachos are huge, big enough for three people to share. Other appetizers include sweet potato fries and stuffed mushrooms, as well as the Espinaca, which is creamy cheese sauce with jalapeños, cayenne pepper, spinach, and salsa served with tortilla chips for dipping. Want a good hearty meal? Grab the Oatmeal Stout Beef Stew, served in a bread bowl

## Anheuser-Busch in The Granite State

Although this book is about the great craft beer produced in New England and the places where you can go to get that great craft beer, I feel obligated to address the fact that most people are still likely to choose a mass-produced lager like Budweiser over a hoppy IPA while out at the bar. And there's nothing wrong with that—beer lovers don't have to like just craft beer.

The largest brewing company in the US is Anheuser-Busch—producer of Budweiser, Bud Light, and Michelob, among other beers—and they have 12 breweries in the US, including one at 221 Daniel Webster Hwy., in Merrimac, New Hampshire. The brewery can package eight million 12-ounce bottles or cans a day, if needed. That is more beer than nearly every brewery in New England brews in a year.

The New Hampshire brewery hosts tours throughout the year. The times change by month, so log onto www.budweisertours.com to see when the tour takes place. The in-depth, guided tour is free, and it includes free beer samples, soda, and snacks. It typically lasts about one and a half hours, and photography is usually not allowed. On the first Saturday of the month from 1 to 3 p.m., they allow people take photos of themselves and one of the Clydesdales.



(see recipe, page 313). It is a classic beef stew made with Milly's Oatmeal Stout. Milly's also offers 8-inch flatbread pizzas, 12-inch pizzas, burgers, salads, wraps, and quesadillas. There are also plenty of sandwiches. Best bargain? Get two beer-steamed hot dogs for $5. The dogs are steamed in porter. If you have room, grab a brownie sundae or a root beer float for dessert. The chocolate porter and the brownie sundae would be a perfect food pairing.

At night, Milly's Tavern turns into a nightclub, with dancing, live music, and DJs taking over. Don't worry, the beers are still available.

### MOAT MOUNTAIN SMOKE HOUSE & BREWING COMPANY

3378 White Mountain Hwy., Rte. 16, North Conway, NH; (603) 356-6481; MoatMountain.com
**Draft Beers:** 6

The Moat Mountain Smoke House and Brewing Company is worth making a trip to North Conway. And you will not have to worry about trying to find a place to stay—you can reserve one of the five rooms they have in their own inn. The Moat

Mountain has an eclectic mix of beers that includes several lagers and some higher-alcohol beers.

Year-round beers include the **Moat Czech Pilsner,** the **Moat Ale,** the **Moat Stout,** and the **Hoffman Weiss.** Even better are the seasonals and special releases. The **Moat Pilsner** (a different beer than the Czech Pilsner) and the **Moat Lager** will satisfy those who enjoy lagers. The **Moat IPA** is a 7 percent alcohol by volume (ABV) English-style IPA, and the **Moat Blueberry** is a solid blueberry ale. The **Smoke House Porter** is excellent, and the **Moat Oktoberfest** is spot on for the style. Moat also brews the perfect beer for a pub that specializes in smoked meat, the **Rauchbier,** a German-style smoked ale.

Moat also brews some bigger beers, such as the **Moat Bock,** an 8.5 percent German-style bock. The 8.9 percent ABV **Belgian Triple** is a classic Belgian ale. The **Moat Imperial Stout** is the brewery's strongest beer at 9 percent ABV.

Moat Mountain is more than a brewery; it is also a great place to get some barbecued and smoked meat. The appetizers are different from many restaurants and include the Texas-style brisket and Andouille chili, curried crab and corn bisque, New England–style hush puppies (made with local maple syrup), and the Moat Mountain Pot Stickers. Nachos and quesadillas are also available. Smoke House Burgers are half-pound burgers with tons of toppings available, and there are many sandwiches, such as the blackened catfish and the barbecued Reuben, which substitutes beef brisket for the traditional corned beef.

But if you really like meat, get the Combo Platter, which includes a half-rack of ribs, a quarter chicken, and your choice of beef brisket or smoked pork. It is served with skillet corn bread and cole slaw. All the barbecue sauces used are made on-site.

The great thing about Moat Mountain is that they have the small on-site inn, which makes for an easy overnight trip. All the rooms feature king-size beds and flat-screen televisions. Plan ahead, though—there are only five rooms. Also, if you have pet allergies, keep that in mind because the inn owner's dogs are often inside the inn.

Moat Mountain also sells beers to go in the form of growlers, and you can often find their beers on draft in other bars throughout New Hampshire. Their canned beers also have limited distribution.

## PORTSMOUTH BREWERY

56 Market St., Portsmouth, NH; (603) 431-1115; PortsmouthBrewery.com
**Draft Beers:** 10

The Portsmouth Brewery is known nationally for brewing one of the most sought-after beers in the world, **Kate the Great** (more on her later). Brewmaster Tod Mott and his crew of brewers create some great beer, and the Portsmouth Brewery is one of the five best brewpubs in all of New England.

Founded in 1991 by brother and sister Peter and Janet Egelston, along with Janet's husband, Mark Metzger, the Portsmouth Brewery has set itself above most other brewpubs with a solid lineup of beers from the top to the bottom, as well as several guest taps from other New Hampshire breweries. They also have several Smuttynose Brewing Company beers on tap. Peter Egelston owns Smuttynose, also located in Portsmouth. You'll most likely find something new on top every time you visit. They have a huge list of beers to choose from, from English milds to German alts to Belgian-style ales. Mott brews almost any style you can think of.

The year-round beers include the **Dirty Blonde Ale** and the **Black Cat Stout,** but if you really want to get adventurous, try the other beers on tap. If you're a hophead, the best beer may be the **5 C's,** a west-coast IPA brewed with Cascade, Centennial, Chinook, Columbus, and Crystal hops (and a little Simcoe). Like an IPA with a twist? Grab the **Ginga Ninja IPA,** an IPA brewed with ginger. Or, maybe Belgian ales are for you. The **St. Danmon Trippel** is fantastic, and the **Biere de**

### Kate the Great Day

Every February or March, beer geeks from all over gather on the streets of Portsmouth for one reason—Kate the Great. Kate the Great is Portsmouth Brewing Company's Russian imperial stout. It is released on one day each year. There is a lottery ahead of time to get bottles, but people still gather for their chance to taste this beer before it taps out, usually by 5 p.m. the same day.

**Miele** is a great beer to give to those who say they don't like beer—it has a wine-like quality, and the honey used in the beer is a winning flavor combination. Portsmouth Brewery also has several lagers, including the **Oktoberfest** and the **Pils Von Faust.** But, you cannot talk about the Portsmouth Brewery without mentioning Kate the Great. This 10.5 percent alcohol by volume is one of the best beers brewed in the world. Bold, full-flavored, and oh so tasty.

The great thing is, while you're enjoying the beer, Portsmouth Brewery also serves up some really good food. The food is pretty much straightforward pub-style food, but done really well. The crispy fried calamari is a winner for an appetizer, and the nacho plate is perfect for a group of four, and even more. The bratwurst burger is a great sandwich, and the pastrami on rye is as good as any deli's. The Old Brown Dog Hanger Steak, made with an Old Brown Dog beer marinade, is a good option if you want something more than a sandwich (see recipe, page 313).

The Portsmouth Brewery also offers tours, and everyone who takes a tour will get a 50 percent discount on a platter of beer samples. Before leaving make sure to stop at the brewery shop. Growlers of beer are available at the bar, but 22-ounce bottles, as well as shirts, glasses, and other beer-related gear are available in the store.

### SCHILLING BEER COMPANY

18 Mill St., Littleton, NH, (603) 444-4800, SchillingBeer.com
**Draft Beers:** 12

Some breweries specialize in Belgian-style ales, while others take inspiration from the historic German beers. The Schilling Beer Company, a brewpub in Littleton, New Hampshire, though, takes inspiration from both, as well as other European countries, to create its portfolio of popular beers. The brewpub usually has five of its own beers on tap, as well as a guest tap list from some of the best breweries in New England and beyond.

The rotating list of beers brewed by Schilling include the **Besserwissier** (dunkelweizen), **Clevaux** (Belgian pale ale), **Dr. Oovert** (Belgian strong ale), **Düsseldorf Alt, Erastus** (Belgian tripel), **Heller Weizenbock, Herkules** (kolsch), **Kamaradrie** (Baltic porter) **Nouveau Monde** (Belgian witbier), **RBS—Rustic Belgian Brown, Schlaumeier** (hefeweizen), and the **Smoked Kristall** (smoked kristalweiss).

Along with its beers, Schilling also makes and serves food, mostly pizzas served out of their handmade wood-fired oven which is pretty much in the middle of the restaurant. Schilling specializes in pizzas, as well as calzones and strombolis. They also offer rotating entrees, and entrée-size salads.

Schilling Beer Company is open seven days a week—Monday through Thursday, 3 to 11 p.m.; Friday and Saturday, noon to 11 p.m.; and Sunday, noon to 10 p.m. They do not offer growlers to go.

## SEVEN BARREL BREWERY

5 Airport Rd., West Lebanon, NH; (603) 298-5566; 7Barrel.com
**Draft Beers:** 8

Greg Noonan is most known in New England brewing circles for opening the Vermont Pub & Brewery in Burlington, but he is also the founder of the Seven Barrel Brewery in tiny West Lebanon, New Hampshire. Both pubs have similar qualities—good beer and good food.

The name of the brewery comes from the original brewing system, which was a seven-barrel system. The Seven Barrel Brewery usually has eight beers on draft at all time, which include the **Champion Reserve IPA, New Dublin Brown, R.I.P. Stout, The Red #7,** and the **Quechee Cream Ale.** The cream ale, in particular, is worth trying. It is a light but flavorful beer. Seasonals include the **Octoberfest** and **Spring Ale.** Other beers include the **Double IPA,** the **Mick Jack Porter,** the **Hanover Lager,** and **Al's Bock.** The Seven Barrel Brewery also has a line of higher-alcohol beers called the **Conan the Destroyer Series.** These beers are more high octane than those typically brewed at Seven Barrel and styles include an imperial coffee stout and an imperial brown ale.

Just like the Vermont Pub & Brewery, the Seven Barrel Brewery is heavy on pub-style food. Starters include the Pub Cheese Plate, which includes Grafton Village Cheddar, Gafford's Smoked Gruyère, and Vermont Chevre, served with a crispy baguette, pickled vegetables, house chutney, and honey Dijon mustard. Another standout is a French-Canadian original, poutine, which is french fries smothered in onion gravy and local cheese curds. Entrees include the Cock a'Leekie Pie, which is a pie stuffed with chicken, leeks, carrots, potatoes, and celery and topped with gravy. The Baked Chicken Statler is another possibility. It is a pan-seared, semi-boneless chicken breast with thyme and sautéed mushrooms. You can also get Bratwurst n' Beer, which is a bratwurst steamed in beer, or grab the Toad-in-the-Hole, which is made of pork sausages, sautéed onions, and mild cheddar cheese baked inside a puff pastry.

The Seven Barrel Brewery also frequently hosts live bands, so you can always get a good meal and beer while listening to music. And do not forget to grab a growler of your favorite beer on the way out.

## THE BARLEY HOUSE

132 North Main St., Concord, NH; (603) 228-6363; TheBarleyHouse.com
**Draft Beers:** 13 **Bottled/Canned Beers:** 35

The Barley House has a great spot, located right across the street from the New Hampshire State House in Concord. After a day of politicking, a beer and a burger is a must. The Barley House is a great little beer bar that has been voted "Best of . . ." in several categories by local entertainment publications, and it really earns those designations.

Although they only have 13 beers on tap, they are all worth drinking. They typically have beers from Otter Creek, Peak Organic, Lagunitas, and a beer brewed just for them by Harpoon. The bar offers sample platters, and what they call the Dublin Double, which consists of two 10-ounce taster pints of two different beers of your choice. The bottled list is split up between big bottles (22-ounce bombers and 750 ml bottles) and 12-ounce bottles. The larger bottles are a little more geared to beer geeks: They typically have beers from Brewery Ommegang, Brewdog, Chimay, Rogue, Unibroue, and White Birch. The 12-ounce bottles feature mostly mass-produced beers, but Samuel Adams and Long Trail beers are often available.

Food-wise, the Barley House has several decent options. Small plates include crab bacon sliders, which are topped with house-cured bacon, egg, and Cajun mayo on a brioche bun. Other options include wild boar cranberry sausage and Blarney Puffs, which are cheddar, scallions, and potatoes in a fried dumpling, covered with a Guinness cheese sauce. A little too heavy for you? Salads are also available, including the Apple, Craisin, and Spicy Walnut salad, made with mixed greens and cider mustard vinaigrette.

The Barley House is known for making great burgers, which are ground daily. There are several burgers to choose from, including the BBQ bacon bison burger. Another burger to consider is the Bailey Ballpark Burger, which is a pork and beef patty with house beer mustard and smoked Gouda. Many of the entrees offered by the Barley House are made with beer or some sort of liquor. They offer tequila-cilantro-lime sea scallops, Irish whiskey steak, Guinness beef stew, and Smithwick's Curry Fish and Chips. And do not forget to leave room for dessert. The homemade bread pudding with maple whiskey sauce and the crème brûlée with vanilla custard and caramelized sugar are both delightful ends to a good meal.

## BLUE MERMAID ISLAND GRILL

409 The Hill, Portsmouth, NH; (603) 427-2583; BlueMermaid.com
**Draft Beers:** 8 **Bottled/Canned Beers:** About 20

The Blue Mermaid Island Grill is the closest you will get to the Caribbean without leaving Portsmouth—and they also happen to have great beer. The Mermaid is within walking distance of several other good beer bars, as well as the Portsmouth Brewery, so if you're in town, be sure to make a day of it.

The draft list is on the small side, with only eight beers on tap. The beers, for the most part, are beers from New England, such as Moat Mountain, Shipyard, Smuttynose, and Throwback. They also often switch out the tap list, making sure there are at least a few seasonals available. The bottled list includes Samuel Adams, Sierra Nevada, and imports such as Gulden Draak and Piraat Ale, both from Belgium.

Food-wise, the Blue Mermaid's menu is quite different from most beer bars. That difference is noticeable right away looking at the small plates or appetizers. There are several interesting options, such as wasabi rangoons; orange ginger egg rolls; and the Mermaid Fundito, a dip made with cheddar cheese, pale ale, fire-roasted tomatoes, and chili, served with crusty bread for dipping. Entrees include the plantain--encrusted cod and the Rasta Pasta. The Rasta Pasta is made with penne pasta, sautéed with onions, baby spinach, and roasted tomatoes, served in a chili pesto cream sauce. Other dishes include the New World Paella, made with chicken, shrimp, sausage, and mussels, sautéed in a curried rice; and pan-blackened mahi mahi.

Brunch is also served on Sunday from 10 a.m. to 2 p.m. Items available include lobster frittata, which is three eggs, roasted tomato, goat cheese, spinach, and lobster. Another option is the Green Eggs and Ham, which is made of three scrambled eggs, jack cheese, ham, and jalapeño pesto, served in a tortilla wrap with goat cheese.

## PORTSMOUTH GAS LIGHT CO.

64 Market St., Portsmouth, NH; (603) 431-9122; PortsmouthGaslight.com
**Draft Beers:** 21 **Bottled/Canned Beers:** About 20

The Portsmouth Gas Light Co. is a multifaceted establishment. It's one part restaurant/pub with good food and beer and one part pizzeria with a big selection of pasta (the outdoor deck also has a smaller menu and live music), and the "Third Floor" is a nightclub. Needless to say, the Gas Light has something for everyone, especially beer lovers.

The pub area has 12 beers on tap, as well as a selection of bottled beers. The pizzeria has another 8 beers on tap, while the deck has 1 additional draft. All the beers and bottles are available throughout the building. The beers are split up between New England beers and beers from other parts of the country. Breweries often available include Allagash, Berkshire Brewing Company, Shipyard Brewing Company, Full Sail Brewing Company, and a brewery I have never seen on tap anywhere else in New England, Hinterland Brewery from Wisconsin.

The menus are different in all three eating locations (the nightclub does not serve food), but the street-level grill serves up some of the best food in Portsmouth. Appetizers include the Louisiana-style grilled sea scallops and the quarter-pound Maine lobster cake. They also offer several salads, including the Tomato and Watermelon Salad, which features tri-colored tomatoes tossed with fresh mint and basil chiffonade, diced watermelon, and feta cheese topped with just a little olive oil. Portsmouth Gas Light also offers a large wood-fired-grilled menu. Steaks, ribs, chicken, and mahi mahi are all available from the grill. Downtown Pizza, like its name implies, is all about the pizza. Sure, you can get a regular pepperoni pizza, but why not order one of their specialty pizzas, such as the Congress, which is topped with mounds of pepperoni, sweet sausage, onions, green peppers, mushrooms, and black olives? If you're feeling really hungry, try the Navy Yard, which is topped with cheddar and mozzarella cheese, piles of ground beef, and bacon.

## STRANGE BREW TAVERN

88 Market St., Manchester, NH; (603) 666-4292; StrangeBrewTavern.com
**Draft Beers:** 82 **Bottled/Canned Beers:** 30

The Strange Brew Tavern is a downtown Manchester destination for those looking for good beer and live music. Not only do they feature the most beers on tap in all of New Hampshire, 82 beers over two floors, but the tavern also hosts live bands six nights a week.

The beer selection is large, but for the most part, the beers are more mainstream craft beer, like Magic Hat, Samuel Adams, and Shipyard. They also feature several New Hampshire breweries, such as Redhook, Smuttynose, and Woodstock. Other breweries often featured include Blue Point, Dogfish Head, and Victory. Strange Brew also offers up a few imports, such as beers from Unibroue, as well as Smithwick's and Dos Equis. Can't decide what beer to get? Order the sampler, in which you can get five small glasses of beer of your choice for $8, only available on Wednesday and Sunday. Most nights, Strange Brew also offers drink specials, with discount beers.

To go along with the beer, Strange Brew also offers some delicious pub food. Appetizers include fried pickle chips or fried artichoke hearts, as well as the Beer Cheese Platter, which features pub cheese mixed with red ale. If there is a group, the best option is probably the Combo Platter, which features potato skins, jalapeño poppers, mozzarella sticks, and chicken tenders. In addition to the many sandwiches, burgers, and wraps on the menu, there are salads available, including the Strange Brew Chopped Salad, which is made of grilled chicken, bacon, eggs, zucchini, squash, caramelized red onions, Swiss cheese, romaine lettuce, and sweet ranchero dressing. Entrees include Guinness meat loaf and mashed potatoes, Blue Moon Beer Batter Scallops or Blue Moon Beer Batter Fish and Chips, fried fish tacos, and jambalaya.

Along with live music, every Thursday night Strange Brew hosts trivia nights where teams compete for a $100 gift certificate to the Portsmouth Brewery.

# Connecticut

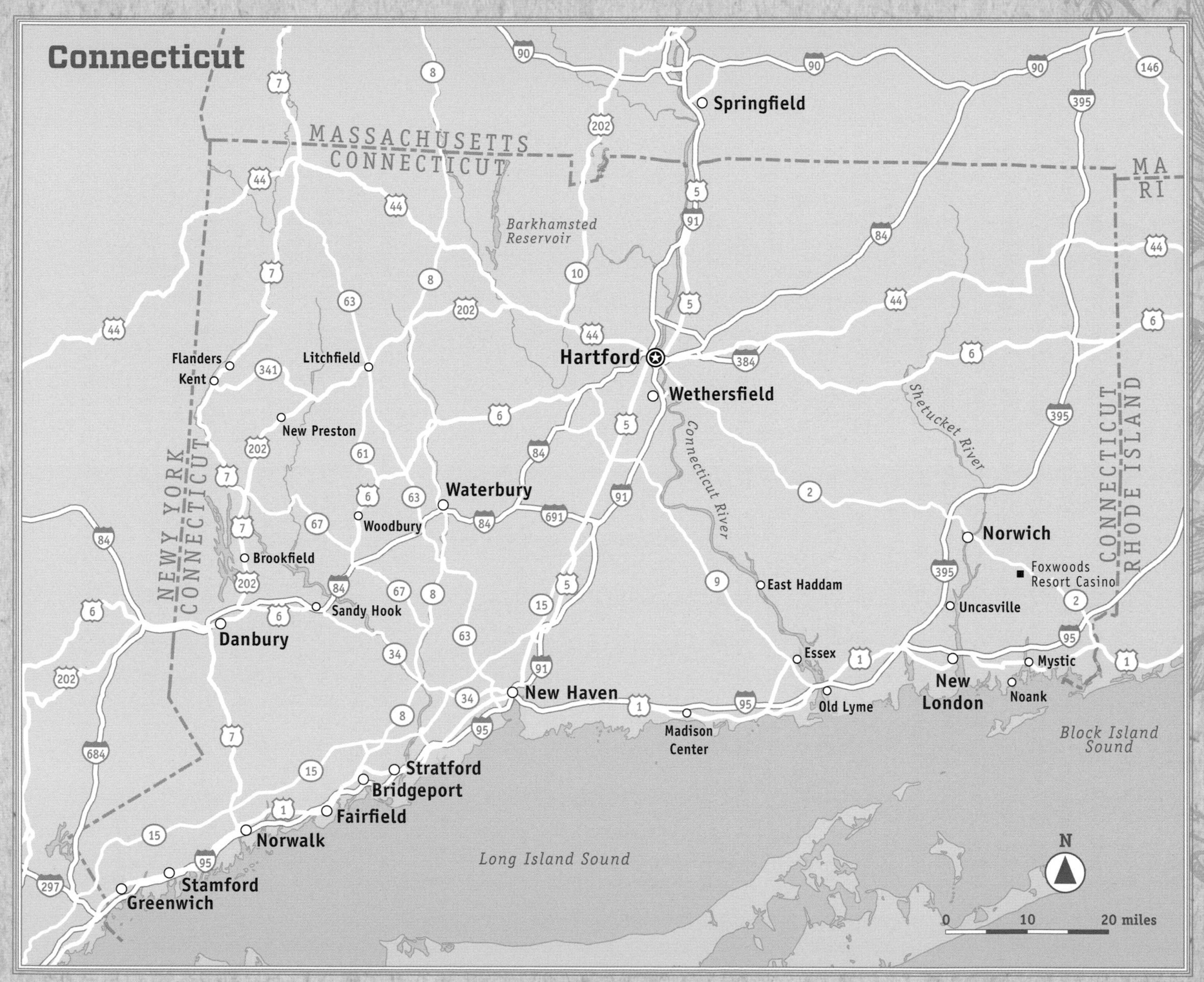

# Connecticut

Connecticut might be a slow starter in the craft beer boom that is taking over New England, but they are showing some signs of becoming bigger and better than ever.

The New England Brewing Company has added some wonderful beers to its already solid lineup, and Thomas Hooker Brewing Company is still chugging along, brewing their old classics while adding some newer beers to appeal to the beginner craft beer enthusiast.

There are plenty of good brewpubs, including the Tullycross Tavern & Microbrewery and the well-established Willimantic Brewing Company to keep Connecticut beer lovers happy. And don't forget about New Haven; a new beer bar seems to pop up in the city at least once a year, adding to an already blossoming craft beer scene.

## BACK EAST BREWING COMPANY

1296A Blue Hills Ave., Bloomfield, CT; (861) 242-1793; BackEastBrewing.com
**Founded:** 2012 **Founders:** Edward Fabrychi Jr., Tony Karolowicz **Brewer:** Mike Smith
**Flagship Beer:** Back East Ale **Year-round Beers:** Golden Ale, Misty Mountain IPA, Porter
**Seasonals/Special Releases:** Octoberfest, Spring Ale, Summer Ale, Winterfest, Imperial Stout, Hammer of the Gods series **Tours:** Sat, noon, 1, 2, and 3 p.m.; $3. Tasting room hours, Wed through Fri, 4 to 7 p.m.

Edward Fabrychi Jr. grew up in Connecticut, but moved out to San Diego, a hot bed for craft brewing. He was inspired and wanted to open his own brewery. When he returned to Connecticut, he told his cousin Tony Karolowicz of his dream, only to find that he also dreamed of opening his own brewery. In 2012, that dream was realized when they opened Back East Brewing Company, a canning brewery in Bloomfield.

The pair, along with their head brewer Mike Smith, created four well-received year-round beers, a full compliment of seasonals, and other special releases. The flagship beer is the **Back East Ale,** a sweet, but easy drinking amber ale. The **Golden Ale** is a crossover beer—the kind of beer a craft beer drinker will drink, but one light enough with mild flavors that those who prefer mass-produced lagers, can still drink without having their taste buds shocked. The **Misty Mountain IPA** is a well-hopped, floral IPA with grapefruit notes. At 7 percent alcohol by volume (ABV) it is

### Beer Lover's Pick

**Porter**
**Style:** Porter
**ABV:** 6 percent
**Availability:** Year-round
Porters are an often overlooked style. But, Back East's version proves that more should be brewed. This Porter has flavors of chocolate and caramel and it's smooth, creamy, and less roasty than stouts. It's a pleasurable beer.

pushing into double IPA levels, but it does not drink big. The **Porter** is exactly what the style calls for.

Seasonals include the **Summer Ale,** a 4.9 percent pale ale; the **Spring Ale,** which is an Irish Red Ale; the **Winterfest,** which is brewed with cinnamon and local honey; and the **Octoberfest**, which is Back East's version of the classic German style.

In 2014, Back East introduced the **Hammer of the God series,** which are higher-alcohol beers. The first beer in the series is the **Palate Mallet,** a tongue-blistering double IPA.

While Back East cans most of its beer, each October it releases its 10.5 percent ABV **Imperial Stout** in caged and corked bottles.

The Back East Brewing Company's tasting room is open Wednesday through Saturday. Samples are free. Tours are every hour on the hour from noon to 3 p.m. on Saturday and cost $3, which includes a tasting glass and samples. The brewery also sells T-shirts, polo shirts, glasses, tap handles, and other items.

Connecticut

## BEAVER BEER COMPANY

Based in Westport, CT, brewed at Paper City Brewing Company, Holyoke, Mass.; BeaverBeer.com

**Founded:** 2013 **Founders:** Rob Anson, Bill O'Brien, Baxter Urist **Brewer:** None **Flagship Beer:** None **Year-round Beers:** Blonde, Brewnette, Big Red **Seasonals/Special Releases:** Oaked Brown **Tours:** None

So many breweries, it seems, are started by young people. This isn't the case with the Beaver Beer Company, which was launched in 2013 by three friends in their 60s after enjoying a few beers together. The group, Ron Anson, Bill O'Brien, and Baxter Urist, sought to create balanced beers rather than the bitter IPAs that

**Oaked Brown**
**Style:** Brown Ale
**ABV:** 5 percent
**Availability:** Winter
The Oaked Brown is different than many oaked beers, with it only being 5 percent ABV. The chocolaty, caramel malt flavors blend well with the vanilla notes the oak imparts in the beer.

dominate the craft beer market. The result is four easy drinking beers—three year-round and one winter release.

The **Blonde** is a 4.5 percent alcohol by volume (ABV) blonde ale. It is mild, smooth and has a slight Belgian yeast character. The **Brewnette** is a Vienna Lager, similar to a Samuel Adams Boston Lager. It has almost a doughy flavor from the malts. The hops add just a hint of spice in the finish. The **Big Red** is a red ale. It's the strongest beer produced by Beaver, coming in at 6 percent ABV. The only other beer brewed is the **Oaked Brown,** a brown ale aged in oak.

If there is one issue with Beaver Beer is that all of their beers are overly carbonated. The flavors aren't affected, but it takes forever to pour a beer in the glass. Beaver Beer is contract brewed at the Paper City Brewing Company in Holyoke, Massachusetts. They do not host tours.

## BEER'D BREWING COMPANY

22 Bayview Ave, #15, Stonington, CT; (860)857-1014; BeerdBrewing.com
**Founded:** 2012 **Founders:** Precious S. Putnam, Aaren M. Simoncini **Brewer:** Aaren M. Simoncini **Flagship Beer:** None **Year-round Beers:** Whisker'd Wit is the beer most likely to be found throughout the year. The rest are constantly rotating **Taproom hours:** Fri, 5 to 9 p.m.; Sat and Sun, 1 to 5 p.m.

Beer'd Brewing Company, named for co-founder and brewer Aaren M. Simoncini's furry face, is a tiny nano brewery/tap room located in an old mill in Stonington. Although small, the brewery is prolific, brewing dozens of different beers throughout the year. You could visit the taproom every week and there could be different beers available on tap at one time. The **Whisker'd Wit,** a Belgian-style witbier, is the one you'd be most likely to find repeatedly.

Throughout the year, Simoncini may brew 25 to 30 new beers. Since the brewery was founded in 2012, they have already brewed 10 different double IPAs, such as **Bumper Crop** and **Hobbit Juice.** They also have brewed the **Midnight Oil,** an oatmeal stout; **Anomaly,** an American black ale; **Ghost Eagle,** an American pale ale; and **Trouble,** a Belgian-style tripel.

The brewery's tap room is open Friday through Sunday. There are no tours available because the entire brewery is open from the tasting bar. All samples are free, and Beer'd offers growlers and half-growlers to go. Nearly 100 percent of beer sold is in the form of growlers and half-growlers.

Beer'd beers are only available off-site at two restaurants in Mystic, the Pizzetta and the Engine Room. Being in an old mill, there is plenty of off-street parking at Beer'd, and typically there are three to five beers on tap at all times, although sometimes it can slip to one or two in a particular busy time since the brewery can only brew 98 gallons of beer at a time.

## BROAD BROOK BREWING COMPANY

2 North Rd., East Windsor, CT; (860) 623-1000; BroadBrookBrewing.com
**Founded:** 2012 **Founders:** Tom DeAlbi, Eric Mance, Tom Rossing **Brewer:** Tom Rossing
**Flagship Beer:** Broad Brook Ale **Year-round Beers:** Chet's Pale Ale, No B.S. Brown Ale, 7th Heaven IPA, Dark Star IPA, Porter's Porter, Chocolate Oatmeal Stout, Hopstillo IPA
**Seasonals/Special Releases:** Rhino Red Ale, Ping Dragon WIT, Oktoberfest Ale, 6 Balls Alt, Homewrecker Holiday Ale, Tobacco Valley Series **Taproom hours:** Wed, 3 to 7 p.m.; Thurs, 3 to 8 p.m.; Fri, 2 to 8 p.m.; Sat, noon to 7 p.m.; Sun, noon to 5 p.m.

Founded by friends Eric Mance, Tom DeAlbi, and Tom Rossing, the Broad Brook Brewing Company in East Windsor, has one of the largest beer portfolios in all of Connecticut. The brewery, which operates a tap room, brews more than a dozen beers, a combination of year-round, seasonals and special releases.

The brewery's flagship beer is the **Broad Brook Ale** a 6.1 percent alcohol by volume (ABV) red ale. It is malty and sweet, with a slight grassy hop kick in the finish. The brewery's best beer is probably the **7th Heaven IPA,** a 7 percent ABV IPA brewed with seven different hop varieties. Some IPAs are supper hoppy, while others are sweet. This is just a plain good IPA that is easy to drink and tasty. Other year-rond beers include the **No B.S. Brown Ale,** which is a hoppy brown; the **Dark Star IPA,** another IPA, **Porter's Porter,** which is, shockingly based on the name, a porter; the **Hopstillo IPA;** and the **Chocolate Oatmeal Stout,** which tastes like a good breakfast beer.

Broad Brook also brews several seasonals, including the **Pink Dragon WIT,** which is a Belgian witbier turned pink thanks to the addition of hibiscus flowers. The **Rhino Red Ale** is an Irish Red Ale, while the **Oktoberfest Ale** is Broad Brook's version of an Oktoberfest beer (traditionally lagers). The **Homewrecker Holiday Ale** is a 6.7 percent ABV winter warmer, and the **6 Balls Alt,** a traditional German altbier. Broad Brook also releases the **Tobacco Valley Series,** which are often more off-the-wall beers. The series includes the **Season of the Witch,** an imperial brown ale brewed with local honey; and the **Robust Porter.**

Broad Brook is open Wednesdays through Sundays for tastings, growler fills and tours. You can buy full pints or taster flights of several of the 10 beers on tap. Food is not available, but visitors can bring their own food, or order from numerous area restaurants that deliver to the brewery. Free wi-fi is also available.

Along with growlers (which are available in select stores), people can buy shirts, hats, glasses and other Broad Brook beer gear.

### BLACK HOG BREWING CO.

115 Hurley Rd., Building 9A, Oxford, CT; (203) 262-6075; blackhogbrewing.com
**Founded:** 2010 **Founders:** Jason and Tom Sobocinski **Brewer:** Tyler Jones Flagship **Beer:** Marauder IPA **Year-Round Beers:** Ginga' Ninja; Granola Brown Ale; Coffee Milk Stout; Piglet IPA; Easy Rye'Da **Seasonals/Special Releases:** S.W.A.G.; Ghost Rye'Da IPA; Piper Saison; Autumn Nugget; Hog Water IPA; Iron Hog; Bacchanalian Barley Wine; Iron Hog; CT Wet Hop "Love Bomb;" Rosemary Dunkelweizen; Mosaic; Strawberry Gose; Peace Gose; Lime Maguey; Brett Golden Sour; La Rouge Trios; Brown Brett Braggot **Tours:** Wed 4-6 p.m.; Fri 2-7 p.m.; Sat noon-6 p.m.; Sun 1-5 p.m.

Black Hog Brewing Co., formerly Cavalry Brewing, was founded in 2010 by brothers Jason and Tom Sobocinski. The two share a passion for food and drink, and with Jason's experience in the food industry and masters in gastronomy combined with Tom's financial know-how the two form the perfect team. An old family friend and former Brewer at The Portsmouth Brewery in New Hampshire, Tyler Jones, contacted the brothers as he prepared to move to New Haven, and together they planned to open a brewery. They sought to celebrate food and family, and since they were all passionate about their work they wanted a name they were passionate

**Big Wally Porter Easy Rye'Da Rye Session IPA**
**Style:** IPA
**Availability:** Year-Round
There is a trend in beer today to imperialize everything and make it bigger. The Big Wally Porter is an example of how good a beer can be when brewed traditionally. This beer has some light roasty undertones, with hints of chocolate and some yeasty flavors. It is a smooth and creamy beer, and the low alcohol means you can enjoy at least one or two more.

about as well. A family tradition is to roast a Berkshire hog at every celebration, and thus to celebrate their business they dubbed it "Black Hog Brewing."

The Black Hog Brewing tasting area is located in a 3500 square foot brewery. They offer sample flights, merchandise, and 32 ounce squealer fills. They have 8 taps and offer Nitro Coffee Milk Stout year-round. They also offer the brewery-exclusive Disco Pig Series, barrel-aged brews with nontraditional flavors. Come on down, take a tour, and try to beat Tyler's high-score on Galaga on the brewery arcade machine! Bear in mind, while supervised children are welcome, animals are not.

## CHARTER OAK BREWING COMPANY

1 Smith Ridge Rd., New Canaan, CT; (203) 972-9058; CharterOakBrewing.com
**Founded:** 2012 **Founder:** P. Scott Vallely **Brewer:** P. Scott Vallely **Flagship Beer:** None
**Year-round Beers:** 1687 Brown Ale, Royal Charter Pale Ale, Wadsworth India Pale Ale
**Seasonals/Special Releases:** None **Tours:** None



Businessman P. Scott Vallely decided to close his paper factory in 2010, but he wasn't ready to retire. The longtime homebrewer decided to open up his own brewery.

Charter Oak brews four year-round beers—the **1687 Brown Ale,** the **Royal Charter Pale Ale,** the **Wadsworth India Pale Ale.,** and the **Sanford Tavern Extra Special Bitter.** The 1687 Brown Ale is 5.5 percent alcohol by volume (ABV). It

### Beer Lover's Pick

**Wadsworth India Pale Ale**
**Style:** IPA
**ABV:** 6 percent
**Availability:** Year-round
The Wadsworth India Pale Ale is a west coast IPA, full of citrusy hops, but with a sweet, almost caramel like flavor from the malts. This is a solid beer, it won't knock anyone's socks off, but it won't disappoint anyone.

uses seven different types of malts, striving for a malt complexity not often found in American brown ales. There's a little more hop flavor than in English brown ale, but not quite as much as many American brown ales. The Royal Charter Pale Ale is also 5.5 percent ABV. It's a pretty standard west coast pale ale—citrusy hops, decent malt backbone. It is easy to drink and good to pair with moderately spicy food. The Wadsworth India Pale Ale is a 6.5 percent ABV IPA.

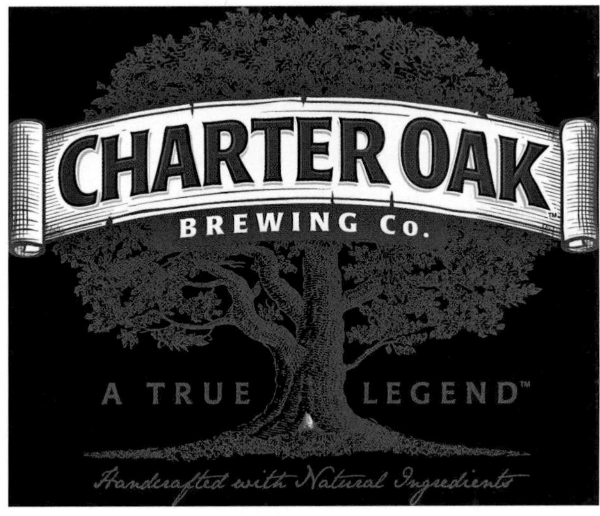


### COTTRELL BREWING COMPANY

100 Mechanic St., Pawcatuck, CT; (860) 599-8213; CottrellBrewing.com
**Founded:** 1996 **Founder:** Charles Cottrell Buffum Jr. **Brewer:** Charles Cottrell Buffum Jr. **Flagship Beer:** Old Yankee Ale **Year-round Beer:** Mystic Bridge IPA **Seasonals/Special Releases:** None **Tours:** Mon through Wed, by appointment only; Thurs, 3 p.m.; Fri, every half-hour, 3 to 6 p.m.; Sat, every half-hour, noon to 5 p.m.

The Cottrell Brewing Company has to be doing something right. Cottrell has been in existence for 15 years, and during that time, they've been brewing only two beers. If a brewery can succeed for 15 years by brewing only two beers, the beers must be fantastic. Luckily for Cottrell Brewing Company, that is indeed the case.

The **Old Yankee Ale,** in particular, is fabulous. It's an amber ale, which is typically a boring style that a lot of beer lovers ignore. But, do not sleep on this particular amber ale. Old Yankee is probably the best amber ale being brewed in New England today. The **Mystic Bridge IPA** is relatively mellow at 6 percent alcohol by volume (ABV). It is not quite a west coast IPA or an English-style IPA—it seems to

## Beer Lover's Pick

**Old Yankee Ale**
**Style:** Pale Ale
**ABV:** 5 percent
**Availability:** Year-Round

The Old Yankee Ale is a classic example of an east coast pale ale. Not as hoppy as its west coast counterparts, this beer is no less complex. The malt is sweet and caramel-like, with a little hint of doughy yeast flavor. The hops are there, providing a wonderful balance to keep the sweetness at a pleasant level without becoming cloying. This beer ends on a sweet note, unlike a lot of dry pale ale. At 5 percent alcohol by volume, this is a great daily drinking beer.

be somewhere in the middle. It's easy drinking, slightly earthy, but with just a hint of grapefruit character from the hops. The IPA's name came from the local Mystic River Bridge.

The Cottrell Brewing Company is housed in a piece of both Connecticut and Cottrell family history—the former C.B. Cottrell & Sons Inc. factory, a printing press facility that printed nearly every magazine of note in the late 1800s and early 1900s. The founder of that company, Calvert B. Cottrell, is Buffum's great-grandfather. The brewery only takes up about 9,000 square feet of the 350,000-square-foot factory.

To see part of the history, attend one of the several tours Cottrell Brewing Company hosts throughout the week. The tour features a discussion of the brewery's history, as well as the process of brewing the beer, and also includes a tasting. The beer is also available for sale.

## FIREFLY HOLLOW BREWING

139 Center St., Bristol, CT; (860) 845-8977; FireflyHollowBrewing.com
**Founded:** 2013 **Founders:** Dana Bourque, Bill Collins, Rich Loomis **Brewer:** Dana Bourque
**Beers:** Emily's Choconut Porter, Red Lantern, Lizard Breath, Corn Flakes IIPA, Toad Stool Oat Stout, Ram Shackle Golden Mild, Moon Rise Amber, Photon Imperial Crimson, Ye Olde' Twinkler Barleywine **Taproom hours:** Thurs and Fri, 2 to 8 p.m.; Sat, noon to 8 p.m., Sun, noon to 5 p.m.

Maybe not all of Firefly Hollow Brewing's beer names make them seem the most appetizing (Toad Stool Oat Stout), but it's the liquid and not the name that is important. And in that aspect, Firefly Hollow has that down, with a strong lineup of beers available at its Bristol taproom.

The beer list is constantly changing, so some of the listed beers may not be available all of the time. But some of the rotating beers include the **Red Lantern,** traditional Irish red ale; the **Lizard Breath IPA,** a 6.6 percent alcohol by volume (ABV) IPA that is packed with hops, but is also brewed with flaked oats, giving it some creaminess not found in many IPAs; and the **Moon Rise Amber,** a hoppy amber ale. Other beers include the **Cone Flakes IIPA,** a 7.7 percent ABV double IPA that is bursting with citrus and floral flavors from the hops. **Emily's Choconut Porter** is aged on cacao nibs and brewed with roasted coconut. The **Ye Olde' Twinkler** is a sweet, malty 9 percent ABV barley wine, while the **Proton Imperial Crimson** is a hoppy strong ale. The **Toad Stool Oat Stout** has strong roasted coffee flavors and is brewed with oat and barley flakes, making it quite a creamy beer, while the **Ram Shackle Mild** is a tasty sessionable ale.

Firefly Hollow's taproom is open Thursday through Sunday for samples, full-pints, and growler fills. Although no food is available, feel free to stop at a local restaurant and bring in some food to enjoy while enjoying some tasty pints.

## HALF FULL BREWERY

43 Homestead Ave., Stamford, CT; (203) 658-3631; HalfFullBrewery.com
**Founded:** 2012 **Founder:** Conor Horrigan **Brewer:** Jen Muckerman **Flagship Beer:** None
**Year-round Beers:** Bright Ale, IPA, Toasted Amber Ale **Seasonals/Special Releases:** American Pale Ale, Pumpkin Ale, Chocolate Coffee Brown Ale, Peach Wheat, Imperial American Pale Ale **Taproom hours:** Wed through Fri, 4 to 7 p.m., Sat 1 to 5 p.m.

Conor Horrigan is a former Wall Street drone who, in 2008, decided he needed do something different in his life. He decided he wanted to start a brewery, and four years later, the Half Full Brewery was born. The brewery has a tap room, although they hope to start canning its year-round beers by the time this book is published.

The year-round beers, called Inspirational beers, are the **Bright Ale,** the **IPA,** and the **Toasted Amber.** The Bright Ale is a blonde/pale ale hybrid, meant to be an accessible beer for those new to craft beer. It is a 5.2 percent alcohol by volume (ABV) ale with a light body, but with nice grapefruit aroma. The Half Full IPA is actually a rye IPA. It's piney and earthy, and the rye adds a nice dry spiciness to the finish. The Half Full Toasted Amber ale has chocolate notes and end with a toasted sweetness. This beer is for malt lovers.

Half Full also brews several seasonals, called Experiental beers. The **American Pale Ale** is available August to October. It is a 5.5 percent ABV pale ale, dry hopped and mildly bitter. The **Pumpkin Ale** is available mid-September through Thanksgiving. This 6.5 percent ABV pumpkin ale is brewed with pumpkin, as well as tea, cinnamon sticks and nutmeg. The **Chocolate Coffee Brown Ale** is available from November to January. The beer is brewed with local coffee and chocolate malts. Other beers include the **Peach Wheat,** a wheat beer brewed with peaches, and the **Imperial American Pale Ale,** a 9 percent ABV beer.

On the third Wednesday of every month, Half Full hosts a rare beer night where they tap some experimental beers. The events cost $30 to attend and tickets are available on Half Full's website. The brewery hosts growler fills and samples Wednesday through Friday from 4 to 7 p.m., as well as Saturday from 1 to 5 p.m. A free tour is available at 3 p.m. The brewery also sells T-shirts, hats, key chains, cooler bags, sweatshirts, stickers, posters, and glassware.

### THE HARTFORD BETTER BEER COMPANY

Hartford, CT (corporate office only); (860) 684-5481; HartfordBetterBeer.com
**Founded:** 1991 **Founders:** Mike Harney, Phil Hopkins, Les Sinnock **Brewer:** Contract brewed **Flagship Beer:** Arch Amber Ale Year-round Beers: Arch IPA, Praying Mantis Porter **Seasonals/Special Releases:** None **Tours:** None

The Hartford Better Beer Company is a nostalgia beer company. It started as Connecticut's first brewpub in 1991, called the Hartford Brewery Limited. However, the brewery went out of business in 2000. But, now, that same brewpub's most popular beers are in 12-ounce bottles and are available throughout the state, which is perfect for those who miss drinking a cold pint of the beers they used to have available on the premises.

The beers are now brewed by the Shipyard Brewing Company in Portland, Maine. Shipyard's master brewer Alan Pugsley trained the original brewers at the Hartford Brewery Limited, and they brewed the beers using the Pugsley system. That means the beers, which are brewed to the original specifications, should taste exactly how people remember them.

The **Arch Amber Ale** was by far the most popular beer at Hartford Brewery Limited. It is a decent, if not a little old-fashioned, amber ale. Flavor-wise, the yeast gives it a little bit of a bready taste, while the malts add a little caramel flavor to it. There is also a decent kiss of hops on the finish. This is one of those old New England types of beers that a lot of the older breweries and brewpubs still have. The **Arch IPA** is more of an English-style IPA, in that the hops are not an in-your-face attack

## Beer Lover's Pick

**Praying Mantis Porter**
**Style:** Porter
**ABV:** Unknown
**Availability:** Year-round
The Praying Mantis Porter is the Hartford Better Beer Company's best beer. It is a solid, English-style porter. It has nice toasty and roasty aroma, and it tastes of toffee mixed with a little coffee. There is also a hint of chocolate in the flavor, although it is not overwhelming. It is a good, solid beer worth trying.

on your taste buds. Rather, the hops are a little more subtle, with nice hop aromas. This is a more malt-forward beer. The malt is not overwhelmingly sweet, but still overwhelms the hops. The **Praying Mantis Porter** is a straightforward, English-style porter. It is not an extreme beer, by any means, but it is true to the style.

Since the Hartford Better Beer Company does not brew its own beers, they do not host tours or tastings.

### NEW ENGLAND BREWING COMPANY

7 Selden St., Woodbridge, CT; (203) 387-2222; NewEnglandBrewing.com
**Founded:** 1989 **Founders:** Dick and Marsha King **Brewer:** Rob Leonard **Flagship Beer:** Atlantic Amber **Year-round Beers:** Elm City Lager, Sea Hag IPA **Seasonals/Special Releases:** 668: The Neighbor of the Beast, Gandhi-Bot Double IPA, Imperial Stout Trooper, Wet Willy Scotch Ale **Tours:** Call ahead to make sure someone is available

The New England Brewing Company has the most eye-catching labels or cans in all of New England. They're hard to miss. After all, a robot version of Gandhi kind of stands out on liquor store shelves. You know what else stands out? The beer inside the cans.

The New England Brewing Company has been around for years, brewing solid, sessionable beers, but seem to have really hit their stride in recent years. All three year-round beers are very good. The **Sea Hag IPA** is a well-done, well-hopped, and nicely balanced IPA. The **Atlantic Amber** is an old-school New England beer, and the **Elm City Lager** is an easy drinking beer.

But it's really their special releases that get the New England Brewing Company a lot of attention. The **Gandhi-Bot Double IPA** (mentioned above) is more than just a funny label. It is a phenomenal double IPA. The beer pours a bright orange, and it is aggressively hopped, with aromas of pine and citrus wafting from the glass. Those aromas continue on into the taste. This is a hop bomb, but there is just enough balance to keep this a drinkable hop bomb. The **668: The Neighbor of the Beast** (play some Iron Maiden while drinking) is a spicy Belgian-style strong pale ale. Like Gandhi-Bot, this is a big beer (9 percent alcohol by volume [ABV]). There are a lot of spices in this beer, and it is sweet, but not cloyingly sweet. This is a great nightcap kind of beer, a sipper. The **Imperial Stout Trooper** was the beer that really put New England Brewing Company on the map for those outside of New England. Again, the labels caught peoples' attention—inspired by Storm Troopers from Star Wars—but the beer itself was worthy of the attention. The labels have since changed after a "request" by George Lucas. The beer itself is a remarkable Russian imperial stout. Flavors of coffee and chocolate abound through this complex beer. The **Wet Willy**

## Beer Lover's Pick

**Gandhi-Bot Double IPA**
**Style:** Double IPA
**ABV:** 8.8 percent
**Availability:** Rotating

A big hop bomb in a can? Oh yeah, this is an awesome beer. The Gandhi-Bot is a hoppy assault on the tongue, and a hophead will love that. The hops add citrus and piney flavors, like a classic double or imperial IPA. The malt is there in the background, but it is just there to provide some body and balance. This is a beer that is all about the hops. If you're eating a spicy dish, this will cut right through it.

**Scotch Ale** is another big beer (10 percent ABV), but it is the best Scotch ale, or wee heavy, brewed in New England today. It is malty beer, with caramel and toffee undertones that are oh so good. Drink this beer only slightly chilled to make sure you get all of the fabulous flavors.

Unlike New England Brewing's other offerings, the Imperial Stout Trooper and Wet Willy Scotch Ale are both bottled. New England Brewing Company also brews several draft-only and brewery-only beers, such as barrel-aged versions of the ones mentioned above. They hold tastings at the brewery, as well as tours (just call ahead to make sure they are not too busy).

### OLDE BURNSIDE BREWING COMPANY

780 Tolland St., East Hartford, CT; (860) 528-2200; OldeBurnsideBrewing.com
**Founded:** 2000 **Founder:** Bob McClellan **Brewer:** Joe Lushing **Flagship Beer:** Ten Penny Ale **Year-round Beer:** Dirty Penny Ale **Seasonals/Special Releases:** Amazing Grace Series, Father Christmas Highland Ale, Highland Wild, Penny Weiz, Stone of Destination, Ten Penny Reserve **Tours:** By appointment

## Cans vs. Bottles

Bad beer comes in cans. That was the normal thought of craft beer enthusiasts over the years. It gives beer a metallic taste, they would say.

Things have changed. More and more craft breweries are releasing their beers in cans. In New England, Baxter Brewing in Maine cans all of their beers, as does the New England Brewing Company in Connecticut. The Alchemist, a popular Vermont brewery, opened up a cannery to can their Heady Topper double IPA. Even more established breweries, Harpoon Brewery and Cisco Brewers, can some of their beers for summer releases.

Cans offer many advantages over bottles. Light is beer's number one enemy. If a beer gets too much light, it turns skunky. Do you want to drink a skunk? Neither do I. Cans solve that problem. They also take up less space than bottles, they're more portable, and unlike bottles, some beaches and campsites allow beer as long as it's in a can. They're also more environmentally friendly. Another advantage? The pop, fizz noise you hear when crack open a can is so much more satisfying than opening a bottle.



A lot of people talk about the different flavors that various yeasts, hops, or malts can add to beers, but perhaps the most important ingredient in beer is water. The Olde Burnside Brewing Company is an extension of owner Bob McClellan's water business. The water he sells has nearly the same mineral quality of Burton-on-the-Trent in England, where the India pale ale was developed. So, in 2000, using his own water, McClellan opened the Olde Burnside Brewing Company, brewing mainly British-inspired beers.

The **Ten Penny Ale,** the brewery's first beer and still its most popular, is a Scottish-style ale. It is a malty beer, but it is not too heavy. It is easy drinking, with slight caramel and roasted flavors. Pick up a growler of this at the local liquor store and share it with friends. Olde Burnside's only other year-round beer is the **Dirty Penny Ale,** which is one of the few, and the best, commercially brewed black and tans. A black and tan is typically a stout blended with a lighter beer, such as a pale ale or a lager. The Dirty Penny is made up of a blend of 60 percent Ten Penny Ale and 40 percent house-brewed stout. It is a phenomenal beer.

Seasonals include the **Penny Weiz,** which is only available during the summer. It is a Belgian-style witbier, although some heather is added to the traditional coriander and bitter orange peel to give it a little more spiciness. The **Father Christmas Highland Ale** is a big, malty beast of a wee heavy, coming in at 9.2 percent alcohol by volume (ABV). This is a sipper, and the perfect beer to leave out for Ol' St. Nick on Christmas Eve to warm him up. The **Ten Penny Reserve,** which is available sporadically at the brewery, is the Ten Penny Ale's big brother. This comes in at a hefty 9.2 percent ABV. This is a full-bodied, creamy Scotch ale.

Other beers include the **Highland Wild,** a 9.6 percent Scottish wild ale, aged in oak barrels. You will not find this style brewed in Scotland, but the sourness works well with the sweet malts. The **Stone of Destination** is an imperial, or double, black and tan ale. The **Amazing Grace Series** is a series of ever-changing beers, usually the Ten Penny Ale aged in various barrels, such as oak barrels used to age Crown Royale. Each one is unique, but worth seeking out (only available at the brewery).

## Beer Lover's Pick

**Dirty Penny Ale**
**Style:** Black and Tan
**ABV:** 5 percent
**Availability:** Year-round

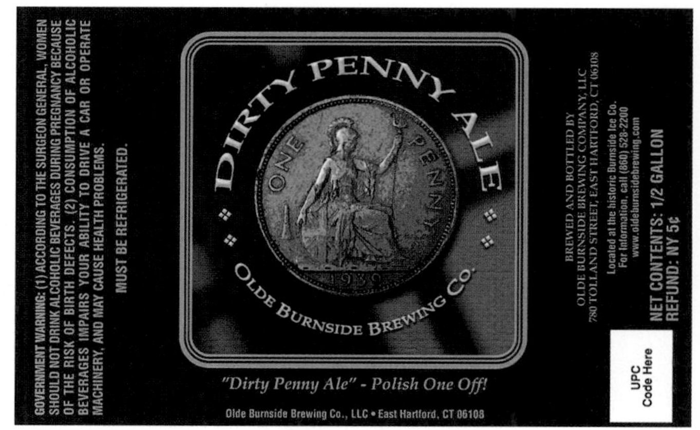


Usually black and tans are created at home using Guinness and Bass, but this version is made using a stout brewed just for this beer, and mixed with Ten Penny Ale. It is a phenomenal beer. It combines the roastiness of the stout with the sweet, caramel, and malty flavors of the Scottish ale that is Ten Penny. It is creamy and has a great body. It is only 5 percent ABV, so you can drink a growler by yourself, or you can be nice and share.

## RELIC BREWING COMPANY

95B Whiting St., Plainville, CT; (860) 255-4252; RelicBeer.com
**Founded:** 2012 **Founder:** Mark Sigman **Brewer:** Mark Sigman **Flagship Beer:** Transatlantic **Beers:** Blackheart Black Lager, The Huntsman Oatmeal Stout, Field Hand Saison, Thrice Tripel, Duality Dubbel, Hypathia Belgian Pale Ale, Queen Annes Revenge Porter, Darkness Falls Dark Saison, Rydale Farmhouse Rye, Rococo Belgian Dark Ale, Prologue **Tours:** None, tasting room is open Thur and Fri, 4 to 7 p.m.; Sat, noon to 4 p.m.

The Relic Brewing Company is one of the bright spots of the Connecticut brewing scene, brewing some of the best beer available in the Constitution State ever since owner/brewer Mark Sigman opened Relic's doors in 2012. Relic brews beers in small amounts, so sometimes when you find a beer you like, you may not be able to buy it again for quite sometime. However, they have plenty of beers that are worth seeking out.

The beer that's closest to being available at all times is the **Transatlantic,** a Belgian-style IPA. Relic brews several Belgian-inspired ales, such as the **Field Hand Saison,** the **Thrice Tripel, Duality Dubbel, Hypathia Belgian Pale Ale, Rydale Farmhouse Rye,** and **Rocco Belgian Dark Ale.** However, they don't limit themselves to Belgian ales. They brew **Blackheart Black Lager,** a wonderful interpretation of a German black lager, the **Huntsman Oatmeal Stout** and **Queen Annes Revenge Porter.**

Relic's beers are only available at limited spots, about a dozen restaurants and a few stores. The beers are available in 22-ounce bottles.

The beers are not easy to miss—they have some of the best artwork on their labels in all of New England. Relic works with local artists to create some truly

**Prologue**
**Style:** Rye lager
**ABV:** 5.6 percent
**Availability:** Spring
Prologue is Relic's spring seasonal, a rye lager. This 5.6 percent alcohol by volume beer is hoppier than a lot of lagers. The rye spiciness plays off the citrusy/piney hops to create a wonderfully refreshing, semi-dry beer, perfect for a nice warm spring day.

stunning labels. Relic doesn't offer tours, but they do have a tasting room where people can come in and sample whatever beers are on tap at the time—usually five to six—as well as buy growlers of their favorite beers. The tasting room is open Thur through Sat.

## SHEBEEN BREWING COMPANY

1 Wolcott Rd., Wolcott, CT; (203) 514-2336; ShebeenBrewing.com
**Founded:** 2013 **Founders:** Patrick Lacerra, Rich Visco **Brewer:** Rich Visco **Beers:** Black IPA, Cannoli Beer, Concord Grape Saison, Rye Porter, Double Rye Porter, Grand Cru, Turbo IPA, West Coast, Bacon Kona Stout, Cucumber Wasabi, Irish Pale, Royal IPA, Pineapple Wheat, German Cerveza, Idaho IPA, Smoked Amber **Taproom hours:** Thur, 5 to 8 p.m., Fri, 5 to 9 pm.; Sat and Sun, noon to 5 p.m.

Beer style guidelines are good, but some brewers like to go outside of the box when it comes to creating their beers. The brewers at Shebeen Brewing Company in Wolcott sure do. Sure, they have some traditional beers, but they also have some pretty non-standard takes on the style.

Shebeen is home to the **Cannoli Beer,** a 5.2 percent alcohol by volume (ABV) ale made with cinnamon, nutmeg, vanilla, and best served with shaved chocolate and powdered sugar on a rim. It is a liquid (and alcohol-infused) cannoli.

For many breweries, that would be the end of their strange beers, but not for Shebeen (Gaelic for illegal brewery). Other left-of-the-dial beers include the **Concord Grape Saison,** a saison brewed with local Concord grape extract; the **Bacon Kona Stout,** a breakfast beer made with Kona coffee, oatmeal, and bacon; the **Cucumber Wasabi,** an ale made with hot wasabi and cool cucumbers; **Pineapple Wheat,** a dark wheat with pineapple juice; **German Cerveza,** a kolsch brewed with agave honey; and the **Idaho IPA,** an India pale ale brewed with all Idaho-grown hops and potato flakes.

Not all of Shebeen's beers are that out there. The **Rye Porter** is a well-done porter with nice rye spicy notes, while its big brother, the **Double Rye Porter** has more roasted, chocolaty flavors. The **Grand Cru** is a Belgian ale brewed with bitter orange peel and coriander. The **Black IPA** is a 6.8 percent ABV beer that is sweet for the style, but actually works, while the **Turbo IPA** is a 7 percent ABV piney double IPA that uses six pounds of hops per barrel. The **West Coast** is a classic west cost pale ale. Other beers include the **Royal IPA** (English IPA), the **Irish Pale,** and the **Smoked Amber.**

Shebeen's taproom is open for growler fills and tours on Wednesday, Friday, Saturday, and Sunday.

## STONY CREEK BREWERY

60 Maple St., Branford, CT; StonyCreekBeer.com

**Founded:** 2012 **Founders:** Ed Crowley Jr., Ed Crowley Sr., Peggy Crowley, Manuel Rodriguez **Brewer:** Andy Schwartz **Flagship Beer:** Docktime Lager **Year-round Beers:** Big Cranky, Cranky, Little Cranky, Docktime Lager **Special Releases:** Sun Juice, Crum, Snow Hole, Crimsang **Taproom hours:** Tues to Thurs, 3 to 8 p.m.; Fri, 3 to 9 p.m.; Sat, noon to 9 p.m.; Sun, noon to 7 p.m.

To start, a lot of things have changed at the Stony Creek Brewery. In 2015 they opened a lovely tasting room right along the docks on the Branford River. They have a beautiful indoor/outdoor taproom, a game pit, dock access and a first-hand look at the canning and bottling lines. They have an experienced crew of people behind their brews. Their founders include a married couple, their son and friend, Ed Sr., Peggy and Ed Jr. Crowley, and Manuel Rodriguez. They have Andy Schwartz as their brewmaster who has brewed at several different breweries throughout the country. Stony Creek offers an array of beers, with perhaps their most interesting being their line of "Cranky" beers. Advertised as just the right fix for your cranky attitude, they have three "Cranky" beers to fit whichever level of crankiness you're feeling. The **Big Cranky** is a double IPA with 9.5% ALC/VOL with big hop flavors. The middle-grade **Cranky** is a regular IPA, and last but not least, the **Little Cranky** is a session IPA. Their **Crimsang** is a take on their own Big Cranky. They add blood orange for a citrus flavor that provides a tart finish. They don't stop there, either. Their flagship beer, **Docktime Lager,** is rich and smooth, blending a solid dose of rye, sterling hops and malt that creates herbal and citrus flavors. This beer leaves you tasting a spicy, yet clean and dry finish.

Their seasonal beers are nothing to make light of, either. The **Seasonal Sun Juice** is a perfect and refreshing brew for summer. It is brewed with wheat, and the Saison yeast provides a silky flavor and texture. Orange peel, grapefruit peel,

**Dock Time**
**Style:** Lager
**ABV:** 4. 8 percent
**Availability:** Year-rounds
While Stony Creek brews mostly IPAs, Dock Time is probably the brewery's best beer. It is crisp, light, and easy to drink.

coriander, and chamomile add a spicy and fruity zest. For autumn, they have their Crum beer. This beer is an interpretation of Apple Crumble. It's a combination of fresh apple cider, oats, cinnamon and nutmeg creating a perfect beer that tastes like Thanksgiving dessert.

Stony Creek Brewery provides a great view and a variety of delicious beers with an ambitious and experienced cast of people behind it all. Whether you're local or just traveling through, it is most definitely worth stopping in.

## STUBBORN BEAUTY BREWING COMPANY

180 Johnson St., Middletown, CT; StubbornBeauty.com

**Founded:** 2014 **Founders:** Andrew Daigle, Shane Lentini **Brewers:** Andrew Daigle, Shane Lentini **Year-round Beers:** How Rye I Am, Kommandmant Lassard, Don't Call me Porter Justice, Speaking in Tongues, Nummy Nummy, Traxx **Taproom hours:** Sat, 1 to 4 p.m.

While most homebrewers play it safe with their first batch of homebrew, brewing a pale ale or maybe an amber ale, Andrew Daigle and Shane Lentini went in the other direction, brewing a big imperial IPA. That imperial IPA was the inspiration for **Nummy Nummy,** one of the beers that Daigle and Lentini brew for the Stubborn Beauty Brewing Company they founded in 2014. The brewery promises "Brewing Outside of the Lines," and with its initial offerings, Stubborn Beauty delivers.

The **How Rye I Am** is an 8 percent alcohol by volume (ABV) saison brewed with large amounts of rye malt. Saisons are typically dry and spicy, and the rye adds to that, while still being a smooth, creamy beer. **Kommandmant Lassard** is a 5.3 percent ABV take on a Germany-style dunkelweizen. This has the banana and clove flavors you would expect from the style, but it has more chocolate flavors than you normally get from a dunkelweizen. The Nummy Nummy is an 8.1 percent ABV imperial IPA, with citrus, grapefruit, and some floral flavor notes from the use of the hops. **Speaking in Tongues** is a black IPA, although this 8 percent ABV beer could be mistaken for a hoppy stout because it is has strong roasted notes and a thick, full body. **Don't Call Me Porter Justice** is a 7.7 percent porter full of chocolate and coffee flavors. Stubborn Beauty Brewing Company also brews **Traxx,** a Belgian golden ale, exclusively for Eli Cannon's Taproom, also in Middletown.

Stubborn Beauty's beers are only available in growlers at the brewery on Saturday from 1 to 4 p.m. They have 32-ounce growlers to fill, and people can bring in clean, capped 64-ounce growlers from other breweries to be filled.

## THIMBLE ISLAND BREWING COMPANY

16 Business Park Dr., Branford, CT; (203) 208-2827; ThimbleIslandBrewery.com
**Founded:** 2012 **Founders:** Mike Fawcett, Justin Gargano **Brewer:** Mike Fawcett **Flagship Beer:** American Ale **Year-round Beers:** Coffee Stout, India Pale Ale **Seasonals/Special Releases:** Unchartered Series **Taproom hours:** Thur and Fri, 3 to 8 p.m.; Sat 11 a.m. to 5 p.m.

Longtime friends Mike Fawcett and Justin Gargano shared an apartment and a passion for home brewing. In 2010, they decided they were going to open their own brewery, and after years of developing recipes, Thimble Island Brewing Company was born in 2012.

The Branford brewery brews three year-round beers. The **American Ale,** Thimble Island's flagship beer, is the only beer available in bottles. The other beers are draft only. The American Ale is a 5 percent alcohol by volume (ABV) red ale. Red ales are on the malty side, which tends to make beer drinkers shy away from them during the hot summer months when lighter, hoppier beers are a more refreshing beverage. The American Ale, however, is on the lighter side of a red ale, so it's good to enjoy anytime of year. The **Coffee Stout** started as a winter seasonal, but it was so popular, Thimble Island added it to its year-round portfolio. The Coffee Stout is 6 percent ABV and uses whole coffee beans from a local coffee roaster to give this beer a kick of coffee goodness. The **India Pale Ale** relies on hops that provide a lot of citrus flavor. There is a decent malt backbone to give it balance, but the citrusy hops almost make this an IPA for the summer time. At 6.9 percent ABV, it's not too big of a beer, either.

Thimble Island also brews a specialty line of brewery only beers called the **Unchartered Series.** These are beers that are only occasionally brewed. They include the **Mutually Assured Destruction Russian Imperial Stout,** a 10 percent ABV imperial stout; the **Sandbar Brown,** a 5.3 percent ABV brown ale; the **Pumpkin Pie Porter,** a 5 percent porter flavored like a pumpkin pie; the **Kolsch,** a 5.2 percent take on the light, refreshing German ale; and the **Ghost Island Double IPA,** a 7.5 percent ABV hop bomb.

Thimble Island's taproom is open Wednesdays through Saturdays and features free tastings and tours (guided tours on Saturday). People can buy growlers, T-shirts, hats and glasses and other brewery swag, as well.

## THOMAS HOOKER BREWING COMPANY

16 Tobey Rd., Bloomfield, CT; (860) 242-3111; HookerBeer.com

**Founded:** 1997 **Founder:** Jack Streich **Brewer:** Mike Yates **Flagship Beer:** American Pale Ale **Year-round Beers:** Blonde Ale, Hop Meadow IPA, Imperial Porter, Irish Red, Liberator Doppelbock, Munich-Style, Old Marley Barleywine **Seasonals/Special Releases:** Nor'Easter Lager, Octoberfest, Watermelon Ale **Tours:** Sat, noon to 5 p.m., $5; first and third Fri of every month, open house from 5 to 8 p.m.

Thomas Hooker Brewing Company has been around for a while, and they walk the line of brewing beers for beer geeks and for those new to craft beer. Named for the founder of Hartford and the state of Connecticut, Thomas Hooker has a wide mix of beers, including lagers, fruit beers, and some big malty beers.

The year-round beers include one of the best New England beers available, the **Liberator Doppelbock.** This is a malty monster of a beer. Along the same lines are the **Imperial Porter** and the **Old Marley Barleywine.** These are the "beer geek" beers—all big beers high in alcohol, complex, and flavorful. The **Hop Meadow IPA** is a very good IPA. It is not too bitter and extremely balanced; the **American Pale Ale** is along the same vein, balanced and easy to drink. The **Irish Red** is spot on for the style. It is not an overly exciting beer, but it goes down easy. The **Munich-Style** is a golden lager, a little light, but still with enough flavor to make it enjoyable. The

**Liberator Doppelbock**
**Style:** Doppelbock
**ABV:** 8 percent
**Availability:** Year-Round
If a double IPA is for hopheads, doppelbocks are for malt heads. This is a big, malty beer with caramel flavors, as well as a toasted, biscuity taste, with hints of dark fruit. It is creamy, and a smooth beer. An 8 percent alcohol by volume beer should not be this easy to drink. Unlike some doppelbocks, you can actually taste the hops in the Liberator, with just a little herbal/grassy notes, particularly in the finish.

**Blonde Ale** has been considered a kind of beginner craft beer—for those who are just starting to drink craft beer, this is a good place to start.

The seasonals include the fantastic **Octoberfest.** It tastes similar to German-brewed Oktoberfests, and it is easily one of the better Oktoberfest beers brewed in New England. The **Watermelon Ale** is what the name says, a watermelon beer. It is a light beer and kind of tastes like watermelon bubblegum. The **Nor'Easter** is a lager brewed with wintery spices.

On the first and third Friday of every month, Thomas Hooker hosts an open house at the brewery from 5 to 8 p.m. For $10, you get a few drinks and a guided tour and get to take home the pint glass you used during the night. All proceeds go to a local charity. Tours are on Saturday from noon to 5 p.m. For $5 you get a fully guided tour and a tasting of all the available beers. The brewery store sells the beers in 12-ounce bottles and in growlers. Clothing, hats, and several other items are also available in the brewery store.

### TOP SHELF BREWING COMPANY

640 Hilliard St., Manchester, CT; (860) 680-4105; TopShelfBrewery.com

**Founded:** 2013 **Founders:** Mike Boney, T.J. Lavery, Joe Frost **Brewer:** Mike Boney **Year-round Beers:** American Ale, Belgian Ale, Irish Ale, Marathon IPA **Seasonals/Special Releases:** Holiday Cheer, Snowed In, Smoked Belgian, Honey Smack **Tours:** Tasting room open Fri, 4 to 7 p.m.; Sat, noon to 4 p.m.

The Top Shelf Brewing Company is straight to the point when it comes to naming its beers. Most of the year-round beers are named for the country of origin for the style. In all, this Manchester brewery, founded by friends Mike Boney, Joe Frost

**Irish Ale**
**Style:** Irish Red
**ABV:** 5 percent
**Availability:** Year-round
Taking the first few sips of the Irish Ale, I wasn't sure if I liked this red ale. But, as I drank it, the flavors of chocolate and dried berries began to come through and this quickly became a beer I enjoyed.

and T.J. Lavery, brews four year-round beers, as well as some seasonals and special release.

The **American Ale** is a classic east coast style pale ale. It is not as hoppy as its west coast counterparts, rather relying on subtle hops and being more malt-forward, similar to English pale ales. At 5 percent alcohol by volume (ABV), it's average in strength, meaning you can have a couple in one sitting. The **Belgian Ale** is an 8 percent ABV Belgian pale ale. Although a little hot (boozy) and sweet, this isn't a bad take on the style. Maybe let it age for a few months to let it mellow a little and you may find yourself with a treat. The **Irish Ale** is an Irish red, coming in at 5 percent ABV, while the **Marathon IPA** is a 6 percent ABV citrusy/piney IPA.

Seasonals include the **Holiday Cheer,** a 6.5 percent ABV porter with strong roasted notes, and the **Snowed In,** a 9.5 percent ABV imperial stout with bitter chocolate and caramel flavors. Other limited release beers include the **Smoked Belgian,** an 8 percent Belgian pale ale with smoked toffee flavors; the **Honey Smack,** a 5 percent ABV that is full of honey; and **Village Charm,** a 6 percent ABV reddish IPA.

Top Shelf's tasting room is open on Friday and Saturday for free samples and tours. Visitors can buy bombers of Top Shelf beers to take home. The beers are also available in several stores.

## TWO ROADS BREWING COMPANY

1700 Stratford Ave., Stratford, CT; (203) 335-2010; TwoRoadsBrewing.com
**Founded:** 2012 **Founders:** Brad Hittle, Phil Markowski, Clement Pellani, Peter Doering **Brewer:** Phil Markowski **Flagship Beer:** Worker's Comp **Year-round Beers:** Honey Spot Road, Road 2 Ruin, Ol' Factory Pilsner, No Limits **Seasonals/Special Releases:** Roadmary's Baby, Route of All Evil Black Ale, Rye 95, Road Jam, Road Less Traveled series **Tours:** Fri, 6:30 p.m.; Sat, 1, 3, and 5 p.m.; Sun, 1, 3 p.m.; $5. Tasting room open Tues to Sat, noon to 9 p.m.; Sun, noon to 7 p.m.

In co-founder/brewmaster Phil Markowski, Two Roads Brewing Company has one of the most respected brewers in all of New England. Markowski is the former brewer at the popular New England Brewing Company in Connecticut, as well as the Southampton Public House in New York. He is also author of the book, *Farmhouse Ales,* about how to brew saisons and farmhouse ales. Add to that the years of experience by co-founder Brad Hittle working for Pabst Blue Ribbon and the years Clement Pellani worked at both Rolling Rock and Labatt USA, and Two Roads Brewing Company has tons of experience in the beer world.

And it shows. They have a solid line-up of both traditional and not-so-traditional beers. They brew five year-round beers, a host of seasonals and a series of off-the-beaten-path-type beers as part of the **Road Less Traveled series.** The

**Road 2 Ruin**
**Style:** Double IPA
**ABV:** 7.6 percent
**Availability:** Year-round
I love double IPAs. The problem is, once you drink a double IPA, your palate is pretty much wrecked for the night—you need to drink something at least as hoppy or even hoppier. But, the Road 2 Ruin is not like that—sure, it's hoppy, but it's not a blistering hop flavor. It's balanced, slightly sweet, and even a little bready. Definitely a beer that does not have to be your last of the night.



brewery's **Worker's Comp** is a saison (Markowski's specialty). It is 4.8 percent alcohol by volume (ABV) and made with coriander. It has less alcohol than the average American saison, but it mimics the original idea of a saison where farm hands were given large amounts of it to drink as they worked throughout the day. The **Road 2 Ruin** is a 7.6 percent double IPA, while the **Ol' Factory Pilsner** is a traditional pilsner. The **No Limits** is a German-style hefeweizen, and the **Honey Spot Road** is a white IPA that uses an American wheat beer base rather than the Belgian wit most white IPAs use.

Seasonals include the **Roadmary's Baby,** a rum-barrel aged pumpkin ale (fall); **Route of All Evil,** a hybrid porter/black IPA (winter); **Rye 95,** a 9.5 percent ABV Belgian tripel brewed with rye (spring) and **Road Jam,** a wheat beer brewed with lemongrass and raspberries (summer).

Two Roads Brewing Company also brews the Road Less Traveled Series. The beers include **Igor's Dream,** a 10.9 percent ABV Russian Imperial Stout; **Conntucky Lightning,** which is brewed using both a sour and regular mash, aged in Bourbon barrels; and **Crazy Pucker,** a Berliner weiss.

Two Roads Brewing Company's taproom is open Tuesdays through Sundays. People can buy tasters of the beers, full pints and growlers or six packs to go. They also sell shirts, glasses, and all other sorts of brewery goods. Tours are held on Fridays, Saturdays and Sundays and cost $5.

Although food is not served, people can bring their own meals in. Two Roads also schedules food trucks to be parked outside of its brewery on Thursdays through Sundays so people can grab food and come on in for a pint. Not a bad deal at all.

### BRU ROOM AT BAR

254 Crown St., New Haven, CT; (203) 495-8924; BarNightclub.com
**Draft Beers:** 5

The Bru Room at Bar is not just a brewpub. It is part of Bar, a full-service nightclub with three separate rooms that fill different roles. The brewpub always has at least five beers on tap.

The year-round beers include the **Toasted Blonde Ale,** which puts a twist on the normally safe style—to get the toasted flavor, brewers throw the malts into the pizza oven and toast them before brewing, giving it a nice, unique flavor never found in a blonde ale. The **AmBAR Ale** is a nice amber ale that features nutty and caramel flavors from the malts, as well as a slight fruitiness from the hops. The **Pale Ale** is a west coast–style pale ale, along the lines of a Sierra Nevada Pale Ale. The **Dam Good Stout** is a nice foreign-style stout, which features undertones of chocolate and coffee. Want more coffee flavor? Grab the **Espresso Dam Good Stout** when it is available. Bru Room features several specialty beers that make occasional appearances. They include the **Big Man IPA,** the **Chocolate Porter,** the **Doctor's Orders Hefeweizen,** the **You Name It IPA,** and the **Raven Haired Beauty,** a 3.7 percent dark mild ale.

The food here is all about the pizza. Except for one salad (which features seasonal greens, pears, pecans, and blue cheese), it's the only type of food available. The pizzas are offered in three bases—the Red Pie, the Red Pie with mozzarella, and the White Pizza with parmesan and garlic. After picking a base, you have 24 options to choose from, including traditional items like pepperoni, onions, and sausage, as well as the not-so-traditional, like mashed potatoes and fresh littleneck clams.

### THE CAMBRIDGE HOUSE

357 Salmon Brook St., Granby, CT; (860) 653-2739; CbhGranby.com
**Draft Beers:** 6

The Cambridge House may not be in the most populous area of Connecticut, but this Granby brewpub is worth making a trek. They brew a large selection of varied beers of numerous styles and strengths. For those who are fans of lighter styles, the **Cooper Hill Kolsch, Berliner Weisse,** and the **Czech Yo'Shelf** (a Czech-style pilsner) are definitely for you.

They brew some hoppy beers, such as the **Abijah Rowe IPA,** or the **BIPA** (Belgian IPA), which are both worth trying. They also brew some malt-heavy beers, such as the **Bock, Pigskin Brown,** and the **Moonbeam Stout,** a 9.8 percent alcohol by volume oak-barrel-aged imperial stout. Other beers brewed by the Cambridge House include the **Alt-45,** the **Farmer's Daughter** (biere de garde), **Oktoberfest,** and **Pumpkin Porter.**

While the beer is obviously what brings people to the Cambridge House, the food will not drive people away. They have a decent size, if not huge, menu. Starters include seared ahi tuna and the Stout Steak Skewers, which are teriyaki- and stout-marinated steak on a stick. Entrees include the Oh Baby Baby Back Ribs, a stout steak, pan-roasted chicken, and jambalaya. The CBH Mac & Cheese is made with several different cheeses, but what really sets it apart is that you can get a half of a lobster tail mixed into it for just a few extra bucks. Throughout the year, the Cambridge House hosts several beer dinners, and also has live music most Fridays and Saturdays, so it is definitely a place you will want to check out.



### CITY STEAM BREWERY CAFE

942 Main St., Hartford, CT; (860) 525-1600; CitySteamBreweryCafe.com
**Draft Beers:** 8 to 10

Not only does City Steam brew good beer and serve good food, they host a comedy club, Brew HA HA, on site at the brewpub. Little-known (at the time) comedians who have performed there over the years include Kevin James, Denis Leary, Jay Mohr, Ray Romano, and Sarah Silverman.

If comedy is not your thing, don't worry, City Steam is still a brewpub. They always have 8 to 10 beers on tap, as well as guest ciders. The beers always on tap include the **Blonde on Blonde Pale Ale,** the **Colt's Light Lager, Naughty Nurse's Amber Ale,** and the **Export Lager.** Feelings are often mixed when a brewpub puts a light lager on draft, but for a brewpub that also doubles as a comedy club, it makes sense because they attract a large crowd of customers who might not have an interest in craft beer. Other beers that are often available include the **Black Silk Stout** (an oatmeal stout), the **Pugnacious Porter** (a big Baltic porter), **White Wedding** (a hybrid of American, Belgian, and German wheat beers), the **Innocence Ale** (an IPA), and the **City Steam Dark Lager.** There is also usually a special Belgian or another strong ale available on draft at all times, as well as seasonal lagers. Growlers are available to go, but each beer costs a different price, so check with your server.

They also have some unique specialty burgers, including the Reuben, which is a burger topped with corned beef, Swiss cheese, Russian dressing, and Asian slaw. City

Steam also has what appears to be the most decadent, heart-stopping burger ever created—the Bacon Triple Decker. It's a bacon cheeseburger sandwiched between two grilled cheese sandwiches. Read that sentence again. If that sounds a little too artery-clogging for you, there is a healthy option section of the menu that includes grilled salmon, grilled fish tacos, and chicken teriyaki skewers. The best seller is the Beer-Braised Pot Roast, braised with house-brewed beer (see recipe, page 315). In 2013, City Steam started bottling some of its beers and they are available in Connecticut and Massachusetts.

### SBC RESTAURANT & BREWERY

Three locations in Milford, Southport, and Stamford; Milford, (203) 874-BEER; Southport, (203) 257-BEER; Stamford, (203) 327-BEER; SouthportBrewing.com
**Draft Beers:** 9

Chain brewpubs can often be a little disappointing. A lot of them have bland beer and boring food. The Southport Brewing Company, or SBC for short, is different. With three locations throughout Connecticut, they do a great job of brewing quality beers and also offer a solid menu.

In all, SBC brews 27 different beers, with 9 different ones on draft at a time. They also make it easy for the novice beer drinker, or those not familiar with the beers. SBC breaks up their beer menu into three tiers. Tier One is light, easy-drinking beers. Tier Two beers are a little more complex, more flavorful, and made to enjoy with food. Tier Three is the more complex beers, designed more for those who are experienced craft beer fans. SBC also lists what mainstream beer the various beers on the menu are most similar to. For example, if you are a fan of Corona, you may want to grab a **SBC Light** from Tier One. If you are a fan of the Samuel Smith's Taddycaster Porter, grab the **SBC Porter** from Tier Three. Harpoon IPA fan? The **SBC IPA** from Tier Two is for you.

The menu is huge and varied. Their mussels are sautéed in the **Big Head Blond Ale,** and SBC offers calamari in three styles: Crispy is the traditional method; the Z-Bar is fried with hot peppers, garlic, and artichoke hearts; and the Sticky is cooked with a sweet chili sriracha glaze with sesame seeds and green onions. Entrees include the SBC Barbecue, a full rack of baby back ribs or a mix of ribs and grilled chicken, all based in beer-infused barbecue sauce. SBC also offers pizza, such as the Loaded Potato Pizza that is topped with mashed potatoes, bacon, scallops, and cheddar and jack cheeses, all topped with sour cream. SBC also has the largest dessert menu of any brewpub I've ever seen. Options include cheesecake, Key lime pie, cinnamon crème brûlée, and chocolate lava cake.

On Sunday from 11:30 a.m. to 2 p.m., SBC offers brunch. Brunch options include many different egg Benedicts, breakfast burritos, omelets, breakfast quesadillas, breakfast sandwiches, steak and eggs, and several different champagne cocktails. In 2013, SBC started bottling several of its beers and they are available in Connecticut and Massachusetts.

### WILLIMANTIC BREWING COMPANY

967 Main St., Willimantic, CT; (860) 423-6777; Willibrew.com
**Draft Beers:** 8 to 10 house beers, 40 overall

The Willimantic Brewing Company is located in a historic post office. It has one of the best mixes of beers around—8 to 10 house-brewed beers and another 30 to 32 guest craft beers.

The only flagship beer is the **Certified Gold,** but the rest are a rotation of IPAs, stouts, porters, red ales, amber ales, blonde ales, wheats, sours, and barrel-aged beers. Get the sampler platter of beers when you go—it is by far the best way to try as many of the beers as you possibly can. Highlights include the **E-Mail IPA,** an English-inspired hoppy IPA; the **Dyvil Hopyard Double IPA,** a Belgian-style double IPA; and the **Autobahn Mail Alt,** a German-style altbier. They also try to introduce a new beer at least once a month using different combinations of hops, malts, yeast, and what founder David Wollner describes as "esoteric ingredients" (such as vanilla, tea, and pineapple).

Guest drafts include several beers from local breweries, as well as Belgian ales and beers from throughout the US. Sierra Nevada Brewing Company, Stone Brewing Company, and Dogfish Head Craft Brewery often find their way onto the tap list.

The menu is huge, and there's also a large number of gluten-free items available. Don't want an entree? Grab one of the many flatbread pizzas or sandwiches available. The Beer Tap Beef Sandwich is one of the better options. The sandwich is made up of thinly shaved steak, melted Swiss cheese, and balsamic beer-glazed onions served on a kaiser roll. Willimantic uses beers in many of their dishes. Along with the onions, they make Beer-B-Que sauce, onion soup, brewer's bread, and sweet beer butter from their house-brewed beers.

Willimantic Brewing Company's beers are also available to go in the form of growlers. Growlers start at $12.95 each, but they can increase in price for some of the higher-alcohol beers.

## THE CASK REPUBLIC

179 Crown St., New Haven, CT; (475) 238-8335; TheCaskRepublic.com
**Draft Beers:** 53 plus 1 cask line **Bottled/Canned Beers:** More than 125

The Cask Republic has become a beer destination for Connecticut beer lovers. The 53-beer draft list is impressive, featuring a wide variety of beers from the US and beyond. If there is an American brewery that you enjoy, and it is available in Connecticut, they have it.

The draft list is broken up by style, so it's easy to navigate. They also have a good mix of big beers and easier to drink, lighter beers. They also have plenty of quality imports. The menu always features some draft specials, when a beer is available at a lower price. The Cask Republic also features several different flights of beers, in which you get four 5-ounce beers, such as the IPA Flight, or the Stone Brewing Company Flight. The bottled beer list is even more impressive. They also have a large imported bottle selection, including a bigger-than-average selection of Italian craft beers (an extremely underrated beer country), and several Japanese beer options. The Cask Republic also has a large selection of Belgian ales and has a few gluten-free beers on the menu.

The Republic also has separate lunch and dinner menus. The lunch menu features smaller, quicker meals, with salads, soups, small plates, sandwiches, and burgers. The Grilled Sausage Plate, which features bratwurst, knockwurst, apple bacon, sauerkraut, and potatoes steamed in lager, is a highlight. If you skipped breakfast, grab the Breakfast Burger, which is topped by a fried egg, applewood-smoked bacon, and tomato jam. Dinner appetizer highlights include the oyster sliders and the seared ahi tuna. There are also plenty of salads, including the warm duck confit salad, which is made up of endive, arugula, red onions, grapes, Granny Smith apples, goat cheese, and caramelized honey vinaigrette. The sandwich you have to try is the German Pretzel Sandwich, which is composed of a breaded pork cutlet, German sauerkraut, and Chimay cheese sauce, all on a giant pretzel bun. One of the standout entrees is the Grilled Extra-Hoppy-Beer-Marinated Half Chicken, served with grilled mash potatoes, sautéed greens, and herb pan gravy (see recipe, page 314).

### ELI CANNON'S TAP ROOM

695 Main St., Middletown, CT; (860) 347-3547; EliCannons.com

**Draft Beers:** 33 **Bottled/Canned Beers:** About 40

Eli Cannon's is probably the best beer bar in the great state of Connecticut, but what really sets it apart from other bars is the dessert menu. Yes, that's right, the dessert menu. There are many great beer bars throughout New England, but none offer the truly creative desserts that Eli Cannon's serves up on a regular basis. Not only does the dessert menu include adult-only and kid-friendly floats, it includes the Fried Cheese Cake Burritos; the Gourmet Pop Tart Sandwiches, which are chocolate Pop Tarts stuffed with white chocolate pretzel peanut butter; and the S'Mores Bread Pudding.

Okay, now for the beer.

Eli Cannon's has 33 beers on tap, and the choices change nearly daily, which will make you want to come back every day to see what you might be missing. The draft list is a good mix of American, Belgian, British, and German beers. They typically have beers from some of the best breweries in the country, such as Dogfish

Every November, Eli Cannon's hosts a Christmas Tree Lighting ceremony. Along with the ceremony, there's snow, "hot elves," and presents for the kids. People are also asked to bring a toy to donate to local charities, and there will be much merry and mirth happening as you enjoy the numerous beers available.

Head, Flying Dog, and Brooklyn Brewery. They also have beers not often available in New England, such as Cooperstown Brewing Company from Cooperstown, New York. New England is usually well-represented with beers from Allagash, Redhook, and Bar Harbor on draft. They also have beers from Ayinger, Delirium Tremens, Wells & Youngs, and Corsendonk. The bottled list is just as varied, so if you can't find a beer you like at Eli Cannon's, you're not really trying.

Now, back to the food.

If you can hold off eating dessert to start your meal, start with a real appetizer. Eli Cannon's has wings, which is not unusual for a bar. What is unusual is the number of different sauces they have available—14, from mild and sweet to hot and spicy, or hot and sweet—pretty much every heat level up to Atomic. Be careful, if the sauce is too hot, no returns. Their baskets of fries are almost as varied—they are served in nine different styles, including Smokers, which are topped with chipotle sauce, jalapeños, cheese, and ranch dressing. Another option is the Porkies Revenge, which are fries covered in barbecue pulled pork and cheese.

Sandwiches include a half-dozen different types of Philly cheesesteaks, as well as the Yogi's BLT, which is made with bourbon teriyaki grilled salmon, bacon, greens, tomatoes, and lemon caper mayonnaise. Burgers are also available. Entrees include macaroni and cheese made with smoked gouda, gruyère, cheddar, Monterey jack, and Parmesan cheeses. Garlic shrimp and shepherd's pie are also options, as is the Caribbean Pasta, which is sautéed chicken tossed in a creamy Caribbean jerk sauce served over pasta. Or do what I would do—order a dessert and a stout and enjoy.

### MIKRO CRAFT BEER BAR

300 Whitney Ave., Hamden, CT; (203) 553-7676; MikroBeerBar.com
**Draft Beers:** 18 **Bottled/Canned Beers:** About 100

The MiKro Craft Beer Bar is proof that good things can come in small packages. The bar only seats 58 people. But, if you are lucky enough to be one of those select few to get a seat inside, you will be treated to a superb draft and bottled list of beer.

MiKro has 18 beers on draft, heavy on New England beers, including Cisco Beer and Harpoon Brewery from Massachusetts, Long Trail Ales and Otter Creek Brewing Company from Vermont, and Sebago Brewing Company from Maine. Other breweries often featured include River Horse Brewing Company from New Jersey, Rogue Brewery from Oregon, and Rodenbach Grand Cru from Belgium. The bottled list includes beers in almost every single style from almost every major American brewery, as well as several larger-format bottles, 750 ml and even 3-liter bottles, from Europe, mainly Belgium.

Throughout the year, MiKro hosts several tap takeovers, where a particular brewery will have several of its beers on tap, often at discounted prices. They also host beer dinners where a brewery will work with the chef to create a dinner in which each beer is matched perfectly with the dish being served. MiKro takes pride in creating a menu that is beer-friendly. Each and every dish is perfect to eat with the various beers on tap.

Start light with a snack, such as deviled eggs, fried chick peas, house-made pretzels, and charcuterie plates. Or order small plates such as beet salad, poutine, chicken wings, and Local Burrata, which is made with cream-filled mozzarella, olive oil confit tomatoes, arugula, basil oil, and balsamic vinaigrette. MiKro also has several whole-wheat flatbreads, with toppings like Yukon Gold potatoes, mushrooms, and pork belly. Sandwiches are always an option, including the Kobe beef hot dog or the P.B.L.T., which is topped with roasted pork belly, smoked bacon, Bibb lettuce, tomatoes, and roasted garlic mayonnaise.

Entrees, or, as MiKro calls them, "Large Plates," include smoked trout with dill crème fraîche, pickled red onions, squash puree, local apples, and crispy sweet potatoes. Highlights are the Shrimp + Grits, which is cheddar grits served with shrimp, smoked bacon, green onions, and pickled green tomato relish; and pan-roasted chicken breast, which is served with roasted sweet potato, quinoa, Swiss chard, and cilantro-pumpkin seed pesto. There is a different dessert available daily.

### PRIME 16

172 Temple St., New Haven, CT; (203) 782-1616; Prime16.com
**Draft Beers:** 20, plus 2 casks **Bottled/Canned Beers:** More than 40

Enjoying a good beer while munching on a burger is a time-honored tradition, but Prime 16 takes the pairing to an all-new level: they combine great craft beer with grass-fed beef burgers. Talk about a perfect pairing.

Prime 16 has 20 beers on draft, as well as more than 40 different craft beers in bottles and cans. Combine that with one of the best burger menus around, and it makes for a perfect night. They also typically have two beers on cask at all times. The draft list is varied, with beers for all tastes, ranging from fruit beers to hoppy American IPAs to many different Belgian ales; if you can't find a beer you like, you really aren't trying that hard. The bottled list features many of the top breweries in the country, as well as local favorites.

The burgers are the stars of the menu. There are several beefless burgers, including the lamb burger and the wasabi-glazed salmon burger. Of course, if you call yourself a burger place, you'd better have some unusual, but tasty, burgers on the menu.

Prime 16 does. The Maui Burger has pineapple, Maui onions, tropical mayonnaise, and applewood bacon. The New York Steak Burger is another interesting creation. It's topped with cracked pepper, wilted spinach, blue cheese crumble, and tobacco-fried onions. If there isn't a burger on the menu that catches your attention, you can always build your own burger—pick the toppings of choice to make the perfect burger just for you.

Prime 16 hosts plenty of special events throughout the year. They do a tap take-over at least every other month, and they host both beer and bourbon dinners. In addition, Monday is $3 beer night, and there are free beer tastings every Wednesday starting at 9 p.m. Happy hour, Monday through Friday from 4 to 7 p.m. and Saturday 2 to 4 p.m., features half-price beers. Prime 16 is a perfect night out; just make sure to get there early on a Saturday night or risk standing up all night, then grab a burger and a beer and have fun.

# Rhode Island

Rhode Island is New England's smallest state in terms of size and the beer scene, but it isn't without merit. The Coastal Extreme Brewing Company, brewers of Newport Storm beers, brews several excellent beers, from their year-round beers to their special releases, while Narragansett Beer is growing and trying to regain the popularity of its heyday of the 1950s. Meanwhile, Providence is quickly developing a growing beer scene with a pair of brewpubs and several beer bars, making it a nice weekend stop for visitors and a beer haven for local beer lovers.

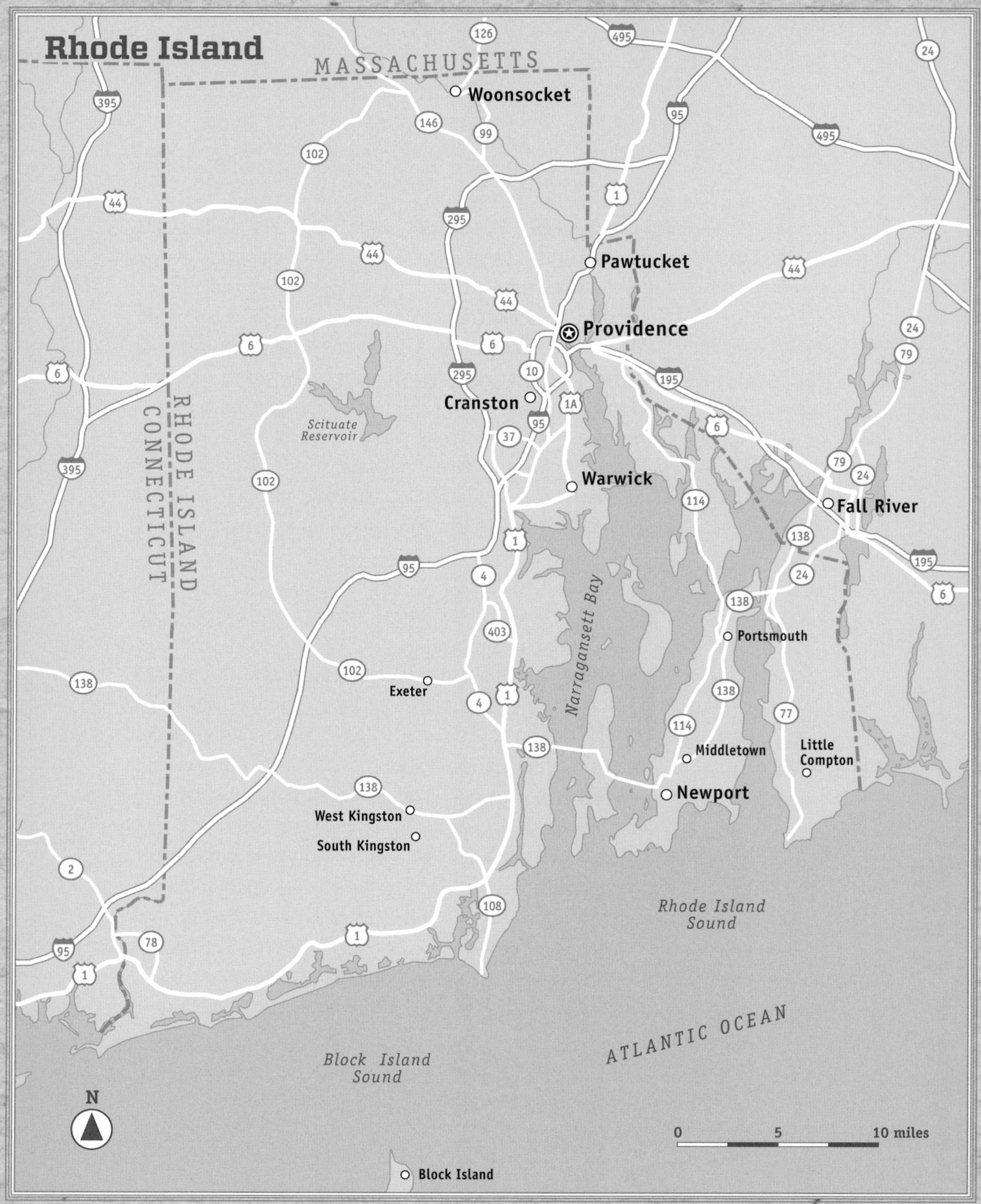
Rhode Island
MASSACHUSETTS
RHODE ISLAND
CONNECTICUT
Woonsocket
Pawtucket
Providence
Cranston
Warwick
Fall River
Portsmouth
Middletown
Newport
Little Compton
Exeter
West Kingston
South Kingston
Scituate Reservoir
Narragansett Bay
Rhode Island Sound
Block Island Sound
ATLANTIC OCEAN
Block Island
N
0
5
10 miles

**BUCKET BREWERY**

545 Pawtucket Ave., Pawtucket, RI; (401) 305-0597; BucketBrewery.com
**Founded:** 2012 **Founders:** Erik Aslasken, Nate Broomfield, Ron Klinger, T.J. O'Connor, Andrew Powers **Brewers:** Erik Aslasken, Nate Broomfield **Flagship Beer:** Pawtucket Pail Ale **Year-round Beers:** Park Loop Porter, Rhode Scholar, Thirteenth Original Maple Stout **Seasonals/Special Releases:** Consistently Inconsistent, a series of one-off beers **Tours:** Sat, 2, 3, and 4 p.m.; $10.

The Bucket Brewery got started as many breweries did—homebrewing. Erik Aslasken and Nate Broomfield were good friends and homebrewing partners. Soon, they began brewing so much beer, they couldn't keep up with drinking it, so after bringing on more partners—Ron Klinger, T.J. O'Connor, and Andrew Powers—they launched the Bucket Brewery.

The brewery is located in one of the many old mills that populate Pawtucket. There, Aslasken and Broomfield work on four year-round beers and a series of one-off beers called **Consistently Inconsistent,** each time you visit the Pawtucket Avenue brewery there's a good chance there will be a new Consistently Inconsistent beer available.

The **Pawtucket Pail Ale** is a not-so-traditional take on a pale ale. While most pale ales are hop forward, this beer uses caramel malts to provide a sweetness not usually found in pale ales that blend well with the nicely piney hops. A truly balanced beer. The **Rhode Scholar** is a kolsh, a German-style of ale that isn't brewed enough. It's light, crisp and refreshing, with hints of lemon and pepper. It's light enough for those who may not be the biggest beer aficionados, but complex enough that a beer geek will enjoy picking out the subtle flavors. The **Park Loop Porter** is the Bucket's biggest year-round beer, a 7.8 percent alcohol by volume English-style robust porter. This beer is bursting with chocolate and toffee flavors. The **Thirteenth Original Maple Stout** is lighter in body than the average stout, but don't let the light body fool you. This beer is full of flavor, dark roasted chocolates, and the maple that's in the name adds prominent flavors. What is a standout is the smoky flavor you don't expect in a stout.

The brewery's tasting room is open from noon to 5 p.m. every Saturday. A tasting costs $2 and you get a sample of all available beers (year-round and anything else they have available). Tours are at 2, 3, and 4 p.m. and cost $10. The $10 pays for your tour, the tasting of all available beers, and a Bucket Brewery glass.

**Thirteenth Original Maple Stout**
**Style:** American Stout
**ABV:** 6.4 percent
**Availability:** Year-round
If you like smoky beers, this is a treat. It doesn't reach the levels of a rauchbier (German-smoked lager), but it adds a nice complimentary flavor to the maple and roasted notes in this beer. The lighter body also makes it one of the easier drinking stouts you can drink.

Also available at the brewery are men's and women's T-shirts, thermals, bumper stickers, and glasses. Growlers are available at the brewery, but Rhode Island state law limits it to one per person.

The beer is only available in Rhode Island at a number of liquor stores and restaurants.

## COASTAL EXTREME BREWING COMPANY

293 JT Connell Rd., Newport, RI; (401) 849-5232; NewportStorm.com
**Founded:** 1999 **Founders:** Brent Ryan, Derek Luke, Mark Sincliar, Will Rafferty **Brewer:** Derek Luke **Flagship Beer:** Newport Storm Hurricane Amber Ale **Year-round Beer:** Rhode Island Blueberry Ale **Seasonals/Special Releases:** Regenschauer Oktoberfest, Spring Ale, Summer Ale, Winter, Cyclone Series, Annual Release Series **Tours:** Every day except Tues, noon to 5 p.m.; guided tours at 3 p.m.; $7 per person, plus tax

The Coastal Extreme Brewing Company, better known as Newport Storm, is the only full production brewery in the state of Rhode Island, and an excellent brewery at that. Coastal Extreme does not get as much love from beer geeks as they really should. They produce some of the most drinkable beers available in New England.

The brewery's flagship offering, the **Newport Storm Hurricane Amber Ale,** is a remarkably drinkable beer. It might be the best amber ale being brewed anywhere;

it is a beer that can attract those casual beer drinkers, and still have enough flavor that craft beer lovers will still want to seek it out. Newport's only other year-round beer is the **Rhode Island Blueberry Ale,** which is better than most other beers for the style.

Coastal Extreme brews four seasonals, called the **Storms of the Season.** The **Summer Ale** is a really nice, hoppy summer beer. The **Winter** is a dark, roasty porter, while the **Spring Ale** is a roasty red ale. The **Regenschauer Oktoberfest** is a traditional German-style Oktoberfest, rich and malty. Throughout the year, Coastal Extreme also brews the **Cyclone Series.** Each one of the beers is produced in limited qualities, is a different style, and is named for different Atlantic hurricanes. The styles vary and in the past have included various types of pale ales, a winter warmer, and even a rum barrel–aged beer. At the end of the year, Coastal Extreme brews an anniversary beer, and the name is simply the year—'09, '10, '11, etc. The beers are usually higher-octane beers, packaged in 750 ml, strikingly blue bottles, with a waxed top so the beer can be cellared and enjoyed for years, to see how the beer ages and matures.

Also at Coastal Extreme is the Newport Distillery, which produces Thomas TewRum. Coastal Extreme hosts tours daily (except for Tuesday). A guided tour begins at 3 p.m., but self-guided tours are anytime from noon to 5 p.m. The tours cost $7, and you get to try four different beers and get a Newport Storm tasting

**Hurricane Amber Ale**
**Style:** Amber Ale
**ABV:** 5.2 percent
**Availability:** Year-Round
The Hurricane Amber Ale may be what many people consider a boring style (amber ale), but this is one fantastic beer. It is darker than many amber ales, and it has a full body thanks to the sweet malts, with a creamy head and mouthfeel. At the same time, there is just a hint of hops, which is just enough to give this beer a nice balance.

glass. You can also tour the distillery, which costs an additional $9. Coastal Extreme also hosts several events throughout the year, such as the Hoppy Holiday, which is an on-site beer festival.

## FOOLPROOF BREWING COMPANY

241 Grotto Ave., #1, Pawtucket, RI; (401) 721-5970; FoolproofBrewing.com

**Founded:** 2012 **Founder:** Nick Garrison **Brewer:** Damase Olsson **Flagship Beer:** Barstool **Year-round Beers:** Backyahd, La Ferme Urbaine, Raincloud **Seasonals/Special Releases:** King of the Yahd, Revery **Tours:** Sat, 1, 2, 3, and 4 p.m.; $10. Tastings on Fri, 5 to 7 p.m.; $7

Many breweries offer food parings for their beers, but the Foolproof Brewing Company is unique in that they offer experience parings for each of their beers.

Foolproof likes to say that their beers are meant to be part of an overall experience. The **Backyahd IPA,** for example, is meant to be enjoyed while sitting outside on a nice day, maybe with a big porterhouse on the grill; or the **Barstool,** meant to be enjoyed when your throwing a few back with your buddies while sitting at your neighborhood bar while the game is on the big-screen TV in front of you.

But, to be part of a good experience, you need good beers, and Foolproof's beers more than fit the bill.

The Barstool is an American golden ale—it's light at 4.5 percent alcohol by volume (ABV), easy to drink, and much more flavorful than the average golden ale. The Backyahd is a dependable, go-to IPA, always good to have in the fridge. The Rain

**Backyahd**
**Style:** IPA
**ABV:** 6 percent
**Availability:** Year-round

This is exactly what you expect from a 6 percent ABV. The hops don't scorch your tongue. They add pleasant flavors and just a hint of bitterness, while the malt backbone adds perfect balance. I enjoyed several of these while grilling and I plan on doing that again and again.

Cloud is a wonderful robust porter, full flavored with roasted coffee notes, a hop of dark chocolate bitterness and, at 6.5 percent ABV, not as strong as many robust porters. The **La Ferme Urbaine,** a saison, was originally a special release, but it was so popular it became a year-round beer. It's a French farmhouse style ale. Yeasty and fruity with a dry finish, it's spot on for the style.

While Foolproof's year-round beers are available in 12-ounce cans, its special releases are in 22-ounce bombers. The special releases are the **King of the Yahd,** a souped up version of the Backyahd. This double IPA comes in at a hefty 9.5 percent ABV. It's not Foolproof's biggest beer. That honor is reserved for **Revery,** a 10.7 percent ABV imperial stout.

Foolproof offers tours every hour on the hour from 1 to 4 p.m. on Saturday. Tours are $10 and include samples. Tastings are available Friday from 5 to 7 p.m. for $7. The brewery store is fully stocked with hats, beanies, sweat shirts, CANdles, and other swag. Rhode Island law prevents breweries from selling beer, but it does allow them to sell up to 72 ounces of samples for people to bring home.



## GREY SAIL BREWING OF RHODE ISLAND

63 Canal St., Westerly, RI; (401) 315-2533; GreySailBrewing.com
**Founded:** 2011 **Founders:** Alan and Jennifer Brintin **Brewer:** Josh Letourneau **Flagship Beer:** Flagship Beer **Year-round Beers:** Flying Jenny Extra Pale Ale **Seasonals/Special Releases:** Autumn Winds, Hazy Day, Leaning Chimney **Tours:** Sat, 1 to 5 p.m.; free. Tasting room open Fri, 3 to 6 p.m.

Alan and Jennifer Brintin shared a dream of opening a brewery for almost 15 years. But then reality hit. Children came, and with that came responsibility. But, finally, in 2011, the couple opened Grey Sail Brewing of Rhode Island, and they haven't looked back.

Grey Sail brews two year-round beers, the aptly named **Flagship Beer** and the **Flying Jenny Extra Pale Ale.** The Flagship Beer is a cream ale. Cream ales are brewed like lagers, but use ale yeast. They're an under-represented style in the craft beer world, but they can be fabulously easy-drinking, tasty beers. Grey Sail's Flagship Beer, which is 4.9 percent alcohol by volume (ABV), is light and refreshing with plenty of flavor. The Flying Jenny Extra Pale Ale is a 6 percent ABV hoppy pale ale (close to an IPA). Full of citrus and floral flavor notes with a grainy, almost bready malt backbone, this is a well-done beer worth trying. Both of Grey Sail's year-round beers are available in 12-ounce cans.

Grey Sail also offers several seasonals. **Hazy Day** is a Belgian wit, smooth, light and spicy. It is the summer seasonal. The **Autumn Winds** is an ale brewed like an

**Leaning Chimney**
**Style:** Robust porter
**ABV:** 6 percent
**Availability:** Year-round
The Leaning Chimney is a 6 percent ABV robust porter. The malts are peat-smoked, giving this beer a pleasant smokiness, which blends well with the flavors of dark chocolate and the slight roasty coffee flavors.

Oktoberfest. It has a biscuity taste from the malts with just a hint of hops in the finish. The **Leaning Chimney** is a robust porter available during the winter. Grey Sail's tasting room is open on Friday for growler fills. Tours are available on Saturday from 1 to 5 p.m.

## NARRAGANSETT BEER

60 Ship St., Providence, RI (corporate office); (401) 437-8970; NarragansettBeer.com
**Founded:** 2005 **Founder:** Mark Hellendrung **Brewer:** Contract brewed **Flagship Beer:** Narragansett Lager **Year-round Beers:** Narragansett Light **Seasonals/Special Releases:** Narragansett Bock, Fest Lager, Narragansett Porter, Summer Ale, Imperial Series **Tours:** None

"Hey neighbor, grab a 'Gansett." That saying was synonymous with the former Narragansett Brewing Company in the 1950s and 1960s. Pittsburgh had Yuengling, but New Englanders had Narragansett. That was our beer.

But as breweries started consolidating, Narragansett was sold, and eventually it went away, until 2005 when Mark Hellendrung and a group of investors bought back the rights to the name, hired back former brewer Bill Anderson to re-create the original recipe, and brought the 'Gansett name back home. Narragansett is actually brewed in New York, but Hellendrung is trying to sell enough beer that he can open a full brewery in Rhode Island. Until then, more and more bars throughout the state are carrying the classic Narragansett "Tall Boys," the 16-ounce cans.

The classic **Narragansett Lager** is cheap, easy to drink, and just plain tasty. Nothing flashy here. This is a straightforward American lager, but with more flavor than you see from the big boys in St. Louis, Milwaukee, and Golden, Colorado. However, where Narragansett really excels is their seasonals. They have found a niche of doing quality, straightforward interpretations of relatively simple styles. Again, no flash, no twists, just darn good beer. The **Fest Lager** is an Oktoberfest-style beer, available during the fall. It is the kind of beer that goes down easy. It may not be as full-bodied as the German counterparts, but it is about half the price, and it will not be a letdown. When snow begins to fall, you will see the **Narragansett Porter** popping up on liquor store shelves. This is Narragansett's strongest beer, 7 percent alcohol by volume, and it is a perfect winter beer, dark, creamy, full-bodied with just a hint of heat from the alcohol, just what you want while sitting in front of a fire (or space heater) on a cold January night. The spring seasonal, the **Narragansett Bock,** is their best beer. This is a traditional German-style bock, which is a pleasure to drink. The summer seasonal, **Summer Ale,** is a light, refreshing blonde ale with a touch of hops. It is not uncommon to see someone leaving a liquor store with a few cases of these for a cookout.

Narragansett may be more active than any other New England brewery in terms of getting their name out there. It is almost impossible to find a night on the calendar

### Beer Lover's Pick

**Narragansett Bock**
**Style:** Bock
**ABV:** 6.5 percent
**Availability:** Spring Seasonal
This is close to a traditional German bock, but a little more hoppy. Narragansett excels at doing no-frills, simple styles of beer, and the Narragansett Bock is a perfect example of their brewing philosophy. There is a yeasty, biscuity quality to it, with hints of herbal hops. It is creamy and slightly sweet. Overall, it is a fantastic beer.

when there are no in-store tastings of 'Gansett beers in New England. Every year, Narragansett hosts several contests. One of the most popular is one where entrants submit a tie design. The winning design is then turned into ties and inserted into 12-packs and cases for Father's Day. They also release a "'Gansett Girls" calendar, which features women in 1950s-style pinup clothing and poses.

### PROCLAMATION ALE COMPANY

141 Fairgrounds Rd., West Kingston, RI; (401)787-6450; ProcolmationAleCo.com
**Founded:** 2013 **Founder:** Dave Witham **Brewer:** Dave Witham **Year-round Beers:** Tendril, Zzzlumber **Taproom:** No official times, if beer is available, Sat from noon to 3 p.m. Samples, growler fills available

Proclamation Ale Company is one of the growing number of nano-breweries popping up throughout New England on what seems like a weekly basis. Founder/Brewer Dave Witham only produces about 640 gallons of beer a month on his three-and-a-half gallon system.

The brewery is small, with one small room where all of the brewing equipment is located, and Witham is the sole employee. Although he typically offers tours on Saturday from noon to 3 p.m., he said it is not every Saturday, it's only weekends where he does not have an event or he has enough beer available for both samples and growler fills. There is no brewery store.

Proclamation Ale Company only brews two beers—**Tendril** and **Zzzlumber.** Tendril is described as a "One and a half times IPA," an India pale ale that is stronger than the typical IPA at 7.8 percent alcohol by volume (ABV), but lower than the double, or imperial, IPAs you see on the market. The Tendril has flavors of pine, citrus, pear, and tropical fruit. The malt background is just enough to give the beer a little sweetness so the hops don't overwhelm your palette. The Zzzlumber is a "Dutch imperial stout," a 10 percent ABV, dark as night beer. It has roasted, coffee-like flavors, with hints of chocolate, vanilla, Bourbon, and oakiness.

Proclamation Ale Company beers are only available at select establishments near West Kingston and in growlers at the brewery.

### RAVENOUS BREWING COMPANY

840 Cumberland Hill Rd., Woonsocket, RI; (401) 216-5331; RavenousBrew.com
**Founded:** 2012 **Founder:** Dorian Rave **Brewer:** Dorian Rave **Beers:** Coffee Milk Stout, Blackstone Pale Ale, IRA, Black Harvest Stout, Saison **Taproom:** Taproom hours and days vary so check website before planning to go. Tours are $8 and include a glass.

The Ravenous Brewing Company is a nano-brewery located in one of Rhode Island's biggest cities, Woonsocket. Founded in 2012 by Dorian Rave (one of the best brewer names in New England), the brewery offers several beers available on tap and in growlers at the Cumberland Hill Road brewery.

The beers include the **Coffee Milk Stout, Blackstone Pale Ale, IRA, Black Harvest Stout,** and the **Saison.** The Coffee Milk Stout is a 5 percent alcohol by volume (ABV) milk stout brewed with coffee from local coffee roasters. Milk stouts use lactose sugar to give the beer more body without raising alcohol and this beer takes advantage of it, feeling like a more robust beer. The Blackstone Pale Ale is brewed to honor the Blackstone Region, which Woonsocket is part of. It's a classic pale ale, brewed with Cascade hops to give it a spicy flavor with a floral aroma. Other beers include the IRA, the Indian Red Ale, kind of like a hopped-up red ale, or maybe a red IPA. The Black Forest Stout is a dry stout and the saison is a 7.7 percent ABV version of the style.

Ravenous opens for tours, most often on Saturday, but the hours and days change, so check the website before going. Tours are $8, and you get to keep the glass. Growler fills are also available, as well as 32-ounce howlers.

## REVIVAL BREWING COMPANY

Based in Providence, RI, brewed at two locations; (401) 523-9923; RevivalBrewing.com
**Founded:** 2011 **Founder:** Owen Johnson, Sean Larkin **Brewer:** Sean Larkin **Flagship Beer:** Revival Saison **Beers:** Juliet 484, Double Black IPA, Larkin's Dry Irish Stout, Imperial Oktoberfest **Tours:** None

The Revival Brewing Company has the most well-known Rhode Island brewer creating its recipes and making sure its beers are made correctly in Sean Larkin. Larkin is the former brewery of the well-respected Trinity Brewhouse, a brewpub in Providence. He also created several of the recipes that Narragansett Beer uses as seasonals. Revival brews beer both at Trinity Brewhouse and the Cottrell Brewing Company in Connecticut.

The flagship beer is the **Revival Saison,** which is an American take on the Belgian style. It is brewed with traditional Belgian malts and yeast, but then liberally hopped with Pacific Northwest hops. The **Larkin's Dry Irish Stout** is based on an old family recipe. It's a 5.5 percent alcohol by volume (ABV), version of the style, slightly stronger than the typical beer of the style. **Juliet 484** is named for a submarine that is sunk in Providence Harbor. It is Revival's biggest beer. The imperial stout is 9.5 percent ABV. Another big beer is the **Double Black IPA,** which is 8 percent ABV.

**Double Black IPA**
**Style:** Black IPA
**ABV:** 8 percent
**Availability:** Winter
This black IPA does a good job of blending the roasted malts that provide a slight chocolate flavor, with the citrusy, lemony hops provided by the Chinook and Simcoe hops. At 8 percent ABV it's strong, but the alcohol is hidden, making it a smooth, easy to drink beer at its strength.

Also available on a rotating basis is the **Imperial Oktoberfest.** Oktoberfests typically are 5 to 6 percent ABV. The Revival version is 7 percent. It's a tad sweet, but better than many other imperial Oktoberfests available.

### CODDINGTON BREWING COMPANY

210 Coddington Hwy., Middletown, RI; (401) 847-6690; Newport-Brewery.com
**Draft Beers:** 7

The Coddington Brewing Company provides an option for those who want to visit beautiful Newport but do not want to pay the high prices that most of the restaurants in the area charge. Add the fact that Coddington brews some quality beer, and you have a good alternative to the expensive Newport dining scene.

The Coddington Brewing Company offers a rotating selection of seven different beers on tap at all times. The selection is varied, ranging from lighter beers to heavy beers and pretty much everything in between. For those who prefer the lighter end of the beer spectrum, the **Golden Ale,** the **Blueberry Blonde,** the **Raspberry Cream Ale, Watermelon Ale,** and the **Vienna Lager** should be right up your alley; although light, they pack plenty of flavor. If you'd rather have a bigger beer, go for the **ESB, IPA, Irish Red Ale, Maibock,** or the **Nut Brown Ale.** Coddington also offers seven bigger beers, such as the **Belgian Triple,** the **Barley Wine,** and the **Doppelbock,** which are all higher than 7 percent alcohol by volume (ABV).

Stout lovers will rejoice in the fact that Coddington offers two of the most traditional stouts brewed in New England: Their **Irish Stout** and **Oatmeal Stout** are both under 4 percent ABV, which is the traditional level for the style. Although low in alcohol, they both retain their flavor. Other beers available include the **Chocolate Porter, English Mild, Maibock, Oktoberfest, Scotch Ale, Scottish Heavy, Winter Lager,** and **Winter Wheat.**

Worked up an appetite? Codington sports a rather large food menu. William Coddington's Turkey Platter is a cross between an entree and a sandwich. The platter has roasted sliced turkey breast, served with red bliss mashed potatoes, stuffing, gravy, and cranberry sauce, all served on top of toast points. If you can handle the heat, try the hot and spicy Calamari Fra Diavolo, which is made of fried calamari tossed in a hot and spicy tomato broth with peppers and onions, all tossed in linguine. Coddington also serves 14-inch pizzas, perfect for two people to share. All traditional toppings are available, or get one of the special pizzas, such as the Chourico & Peppers, which is topped with chourico, green peppers, onions, mushrooms, mozzarella cheese, and red sauce.

Coddington also sells growlers of most of their beer, although some of the higher-alcohol beers and the stouts may not be available.

## MOHEGAN CAFE & BREWERY

213 Water St., Block Island, RI; (407) 466-5911
**Draft Beers:** 6

Mohegan Cafe & Brewery provides a much-needed service to Block Island residents and visitors: They brew quality beer, offering an alternative to the usual mass-produced lagers that dominate the local landscape. The brewpub typically has six rotating drafts from 12 different Mohegan beers. These beers include some lighter offerings, like the **Amber Ale, Apricot Amber** (the amber with apricot flavor added), and the **Summer Wheat.** The **BIPA** (Block Island Pale Ale) is a popular beer, while the **Block Island IPA** is a decently hopped, easy-drinking beer. The **Mohegan Pilsner** is a pretty, golden beer, and goes down easy.

Other beers include the **Black Buck Porter,** the **Black Buck Stout,** and the **Striper English Ale.** Mohegan's strongest beer is the **Joe's High Octane,** an 8 percent alcohol by volume English strong ale. Or perhaps you enjoy spicy food. How about spicy beer? Why not order the **Chili Pepper Ale** and find out?

The Mohegan Cafe & Brewery serves some of the best seafood on the island. The Lone Star Crab Cakes, coconut shrimp, fried calamari, shrimp cocktail, and mussels Chardonnay are all standout starters, as is clam chowder. Lunch options include fish and chips, a fried clam plate, and an open-faced steak sandwich. Burgers are also available all day. Entrees (available at dinner), include seafood scampi, cedar-smoked salmon, baked stuffed tilapia, and curried eggplant risotto.

## TRINITY BREWHOUSE

186 Fountain St., Providence, RI; (401) 453-227; TrinityBrewhouse.com
**Draft Beers:** 10

The Trinity Brewhouse is in the perfect location in Providence to grab a beer and a bite to eat on your way either to or from an event. Trinity is located right across the street from the Dunkin Donuts Center, just down the street from the Trinity Repertory Theater, and across from the Rhode Island Convention Center.

The Trinity may not be as well-known as Boston-area brewpubs, but do not let their lack of name recognition fool you. Trinity has an eclectic mix of excellent beers always on tap, making it a beer destination. They have 10 house beers on tap, with a featured guest tap from time to time. One thing is for sure: Trinity's beers are never boring. Even common styles are often brewed with a twist.

For example, the **Kolsch,** a wonderfully light German style of beer, is brewed with a Japanese variety of hops called Sorachi Ace, which add lemon flavors that you would never find in a traditional German kolsch, resulting in some fantastic flavor. The **Rhode Island IPA** pushes the boundaries between a regular IPA and a double IPA. The beer is only 7 percent alcohol by volume (ABV), which is at the top range of what most breweries consider a regular IPA, but this beer is hopped like a double IPA with big citrus notes and a lot of bitterness. And somehow, the Trinity Brewhouse balances this beer without putting more fermentable sugars in the beer to raise the alcohol. Like the kolsch, the **Bruins Brown Ale** is a traditional style brewed with untraditional hops. In this case, Trinity uses Galaxy hops, which are known for creating passion-fruit flavors and aromas. This works with the brown ale, giving it a fruity essence not typically found in the beer.

Some of the other standouts include the **White Electric Stout,** which is a coffee-infused stout, the **Russian Imperial Stout,** which comes in at 8.5 percent ABV with huge coffee and chocolaty flavors, and the **Belgo-American Saison.** Other occasional beers include the **Imperial Pilsner, Dark Wheat, REDRUM Imperial Red Ale,** and the **Wolf's Breath Winter Warmer,** a huge malty barleywine.

Food-wise, Trinity Brewhouse does not offer entrees, but they have a large selection of appetizers, soups, salads, pizzas, burgers, and sandwiches. Appetizers include the Double Loaded Ravioli, which are deep-fried pasta-potato raviolis stuffed with cheddar cheese and chives, baked with Monterey jack and Colby cheddar, and topped with sour cream, crumbled bacon, and scallops. The Zuppa di Brew is locally harvested black-shell mussels served with chorizo, onions, and roasted garlic, simmered in a pilsner-seafood broth. Fittingly, several of the sandwich options include items

### Trinity Christmas Party

Joining the Trinity Brewhouse Mug Club gets you many advantages (including large beers at pint prices), and one of the best things you get as a Mug Club member is an invite to the Trinity Christmas Party. Held in December, this event features special winter beers and food prepared for Mug Club members.

prepared with beer. The barbecued pulled pork sandwich features a barbecue sauce that is made with house beer, and the corned beef served on the Reuben is slowly braised in stout.

Trinity also offers growlers of all of its beers to go. In addition, you do not have to be in Rhode Island to get the Trinity IPA. The IPA is bottled and distributed in other states.

## UNION STATION BREWERY

36 Exchange Terr., Providence, RI; (401) 274-2739; JohnHarvards.com
**Draft Beers:** 8

The Union Station Brewery is part of the John Harvard's chain of brewpubs. Some of the same beers are on tap at both the John Harvard's location in Massachusetts and at Union Station, but there is some room for the local brewers to be creative.

A handful of beers you may run into include the **Triple Hop,** which is a hybrid of a Belgian-style tripel and an American IPA. **Ken's Breakfast Stout,** made with coffee, oatmeal, and hints of chocolate, is also worth trying. Union Station has two different porters: the **College Hill Porter** is a typical, straight-ahead porter, while the **Vanilla Bean Porter** is made with vanilla beans and has strong vanilla notes. The **Friar Brown Ale** is a really good brown ale, the **Lucky Penny IPA** is a nicely hopped beer, and the **Hersbruck Pils** is a good, solid pilsner. Buy a growler of your favorite on the way out.

Union Station may not serve up the most adventurous fare in the world, but the menu boasts good pub and comfort-food dishes. Sandwiches include the Lentil Pocket, which is in Syrian bread with feta cheese, shredded lettuce, diced tomatoes, and yogurt dressing. Another tasty option is the fontina and grape grilled cheese sandwich, which also includes rosemary and is served on sourdough bread. Pub-style pizzas and burgers are pretty darn good at Union Station. The Fungus is a burger topped with garlic aioli, crumbled blue cheese, and portobello, white, and shitake mushrooms, while the Three Amigos is a burger made for those who like a little heat with their meat. It is topped with fried cherry peppers, capicola, chipotle and chili aioli, and pepper jack cheese. But the best meal may be the Rhode Island Clam Bake, which includes cod, littleneck clams, mussels, chorizo, corn, potatoes, onions, tomatoes, and herbs. Make sure to leave room for some apple crisp, or the butterscotch bread pudding.

### DOHERTY'S EAST AVENUE IRISH PUB

342 East Ave., Pawtucket, RI; (401) 725-1800; Dohertys.com
**Draft Beers:** 82 **Bottled/Canned Beers:** Around 60

There are tons of faux Irish pubs throughout New England. Heck, you can't walk a block in Boston without seeing one. The problem is most of them have a boring atmosphere, and the only thing Irish about them is Guinness on tap and green beer on St. Patrick's Day. Doherty's East Avenue Irish Pub is a step above those pubs. This is a beer destination worth seeking out in Pawtucket.

Doherty's has more than 80 beers on draft (yes, Guinness is one of them), but they also have plenty of good beers from breweries such as Harpoon, Samuel Adams, and Coastal Extreme Brewing. Beers from Heavy Seas and Brooklyn Brewing Company also often find themselves on the draft list. The bottled list is just as good as the draft list.

Food-wise, Doherty's is mainly pub-style food, and there really is not much as far as Irish cuisine available, except for shepherd's pie and bangers and mash.

Appetizers include chicken wings and chicken tenders, fried calamari, and jalapeño poppers. Also available are Chinese pot stickers and Mussels Zuppa, which are Prince Edward Island mussels served in a zesty zuppa sauce. Doherty's also has several burgers and grilled chicken sandwiches on the menu. The highlights include the Old Smoker, which is meat braised with barbecue sauce, topped with your choice of cheddar cheese and bacon or mushrooms and Swiss.

### ENGLISH CELLAR ALEHOUSE

165 Angell St., Providence, RI; (401) 454-3434; Englishcellaralehouse.com
**Draft Beers:** 12 **Bottled/Canned Beers:** Around 150

England is known for having one of the best pub cultures in the beer drinking world, but it also happens to be on the other side of the Atlantic Ocean. So to get your English pub fix, head to the English Cellar Alehouse in Providence. The bar has plenty of really good English beers, as well as beers from other parts of the world, too. The English Cellar Alehouse also features some traditional English-style pub food, as well as good ol' American cuisine.

The draft list features several English ales, including Newcastle, Old Speckled Hen, Young's Double Chocolate Stout, and Boddingtons. Other English ales are often available in bottles, including Hobgoblin, several beers from Well's and Young's, Fullers, and Samuel Smith's. Non-British beers often include Brooklyn Brewing, Flying Dog, and North Coast from the US; Warsteiner and Spaten from Germany; and Kasteel, Rochefort, and Maredous from Belgium. Along with beer, the English Cellar Alehouse has a large selection of single malt scotches, bourbons, and some interesting-looking mixed drinks, many of which have very British-sounding names, such as Scotland Yard, Summer on the Thames, and Westminster Abbey.

The English influence carries on to the menu. Appetizers include such dishes as stout onion soup, Newcastle Steak on a Stick, and Scottish Eggs, which are soft-boiled eggs wrapped in bacon, breaded, and fried. The original James Bond was Scottish, not English, but the English Cellar Alehouse still offers a burger named after the famous movie spy. The James Bond Burger is an 8-ounce beef patty, topped with fried onions, barbecue sauce, and cheddar cheese. British classics like bangers and mash, fish and chips, chicken pot pie, and shepherd's pie are also available.

If you are a fan of the English Premier League, the English Cellar Alehouse is the place to go to watch football (soccer, to us). If there are no English games available, the New England Revolution will be on the screen. Head in for a beer and watch the game.

### JULIANS

318 Broadway, Providence, RI; (401) 861-1770; JuliansProvidence.com
**Draft Beers:** 20 **Bottled/Canned Beers:** About 50

If you happen to be a beer geek, Julians is the place to go in Providence. They may not have the largest beer selection in the city, but they do have the largest selection of hard-to-find beers, both in bottles and draft, with both rare and expensive beers not seen at many bars.

The draft list often includes beers from the Baladin brewery in Italy. Baladin makes some fantastic Belgian-style beers, but typically, even at a liquor store, the bottles can range from $25 to $45. Getting it on draft is a much better deal, because you can try one glass before making the commitment to such an expensive bottle. Typically, Julians will have beers from Belgium and Denmark on draft, as well as some great American craft beer like Bear Republic and Sixpoint. They also do not forget about the only production brewery in Rhode Island, usually having at least one Coastal Extreme beer on the list. The bottled list is much of the same. There are more Baladin beers, and some rare British beers such as several different versions of the Harviestoun Old Dubh, Cantillon, and Mikkeller. American craft beers are also represented, with Ballast Point, Brooklyn Brewery, and Victory often available.

Beer Event

### Stout and Porter Dinner

Every year, Julians hosts several beer dinners, but our favorite is the Stout and Porter Dinner, held in December. Chef Michael McHugh prepares dinners that complement the bold flavors of coffee, chocolate, and often bourbon from barrel-aging, found in all the world-class dark beers paired with each dish. Past pairings include Smuttynose Brewing Company's Robust Porter with butternut squash ravioli and B.O.R.I.S., the Crusher Imperial Stout from Hoppin' Frog, with roasted duck.

Julians also offers some pretty tasty food to go with their excellent beer selection. Popcorn and beer go together like peanut butter and jelly, but Julians' Bacon Fat Popcorn is an entirely different, albeit delicious, beast. Their version involves Parmesan cheese, smoked sea salt, pork cracklins, and crispy garlic gremolata. For an entree, try the excellent House Corned Beef, served with roasted fingerling potatoes, maple glazed carrots, and caraway stout braised cabbage. Desserts are a must at Julians. The Root Beer Roasted Sweet Potato Pie, the Deep Fried Cherry Cinnamon Buns, and Chocolate Marshmallow Pound Cake are all tasty. And if you are up early, Julians serves brunch daily. Brunch options included a scrambled egg pizza and Ilan's Israeli Breakfast, which is two eggs poached in a spicy house pomodoro with home fries and garlic bread.

## POUR JUDGEMENT BAR & GRILL

32 Broadway, Newport, RI; (401) 619-2115; PourJudgement.com
**Draft Beers:** 18 Bottled/Canned Beers: 20

The Pour Judgement Bar & Grill is a neighborhood bar, always filled with locals. But, unlike many typical neighborhood bars, the Pour Judgement happens to pour a lot of great beer. The draft list usually includes beers from Clipper City Brewing Company, Coastal Extreme Brewing Company, Magic Hat Brewing Company, and Samuel Adams. Ithaca and Stone beers are also sometimes available. The bottled list is broken down between larger-format bottles and normal-sized 12-ounce bottles. The larger bottles are great for sharing (I don't share, but you can). There are typically beers from Unibroue, Lagunitas, and several of the 750 ml Dogfish Head beers.

Pour Judgement's food is pretty much straight-up pub fare; sometimes you just want a cold beer and a tasty, simple meal. Starters include chili, Southwest eggrolls, and steamed littleneck clams served in three different styles, including Italian with herbs, garlic, lemon, and dry vermouth. The lunch menu is packed with several grilled sandwiches, which include chicken salad with sliced almonds and dried apricots, as well as the black bean burger with guacamole and herb sour cream. Entrees are straightforward, but delicious. Try the Portuguese cod, which is cooked in white wine, fresh garlic, chourico, peppers, onions, tomatoes, and roasted potatoes. The Pour Judgement serves brunch on Sunday from 10 a.m. to 2 p.m. The brunch menu includes omelets, banana bread French toast, and several types of eggs Benedict, including regular, crab meat Benedict, sirloin Benedict, spinach Benedict, and surf and turf Benedict.

# Beer Festivals

There simply isn't a better way to try a bunch of new beers at one time than going to a beer festival. Want to try a hard-to-find beer before buying it? Interested in sampling some quality craft brew that's not sold locally in your hometown? If you consider yourself a beer lover and you haven't been to a beer fest before, find the nearest event and go. Immediately.

New England is home to some fantastic beer festivals. Be it the wildly popular Extreme Beer Fest or the relatively new Massachusetts Brewer's Festival, there is something out there for everyone. This chapter profiles a 12-pack of the beer festivals everyone should go to at least once. The events are organized by month, but because some events take place more than once a year, and dates can change from year to year, it's best to check each event's website for up-to-date information on when the next festival is taking place.

## February & March

### BEER ADVOCATE'S EXTREME BEER FEST

The Cyclorama at the Boston Center for Arts, 539 Tremont St., Boston, MA; BeerAdvocate.com

Have you ever had a beer brewed with tobacco? How about baby formula or jelly beans? Well, if you go to the Extreme Beer Fest, held every year in February or March at the Cyclorama in Boston, those are just a few of the odd creations you may find. Brewers from around the country pull out all the stops for this beer festival. Sure, sometimes they don't work—tobacco probably doesn't belong in a beer—but when one of them does work, such as the Iced Coffee Stout from Hill Farmstead Brewery in Vermont (a 15 percent alcohol by volume [ABV] beer that sports no alcohol flavor should be impossible), it can be amazing.

Tickets are $40 for each of the Saturday sessions, while the Night of the Barrels usually costs about $10 extra. The ticket gets you a tasting glass, a festival program, and unlimited 2-ounce samples. Food is sold separately. Keep an eye out for when tickets go on sale because they tend to sell out fast. There are three sessions: a Saturday afternoon session, a Saturday night session, and a special Friday session. The Friday sessions are usually called "Night of the Barrels" and include special beers not available on Saturday, and brewers mingle with the smaller crowd.

### NEW ENGLAND REAL ALE EXHIBITION

14 Tyler St., Somerville, MA; NERAX.org

The New England Real Ale Exhibition is a showcase of cask-conditioned beer, the traditional manner of serving real ale in England. The festival is held in March over a four-day period, beginning on Wednesday and running through Saturday. Tickets are $15 for the first three days, and $10 on Saturday. The ticket gets you in, and then you pay $5 for a glass. You can either keep the glass or return it at the end to get your money back. You can also pick the size of beer you want—full pint, half-pint, or quarter-pint—and you pay a different price for each size. The New England Real Ale Exhibition, or NERAX, as it is known, is the best place to get rare English ales served in the manner they are supposed to be served—at the correct temperature and well-maintained. Along with the English ales, NERAX also features several American beers on cask, mainly from New England. Food from the nearby Redbones barbecue restaurant is available. The saddest moment of the festival is when the Grim Reaper comes out with his scythe, equipped with an eraser. When the Grim Reaper appears, that means one of the casks has been kicked and is no longer available. NERAX also hosts NERAX North in Haverhill in November, which typically features heavier, higher-alcohol winter beers. Both are great times.

## April

### GREAT INTERNATIONAL BEER FESTIVAL

Rhode Island Convention Center, 1 Sabin St., Providence, RI; BeerFestAmerica.com

The Great International Beer Festival (GIBF) bills itself as the largest international beer festival in the US. I'm not sure if that is true, but this festival is huge. True to its size, the festival has a huge party atmosphere with food, unlimited beer, and music. This fest tends to attract a college crowd of newly legal drinkers looking to get drunk, so the afternoon session is more enjoyable for those not looking for a keg party. The night session, though, can still be fun. About 50 breweries from the US and beyond are in attendance at the festival, pouring nearly 200 beers. The festival features a wide range of breweries from New England, as well as pretty much anywhere else. You will also run into beers you normally do not see at festivals, such as Cottrell Brewing Company, Heineken, Innis and Gun, and even Guinness. The GIBF also hosts beer judging, with medals awarded in numerous beer styles, and breweries take great pride in the medals. Tickets are $40 each.

## *May*

### BRATTLEBORO BREWERS FESTIVAL

Chickering Road, Brattleboro, VT; BrattleboroBrewersFest.com

Outdoor festivals can be a joy, and there is no better host for outdoor beer festivals than Vermont. The Brattleboro Brewers Festival is one such event, held in a large field rain or shine—large tents are set up if there is inclement weather. Accompanied by live music, attendees get a chance to try beers from about 30 breweries, including Allagash Brewing Company, Bobcat Brewery, and Switchback Brewing Company. Non–New England beer producers represented include Brewery Ommegang and Brooklyn Brewing Company from New York, and Sierra Nevada Brewing Company and Stone Brewing Company from California. Tickets are $35 each and admission includes a 6-ounce tasting glass and eight beer tickets. More tickets are available for sale. Attendees also vote on the best brewery of the festival.

## *June*

### BEER ADVOCATE'S AMERICAN CRAFT BEER FEST

Seaport World Trade Center, 200 Seaport Blvd., Boston, MA; BeerAdvocate.com

Beer Advocate hosts three festivals throughout the year, and the American Craft Beer Fest is by far the largest. While the other two have about 30 breweries, this one has 100 breweries bringing more than 500 beers for excited beer fans. The American Craft Beer Fest, which runs three sessions—one on Friday night and one each on Saturday afternoon and night—is held inside the gigantic Seaport World Trade Center. After all, you need a lot of space for all these beers. The only problem with the festival—and it's a good problem to have—is that there are so many beers to choose from, you may get a brain cramp trying to decide which one you're going to sample next. Nearly every popular craft brewery from New England and beyond attends this festival. Tickets are $45 online and $50 at the door. For that money you get an unlimited number of 2-ounce samples and a floor guide.

The American Craft Beer Fest is the culmination of Boston Beer Week, a celebration of Massachusetts breweries, brewpubs, and beer bars. With so many craft beer events in Boston and the surrounding areas leading up to the festival, there are usually a number of brewers on hand pouring samples, answering questions, and generally mingling with the crowd.

## July

### VERMONT BREWERS FESTIVAL

On the shores of Lake Champlain, Burlington, VT; VTBrewFest.com

No other beer festival in New England is in a more picturesque location than the Vermont Brewers Festival right on the shores of Lake Champlain. The festival, run by the Vermont Brewers Association, is a showcase of Vermont breweries, of which there are many. It's not limited to Vermont breweries, though—there are many hard-to-find breweries from Quebec, as well as some of the larger craft breweries from other regions in the US. Luckily for all of the festival-goers, the event is spread out in a large outdoor area with plenty of space and breathing room. Just make sure to bring some bug spray—mosquitoes definitely like beer fest attendees.

If you want a break from walking around, go to the Meet the Brewer Tent and attend one of the workshops, such as pairing beer and cheese or pairing beer with chocolate, or learn about sustainable brewing. The best thing about the festival is that after you're done, you're a 10-minute walk from downtown Burlington and great beer bars and brewpubs. Tickets cost $35 and there are three sessions: Friday night, Saturday afternoon, and Saturday night.

## September

### MASSACHUSETTS BREWERS FEST

Seaport World Trade Center; 200 Seaport Blvd., Boston, MA; MassBrewersGuild.com

The Massachusetts Brewers Festival is the best showcase of the truly amazing beers the state produces today. Sponsored by the Massachusetts Brewers Guild, the festival features nothing but Massachusetts breweries. The breweries pull out all the stops, bringing their flagship beers as well as hard-to-get or specially brewed beers. Don't expect to see just the longstanding in-state breweries, either; recent festivals have featured a handful of up-and-coming beer producers. There's a good mix of both breweries and brewpubs from every section of the state—east, west, central, and the coast—with unlimited sampling as part of the $35 ticket price. Lines can get long and sometimes you may not know which brewery you're in line for, but they move quickly and you're pretty much guaranteed to get a good beer when you finally get to the beer table. The festival is also held on the Trade Center's Concourse, so the festival is mostly outside, but with a partially roofed area. There's good food and equally good live music to be had as well. The parking is also some of the cheapest in Boston, $12 to $13, and there is plenty of public transportation in the area.

## BEER ADVOCATE'S BELGIAN BEER FEST

The Cyclorama, 539 Tremont St., Boston, MA; BeerAdvocate.com

The Belgian Beer Fest is Beer Advocate's third beer festival of the year. As the name suggests, it is all about the Belgian ales. The beer is fantastic. The festival features beer from nearly every world-class brewery from Belgium, such as Cantillion, St. Bernardus, and De Struise. If there is an American brewery that specializes in Belgian-style ales, they will be at the festival. Breweries such as Allagash Brewing Company in Maine, Brewery Ommegang in New York, the Bruery and Lost Abbey in California are almost always at the Belgian Beer Fest. There are three sessions of the Belgian Beer Fest. The two Saturday sessions, which cost $50 each, feature all sorts of Belgian ales. The Friday night session, called Night of the Funk, features sour ales, funky beers, and ales made with wild yeast creating unique and strange flavors that are sought out by hard-core beer lovers. The festival is one of the best in Boston every year.

## BOSTON BEER SUMMIT

The Castle at Park Plaza, 130 Columbus Ave., Boston, MA; BeerSummit.com

If you can't get to Germany for Oktoberfest, this fest at the Castle at Park Plaza is the closest thing to it in Boston. This 10-hour festival, which is more like a party, each and every September. The festival costs around $20 and gets you a beer stein and your first Samuel Adams Octoberfest.

Although this is an Octoberfest event, there are plenty of other Samuel Adams beers to choose from. But unlike other festivals, this is about more than just the beer. This is all about fun. There are German bands playing oompah music and American bands playing more mainstream music. German food such as bratwursts and giant pretzels are good to nosh on, while people dressed in lederhosen take part in feats of strength as they see who can hold a full stein of beer the longest. There are other games and contests with plenty of prizes available.

There are not many festivals that are more fun than the Octoberfest. Try to get there and party like you are in Munich.

## October

### KILLINGTON BREWFEST

Killington Resort, Killington, VT; Killington.com

The Killington Brewfest is not as well-known as some of the other beer festivals featured here, but it is still one of the best in New England. The festival is held at the base of the Killington Ski Resort, a beautiful scenic area. There are tons of hotels and restaurants in the area and it is a perfect place to spend the weekend. The festival begins Friday night at the Brewer's Dinner with a specific brewery, and then the kickoff party. The actual festival is Saturday. For $25, you get 12 tasting tickets and a nice little sample beer glass. The samples are 3 ounces each. Most beers cost one ticket while some of the stronger beers, over 8 percent, take two tickets. If you want more tickets, you can buy them, so you do not have to worry about running out. There are usually about 20 breweries pouring about 75 different beers. The festival is big on local breweries, including some that are unavailable outside Vermont, like the Switchback Brewing Company and Northshire Brewing Company. There is plenty of food available, and plenty of live music. Definitely worth a trip.

### NEW HAMPSHIRE BREW FEST

Redhook Brewery, 1 Redhook Brewery, Portsmouth, NH; BrewNH.com

The New Hampshire Brew Fest is the largest yearly beer event in New Hampshire. Each October, thousands of people gather in the field outside the Redhook Brewery in Portsmouth to get a chance to sample beers from more than 30 different brewers who bring more than 100 beers. The tickets cost $25, and, for that money, you get unlimited beer samples in a 5-ounce tasting glass. Many of the participating breweries are smaller breweries, such as the Elm City Brewing Company, Moat Mountain Smokehouse and Brewery, Tuckerman Brewing Company, and Throwback Brewing Company, all from New Hampshire. Along with the beer, there is a ton of food to buy, and it is always a good idea to eat at a beer festival. A good base of food allows you to sample more beers. There is also live music. This is an outdoor festival, so make sure you dress appropriately in case of chilly weather. You cannot go out to your car to get a sweater and then come back. Once you are out, you are out.

## November

### MAINE BREWERS FESTIVAL

Portland Exposition Building, 239 Park Ave., Portland, ME; MaineBrew.com

The Maine Brewers Festival is a showcase of the greatness of Maine breweries. The festival hosts nothing but Maine brewers, but rest assured, there is more than enough beer to go around. Maine has some fantastic breweries, and they all strive to bring their best beers to the Maine Brewers Festival. Tickets are $36 and get you a 6-ounce logoed beer glass and 12 beer sampling tickets. You cannot buy additional tickets, so choose wisely. It's a good idea to get a list of beers ahead of time so you can pick the ones you really want to try. The festival features the larger breweries, such as Allagash Brewing Company and Shipyard Brewing Company, as well as smaller ones such as Federal Jack's and the Oxbow Brewing Company. There is also plenty of food available. A nice feature at the Maine Brewers Festival is the fact they have designated driver tickets. The tickets are the same price, but instead of beer tickets, they get food and non-alcoholic beverage coupons to use.

## Beer Fest Etiquette

Okay, you bought those tickets for the beer festival—now what?

Here are a few simple rules to help guide you through the festival experience. (I've followed them relatively closely throughout the years, with some trial and error.)

**Always hydrate.** Lack of hydration is always a killer at a festival. You're surrounded by hundreds of people in cramped quarters making you sweat and you're drinking beer—you will dehydrate if you don't drink water. Drink a couple glasses of water before the festival, and keep a bottle of water with you while at the festival. If you don't have water on you, drink the water that you rinse your glass with between tastings. It's a good way to keep your palate fresh and to stay hydrated.

**Eat.** Give yourself a good base before you start drinking a lot of beer. Eat a good breakfast and grab lunch before the festival, or eat something at the festival. Drinking on an empty stomach is never a good idea. You want to enjoy the different beers, and if you're drinking on an empty stomach, about halfway through you'll start forgetting what's in your glass.

**Don't be stupid.** Yeah, this sounds easy, but you'd be amazed by how some people act at a festival. It's a beer fest, not a drunk fest. Sure, beer gets you intoxicated, but don't get out of control, make a spectacle of yourself, and get dragged out by security. All your friends will know about it on social media before you even get over your hangover the next day.

**Don't stand and talk to the brewer.** One of the highlights of going to a beer festival is getting to meet the man or woman who brewed your favorite beer. I get that. But, while you're spending 15 minutes talking to the brewer and getting your glass refilled over and over, no one else can get his or her glass filled. Wait until there isn't much of a line, or if you really want to talk to the brewer, stand off to the side to let other people get their beer. Remember, if you want to meet him or her, there are probably dozens of others at the festival who also want to meet the brewer.

**Have fun.** That's the main part of a beer festival. Don't waste the whole time writing tasting notes on paper, or typing them into your iPhone. You can't judge a beer fully on a 2-ounce sample anyhow. I keep the brewery program handy and put a check next to a beer I like and want to try again. Review the beer later and enjoy it now.

# BYOB: Brew Your Own Beer

Are you sick of going to the liquor store and spending more and more money for beer? Do you want to unleash your inner brewer and concoct your own craft beer? Just make your own!

Homebrewing is a fun hobby, and it allows you to brew a beer exactly how you want it. The start-up cost is not cheap, but you will more than make up the difference when you are making beer for pennies at home.

This chapter includes profiles of several places where you can go to try brewing before making the investment, or if you want to brew your own beer but don't have the space at home. And for established homebrewers, there are a few homebrew recipes for you to try.

## Brew-on-Premises

### BARLEYCORN'S CRAFT BREW

21 Summer St., Natick, MA; (508) 651-8885; BarleyCorn.com

Barleycorn's is a brew-on-premises (BOP) business, which allows you to pick a type of beer you want and then brew it. Don't worry, owner Dan Eng or his assistants will lead you by the hand all the way from start to finish. Eng started Barleycorn's in 1990 after he was inspired by similar businesses on the west coast. It's a great way to get a taste of brewing without having to make your house smell like a brewery. Eng has dozens of different beer recipes with all of the ingredients on site. He is also quick to follow beer trends—if a particular style of beer is becoming popular, he will add a recipe to his portfolio. Eng will then lead you step by step through the brewing process, beginning with mixing the ingredients, grinding the malts, and then putting it in the kettle and adding all the ingredients at the exact time to get the beer you want. You then leave the beer at Barleycorn's and come back in a few weeks (the length of time depends on the style) to bottle the beer. A single bottling session yields about six cases of 12-ounce beers. Price-wise, brewing a batch of beer will range from $150 to about $200, although some batches will get as high as $250.

One exciting feature is that Eng invites professional brewers a few times a year to bring in specially created recipes. During these visits, the brewer leads a group of people through a collaborative brewing session where they brew all the different styles at once. Then, you come back a few weeks later to bottle the beers and get a mix of all the different beers. Barleycorn's also hosts collaborative brewing events where people come in and brew several batches of a popular beer, such as a pumpkin ale, and come back to bottle and buy as much as they want a few weeks later. In addition to beer, Barleycorn's also has wine-making and soda-making equipment.

### CORK & BREW

35 North Main St., Southington, CT; (860) 863-5655; CorkAndBrew.com

Cork & Brew is a little different than other brew-on-premises businesses. While most BOPs have dozens of recipes, usually using all grain ingredients, Cork & Brew is more of a beginner's BOP. They have 10 different recipes, all made from Fiesta Brew kits. That makes it easier, because everyting is in one place, and easy to mix. The whole process takes about an hour to brew, and then you come back three weeks later and bottle your product. The beers available include a blonde ale, cream ale, red ale, brown ale, bock, pale ale, and stout. Along with the 10 base recipes, you can add extract flavors, such as various fruits, so you can have a raspberry stout or a number of other flavors. When you bottle the beer a few weeks later, you get about 60 12-ounce bottles. The price is right, too, ranging from $119 to $125 for a batch of beer. Along with beer, Cork & Brew also does wine and soda making. They also host homebrew parties where groups of people come in and do a group brew, sometimes of different types of beer, so each person can get a bigger variety.

### DEJA BREW INC.

510B Boston Turnpike Rd., Shrewsbury, MA; (508) 842-8991; Deja-Brew.com

Brewing your own beer on-site at Deja Brew in Shrewsbury is a great experience. They have one of the most varied selections of beer recipes around, and they lead you through the entire process of brewing beer—from picking the right hops and grains, to mashing in, to putting the hops in at the right time during the boil, and, of course, the best part, bottling the beer. Deja Brew offers dozens of beer recipes (as well as 12 wine recipes, if you are so inclined) and has a more diverse selection of choices than many BOP buisinesses. They have beer for every taste, including mild, lower-alcohol beers such as bitters and brown ales, as well as lagers like Oktoberfests and pilsners. They offer IPAs, pale ales, and speciality beers, including gluten-free beers.

They also offer many higher-octane beers, usually clones or approximations of famous craft beers. Are you a big fan of Dogfish Head's huge World Wide Stout (which comes in at 18 percent alcohol by volume [ABV])? Then brew the Deja Wide Stout. Are you a hophead who absolutely loves Stone Brewing Company's Double Bastard Ale? Deja Brew has a version called Dave's Double Bastid. The costs range from a low $135 for one of the English bitter recipes to a high of $335 for a 9.5 percent ABV, 124 international bittering units double IPA.

For the money, you will get approximately 72 22-ounce bombers of beer. For $325 and the cost of bottles and labels (about $400 total), you would get 75 bottles of Deja Wide Stout. To buy the equivalent quantity of Dogfish Head World Wide Stout, it would cost more than $1,000. Quite the savings. When the beer is ready (usually in a couple of weeks), you go back and bottle the beer, which typically takes half an hour. You can also pick your own labels. Deja Brew also hosts several beer events a year, as well as a chili cookoff.

## HOPSTERS BREW & BOARDS

292 Centre St., Newton, MA; 617-916-0752; Hopsters.net

Hopsters Brew & Boards is like no other brew-on-premises (BOP) business in New England. Sure, you can go there and brew a batch of your own beer, just like any other BOP. However, unlike others, you can also go there and grab lunch or dinner, watch a game on the big screens, listen to music, or grab a few pints of beer. Hopsters Brew & Boards is a hybrid BOP and bar. Founder Lee Cooper wanted to make it Hopsters a full experience for his customers.

As for brewing beer, customers can either brew one of the prepared recipes developed by Hopsters' brewers, or they can brew a recipe of their own. The batch of beer is about seven and a half gallons. A prepared recipe can run between $150 to $230 and that will yield three cases. Some of the $150 beers include an American pale ale, a crystal wheat, and an Irish red. Recipes that cost $200 include an almond breakfast stout, coconut porter, and vanilla Bourbon barrel stout. The most expensive recipes ($230) include an oak-aged tripel and an oak-aged imperial pale ale.

As for food and beer, Hopsters is the best destination in the immediate Newton area. They have 16 beers on tap, all local to New England breweries such as Jack's Abby Brewing, Notch Brewing, and Wormtown Brewery. Hopsters hopes to begin offering house-brewed beers in the future. Food-wise, they offer cheese and meat boards featuring artisanal meats and cheeses, as well as soups, flatbreads, and sandwiches such as the Pork Belly BLT and hot pastrami.

Hopsters is open Tuesday through Friday from 11:30 a.m. to 3 p.m. and again from 5 p.m. to midnight. It is open Saturday and Sunday from 11 a.m. to midnight.

### INCREDIBREW

112 Daniel Webster Hwy. South, Nashua, NH; (603) 891-2477; IncrediBrew.com

Brew-on-premises businesses are now found almost everywhere throughout the country, but incrediBREW of Nashua, New Hampshire, was the first, founded in 1995. They are also the cheapest BOP business in New England. The cost to brew a beer ranges from $130 for a few recipes, such as the Beechwood Lager (a Budweiser-like beer), to the most expensive at $195 for a big, 11 percent alcohol by volume barleywine. In all, incrediBREW offers about 100 different recipes, ranging from low-alcohol bitters to Belgian-style quads, and pretty much everything in between. They also offer numerous clone recipes, or recipes inspired by commercial beers, including several beers you do not see at other brew-on-premises locations. Some of the clones include Amstel Light, Corona, Michelob, and Heineken. Other beers are inspired by craft beers, such as Arrogant Brewer, which is based on Stone Brewing Company's Arrogant Bastard Ale; Something Wicked, based on Pete's Wicked Ale; Catfish Head 60 Minute IPA, based on Dogfish Head's 60 Minute IPA; and Stella or Try, based on Stella Artois. Other recipes include Belgian whites, a wheat wine, and a barrel-aged porter. Also available are bitters, bocks, brown ales, several lagers, pale ales, IPAs, stouts, pilsners, and several honey beers.

The brewing can take an hour or two and you come back two weeks later to bottle the beer. For the money, it is a good deal. You brew 13.5 gallons of beer, which equals 72 22-ounce bottles. The bottles cost $12 for a case, so expect to add a few extra bucks to the final cost. Like other brew-on-premises businesses, incrediBREW offers several brewing nights where groups get together and brew several beers at once. They also offer wine and soda brewing sessions.

## Beer Recipe

### WILL MEYERS' SGT. PEPPER CLONE

There probably is not a better food beer brewed in New England than Cambridge Brewing Company's Sgt. Pepper, which is a saison brewed with peppercorns. When you drink this beer with a good meal, do not put pepper on the food, just take of sip of this. Cambridge Brewing Company's Brewmaster Will Meyers shared a homebrew clone recipe of his Sgt. Pepper. This recipe will make 5 gallons for all-grain homebrewers.

**Grist**

*3.6 pounds German pils*
*2.75 pounds German wheat*
*2.75 pounds North American pils*
*0.5 pounds North American rye malt*
*0.5 pounds Belgian Caravienne 20°L*
*Rice hulls*

Mash with single-infusion to target conversion temp of 152°F; rest for 1 hour or until iodine test shows complete conversion. Sparge with 170°F water to collect 6.5 gallons in kettle.

At start of 90-minute boil, add 0.25 ounce Magnum hops pellets at 13.5 percent alpha.

At 10 minutes remaining, add 0.4 ounce Spalt pellets.

With 1 minute remaining add:*

*0.5 ounce green peppercorns*
*0.06 ounce white peppercorns*
*0.3 ounce black peppercorns*

Flameout and rest for 5 minutes, then whirlpool by gently stirring kettle for 5–10 minutes. At end of whirlpool add:

*0.13 ounce green peppercorns*
*0.06 ounce pink peppercorns*

Immediately chill with wort chiller to 64°F, transfer gently to fermenter and aerate, and pitch yeast. We use a proprietary yeast strain, but recommend a well-attenuating saison yeast with considerable spicy flavor profile such as White Labs WLP566 Saison II or WLP 568 Saison Blend.

Target OG: 1.054/13.5°P

Target FG: 1.008/2.0°P

* Peppercorns should be purchased whole, then crushed in a spice mill moments before adding to kettle.

COURTESY OF WILL MEYERS, BREWMASTER AT CAMBRIDGE BREWING COMPANY (P. 73)

# In the Kitchen

## *Pairing Beer with Food*

Beer offers a wide variety of flavors, so you can actually match and contrast flavors with your food. Wine, on the other hand, is pretty much limited to contrasting flavors. Paring beer with a dish is not too difficult. Just remember a simple rule of thumb: Pair heavy foods with heavier beers, and lighter food with lighter beer. Below, we suggest some specific New England beers to pair with your meal.

**Beef:** A Belgian quad is good for beef, but if it is grilled, go with a brown ale. The caramelized meat and the caramel malts used in the brown ale will make your taste buds sing. *Pick: High & Mighty's Home for the Holidays*

**Chicken/Turkey:** Saisons are the easiest pairings for lighter meat like chicken and turkey. They just seem to be made for each other. *Pick: Pretty Things Beer & Ale Project's Jack D'Or*

**Chocolate:** You can go different directions with this. Grab a stout and the roasty chocolate and coffee malts can work perfectly. Or go with a really sweet fruit beer; it can taste like you are having a chocolate-covered fruit treat. *Pick: Samuel Adams Chocolate Bock*

**Pasta with Red Sauce:** Let wine have this one. It is not always about beer.

**Pizza:** Go with a good lager. The clean lager taste will not detract from the goodness that is pizza. *Pick: Cisco's Summer of Lager*

**Pork:** A German-style lager, or even a bock, always goes well with pork. This is a classic pairing. *Pick: Narragansett's Bock*

**Salads:** Choose a lighter Belgian ale. It will cut right through the vinegar used in most dressings, and it will not be too strong and overwhelm the veggies. *Pick: Harpoon's Belgian Pale Ale*

**Seafood:** Go with something light, maybe a hefeweizen or American wheat ale, with fish. With lobster and shrimp, the perfect beer is a Belgian-style witbier. *Pick: Allagash White*

**Spicy Food:** You can go two different ways with spicy foods. Go with a really hoppy beer to cut through the spice, or try something sweet to balance it all out. *Pick: Squam's Golden IPA*

## *Food Recipes*

There are a lot of recipes that call for wine to be used as an ingredient, but more and more restaurants are using beer in their food. It just makes sense—beer adds a wider range of flavors than wine can. Depending on the style of beer you add to your recipe, you can get sweet, fruity, or bitter flavors, notes of chocolate or coffee, and anything and everything in between. Beer offers up more diversity than wine ever could.

This chapter offers several recipes that feature beer as an ingredient, ranging from classic New England dishes such as beer-battered fish and chips to desserts such as stout brownies. Enjoy!

### BARRINGTON BREWERY'S CHEDDAR ALE SOUP

Beer and cheese, especially cheddar, is a great pairing. But what is even better is when both are combined into one bite. The Barrington Brewery's Cheddar Ale Soup is a perfect starter to any meal. It's not too heavy, but it has tons of flavor. Makes 5 gallons.

*2 red peppers, diced*
*2 onions, diced*
*¼ cup Dijon mustard*
*1½ cups chicken stock*
*1½ pitchers blonde ale (6–8 cups)*
*Few dashes of Worcestershire sauce*
*1 handful chives*
*3 gallons milk*
*1 (1-pound) box cornstarch, mixed with water*
*2½ pounds American cheese*
*5 pounds white cheddar cheese*

Mix peppers, onions, Dijon mustard, chicken stock, blonde ale, Worcestershire sauce, and chives together and bring to a boil.

Then add milk, cornstarch, American cheese, and cheddar cheese into the mix.

Heat until cheese is melted and then serve.

COURTESY OF BARRINGTON BREWERY (P. 72)

### SHIPYARD BREWING COMPANY'S PEAKS ISLAND MUSSELS

The Shipyard Brewing Company is most known for its Portland brewery. But they also have several small brewpubs, and naturally they use beer in many of their recipes. Mussels, a New England staple, taste even better when cooked in a delcious beer-infused broth. Here is Shipyard's version of the dish.

*2 tablespoons olive oil*
*½ cup diced onion*
*4 cloves chopped garlic*
*4–6 pounds mussels*
*8 ounces Shipyard Export Ale*
*2 tablespoons butter*
*10 basil leaves, sliced thin*
*10–12 chopped kalamata olives*
*1 cup diced tomatoes*
*2 tablespoons capers*
*Salt and pepper*
*Chopped parsley*
*4–6 lemon wedges*
*½ cup feta cheese*

In a hot sauté pan, heat olive oil and cook the onions and garlic until they start to brown a bit.

Add mussels and Shipyard Export Ale, cover, and cook for 3–4 minutes.

Add butter, basil, olives, tomatoes, and capers, and toss in Export mix. Add salt and pepper to taste.

Put in serving bowl and garnish with parsley, lemon wedges, and feta cheese.

COURTESY OF SHIPYARD BREWING COMPANY (P. 137)

## THE INN ON PEAKS ISLAND'S SHIPYARD PUMPKINHEAD ALE PANCAKES

The Inn on Peaks Island is part of the Shipyard Brewing Company's family of restaurants. Its chef, Chris Gordon (2008 Maine Chef of the Year), uses Shipyard's absurdly popular Pumpkinhead Ale to show that beer can be for breakfast, too, with this recipe for Pumpkinhead Ale Pancakes.

*1 cup all-purpose flour*
*½ cup Shipyard Pumpkinhead Ale*
*½ teaspoon baking powder*
*½ teaspoon baking soda*
*½ teaspoon cinnamon*
*½ teaspoon nutmeg*
*½ cup pumpkin puree*
*½ cup milk*
*Pinch clove*
*2 eggs*
*¼ cup melted butter*
*1 teaspoon vanilla extract*

Whisk all ingredients together until blended well. Spray non-stick frying pan with pan spray.

Place half cup batter in center of frying pan on medium heat.

Cook until bubbles form on pancake, then flip (about 2 minutes on each side).

Serve with Reed's Maple Syrup.

COURTESY OF SHIPYARD BREWING COMPANY (P. 137)

### GARDNER ALE HOUSE FISH & CHIPS

There is no dish on more brewpub menus throughout New England than beer-battered fish and chips. The Gardner Ale House, even though nowhere near the ocean, makes some of the best fish and chips around.

*2 (5-ounce) haddock fillets*

*oil for frying (amount depends on deep fryer or pan)*

**Corn Flour**

*½ ounce corn flour*
*3 ounces of Old Bay seasoning*

**Beer Batter**

*1 gallon Gardner's Summer's End, or another kolsch beer*
*1 gallon white flour*
*2 ounces Old Bay seasoning*

For the corn flour, blend corn flour and seasoning together.

For the batter, whisk beer, flour, and seasoning together until it forms into well-blended batter.

Coat both pieces of fish with corn flour. Shake off any extra flour.

Coat fish with beer batter, letting the extra batter run off.

Heat oil to 350°F in a deep fryer or pan. Slowly drop coated fish in the oil. Let the fish cook for 3 or 4 minutes until golden brown on one side.

Flip the fish over and let it cook the rest of the way, approximately another 3 minutes. When fully cooked, remove from the fryer with tongs and let it drain in a fryer basket.

Serve with fries, coleslaw, tartar sauce, and a lemon wedge.

COURTESY OF RICHARD WALTON, OWNER/PRESIDENT OF MOON HILL BREWING INC. AND GARDNER ALE HOUSE (P. 75)

### MILLY'S TAVERN OATMEAL STOUT BEEF STEW

Milly's Tavern of Manchester, New Hampshire, like all of New England, suffers through some harsh winters. What better way to warm up than a crock of beef stew? Milly's version of beef stew uses a hearty stout in its recipe. The roasted coffee flavors of the stout add just a little taste in the background to make you take notice of something different than you'd expect.

*3 pounds stew beef*
*1 tablespoon olive oil*
*1 tablespoon chopped garlic*
*½ cup flour*
*2 pints Milly's Oatmeal Stout (or substitute), divided*
*¼ cup beef base*
*3 large potatoes, chopped*
*3 large carrots, chopped*
*Water as needed*
*2 tablespoons black pepper*
*6 bay leaves*
*1 tablespoon dried thyme leaves*
*3 tablespoons dried rosemary leaves*

Brown the beef in a mixture of the olive oil and garlic in a pot. Add flour and stir, browning the beef for another minute. After that minute add 1 pint of stout. Then add beef base, potatoes, and carrots. Bring to a boil.

In a sachet bag, add the herbs and black pepper. Simmer covered for an hour. Add remaining 1 pint of stout. Serve.

COURTESY OF MILLY'S TAVERN (P. 230)

### PORTSMOUTH BREWERY'S OLD BROWN DOG HANGER STEAK

There is almost no better pairing than a nice slice of beef and really good brown ale. Portsmouth Brewery's Chef Todd Sweet takes that to the next level with his recipe for the Old Brown Dog Hanger Steak, for which he makes a marinade incorporating the brewery's Old Brown Dog beer. The nutty and caramel flavors latch right on to the caramelization of the beef to create a beautiful flavor combination.

*1 cup Old Brown Dog*
*2 tablespoons tamari sauce*

*2 tablespoons Worcestershire sauce*
*2 tablespoons brown sugar*
*1 shallot, minced*
*2 stems fresh thyme, minced*
*2 stems rosemary, minced*
*1 clove garlic, minced*
*¼ cup olive oil*
*1 pinch red pepper flakes*
*1 tablespoon Dijon mustard*
*1 teaspoon black pepper*
*4 (10-ounce) hanger steaks (or substitute beef tips)*

Combine all ingredients and pour over the steaks. Mix well, then marinate at least overnight before grilling to desired temperature.

When serving, cut against the grain. Serve with Gorgonzola Sauce (recipe follows).

**Gorgonzola Sauce**

*2 cups heavy cream*
*¼ cup gorgonzola crumbles*
*Dash Worcestershire sauce*
*Dash Tabasco*
*Fresh ground black pepper to taste*
*1 teaspoon lemon juice*

Reduce the heavy cream by half over medium heat in a small sauce pan.

Whisk in the cheese over the heat, removing it from the heat just as it is melted.

Add remaining ingredients and adjust seasoning.

COURTESY OF PORTSMOUTH BREWERY (P. 233)

### THE CASK REPUBLIC'S GRILLED EXTRA-HOPPY-BEER-MARINATED HALF CHICKEN

The Cask Republic in New Haven, Connecticut, is one of the best beer destinations in the state—and the food is pretty darn tasty, too. The hops in an IPA or other hoppy beer in this recipe will combine nicely with the other ingredients to give this chicken an extra kick. Can be used for a half or full chicken.

*2 quarts extra hoppy beer*
*1 tablespoons Dijon mustard*

*2 tablespoons honey*
*¼ bunch thyme*
*¼ bunch of rosemary*
*3 garlic gloves chopped*
*Juice of 1 orange*
*Juice of 1 lime*
*Juice of 1 lemon*
*½ or whole chicken*
*3 tablespoons butter*
*Salt and pepper to taste*

Combine all ingredients except chicken, butter, salt, and pepper. Marinate the chicken in half the mixture for one day.

Remove chicken and pat dry. Season with salt and pepper and grill both sides.

In a sauté pan, bring the leftover marinade to a boil. Add the ckicken, skin side up, and finish in oven at 400°F for 10–12 minutes.

When chicken is done, remove to serving dish. Take the pan with the hot marinade and add butter, salt, and pepper until thickened. Pour over the chicken.

COURTESY OF THE CASK REPUBLIC (P. 270)

**CITY STEAM BREWERY CAFE'S BEER-BRAISED POT ROAST**

City Steam, a Hartford-based brewpub, is unique in that it brews beer and acts as the place to catch up-and-coming comedians. It also uses some of its house-made beers in many of its food recipes. The Beer-Braised Pot Roast is a restaurant favorite, using its popular Naughty Nurse amber ale as part of the recipe. The flavor of the amber ale does not overwhelm the taste of the meat, and vice versa. This recipe is for a large family gathering, not for a small meal.

*2 bottom flat round cuts of beef*
*6 carrots*
*2 celery stalks*
*4 Spanish onions*
*4 quarts Naughty Nurse or another amber ale*
*8 ounces beef base*
*20 ounces tomato paste*
*8 quarts water*
*8 tablespoons cornstarch*

Trim fat off beef. Slicing against the grain, cut the bottom flats into strips about 1½ inches thick. Cut the strips into cubes about 1½–2 inches thick.

Dice carrots, celery, and onions and add to the beef in the pan.

Combine remaining ingredients and place in the roast pan. Cover with foil and bake at 350°F for 4 hours.

COURTESY OF JAMES DUMOND, CO-OWNER OF CITY STEAM BREWERY CAFE (P. 267)

**SEA DOG BREWING COMPANY'S BARBECUE BLUE PAW SHORT RIBS**

The Sea Dog Brewing Company, a chain of brewpubs and restaurants in Maine and Massachusetts, has a twist on the traditional pairing of brown ales with beef. Instead, they use blueberry ale and real blueberries, giving these short ribs a unique flavor not found in any other dish.

*6–8 pounds short ribs*
*Salt and pepper*
*1 cup diced onions*
*2 tablespoons chopped garlic*
*1 red pepper, diced*
*1 yellow pepper, diced*
*1 jalapeño chili pepper (no pith), diced*
*2 tablespoons olive oil*
*1 cup fresh or frozen blueberries*
*8 ounces Sea Dog Blue Paw Wheat Ale*
*16 ounces any barbecue sauce*
*1 bunch cilantro, chopped, divided*

Season short ribs with salt and pepper. In a hot sauté pan (or on a grill) sear short ribs on all sides. Remove pan from heat and drain the grease. Remove ribs and set aside.

Sauté onions, garlic, and peppers in olive oil until brown. Put meat back in pan and add blueberries, Sea Dog Blue Paw, barbecue sauce, and half the cilantro. Cover and simmer for 1½–2 hours until the meat falls off the bone.

Serve with rice and vegetables and garnish with remaining fresh cilantro. Add salt and pepper to taste.

COURTESY OF SEA DOG BREWING COMPANY (P. 152)

**CAMBRIDGE BREWING COMPANY'S YOU ENJOY MY STOUT BROWNIE**

Beer, particularly imperial stout, is a fantastic pairing for dessert. Imperial stouts often have flavors of chocolate and coffee. Cambridge Brewing Company chef David Drew's You Enjoy My Stout Brownie is a fantastic and decadent dessert. Drew recommends avoiding cheap chocolate and splurging on the good stuff from a local chocolatier.

*½ cup You Enjoy My Stout or any other big imperial stout*
*⅓ cup unsweetened cocoa powder*
*2 ounces chopped Taza 70% Semi-Sweet Baking Squares (or substitute)*
*½ stick butter, melted*
*½ cup canola oil*
*2 eggs*
*2 egg yolks*
*2½ cups granulated sugar*
*1¾ cup all-purpose flour*
*1 teaspoon salt*
*2 ounces roasted cacao nibs (optional)*
*4 ounces chopped Taza 60% stone-ground dark chocolate (or substitute)*

Preheat oven to 350°F. Heat beer in a small sauce pan on high until it comes to just a simmer.

In a large bowl, combine unsweetened cocoa powder and semi-sweet baking squares. Add warm beer to chocolate mix and stir until well incorporated. Next, add butter and oil and gently whisk. Add eggs, egg yolks, and sugar and whisk until fully incorporated.

Gently fold in flour, salt, nibs, and chopped chocolate. Dump into greased 9 × 13-inch baking pan and bake for about 30 minutes.

To check doneness, poke a toothpick into the center of brownies. The brownies are done when the toothpick comes out clean.

Be sure to experiment with different types of beers and chocolates to suit your taste.

COURTESY OF DAVID DREW, EXECUTIVE CHEF AT CAMBRIDGE BREWING COMPANY (P. 73)

# Pub Crawls

The craft beer scene in New England grows more and more with each passing day. It's become easy to visit a craft brewery, take the tour, grab a bite to eat at a nearby brewpub, and if you haven't had your fill of good beer for the day, hit up the local beer bar, all within walking distance. Get together with some friends, develop an itinerary, and start walking, hitting up all the hot spots and trying your favorite beers as you go.

In this chapter, we highlight some of the best beer cities in New England in which to spend a day sampling the best brew the region has to offer. Just remember: Drink in moderation and take a cab if you get tired of walking from place to place, or assign a designated driver before heading out.

## Boston, MA

Boston's Allston neighborhood has two of the best beer bars in all of New England. You will want to make stops at three different venues—the Sunset Grill & Tap and Deep Ellum in Allston and the Publick House in nearby Brookline.

**Sunset Grill & Tap,** 130 Brighton Ave., Allston. The Sunset Grill & Tap is where I cut my teeth on my early journey into beer geekdom. It has the largest beer selection in the greater Boston area, with 113 beers on tap and several hundred bottles and cans. Pretty much every good brewery in the US, and many from other parts of the country and Europe, has at least one beer represented here, either on draft or in bottles. New England is always well represented, with many beers from Clown Shoes and Rapscallion usually available. They also update the seasonal list quite often, so always make sure to take a look before ordering. And you can't leave without having a burger. The burgers are steamed in beer and are the best in the state. The best of the burgers is the Viva La France, which is topped with boursin and grilled portobello mushrooms.

*From there, walk west on Brighton Avenue for about 0.3 miles and take a quick right onto Cambridge Street, where you will see:*

**Deep Ellum,** 477 Cambridge St., Allston. Deep Ellum may not have the huge draft list of the Sunset Grill, but the 28 beers on draft and the 80 bottled and canned beers are all fantastic. They always seem to have some hard-to-find imported beers, such as one of the best lagers brewed today, the Bryggeri Oppigards Well-Hopped

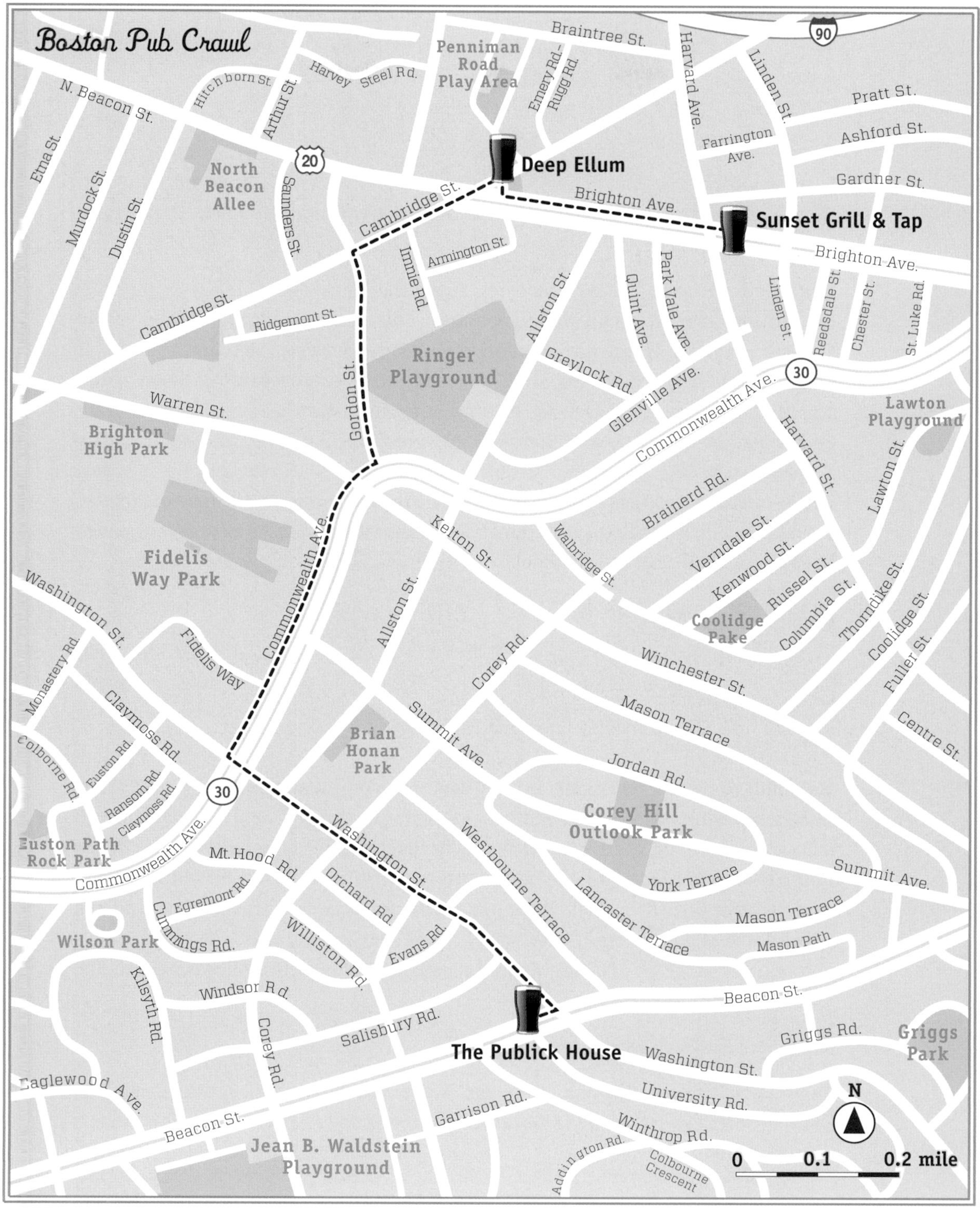

Boston Pub Crawl
Deep Ellum
Sunset Grill & Tap
The Publick House
Braintree St.
90
Penniman Road Play Area
Emery Rd.-Rugg Rd.
Harvard Ave.
Linden St.
Pratt St.
Ashford St.
Farrington Ave.
Gardner St.
N. Beacon St.
Hitchborn St.
Arthur St.
Harvey Steel Rd.
20
North Beacon Allee
Saunders St.
Etna St.
Murdock St.
Dustin St.
Cambridge St.
Brighton Ave.
Armington St.
Imnie Rd.
Ridgemont St.
Allston St.
Quint Ave.
Park Vale Ave.
Reedsdale St.
Chester St.
St. Luke Rd.
30
Ringer Playground
Gordon St.
Greylock Rd.
Glenville Ave.
Commonwealth Ave.
Lawton Playground
Warren St.
Brighton High Park
Harvard St.
Lawton St.
Brainerd Rd.
Fidelis Way Park
Kelton St.
Walbridge St.
Verndale St.
Kenwood St.
Russel St.
Columbia St.
Thorndike St.
Coolidge St.
Fuller St.
Coolidge Pake
Washington St.
Fidelis Way
Corey Rd.
Winchester St.
Mason Terrace
Centre St.
Monastery Rd.
Claymoss Rd.
Colborne Rd.
Euston Rd.
Ransom Rd.
Brian Honan Park
Summit Ave.
Jordan Rd.
Corey Hill Outlook Park
Euston Path Rock Park
Mt. Hood Rd.
Orchard Rd.
Westbourne Terrace
Lancaster Terrace
York Terrace
Egremont Rd.
Cummings Rd.
Williston Rd.
Evans Rd.
Mason Path
Wilson Park
Kilsyth Rd.
Windsor Rd.
Salisbury Rd.
Beacon St.
Griggs Rd.
Griggs Park
Eaglewood Ave.
University Rd.
Garrison Rd.
Winthrop Rd.
Jean B. Waldstein Playground
Addington Rd.
Colbourne Crescent
N
0
0.1
0.2 mile

Lager from Sweden, which is a treat for lager lovers. They also have some good German beers, such as the Aecht Schlenkerla Helles Bock or some Belgian goodies such as the St. Louis Gueuze from Brouwerij Van Honsebrouk. If you want something to munch on, grab a deviled egg, which is pretty much the quintessential pub food, or a giant steamed pretzel.

*When you leave Deep Ellum, either be prepared for a walk, or grab a cab. Your next stop is 1.4 miles away. Just follow Commonwealth Avenue until you reach Washington Street and you will be at:*

**The Publick House,** 1648 Beacon St., Brookline. The Publick House is probably the best beer bar in the greater Boston area. Each beer is hand-picked to give you the best drinking experience possible, the staff is knowledgeable and the beer is served in the proper glassware at all times. The draft list is heavy on Belgian ales, such as N'Ice Chouffe, as well as some fine American craft beer, such as Sixpoint's Gorilla Warfare and Boulevard Brewing Company's Chocolate Ale. The food is nearly as good as the beer selection. Starters include Moules Frites (available in full meal and appetizer sizes), available in four styles, and the potato and cheese croquettes are fabulous. For a meal, go with the grilled marinated steak tips or the spicy pulled pork sandwich.

## Cambridge, MA

Cambridge is perfect for a pub crawl. The city is full of great bars and brewpubs, all within walking distance of one another. This pub crawl incorporates the area's newest beer bar, a brewpub that brews some of the best beer in Massachusetts, and a beer geek haven.

**Meadhall,** 4 Cambridge Center. This bar features more than 100 beers on tap and a small but well-crafted food menu. Even on a busy Saturday night, you should still expect good service. Start with some snacks like the House Made Pork Rinds or the House Made Giant Pretzels—the best in greater Boston. The House Made Long Island Duck Sausage is amazing, but if you want a bigger meal go with the Braised Niman Ranch Lamb Shoulder. Pair it with any of the of New England beers they always have on tap, such as Jack's Abby Brewing's Hoponius Union or a nice Allagash White Ale.

*Head down Broadway until it turns into Hampshire Street, and you will see the Cambridge Brewing Company on your right.*

**Cambridge Brewing Company,** 1 Kendall Sq., Building 100. While at the Cambridge Brewing Company, make sure to look for one of their two barleywines, the Blunderbuss

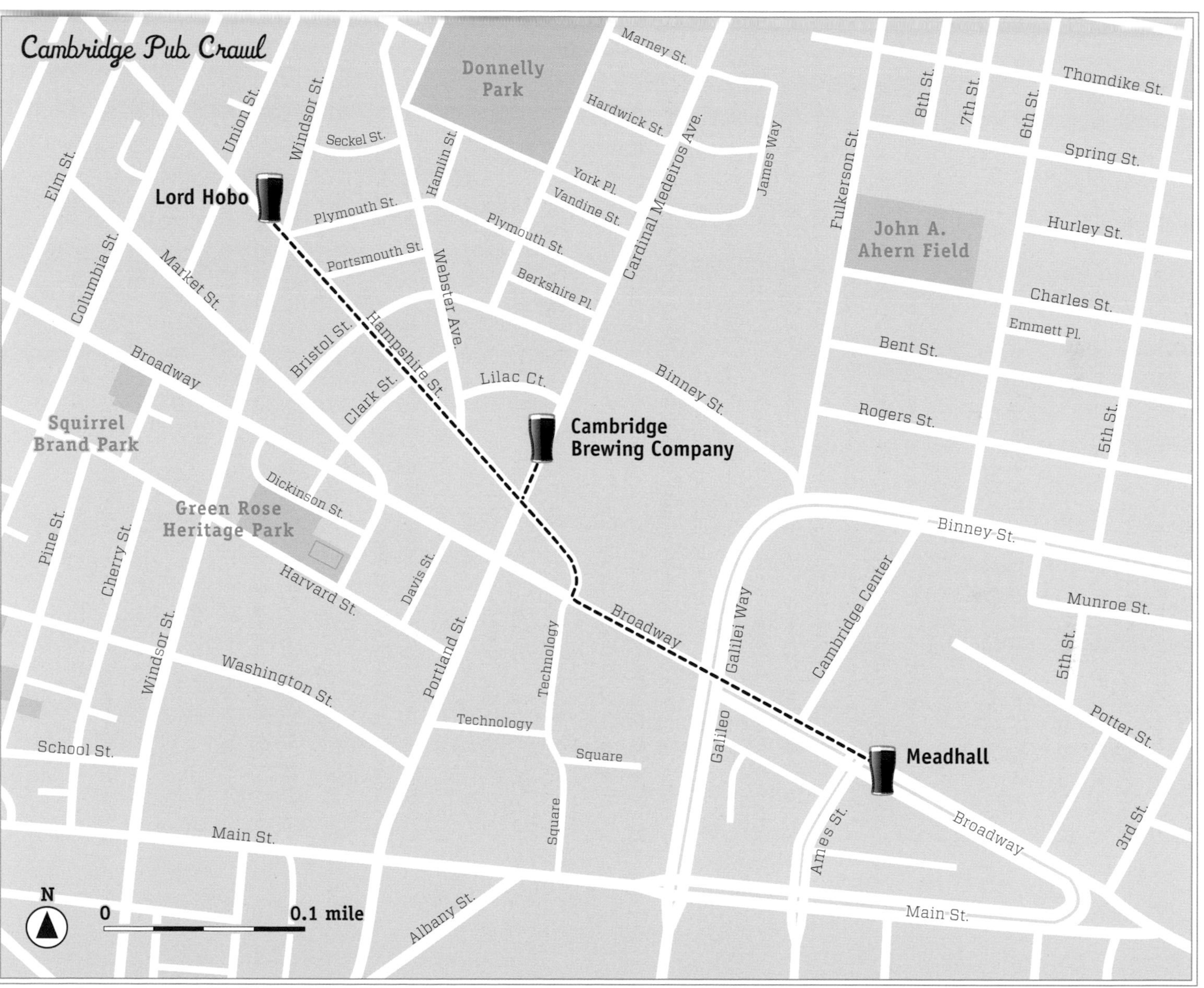

Cambridge Pub Crawl
Lord Hobo
Cambridge Brewing Company
Meadhall
Donnelly Park
John A. Ahern Field
Squirrel Brand Park
Green Rose Heritage Park
Marney St.
Thorndike St.
Hardwick St.
James Way
8th St.
7th St.
6th St.
Spring St.
Union St.
Windsor St.
Seckel St.
Hamlin St.
York Pl.
Vandine St.
Cardinal Medeiros Ave.
Fulkerson St.
Hurley St.
Elm St.
Plymouth St.
Plymouth St.
Portsmouth St.
Webster Ave.
Berkshire Pl.
Charles St.
Emmett Pl.
Columbia St.
Market St.
Bristol St.
Hampshire St.
Bent St.
Broadway
Lilac Ct.
Clark St.
Binney St.
Rogers St.
5th St.
Dickinson St.
Binney St.
Pine St.
Cherry St.
Davis St.
Harvard St.
Cambridge Center
Galilei Way
Munroe St.
Broadway
Windsor St.
Portland St.
Technology
5th St.
Washington St.
Technology
Potter St.
School St.
Square
Galileo
Meadhall
Square
Ames St.
Broadway
3rd St.
Main St.
N
0
0.1 mile
Albany St.
Main St.

or the Arquebus. If you don't want such a big beer, go with the Tall Tale Pale Ale, or if you're there during the summer, order a pint of Spring Training IPA, a great India pale ale. Don't forget to eat. Go with the always table-pleasing nachos or the charcuterie plate to start. Follow that up with the Lobster and Chorizo Pizza or the fabulous Atlantic salmon.

*Leave Cambridge Brewing Company and get on Hampshire Street. Walk for about 5 minutes until you reach:*

**Lord Hobo,** 92 Hampshire St. They might have a small sign, but you can't miss it. The food is excellent at Lord Hobo and the beer selection is top-of-the-line. Grab a fine Belgian ale or maybe a good German lager. A good start is the House Made Turkey Chili, or maybe a plate of artisan cheeses. If you go with the shaved prime rib sandwich or the pork schnitzel for dinner, you will have a very happy stomach. A High & Mighty XPA or maybe the Maine Beer Company's Peeper Ale would go great with those meals.

## Burlington, VT

There may not be a better pub crawl in all of New England than downtown Burlington. The city's brewpubs are close to each other, as well as excellent beer bars. And there are plenty of hotels to stay at nearby.

**American Flatbread,** 115 Saint Paul St. American Flatbread is not only home of the best pizzas in Vermont, they also host the Zero Gravity Pub. The brewmasters produce great beer there, such as the Ripley, a Belgian-style tripel, and the London Calling, a low-alcohol (3.9 percent ABV) session beer, and if nothing on draft catches your eye, they do have a large bottle list, so you should be able to find something you like. If you like pizza, you'll love American Flatbread's selection; they use nothing but local ingredients. Personal favorite: the sausage.

*The next destination is less than one football field away from American Flatbread:*

**Vermont Pub & Brewery,** 144 College St. The Vermont Pub & Brewery is one of the old-time New England brewpubs, so stop there for some New England classics, such as the Burley Irish Stout, one of the best and most traditional Irish dry stouts available in New England. Want to be a little more adventurous? If so, grab the Forbidden Fruit, a tart but extremely refreshing beer brewed with 500 pounds of real raspberries. A plate of local cheeses would be nice to share with someone, or order the portobello mushroom sandwich for yourself.

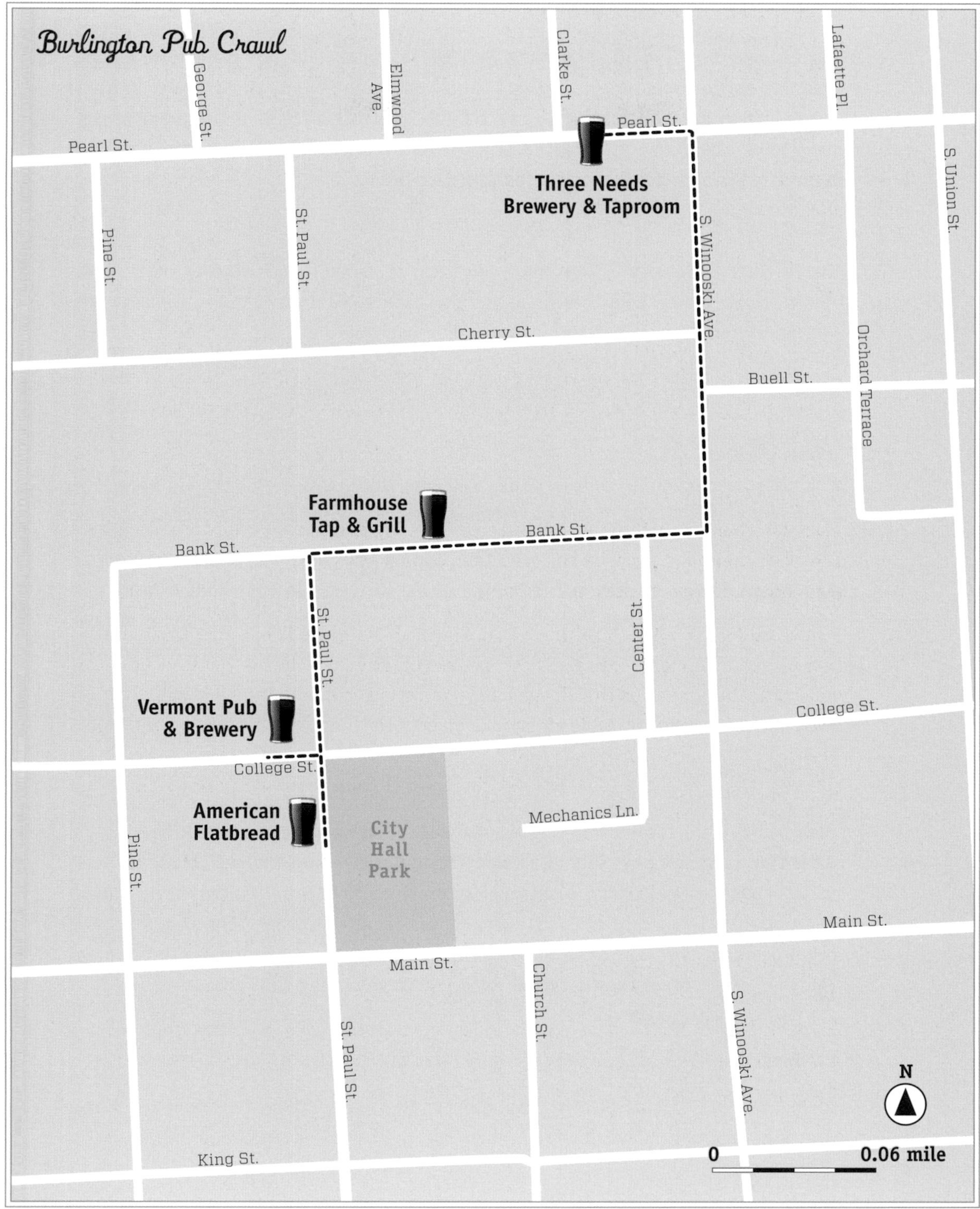

Burlington Pub Crawl
George St.
Elmwood Ave.
Clarke St.
Lafaette Pl.
Pearl St.
Pearl St.
S. Union St.
Three Needs
Brewery & Taproom
Pine St.
St. Paul St.
S. Winooski Ave.
Cherry St.
Orchard Terrace
Buell St.
Farmhouse
Tap & Grill
Bank St.
Bank St.
St. Paul St.
Center St.
Vermont Pub
& Brewery
College St.
College St.
American
Flatbread
City
Hall
Park
Mechanics Ln.
Pine St.
Main St.
Main St.
Church St.
St. Paul St.
S. Winooski Ave.
N
King St.
0
0.06 mile

*It's less than a 0.10-mile walk to:*

**Farmhouse Tap & Grill,** 160 Bank St. Take advantage of the Farmhouse's truly amazing bottle list, or grab some Hill Farmstead on draft, not an easy beer to find. Make sure to order something to eat, because the final stop of the night does not have food. The Vermont Chicken & Biscuits and the Maple Wind Farm Meatloaf are both winners and will fill you up for your last stop.

*The longest walk of the night up next, but it's less than 10 minutes to:*

**Three Needs Brewery & Taproom,** 185 Pearl St. Three Needs doesn't offer food. But when they brew beer this good, you don't really want anything to get between you and your glass. It has the feel of a dive bar, but that adds to the charm. The Dortmunder-style Lager and Milo's IPA are both good, solid beers, but for something a little more exciting, go with the Ich Bin Ein Berliner Weiss.

## New Haven, CT

The craft beer scene is really growing in Connecticut, with new bars and breweries popping up all the time. Nowhere in the state is craft beer as well represented as it is in New Haven.

**Bru Room at Bar,** 254 Crown St. It kind of has a nightclub-type of feel to it, but what is important is that they brew good beer and have good food. Food is always key on a pub crawl, so grab a white pizza topped with bacon and mushrooms and wash it down with a house-brewed pale ale or the AmBAR Ale.

*Walk about 0.1 mile down the street, and stop in at:*

**The Cask Republic,** 179 Crown St. The Cask Republic has an impressive draft and bottle list. There is always at least one beer available on cask. If you're not used to cask beers, it's a totally different way to serve and experience beer. A beer that's served on cask will have different carbonation—some people might think the beer is flat—but the bubbles bring out some interesting flavors, particularly if its served at the proper temperature. Don't worry, if you're not into cask beer, they have 53 other beers on tap. The Cask Republic also holds numerous beer dinners throughout the year, when beers from a certain brewery, such as Blue Hills Brewing Company, are paired with specific dishes.

*The final destination is less than 0.1-mile away at:*

**Prime 16,** 172 Temple St. The final stop of the night should be Prime 16. Make sure you still have room for food when you get here, because they specialize in

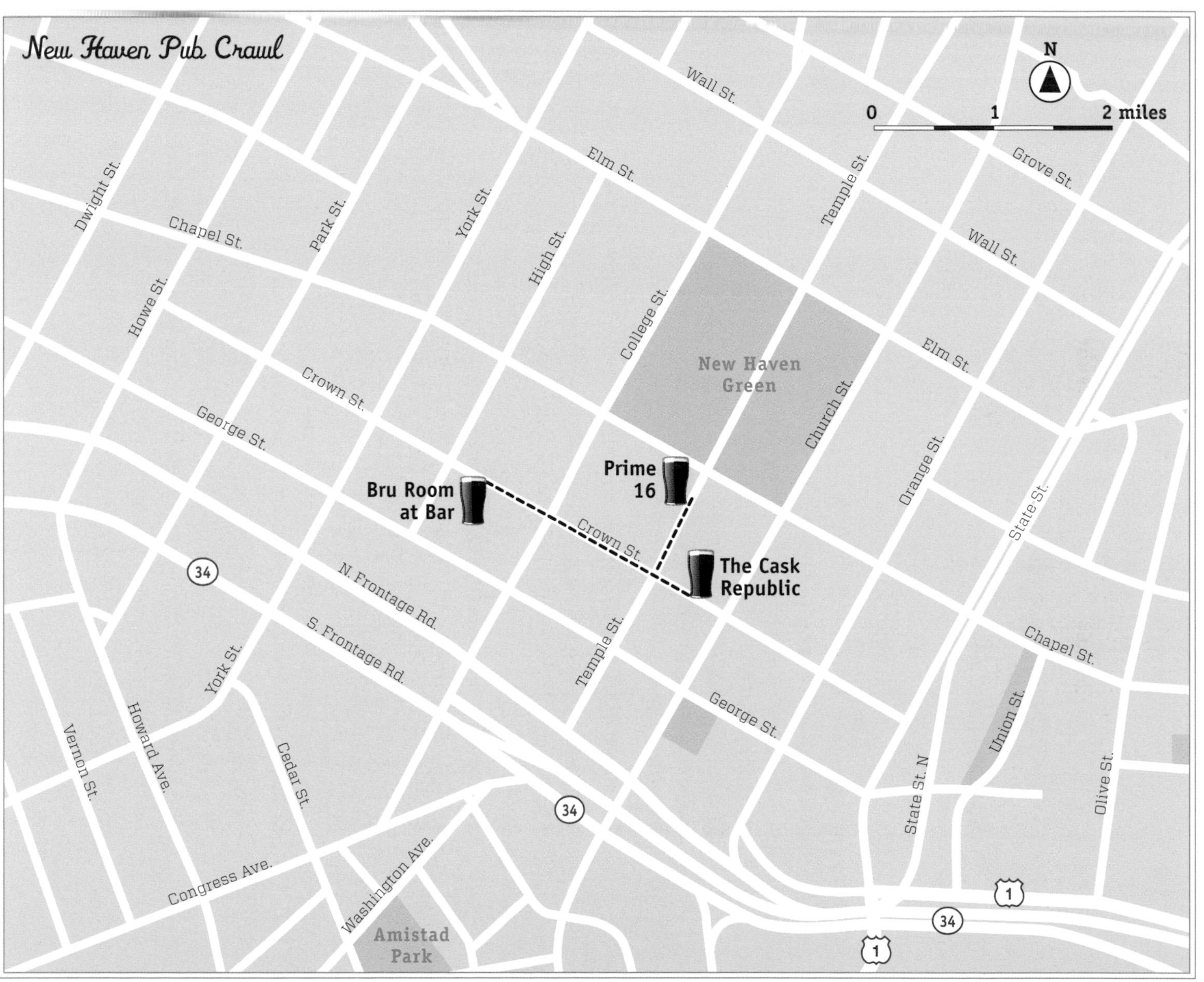
New Haven Pub Crawl
N
0
1
2 miles
Wall St.
Elm St.
Grove St.
Temple St.
Wall St.
Dwight St.
Chapel St.
Park St.
York St.
High St.
College St.
New Haven Green
Church St.
Elm St.
Howe St.
Crown St.
George St.
Orange St.
Prime 16
Bru Room at Bar
The Cask Republic
Crown St.
State St.
34
N. Frontage Rd.
S. Frontage Rd.
Temple St.
Chapel St.
York St.
George St.
Union St.
Vernon St.
Howard Ave.
Cedar St.
34
State St. N
Olive St.
Congress Ave.
Washington Ave.
Amistad Park
1
34
1

gourmet burgers made of beef from grass-fed cows. The Honey Truffle Burger, a beef patty topped with Swiss cheese, applewood bacon, roasted tomatoes, and honey truffle, is excellent, as is the Smoker, which is topped with smoked Canadian bacon, a fried egg, and Vermont cheddar. To wash those burgers down, you need a good beer. Luckily, Prime 16 delivers on that front, too. Try the New England Brewing Company's Elm City Lager or the Victory Brewing Company Headwaters Pale Ale.

## Northampton, MA

Massachusetts beer geeks tend to center around Boston and its suburbs when talking about beer, beer bars, and brewpubs. However, they should not forget the western part of the state, which is home to Amherst, a true craft beer mecca and small college community.

**Northampton Brewery,** 11 Brewster Court. It is one of the oldest brewpubs in all of New England, and they do a great job of brewing beer. They brew beers for pretty much anyone. If you're a fan of lighter beers, try the Paradise City Gold. If you happen to be a fan of big, hop-forward beers, order a Double Take, a 9 percent ABV double IPA. The pub itself is very comfortable, and there is a large bar area. After a few beers there, you'll be in the mood for dinner.

*Take a short 0.3-mile stroll down to:*

**Sierra Grille,** 41A Strong Ave. The Sierra Grille is a combination beer geek and foodie dream. All the available beer is fantastic, and the food is world class—they stand up favorably to any Boston restaurant. Start with the smoked chicken wings or the shrimp in chocolate sauce. Move on to an entree. You start by picking a protein (I go with duck usually) and then a sauce for it to be cooked in (Thai Basil Coconut or Citrus Salsa are both good choices). The draft list always includes Dogfish Head beers, as well as some fine Belgian lambics such as Echte Kriekenbier. It's rare when a restaurant shows as much care for their food as their beer, and this is one of those rare places.

*A 2-minute walk straight down the street leads you to:*

**The Dirty Truth,** 29 Main St. The beer selection is huge, the crowd can get loud, and it's a great way to party and end the night. The crowd is a mixture of college stuents and some townies. The beer list always seems to be heavy on west coast beers, such as Bear Republic and Stone Brewing Company, but some fine New England beers, such as Allagash Black and Smuttynose's Porter, can be found on the large draft list.

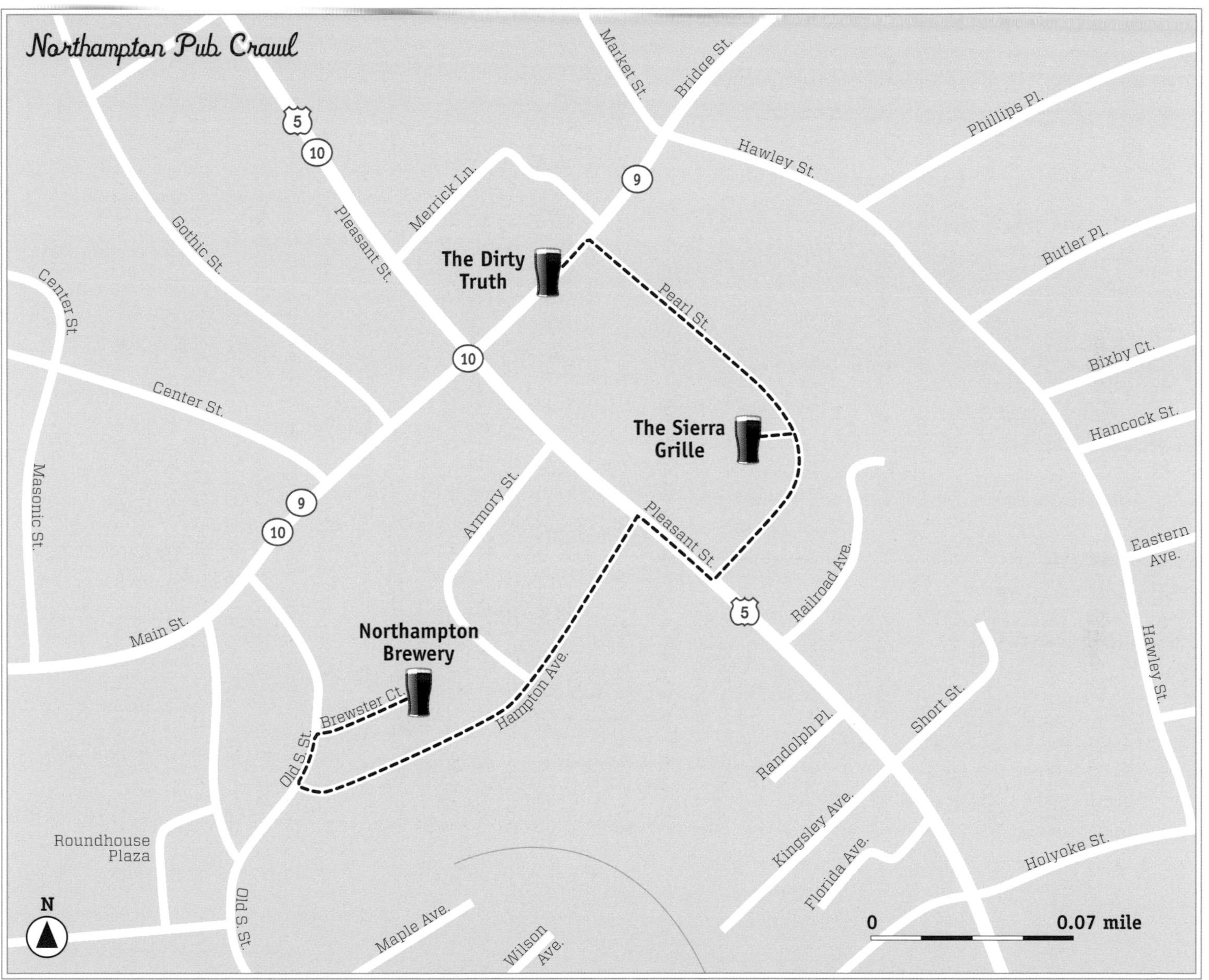
Northampton Pub Crawl
The Dirty Truth
The Sierra Grille
Northampton Brewery
Market St.
Bridge St.
Phillips Pl.
Hawley St.
Merrick Ln.
Gothic St.
Pleasant St.
Butler Pl.
Pearl St.
Center St.
Center St.
Bixby Ct.
Hancock St.
Armory St.
Masonic St.
Eastern Ave.
Railroad Ave.
Main St.
Hawley St.
Brewster Ct.
Hampton Ave.
Old S. St.
Randolph Pl.
Short St.
Kingsley Ave.
Roundhouse Plaza
Florida Ave.
Holyoke St.
Old S. St.
Maple Ave.
Wilson Ave.
0
0.07 mile
N

## Portland, ME

The Old Port section of Portland is full of small antiques shops, touristy stores, and good restaurants. It also has its good share of places for beer lovers, all within less than a mile of each other.

**Three Dollar Dewey's,** 241 Commercial St. This is one of the oldest beer bars in New England. There are tons of local Maine beers on draft, the beer is cheap, and it has a townie feel to it. A pint of Geary's Brewing Company's IPA or a Bar Harbor Real Ale is always a good start to a night. Or go with Maine's best stout, Atlantic's Cadillac Mountain Stout.

*A short, 5-minute walk from Three Dollar Dewey's will lead you to:*

**Gritty McDuff's Brewing Company,** 396 Fore St. Here, order some of the most authentic British-style beers brewed in New England, and make sure to get at least one on cask. They do a great job of serving the beer at the right temperature. Also, do yourself a favor and order the sweet potato fries—they're the best in New England.

*Take a quick stroll to the next stop for a truly different beer experience:*

**Novare Res Bier Cafe,** 4 Canal Plaza. Novare Res is one of the five great New England beer bars. They do everything right, from the beer selection to the food to the knowledgable staff. A trip to Portland would not be complete without going here. They specialize in Belgian ales, so grab a St. Bernardus Abt 12, or maybe a Rochefort 8. They make sure to take care of Maine breweries, too. Marshall Wharf, one of the best breweries not a lot of people know about, always seems to be on tap here, and it would be a shock if there isn't an Allagash beer or two available.

*This next walk will be the longest one of the night at a little more than 0.5 mile, but it should build up your appetite by the time you get to:*

**Sebago Brewing Company,** 211 Fore St. Here, grab some of the fine Sebago beers on draft, and maybe a burger or some nachos to share. Sebago's two best beers are its IPAs. The Frye's Leap IPA is the "regular" IPA, while the Full Throttle is the big, burly, west coast double IPA. At this point you're probably in the mood for some food, so share some pork dumplings or Cajun-dusted Haddock Bites for an appetizer. You can't go wrong with the beer-battered fish and chips or the New York center sirloin if you're hungry enough for a full meal.

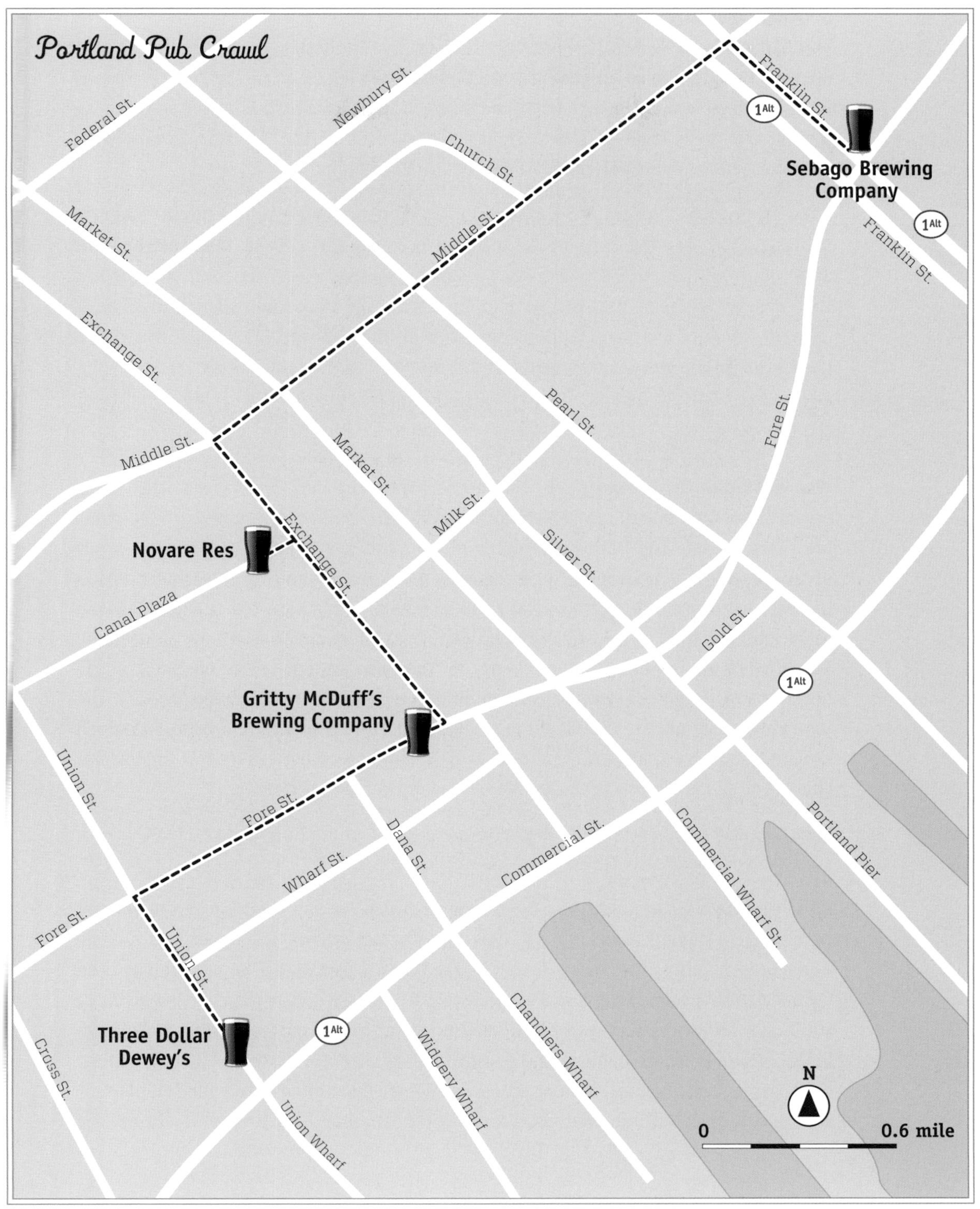

Portland Pub Crawl
Sebago Brewing Company
Novare Res
Gritty McDuff's Brewing Company
Three Dollar Dewey's
Federal St.
Newbury St.
Church St.
Franklin St.
Franklin St.
1 Alt
Market St.
Middle St.
Exchange St.
Middle St.
Pearl St.
Fore St.
Market St.
Exchange St.
Milk St.
Silver St.
Canal Plaza
Gold St.
Union St.
Fore St.
Dana St.
Wharf St.
Commercial St.
Commercial Wharf St.
Portland Pier
Fore St.
Union St.
Cross St.
Union Wharf
Widgery Wharf
Chandlers Wharf
N
0
0.6 mile

## Portsmouth, NH

Portsmouth is a great little beer city. It is by far the best beer destination in the whole Granite State, with the best selection of bars and one of the best brewpubs in all of New England in the Portsmouth Brewery. Portsmouth is also one of those picturesque New England cities, right on the coast of the Atlantic Ocean, with numerous little shops perfect for a day of window-shopping.

**RiRa Irish Pub,** 22 Market Sq. Don't skip RiRa just because it is a chain. They do things right here. The Portsmouth location is housed in a bank that was built in 1809, and you can still see the vault from the seating area. The food is heavy on Irish specialties, so either start with an appetizer like some lamb sliders, or go with a hearty meal of shepherd's pie or corned beef and cabbage. Wash it down with a bomber of Rogue Brewing Company's Dead Guy Ale or grab a Guinness Stout.

*After you leave RiRa, walk by the many small shops, even a store that specializes in the sale of various salts, about 100 feet to:*

**The Portsmouth Brewery,** 56 Market St. The Portsmouth Brewery, the sister brewpub to the Smuttynose Brewing Company, is a world class brewpub. The beers are phenomenal. The Oatmeal Stout is divine, and the Belgian-style Tripel is out of this world. If you happen to be there on a certain day during the winter, either in February or early March, you may get a chance to try Kate the Great, a Russian imperial stout that happens to be one of the best beers in the world. Of course, you will have to wait in line for hours to try it. They also always have some Smuttynose beers on tap, as well as guest taps for various breweries from around the country. The food is also top-notch. The Ploughman's Plate and the Hummus and Baba Ghanoush are both good for sharing. If you or one of your fellow pub crawlers is a vegetarian, this is the place for you because there are many veggie options.

*After you leave the Portsmouth Brewery, turn right and walk approximately 10 feet to your next destination:*

**The Portsmouth Gas Light Co.,** 64 Market St. If you haven't filled up before you get here, the Portsmouth Gas Light Co. has some fantastic food. The appetizers include a personal favorite, the Wood Fired Chicken Legs, as well as a large order of fried calamari. Want something more substantial? Go for the lobster-stuffed haddock or the braised short ribs. If you are in the mood for pizza, grab one from Downtown Pizza, which is located within the Gas Light Company. The Congress Street, topped with pepperoni, sausage, onions, green peppers, mushrooms, and black olives, is nice and filling. With all that good food, you need good beer to wash it down. The

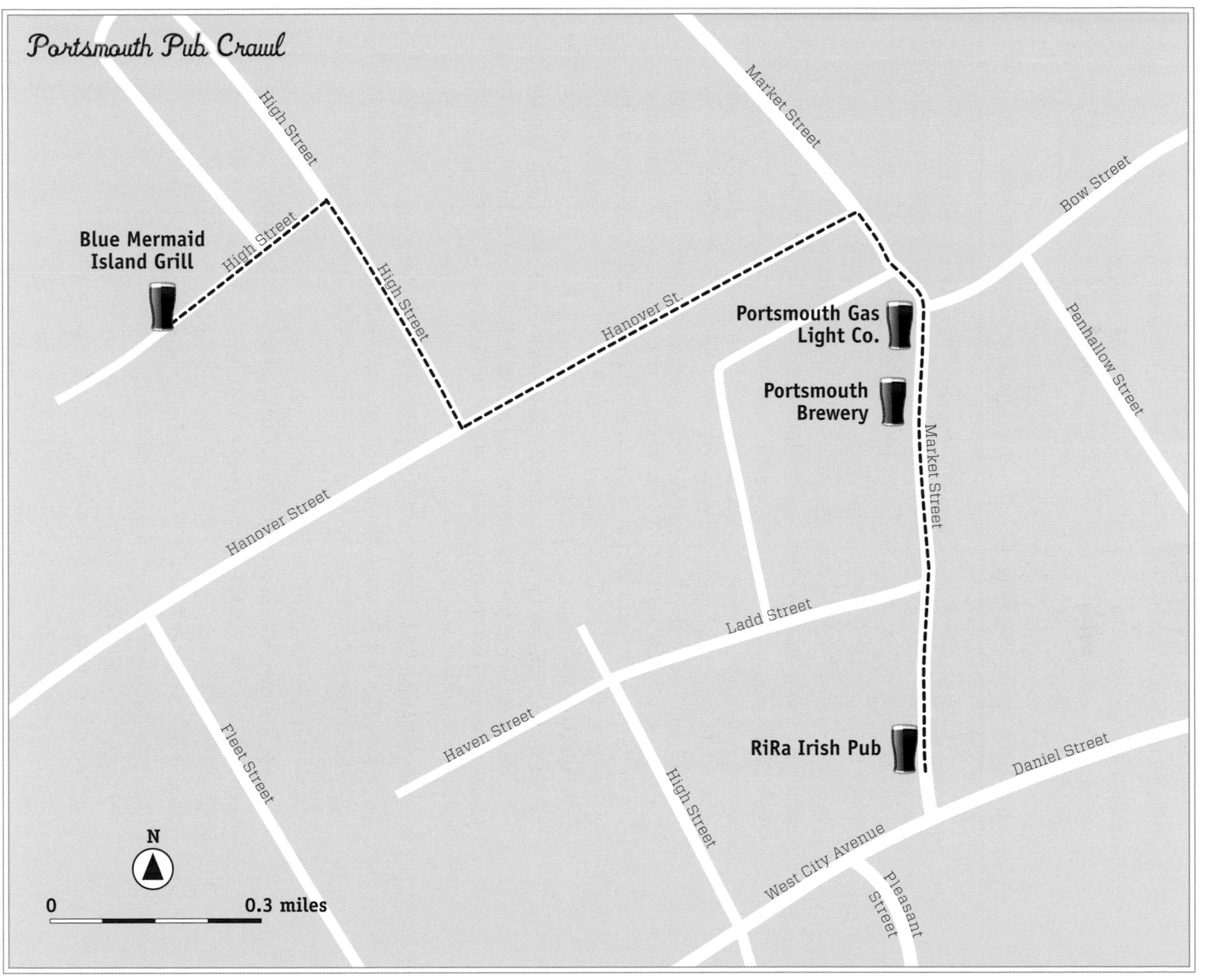
Portsmouth Pub Crawl
High Street
Market Street
Bow Street
Blue Mermaid
Island Grill
High Street
High Street
Hanover St.
Portsmouth Gas
Light Co.
Portsmouth
Brewery
Penhallow Street
Market Street
Hanover Street
Ladd Street
Haven Street
RiRa Irish Pub
Daniel Street
Fleet Street
High Street
N
West City Avenue
Pleasant
Street
0
0.3 miles

Portsmouth Gas Light Company has plenty of good beers, such as the Berkshire Brewing Company's Steel Rail Extra Pale Ale or the Hinterland Cherry Wheat.

*There's one more stop on this pub crawl. Just head on to Hanover Street and walk about 400 feet to High Street, before crawling about another 200 feet to The Hill and a little piece of the Caribbean in Portsmouth:*

**Blue Mermaid Island Grill,** 409 The Hill. The Blue Mermaid is a standout in Portsmouth because it is just so much different than the other locations. While all three of the other destinations feel like beer bars, this has a much brighter and more sunny feel to it. However, they still have really good beer. Most of the Blue Mermaid's eight draft lines are reserved for New England beers. You are likely to find a Peak Organic Local Harvest or Throwback Brewing Company Love Me Long Time Pilsner on draft. Both of those go swimmingly with the islands-inspired menu. If you still have room for food, the Bermuda Triangles Beef Patties and Lobster Quesadillas are fantastic. If you have had enough beer, they also have a large drink menu, which features such tropical coolers as the Mermaid Mai Tai, made with light and dark rums, Triple Sec, orange juice, mango juice, pineapple juice, and sour mix; or the Cocomojorinha, made with Bacardi coconut rum, fresh lime, mint, and simple syrup with a splash of pineapple.

## Providence, RI

Providence may not have the beer reputation of some of the other New England cities featured in this book, but you would be surprised. Craft beer appreciation is growing there, and for those who don't want to travel outside of Rhode Island, this is a nice little pub crawl.

**English Cellar Ale House,** 165 Angell St. As the name implies, this is an English-centric pub, although beer from the US, Germany, and Belgium are well-represented. A good starter would be an Old Speckled Hen—low alcohol, high in flavor, and just a good beer.

*Get ready for some fresh air, because you will have your longest walk of the pub crawl heading to your second stop, a 0.7-mile walk that should only take you about 15 to 20 minutes.*

## How to Taste a Beer

Tasting beer is not as easy as you may think. Sure, you can grab a bottle, pop the top, and take a sip and taste it, but you won't get the whole experience that way.

First off, pour your beer into a glass. A pint glass is fine, or if you're drinking a stronger beer, such as an imperial stout or a Belgian tripel, pull out a brandy snifter or a wine glass.

Now stick your nose in there, almost touching the beer. Notice how it smells. You lose the aroma when drinking from a bottle, and you can't appreciate anything, food or beer, without being able to smell it.

What does it smell like? Is it bready or doughy? That could be from the malts in a lager. Are there aromas of grapefruits or pine? That could be the hops in an IPA. Coffee? Roasted barley malt in a stout could be the cause of that. There are hundreds of aromas you could be detecting.

Look at the beer. Is it dark, light, cloudy? Different beers look different. A cloudy appearance could mean the beer is unfiltered.

Now, the most important part of tasting a beer is actually tasting it. Take a sip. Not a huge one, but not a dainty sip—enough to fill your mouth. Let it sit on your tongue for a second to see what flavors you will pick up. Don't spit it out like wine. You actually need to swallow it. The taste receptors for bitterness are on the back of the tongue, so you can't fully taste a beer without swallowing.

Okay, the next step is to take another sip, and another, and a few more. Have fun—it's beer. Enjoy.

**Union Station Brewery,** 36 Exchange Terr. The walk is worth it once you try some of Union Station's house-brewed beers. It is part of the John Harvard's chain of brewpubs, so the beers are all solid and well-made. Grab dinner there if you're hungry, because the food is excellent. The nachos smothered with cheese and pulled pork are gigantic, and great for a group. If you want a sandwich, the fontina and grape grilled cheese is fantastic, while the lobster mac and cheese is a meal that will leave you stuffed and ready to move to your next bar.

*A 0.25-mile walk will lead you to:*

**Trinity Brewhouse,** 186 Fountain St. The Trinity Brewhouse always has a wide variety of beers, so grab your favorite style, or maybe two. The Rhode Island IPA would go perfectly with a bowl of the Spicy Trinity Chili, and is there a food that says beer more than a grilled sausage platter? Pair it with Trinity's well-done kolsch.

*The final stop on the crawl is Julians, which is a little over 0.5 mile from Trinity. At this point in the crawl, the walk will do you good.*

**Julians,** 318 Broadway. Once at Julians, take advantage of the top-notch draft list or large bottle selection. They have a list of larger-format bottles, such as 750 ml, perfect for sharing at the end of the night.

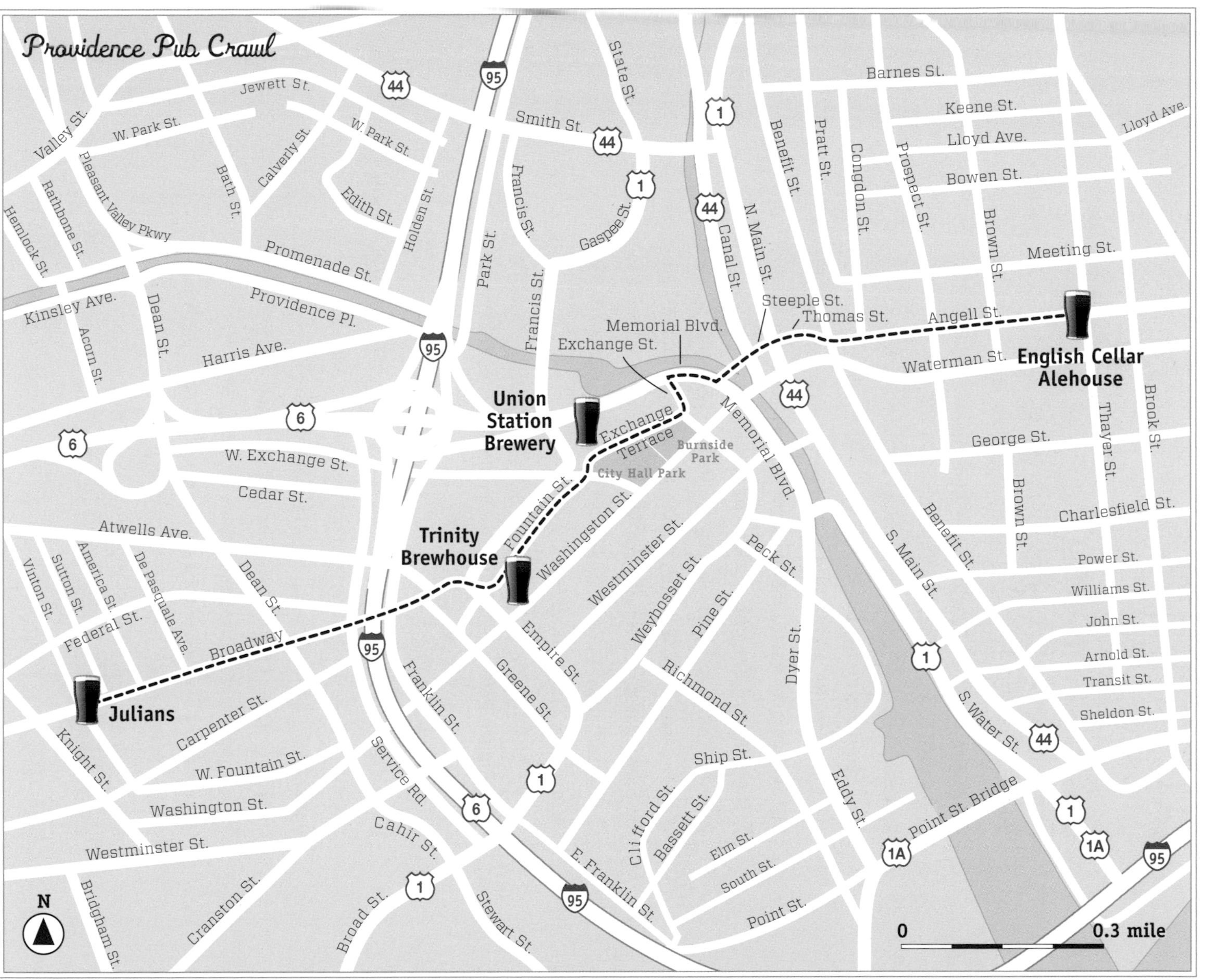
Providence Pub Crawl
English Cellar Alehouse
Union Station Brewery
Trinity Brewhouse
Julians
City Hall Park
Burnside Park
Barnes St.
Keene St.
Lloyd Ave.
Bowen St.
Meeting St.
Angell St.
Waterman St.
George St.
Charlesfield St.
Power St.
Williams St.
John St.
Arnold St.
Transit St.
Sheldon St.
Thayer St.
Brook St.
Brown St.
Prospect St.
Congdon St.
Pratt St.
Benefit St.
N. Main St.
Canal St.
Steeple St.
Thomas St.
Memorial Blvd.
Exchange St.
Exchange Terrace
Fountain St.
Washington St.
Westminster St.
Weybosset St.
Peck St.
Pine St.
Dyer St.
Richmond St.
Empire St.
Greene St.
Franklin St.
S. Main St.
S. Water St.
Point St. Bridge
Eddy St.
Ship St.
Clifford St.
Bassett St.
Elm St.
South St.
Point St.
E. Franklin St.
Stewart St.
Broad St.
Cahir St.
Service Rd.
Cranston St.
Bridgham St.
Westminster St.
Washington St.
W. Fountain St.
Carpenter St.
Knight St.
Broadway
Federal St.
Vinton St.
Sutton St.
America St.
De Pasquale Ave.
Dean St.
Atwells Ave.
Cedar St.
W. Exchange St.
Harris Ave.
Providence Pl.
Promenade St.
Kinsley Ave.
Acorn St.
Hemlock St.
Rathbone St.
Pleasant Valley Pkwy
Valley St.
W. Park St.
Jewett St.
Bath St.
Calverly St.
Edith St.
Holden St.
Park St.
Francis St.
Smith St.
State St.
Gaspee St.
1
1A
6
44
95
N
0
0.3 mile

# Appendix:

## Beer Lover's Pick List

**American Brown Ale,** Out.Haus Ales, Brown Ale, 211

**American Rye,** Banner Beer Company, Rye Beer, 6

**Baby Tree,** Pretty Things Beer & Ale Project, Belgian Quad, 55

**Backyahd,** Foolproof Brewing Company, IPA, 280

**Berliner Weisse,** White Birch Brewing, Berliner Weisse, 223

**Big Wally Porter,** Easy Rye'Da Rye Session IPA, 246

**Black Bear Stout,** Black Bear Microbrewery, American Stout, 116

**Blatant Imperial Stout,** Blatant Brewery, Imperial Stout, 11

**Brother Adam's Bragget,** Atlantic Brewing Company, Braggot, 109

**Cadillac Mountain Stout,** Bar Harbor Brewing Company, American Stout, 111

**Cape Cod Red,** Cape Cod Beer, Red Ale, 19

**Chocolate Oatmeal Stout,** Lefty's Brewing Company, Oatmeal Stout, 38

**Chocolate Oatmeal Stout,** Trout River Brewing Company, Oatmeal Stout, 185

**Clementine,** Clown Shoes Beer, Belgian Wit, 22

**Coffee Porter,** Berkley Beer Company, Porter, 7

**Coffeehouse Porter,** Berkshire Brewing Company, Coffee Porter, 8

**Cogway IPA,** 603 Brewery, IPA, 215

**Curieux,** Allagash Brewing Company, Tripel, 106

**Damariscotta Double Brown,** Sheepscot Valley Brewing Company, Brown Ale, 136

**Daymark,** Rising Tide Brewing Company, Rye Pale Ale, 133

**Declaration,** Backlash Beer Company, Belgian IPA, 4

**Dirty Penny Ale,** Olde Burnside Brewing Company, Black and Tan, 256

**Dock Time Lager,** Stony Creek Brewery, Lager, 259

**Double Black IPA,** Revival Brewing Company, Black IPA, 286

**Double Black Stout,** Redhook Ale Brewery, American Double Stout, 213

**Effinghamburgherbrau,** Prodigal Brewing Company, Lager, 212

**Equinox Pilsner,** Northshire Brewery, Czech Pilsner, 178

**Ever Weisse,** Night Shift Brewing, Berliner Weisse, 48
**Extra Special Oak (Cask),** Element Brewing Company, English Strong Ale, 26
**Farmhouse Pale Ale,** Oxbow Brewing Company, Saison, 129
**Fat Alberta,** Throwback Brewery, Imperial Stout, 220
**The 413 Farmhouse Ale,** Big Elm Brewing, Saison, 10
**Frye's Leap India Pale Ale,** Sebago Brewing Company, IPA, 135
**Gandhi-Bot Double IPA,** New England Brewing Company, Double IPA, 254
**Gnomad,** RiverWalk Brewing Company, Saison, 58
**Golden IPA,** Squam Brewing Company, Double IPA, 218
**Gonzie,** Lawson's Finest Liquids, Pale Ale, 173
**Granite Ledge Stout,** Canterbury Ale Works, Stout, 207
**Grateful Harvest Cranberry Ale,** Harpoon Brewery, Fruit Beer, 30
**Halloween Ale,** Gritty McDuff's Brewery, Extra Special Bitter, 124
**Hampden Pale Ale,** Scantic River Brewery, Pale Ale, 60
**Happy Sol,** Somerville Brewing Company, Hefeweizen, 61
**Headwall Alt,** Tuckerman Brewing Company, Alt, 221
**Heart of Darkness,** Magic Hat Brewery, Oatmeal Stout, 177
**Home for the Holidays,** High & Mighty Beer Company, American Brown Ale, 32
**Hop Monster,** Paper City Brewing Company, Double IPA, 51
**Hoponius Union,** Jack's Abby Brewing, India Pale Lager, 35
**Hurricane Amber Ale,** Coastal Extreme Brewing Company, Amber Ale, 279
**Iced Coffee Stout (Iced Earl),** Hill Farmstead Brewery, Imperial Stout, 170
**Ipswich Dark Ale,** Mercury Brewing Company, Brown Ale, 41
**Irish Ale,** Top Shelf Brewing Company, Irish Red, 263
**Kanc Country Maple Porter,** Woodstock Inn Brewery, Porter, 225
**Lager,** Rapscallion, American Pale Lager, 56
**Laughing Loon Lager,** Oak Pond Brewing Company, Munich Dunkel Lager, 128
**Leaning Chimney,** Grey Sail Brewing of Rhode Island, Robust Porter, 282
**Liberator Doppelbock,** Thomas Hooker Brewing Company, Doppelbock, 262
**Lobster Ale,** Belfast Bay Brewing Company, Amber/Red Ale, 114
**Long Trail Ale,** Long Trail Brewing Company, Altbier, 174

**Midnight Milk Chocolate Stout,** Westfield River Brewing Company, Milk Stout, 68
**Mild at Heart,** Wandering Star Brewing Company, English Dark Mild, 67
**Milk Stout,** Wachusett Brewing Company, Milk Stout, 65
**Mystic Saison,** Mystic Brewery, Saison, 43
**Narragansett Bock,** Narragansett Beer, Bock, 283
**The New Frontier,** Pioneer Brewing Company, Double IPA, 53
**Norm,** Wormtown Brewing Company, Oatmeal Stout, 69
**Notch Session Pils,** Notch Brewing, Pilsner, 49
**Nut Brown Ale,** Peak Organic Brewing Company, Brown Ale, 130
**Oaked Brown,** Beaver Beer Company, Brown Ale, 243
**Oaktoberfest,** Nashoba Valley Winery, Oktoberfest, 45
**The Old Factory Whistle,** Penobscot Bay Brewery, Scottish Ale, 132
**Old Yankee Ale,** Cottrell Brewing Company, Pale Ale, 249
**OktoBrau,** Blue Hills Brewery, Oktoberfest, 12
**Otter Creek Black IPA,** Otter Creek Brewing, Black IPA, 180
**Parsnippitty,** Glass Bottom Brewery, Belgian Tripel, 28
**Pechish Woods,** Cisco Brewers, American Wild Ale, 21
**Peeper Ale,** Maine Beer Company, Pale Ale, 126
**The Plum Island White,** Newburyport Brewing Company, Belgian Wit, 46
**Porter,** Back East Brewing Company, Porter, 242
**Praying Mantis Porter,** The Hartford Better Beer Company, Porter, 252
**Prologue,** Relic Brewing Company, Rye Lager, 257
**Pugsley Signature Series Imperial Porter,** Shipyard Brewing Company, Imperial Porter, 138
**Pumpkin Stout,** Cape Ann Brewing Company, Stout, 17
**Road 2 Ruin,** Two Roads Brewing Company, Double IPA, 265
**Schwarzbier,** Agner & Wolf Brewery Corporation, Schwarzbier, 204
**The Shire,** Candia Road Brewing Company, American Stout, 206
**The S'Muttonator,** Smuttynose Brewing Company, Doppelbock, 216
**SOS,** Cody Brewing Company, Belgian IPA, 24
**Stowaway IPA,** Baxter Brewing Company, IPA, 112

**Stray Dog Lager,** Brewmaster Jack, Golden Lager, 16
**Summer Golden Ale,** Andrews Brewing Company, Blonde Ale, 107
**Switchback Ale,** Switchback Brewing Company, Pale Ale, 184
**Thanksgiving Ale,** Mayflower Brewing Company, Strong Ale, 39
**Thirteenth Original Maple Stout,** Bucket Brewery, American Stout, 278
**Trillium,** Trillium Brewing Company, Saison, 64
**Triplication,** Idle Hands Craft Ales LLC, Tripel, 34
**Tweiss,** Gneiss Brewing Company, Weizenbock, 123
**Utopias,** Boston Beer Company, Strong Ale, 14
**Valor Ale,** 14th Star Brewery, Ale, 168
**Vermonster,** Rock Art Brewery, Barleywine, 182
**Wadsworth India Pale Ale,** Charter Oak Brewing Company, IPA, 247
**Wee Heavy,** D.L. Geary Brewing Company, Scotch Ale, 119
**WheneverFEST! Ale,** Goodfellow's Brewing Company, Oktoberfest, 29
**Whoopie Pie Porter,** Friar's Brewhouse, Porter, 121
**Working Man's Porter,** Henniker Brewing Company, English Porter, 209

# Index


Agner & Wolf Brewery Corporation, 204
Alchemist Cannery, 189
Ale House, The, 84
Allagash Abduction, 199
Allagash Brewing Company, 105
American Flatbread, 196, 322
Amherst Brewing Company, 71
Andrews Brewing Company, 106
Anheuser-Busch, 231
Armsby Abbey, 85
Atlantic Brewing Company, 108

Back East Brewing Company, 242
Backlash Beer Company, 3
Badger Cafe & Pub, The, 155
Bad Martha Beer, 4
Banded Horn Brewing Company, 109
Banner Beer Company, 5
Bar Harbor Brewing Company, 110
Barleycorn's Craft Brew, 303
Barley House, The, 236
Barleywine Festival, 74
Barrington Brewery's Cheddar Ale Soup, 309
Barrington Brewery & Restaurant, 72
Baxter Brewing Company, 111
Beaver Beer Company, 243
Beer Advocate's American Craft Beer Fest, 297
Beer Advocate's Belgian Beer Fest, 299
Beer Advocate's Extreme Beer Fest, 295
Beer and Pemaquid Mussel Fest, 151
Beer'd Brewing Company, 244
Beer Works, 73
Belfast Bay Brewing Company, 113
Berkley Beer Company, 6
Big Elm Brewing, 9
Big Game and Big Beer Dinner, 100
Bissell Brothers, 114
Blackback Pub & Flyshop, 197
Black Bear Microbrewery, 115
Blatant Brewery, 10
Blue Hills Brewery, 11
Blue Mermaid Island Grill, 237, 332
Bobcat Cafe & Brewery, 187
Bog Iron Brewing, 13
Boon Island Ale House, 142
Boothbay Craft Brewery, 117
Boston BeerSummit, 299
Boston pub crawl, 318
Brattleboro Brewers Festival, 297
Bray's Brewpub & Eatery, 143
Brewer's Dinner, The, 152
Brewmaster Jack, 15
Brewster River Pub & Brewery, 188
British Beer Company, 86
Broad Brook Brewing Company, 245
Bru Room at Bar, 266, 324
Bucket Brewery, 277
Bukowski's Tavern, 87
Bunker Brewing Company, 117
Burlington pub crawl, 322

Cambridge Brewing Company, 73, 320
Cambridge Brewing Company's You Enjoy My Stout Brownie, 317
Cambridge Common Restaurant, 89
Cambridge House, The, 266
Cambridge pub crawl, 320
Candia Road Brewing Company, 205
Canterbury AleWorks, 207
Cape Ann Brewing Company, 16
Cape Cod Beer, 18
Cask Republic's Grilled Extra-Hoppy-Beer-Marinated Half Chicken, 314
Cask Republic, The, 270, 324
Charter Oak Brewing Company, 247
Christmas Tree Lighting ceremony, 271
Cisco Brewers, 20
City Steam Brewery Cafe, 267
City Steam Brewery Cafe's Beer-Braised Pot Roast, 315
Clown Shoes Beer, 21
Coastal Extreme Brewing Company, 278
Coddington Brewing Company, 287
Cody Brewing Company, 23
Cork & Brew, 304
Cottrell Brewing Company, 248
Crop Bistro & Brewery, 188

Das Bierhaus, 198
Deep Ellum, 90, 318
Deja Brew Inc., 304
Dirty Truth, 326
Dive Bar, The, 91
D.L. Geary Brewing Company, 118
Dogfish Head Halloween, 91
Doherty's East Avenue Irish Pub, 291
Drop-in Brewery, 165

Earth Eagle Brewings, 226
Ebenezer's Belgian Beer Dinner, 156
Ebenezer's Pub, 155
Element Brewing Company, 25
Eli Cannon's Tap Room, 271
Elm City Brewing Company, 227
English Cellar Ale House, 291, 332

Farmhouse Tap & Grill, The, 199, 324
Federal Jack's Restaurant & Brew Pub, 144
Fiddlehead Brewing Company, 165
Firefly Hollow Brewing, 250
Flying Goose Brew Pub & Grill, 228
Foley Brothers Brewing, 166
Foolproof Brewing Company, 280
Foundation Brewing Company, 120
Founder's Breakfast, 86
Four Quarters Brewing, 167
14th Star Brewery, 168
Friar's Brewhouse, 120

Gardner Ale House, 75
Gardner Ale House Fish & Chips, 312
Geaghan's Restaurant & Pub, 145
Glass Bottom Brewery, 27
Gneiss Brewing Company, 122
Goodfellow's Brewing Company, 28
Great International Beer Festival, 296
Great Lost Bear, The, 157
Great Rhythm Brewing Company, 208
Green Street Grille, 92
Grey Sail Brewing of Rhode Island, 281
Gritty McDuff's Brewery, 123, 328

Half Full Brewery, 250
Harpoon Brewery, 30
Harpoon Brewery (Vermont), 175
Hartford Better Beer Company, The, 251
Henniker Brewing Company, 208
High Horse Brewing, 76
High & Mighty Beer Company, 31
Hill Farmstead Brewery, 169
Hophead Throwdown, 98
Hopsters Brew & Boards, 305
Horseshoe Pub & Restaurant, 93

Idle Hands Craft Ales LLC, 33
IncrediBREW, 306
Inn on Peaks Island's Shipyard Pumpkinhead Ale Pancakes, 311

Jack's Abby Brewing, 34
Jacob Wirth Restaurant, 94
Jasper Murdock's Alehouse, 190
Jimmy the Greek's, 158
John Harvard's Brew House, 76
Julians, 292, 334

Kate the Great Day, 233
Kelsen Brewing Company, 209
Kennebec River Pub & Brewery, 146
Killington Brewfest, 300
Kingdom Brewing, 171
Kretschmann Brewing Company, 36
Kung Fu Christmas, 88

Lawson's Finest Liquids, 172
Lefty's Brewing Company, 37
Liberal Cup Public House and Brewery, 148
Long Trail Brewing Company, 173
Lord Hobo, 95, 322
Lost Nation Brewing, 175

Madison Brewing Company, 191
Magic Hat Brewing Company, 176
Maine Beer Company, 125
Maine Brewers Festival, 301
Maine Brew Pub Cup, 158
Maine Coast Brewing Company, 149
Marshall Wharf Brewing Company, 150
Martha's Exchange, 229
Massachusetts Brewers Fest, 298
Mayflower Brewing Company, 39
McNeill's Brewery, 192
Meadhall, 320
Mercury Brewing Company, 40
MiKro Craft Beer Bar, 272
Milly's Tavern, 230
Milly's Tavern Oatmeal Stout Beef Stew, 313
Moan and Dove, The, 96
Moat Mountain Smoke House & Brewing Company, 231
Moe's Tavern, 96
Moezapalouza, 97
Mohegan Cafe & Brewery, 288
Monk's Cell, 98
Mystic Brewery, 42

Narragansett Beer, 282
Nashoba Valley Winery, 44
Newburyport Brewing Company, 45
New England Brewing Company, 253
New England Real Ale Exhibitio, 296
New Hampshire Brew Fest, 300
New Haven pub crawl, 324
Night Shift Brewing, 47
Northampton Brewery, 77, 326
Northampton pub crawl, 326
Northshire Brewery, 178
Notch Brewing, 49
Novare Res Bier Cafe, 159, 328

Oak Pond Brewing Company, 127
Offshore Ale Company, 78
Oktoberfest, 79, 227
Olde Burnside Brewing Company, 254
One Night Stand, 144
Opa Opa Steakhouse & Brewery, 80
Otter Creek Brewing, 179
Out.Haus Ales, 210
Oxbow Brewing Company, 128

Paper City Brewing Company, 50
Parker Pie Company, 200
Peak Organic Brewing Company, 130
Penobscot Bay Brewery, 131

People's Pint, The, 80
Percival Beer Company, 52
Pioneer Brewing Company, 52
Portland pub crawl, 328
Portsmouth Brewery, 233, 330
Portsmouth Brewery's Old Brown Dog Hanger Steak, 313
Portsmouth Gas Light Co., 237
Portsmouth pub crawl, 330
Post Road Tavern, 160
Pour Judgement Bar & Grill, 293
Pretty Things Beer & Ale Project, 54
Prime 16, 273, 324
Proclamation Ale Company, 284
Prodigal Brewing Company, 212
Providence pub crawl, 332
Publick House, The, 98, 320

Rapscallion, 56
Ravenous Brewing Company, 284
Redhook Ale Brewery, 213
Relic Brewing Company, 257
Revival Brewing Company, 285
RiRa Irish Pub, 330
Rising Tide Brewing Company, 133
RiverWalk Brewing Company, 57
Rock Art Brewery, 181
Roguepalooza, 160
Run of the Mill, The, 151

SBC Restaurant & Brewery, 268
Scantic River Brewery, 59
Schilling Beer Company, 234
Sea Dog Brewing Company, 152
Sea Dog Brewing Company's Barbecue Bluepaw Short Ribs, 316
Sebago Brewing Company, 134, 328
Seven Barrel Brewery, 235
Shebeen Brewing Company, 258
Sheepscot Valley Brewing Company, 136
Shipyard Brewing Company, 137
Shipyard Brewing Company's Peaks Island Mussels, 310
Sierra Grille, 99, 326
603 Brewery, 214
Slumbrew: Somerville Brewing Company, 60
Smuttynose Brewing Company, 215
SoMe Brewing Company, 139
Spencer Brewery, 62
Spring Raft 'n Brews, 147
Squam Brewing Company, 217
Stone Corral Brewery, 182
Stoneface Brewing Company, 218
Stony Creek Brewery, 259
Stout and Porter Dinner, 293
Strange Brew Tavern, 238
Strong Brewing Company, 140
Stubborn Beauty Brewing Company, 260
Sunday River Brewing Company, 153
Sunset Grill & Tap, 100, 318
Switchback Brewing Company, 183

Tap Brewpub, The, 81
The Bag & Kettle Brewpub, 141
The Funky Bow Brewery and Beer Company, 121
The Portsmouth Gas Light Co., 330
Thimble Island Brewing Company, 261
Thomas Hooker Brewing Company, 262
Three Dollar Dewey's, 161, 328
Three Needs Brewery & Taproom, 193, 324
Three Penny Taproom, 201
Three Tides Restaurant, 150
Throwback Brewery, 219
Top Shelf Brewing Company, 263
Trapp Family Lodge Brewery, 193
Tree House Brewing Company, 62
Trillium Brewing Company, 63
Trinity Brewhouse, 288, 334
Trinity Christmas Party, 289
Trout River Brewing Company, 184
Tuckerman Brewing Company, 221
Two Roads Brewing Company, 264

Union Station Brewery, 290, 334

Vermont Brewers Festival, 298
Vermont Pub & Brewery, 194, 322

Wachusett Brewing Company, 64
Wandering Star Brewing Company, 66
Watch City Brewing Company, 83
Westfield River Brewing Company, 67
Whetstone Station Restaurant & Brewery, 195
White Birch Brewing, 222
Willimantic Brewing Company, 269
Will Meyer's Sgt. Pepper Clone, 306
Wolaver's, 179
Woodstock Inn Brewery, 224
Wormtown Brewing Company, 68

Yard House, 101

Zero Gravity Craft Brewery @ American Flatbread, 196